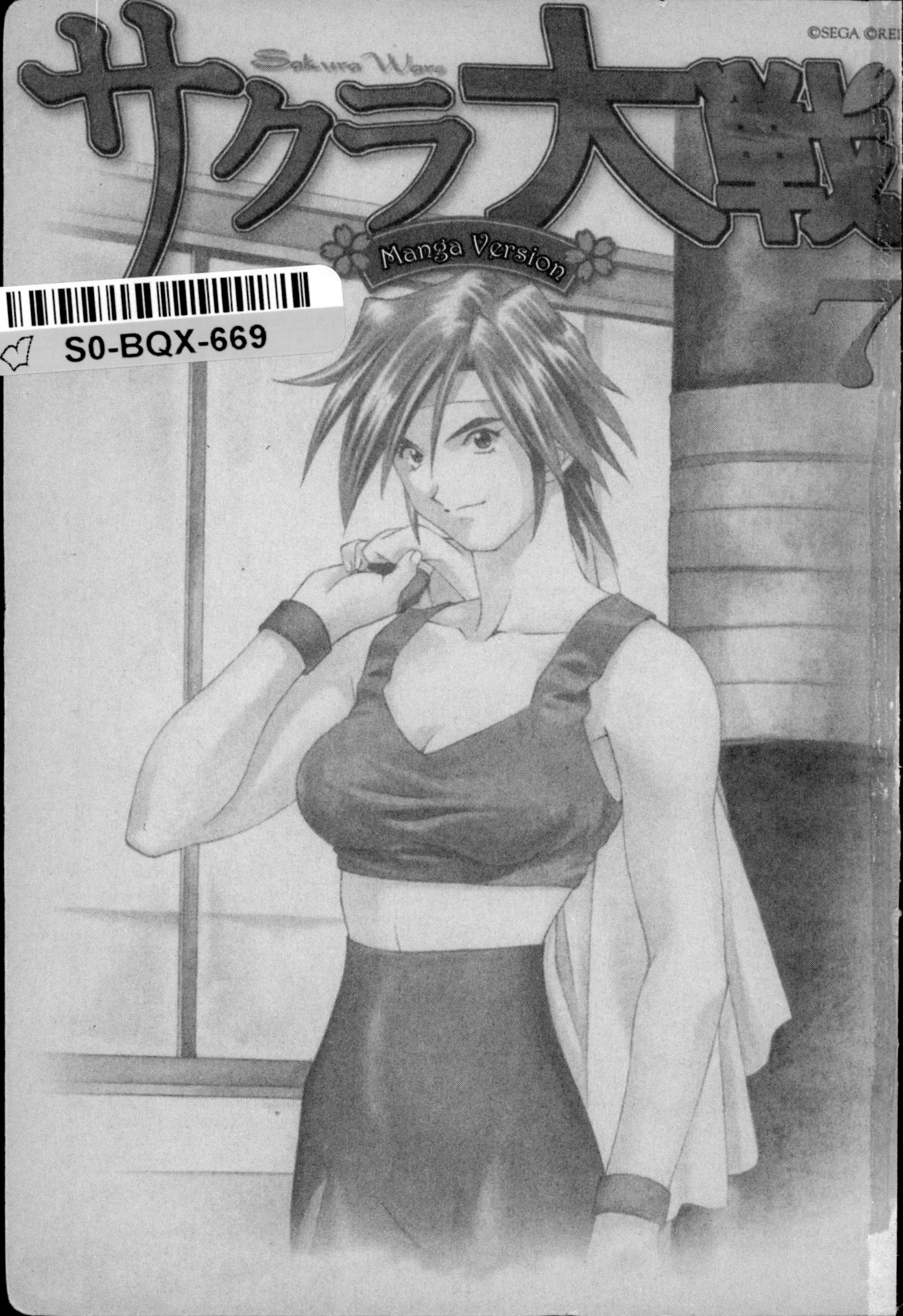
サクラ大戦
Sakura Wars
Manga Version
7
©SEGA ©RE

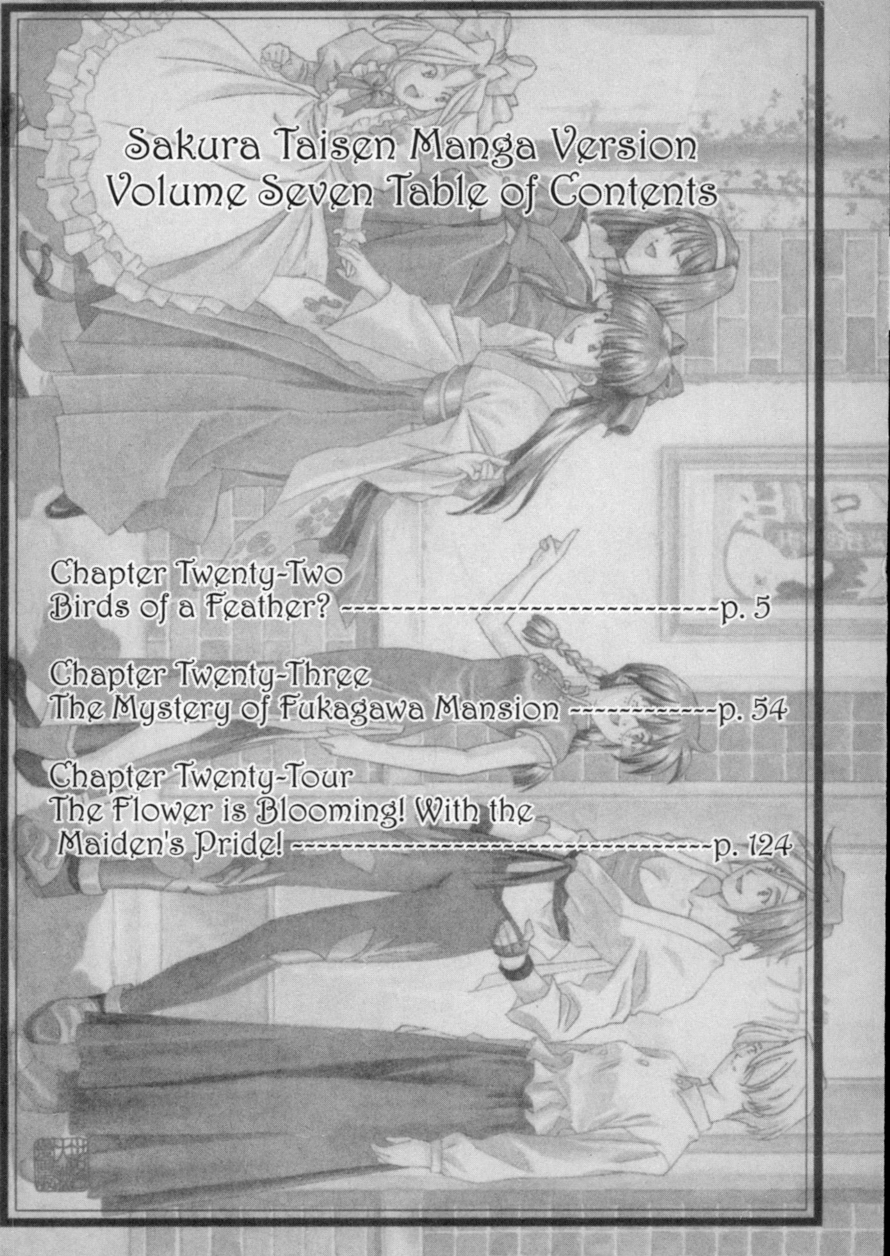

# Sakura Taisen Manga Version Volume Seven Table of Contents

# SAKURA TAISEN™

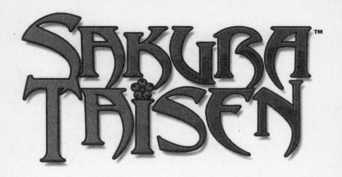

Vol. 7

Story by
Ohji Hiroi

Art by
Ikku Masa

Characters by
Kosuke Fujishima

TOKYOPOP®

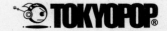

HAMBURG // LONDON // LOS ANGELES // TOKYO

# Sakura Taisen Volume 7
## Story By Ohji Hiroi
## Art By Ikku Masa

Translation - Yuko Fukami
English Adaptation - Lillian Diaz-Przybyl
Copy Editor - Shannon Watters
Retouch and Lettering - Star Print Brokers
Production Artist - Mike Estacio
Graphic Designer - James Lee

Editor - Nikhil Burman
Digital Imaging Manager - Chris Buford
Pre-Production Supervisor - Lucas Rivera
Production Manager - Elisabeth Brizzi
Managing Editor - Vy Nguyen
Creative Director - Anne Marie Horne
Editor-in-Chief - Rob Tokar
Publisher - Mike Kiley
President and C.O.O. - John Parker
C.E.O. and Chief Creative Officer - Stu Levy

A  Manga

TOKYOPOP and 🐸 are trademarks or registered trademarks of TOKYOPOP Inc.

TOKYOPOP Inc.
5900 Wilshire Blvd. Suite 2000
Los Angeles, CA 90036

E-mail: info@TOKYOPOP.com
Come visit us online at www.TOKYOPOP.com

ISBN: 978-1-4278-1034-2

First TOKYOPOP printing: May 2008
10 9 8 7 6 5 4 3 2 1
Printed in the USA

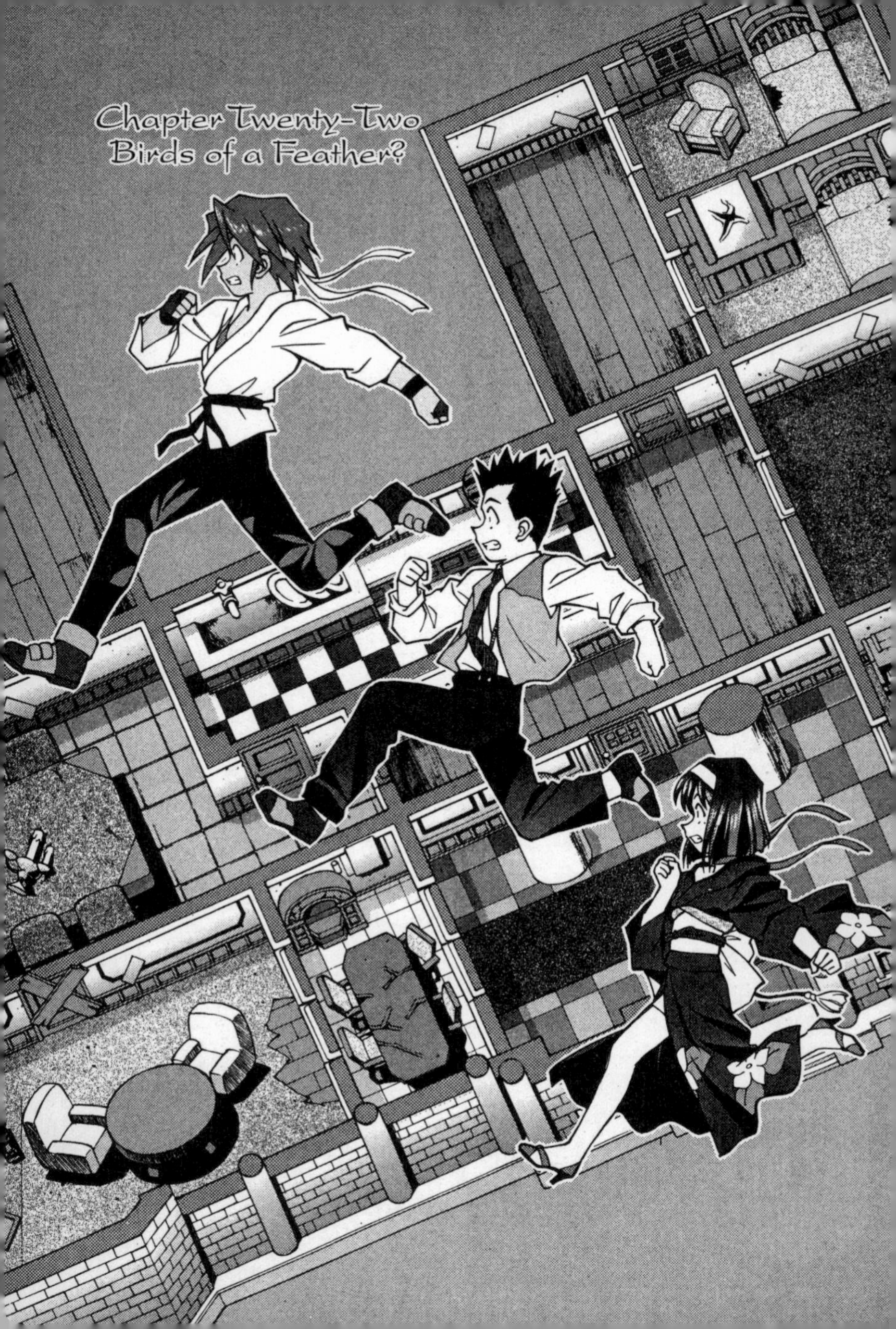
Chapter Twenty-Two
Birds of a Feather?

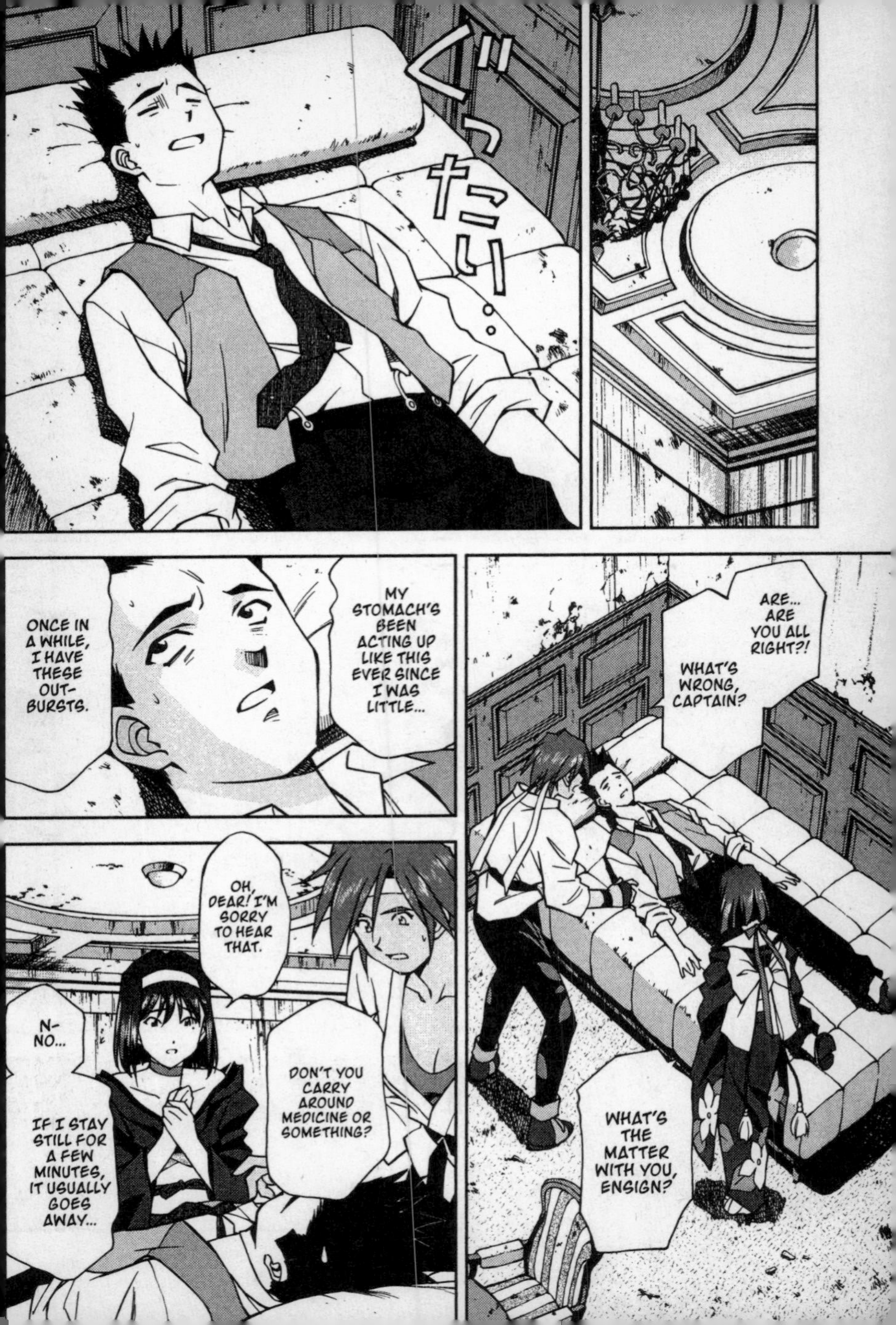
ARE... ARE YOU ALL RIGHT?!
WHAT'S WRONG, CAPTAIN?
WHAT'S THE MATTER WITH YOU, ENSIGN?
MY STOMACH'S BEEN ACTING UP LIKE THIS EVER SINCE I WAS LITTLE...
ONCE IN A WHILE, I HAVE THESE OUT-BURSTS.
OH, DEAR! I'M SORRY TO HEAR THAT.
DON'T YOU CARRY AROUND MEDICINE OR SOMETHING?
N-NO...
IF I STAY STILL FOR A FEW MINUTES, IT USUALLY GOES AWAY...

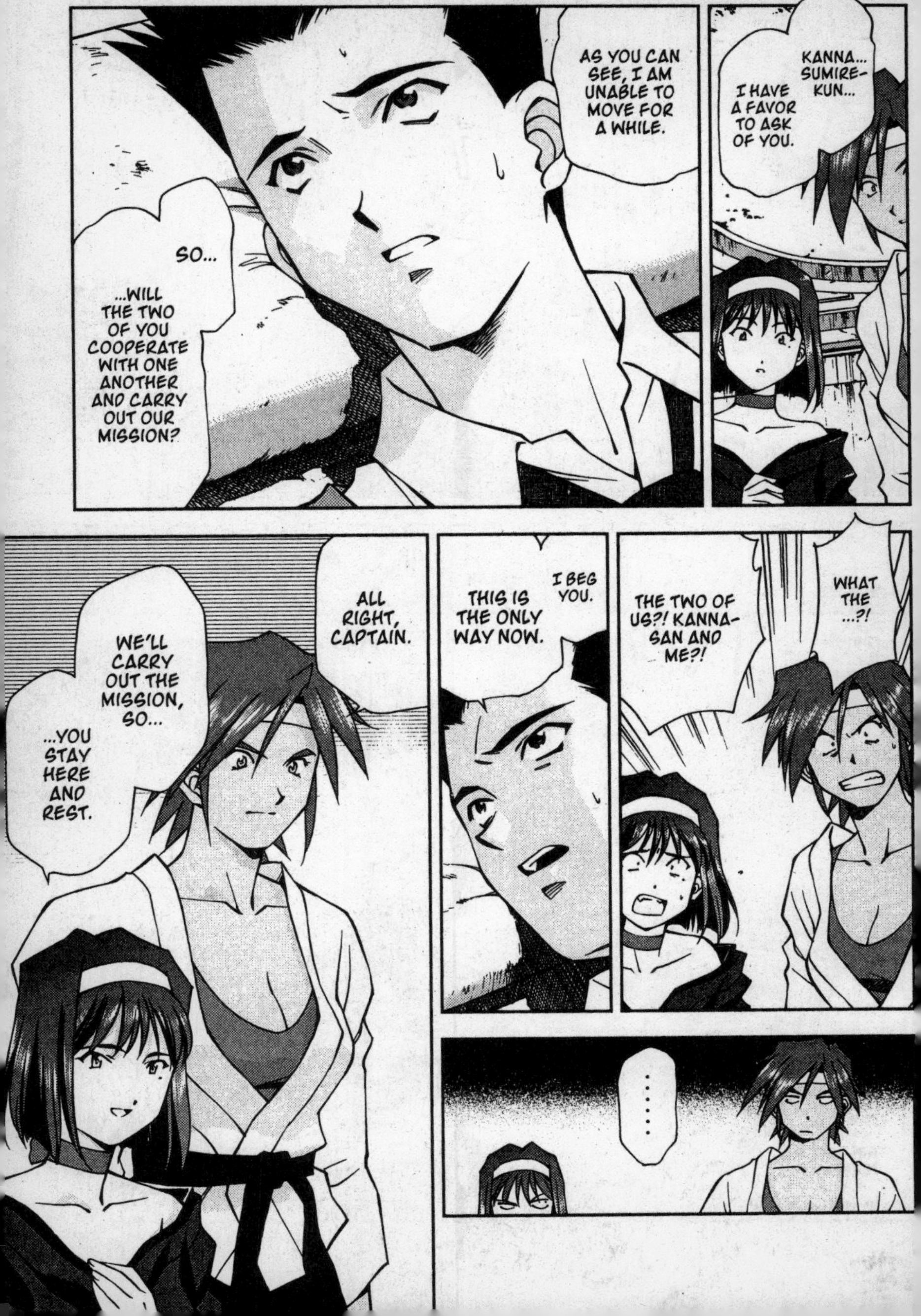
KANNA... SUMIRE-KUN...
I HAVE A FAVOR TO ASK OF YOU.
AS YOU CAN SEE, I AM UNABLE TO MOVE FOR A WHILE.
SO...
...WILL THE TWO OF YOU COOPERATE WITH ONE ANOTHER AND CARRY OUT OUR MISSION?
WHAT THE ...?!
THE TWO OF US?! KANNA-SAN AND ME?!
I BEG YOU.
THIS IS THE ONLY WAY NOW.
ALL RIGHT, CAPTAIN.
WE'LL CARRY OUT THE MISSION, SO...
...YOU STAY HERE AND REST.
......

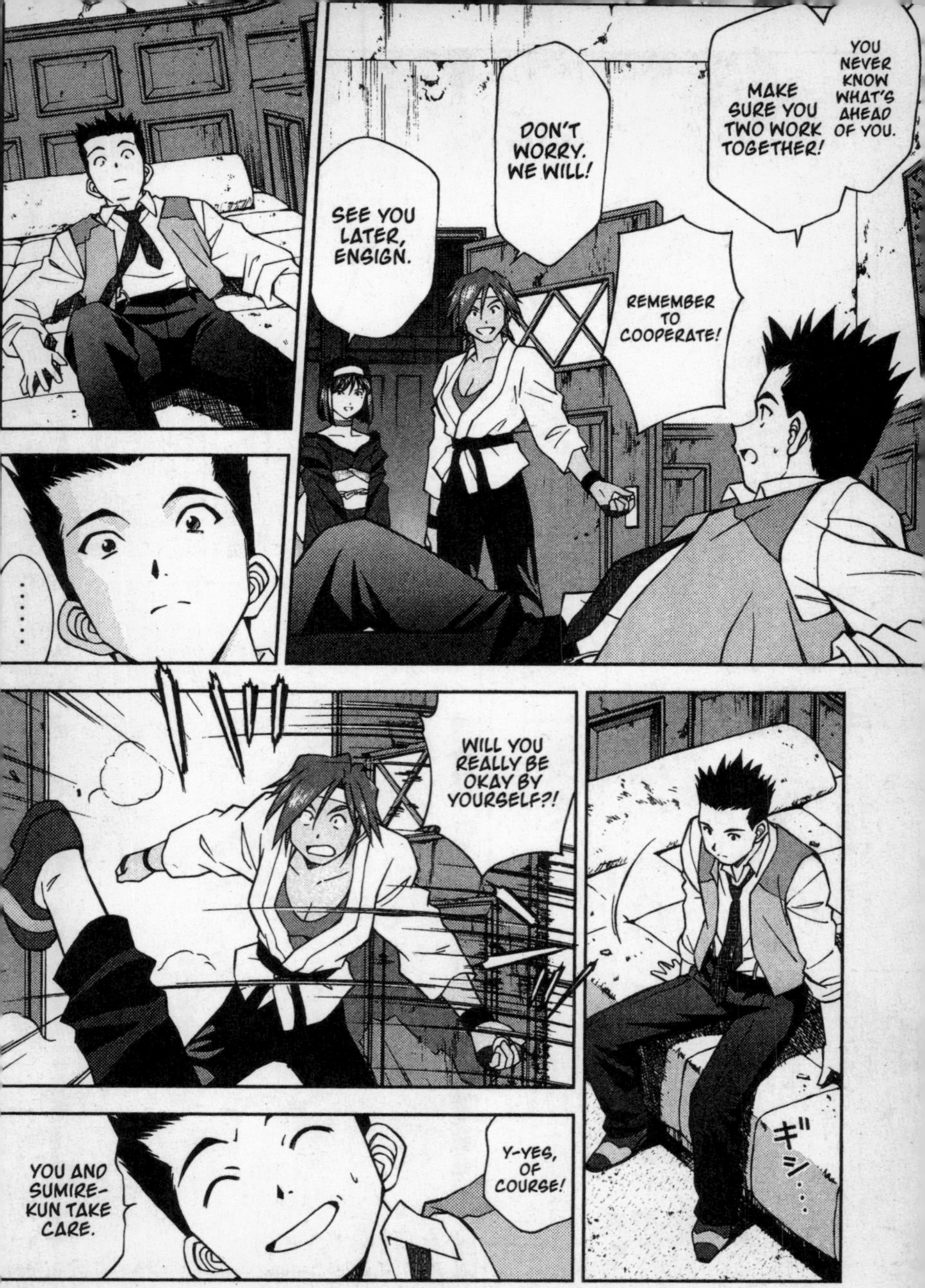
MAKE SURE YOU TWO WORK TOGETHER!
YOU NEVER KNOW WHAT'S AHEAD OF YOU.
DON'T WORRY. WE WILL!
SEE YOU LATER, ENSIGN.
REMEMBER TO COOPERATE!
......
ギシ...
WILL YOU REALLY BE OKAY BY YOURSELF?!
Y-YES, OF COURSE!
YOU AND SUMIRE-KUN TAKE CARE.

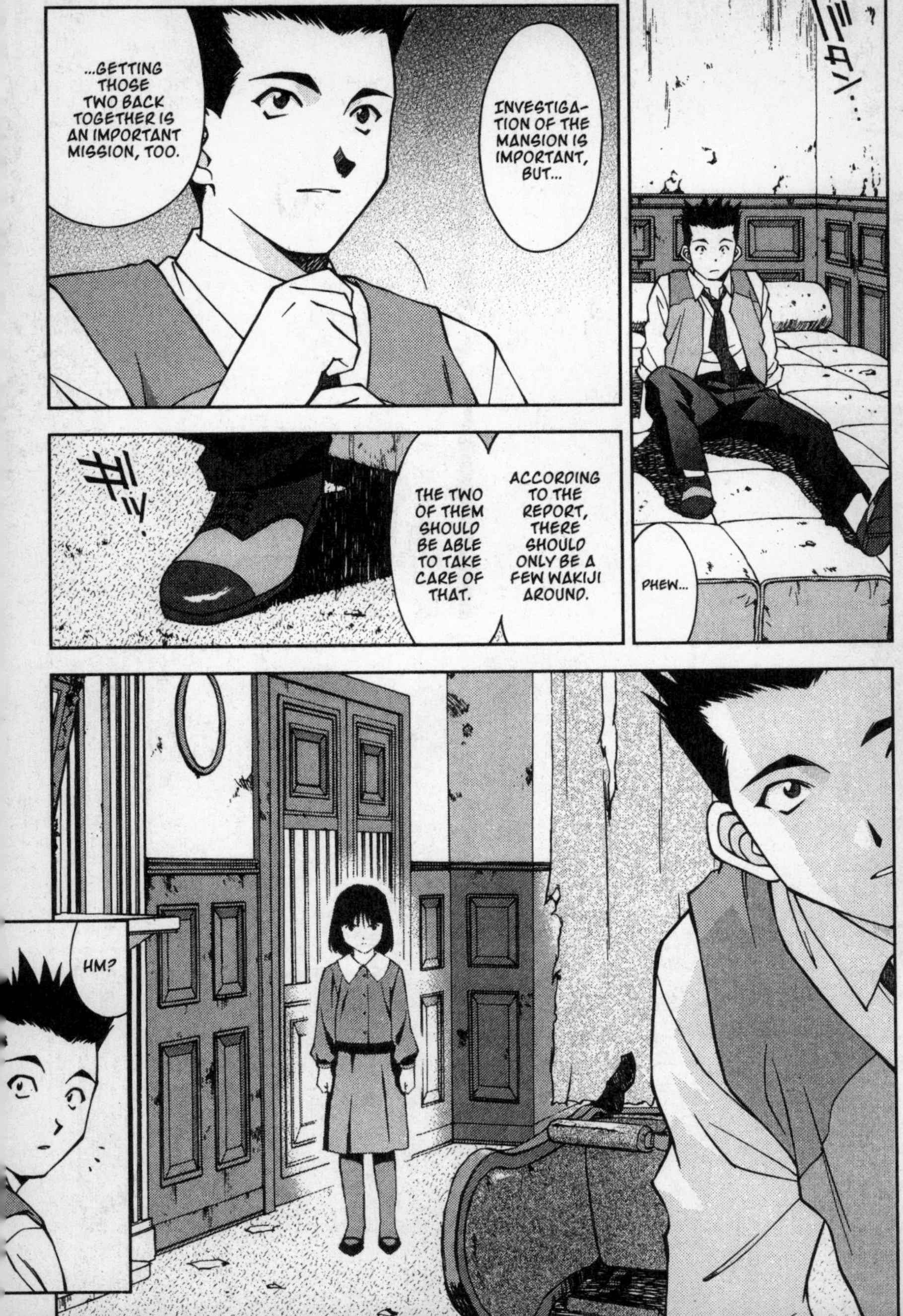
PHEW...
INVESTIGATION OF THE MANSION IS IMPORTANT, BUT...
...GETTING THOSE TWO BACK TOGETHER IS AN IMPORTANT MISSION, TOO.
ACCORDING TO THE REPORT, THERE SHOULD ONLY BE A FEW WAKIJI AROUND.
THE TWO OF THEM SHOULD BE ABLE TO TAKE CARE OF THAT.
HM?

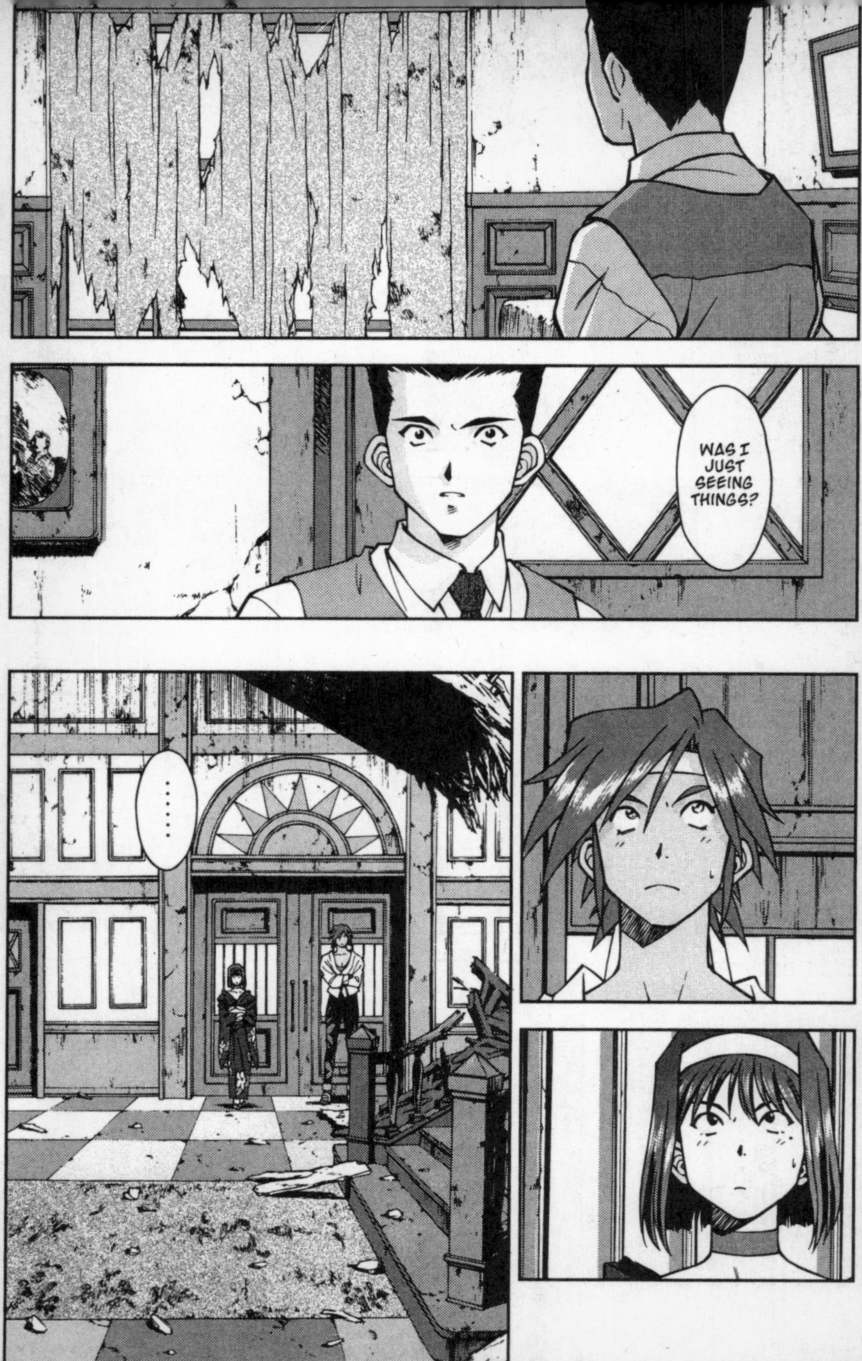
WAS I JUST SEEING THINGS?
......

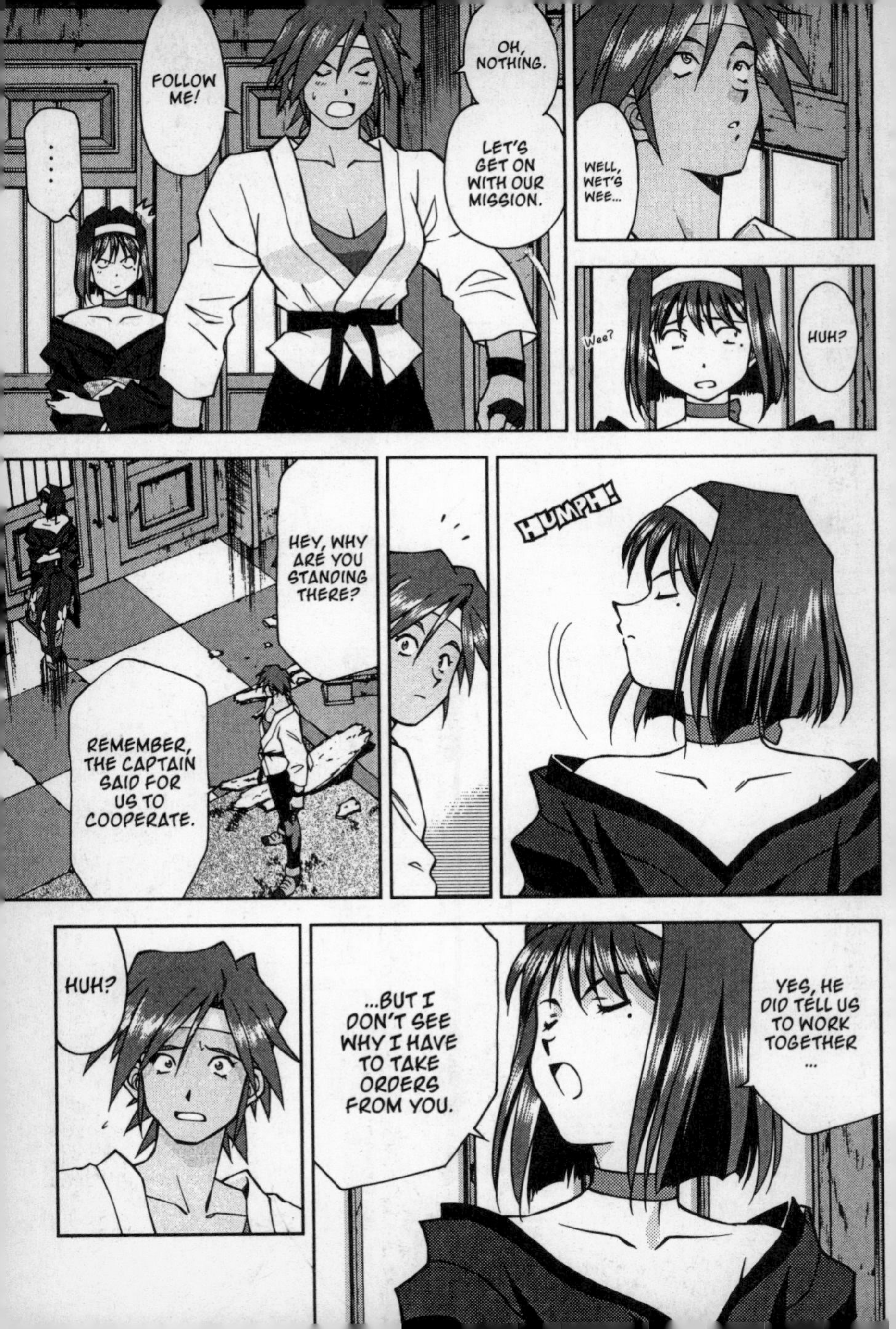
WELL, WET'S WEE...
HUH?
Wee?
OH, NOTHING.
LET'S GET ON WITH OUR MISSION.
FOLLOW ME!
....
HUMPH!
HEY, WHY ARE YOU STANDING THERE?
REMEMBER, THE CAPTAIN SAID FOR US TO COOPERATE.
YES, HE DID TELL US TO WORK TOGETHER ...
...BUT I DON'T SEE WHY I HAVE TO TAKE ORDERS FROM YOU.
HUH?

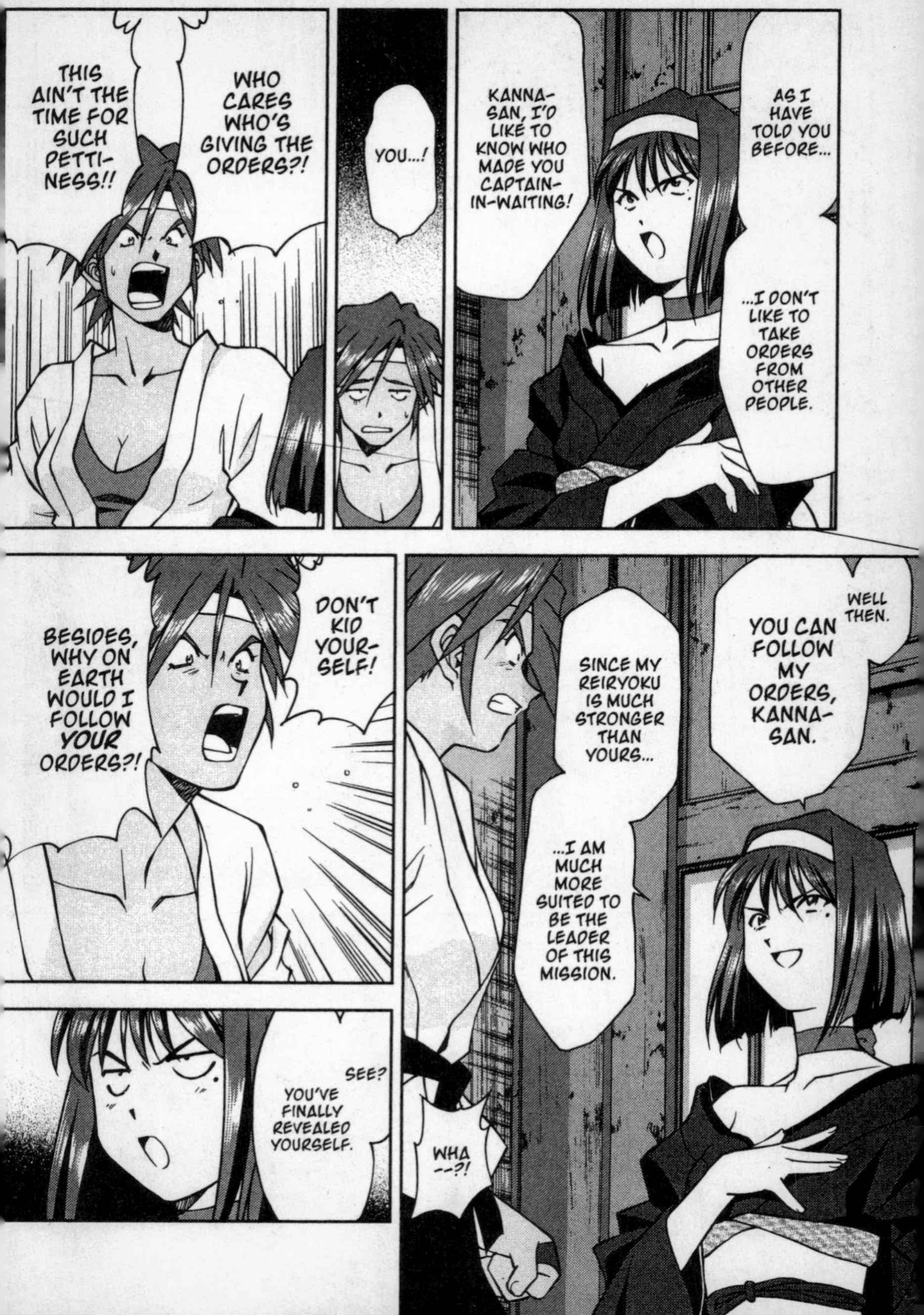
AS I HAVE TOLD YOU BEFORE...
...I DON'T LIKE TO TAKE ORDERS FROM OTHER PEOPLE.
KANNA-SAN, I'D LIKE TO KNOW WHO MADE YOU CAPTAIN-IN-WAITING!
YOU...!
WHO CARES WHO'S GIVING THE ORDERS?!
THIS AIN'T THE TIME FOR SUCH PETTINESS!!
WELL THEN.
YOU CAN FOLLOW MY ORDERS, KANNA-SAN.
SINCE MY REIRYOKU IS MUCH STRONGER THAN YOURS...
...I AM MUCH MORE SUITED TO BE THE LEADER OF THIS MISSION.
DON'T KID YOURSELF!
BESIDES, WHY ON EARTH WOULD I FOLLOW *YOUR* ORDERS?!
SEE?
YOU'VE FINALLY REVEALED YOURSELF.
WHA--?!

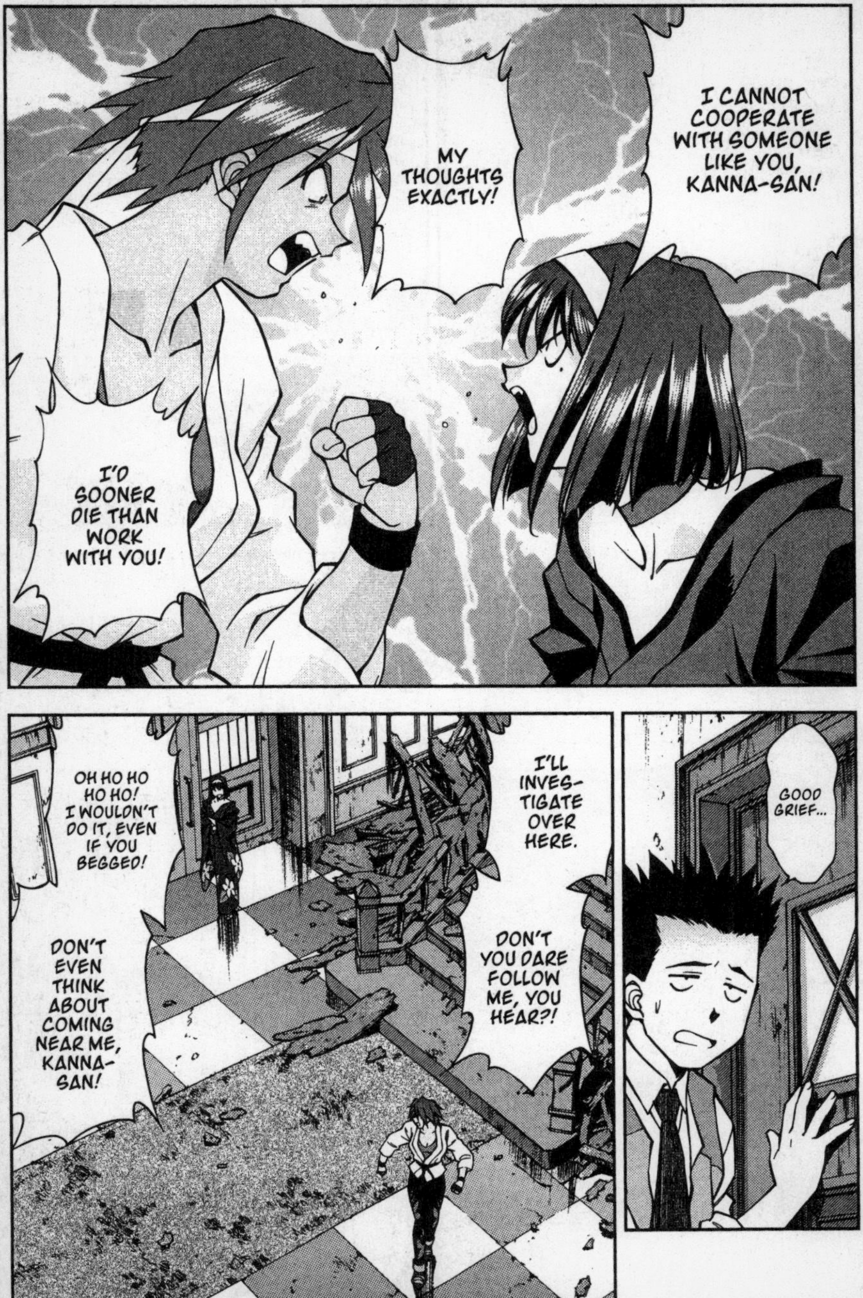
I CANNOT COOPERATE WITH SOMEONE LIKE YOU, KANNA-SAN!
MY THOUGHTS EXACTLY!
I'D SOONER DIE THAN WORK WITH YOU!
GOOD GRIEF...
I'LL INVES-TIGATE OVER HERE.
DON'T YOU DARE FOLLOW ME, YOU HEAR?!
OH HO HO HO HO! I WOULDN'T DO IT, EVEN IF YOU BEGGED!
DON'T EVEN THINK ABOUT COMING NEAR ME, KANNA-SAN!

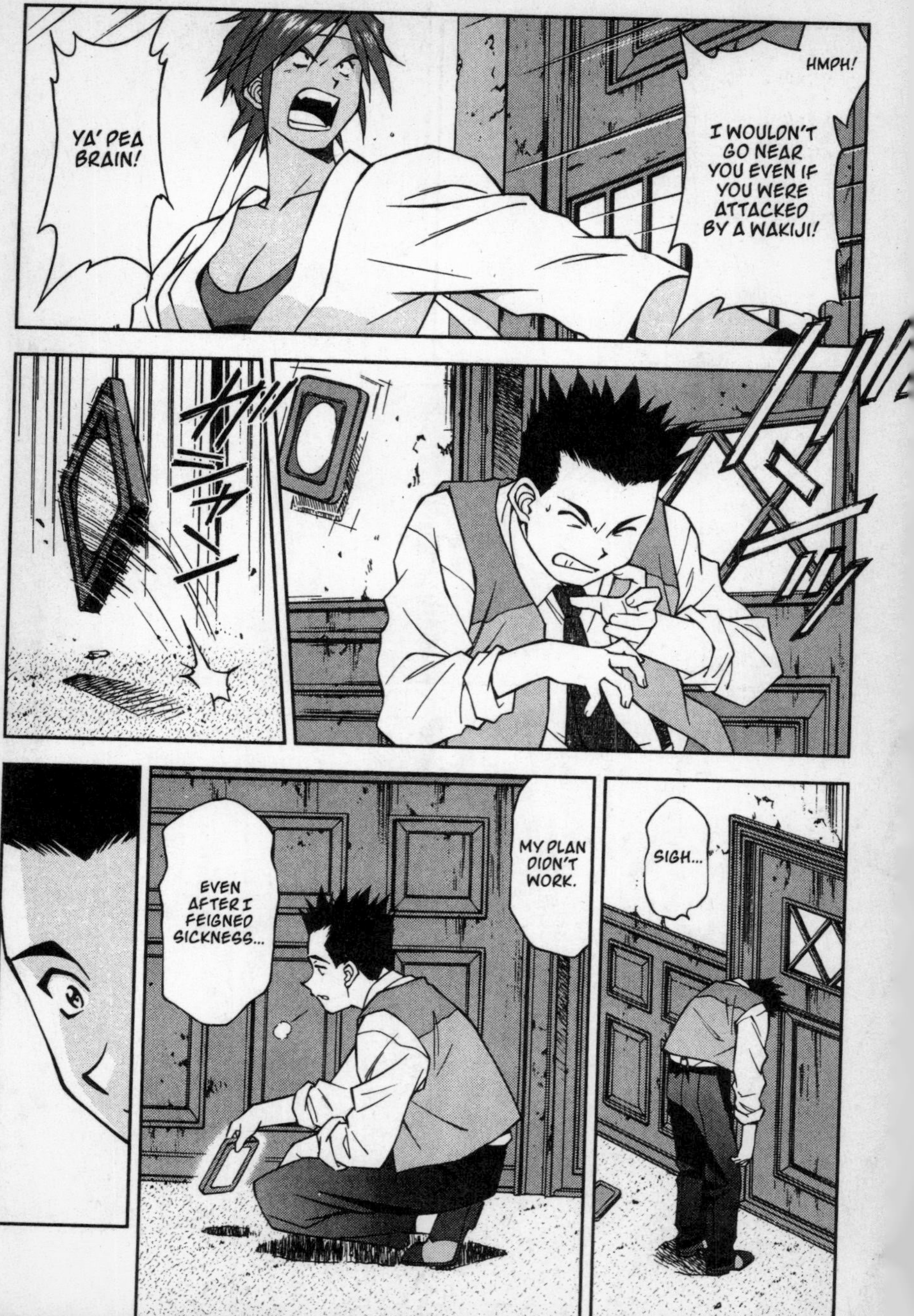
HMPH!
I WOULDN'T GO NEAR YOU EVEN IF YOU WERE ATTACKED BY A WAKIJI!
YA' PEA BRAIN!
SIGH...
MY PLAN DIDN'T WORK.
EVEN AFTER I FEIGNED SICKNESS...

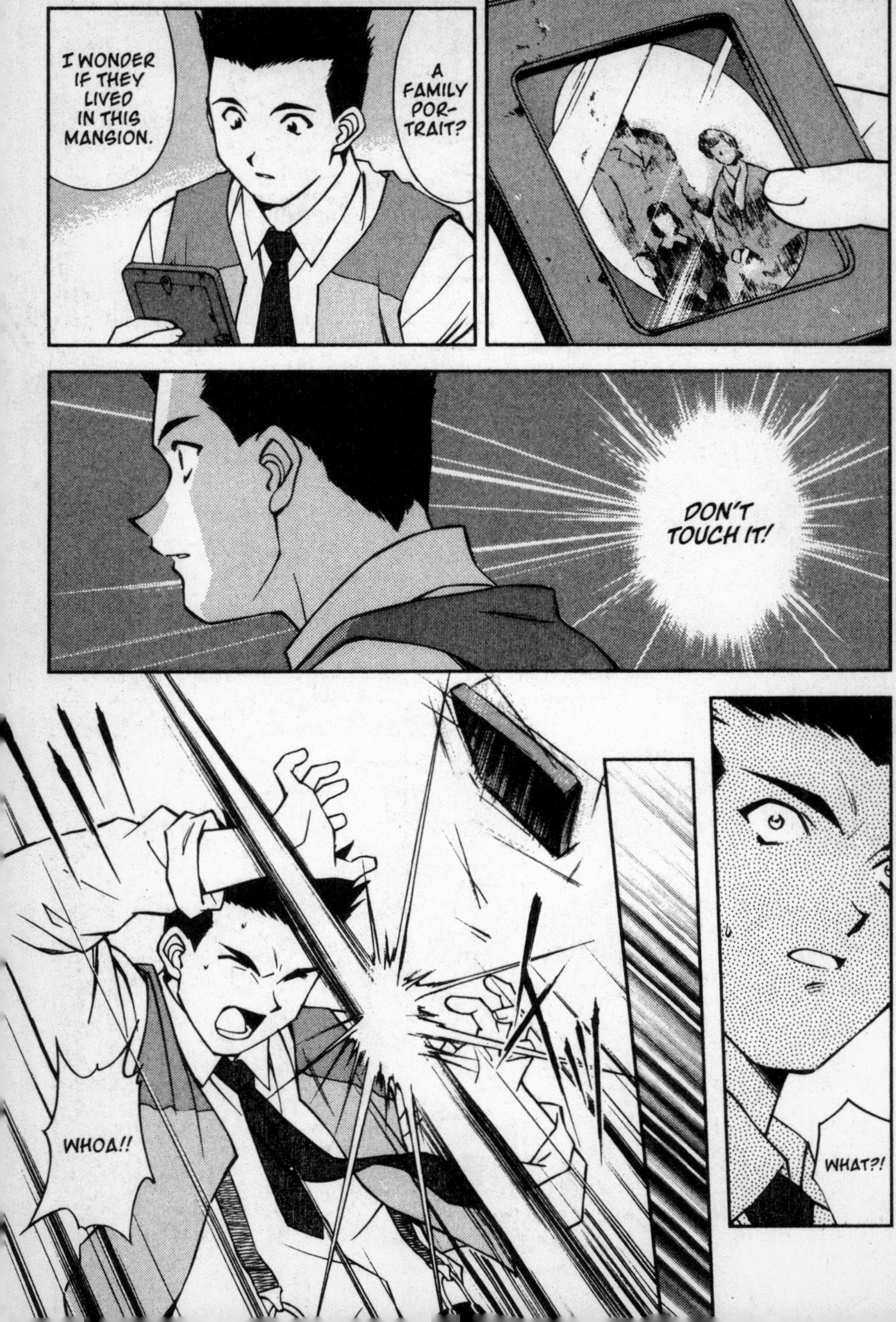
A FAMILY POR-TRAIT?
I WONDER IF THEY LIVED IN THIS MANSION.
DON'T TOUCH IT!
WHAT?!
WHOA!!

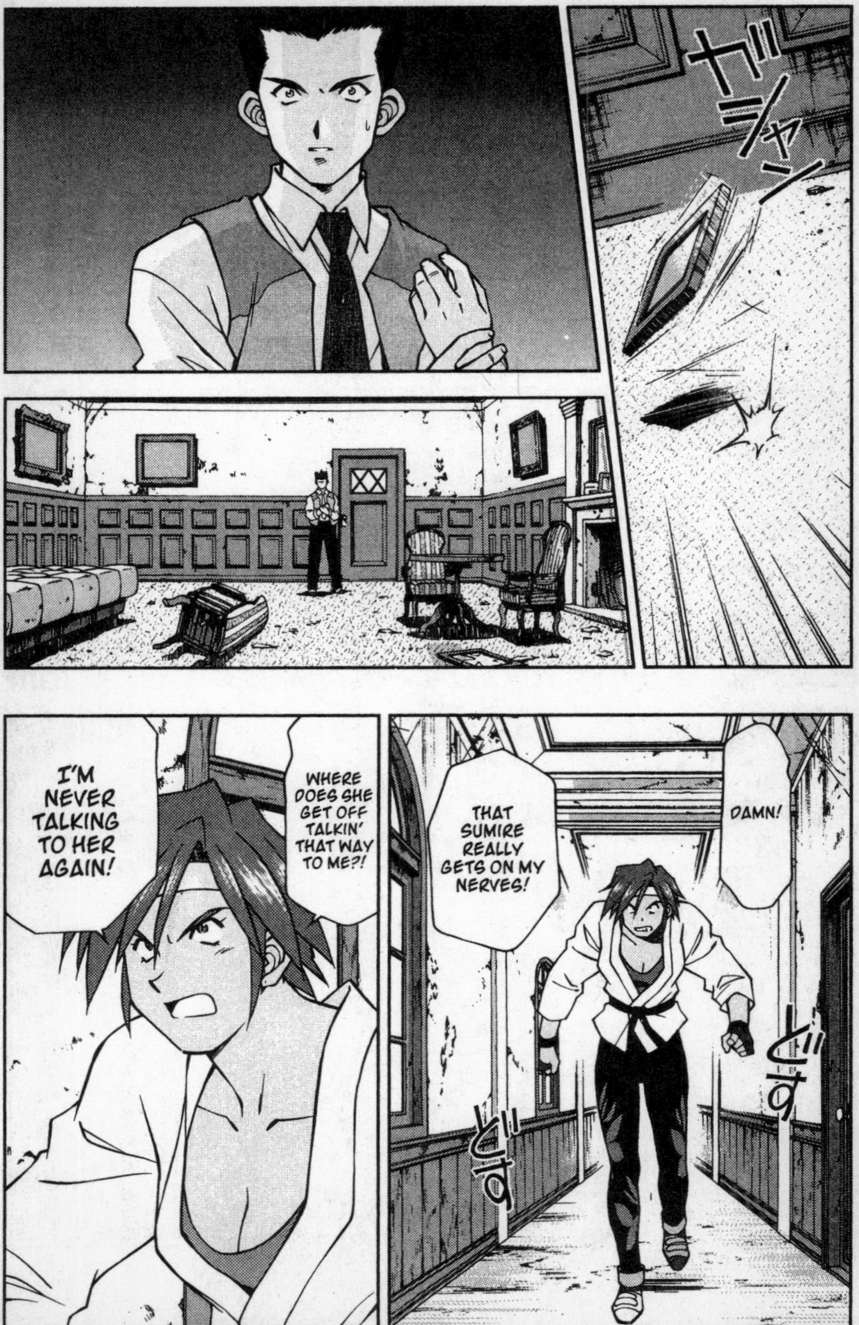
ガシャン
DAMN!
THAT SUMIRE REALLY GETS ON MY NERVES!
どす
どす
WHERE DOES SHE GET OFF TALKIN' THAT WAY TO ME?!
I'M NEVER TALKING TO HER AGAIN!

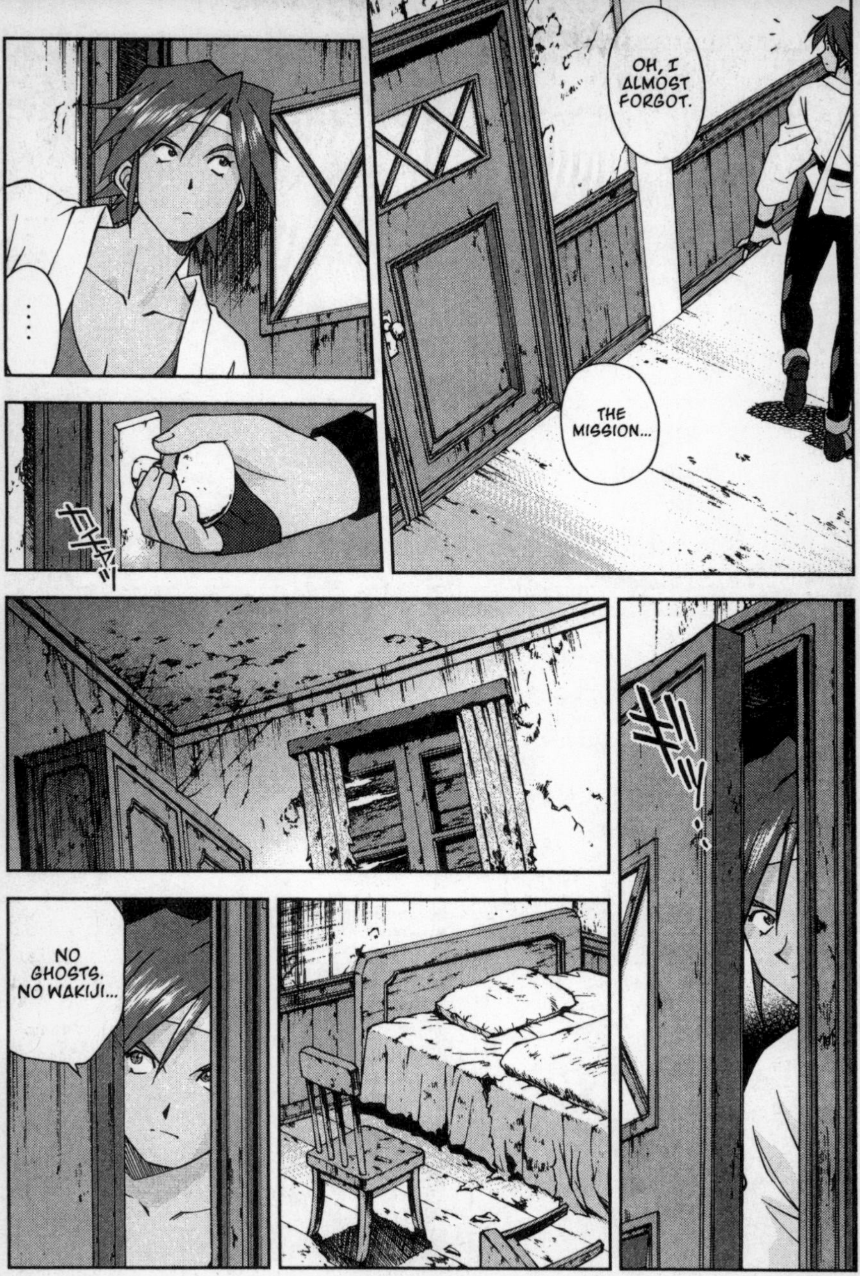
OH, I ALMOST FORGOT.
THE MISSION...
....
NO GHOSTS. NO WAKIJI...

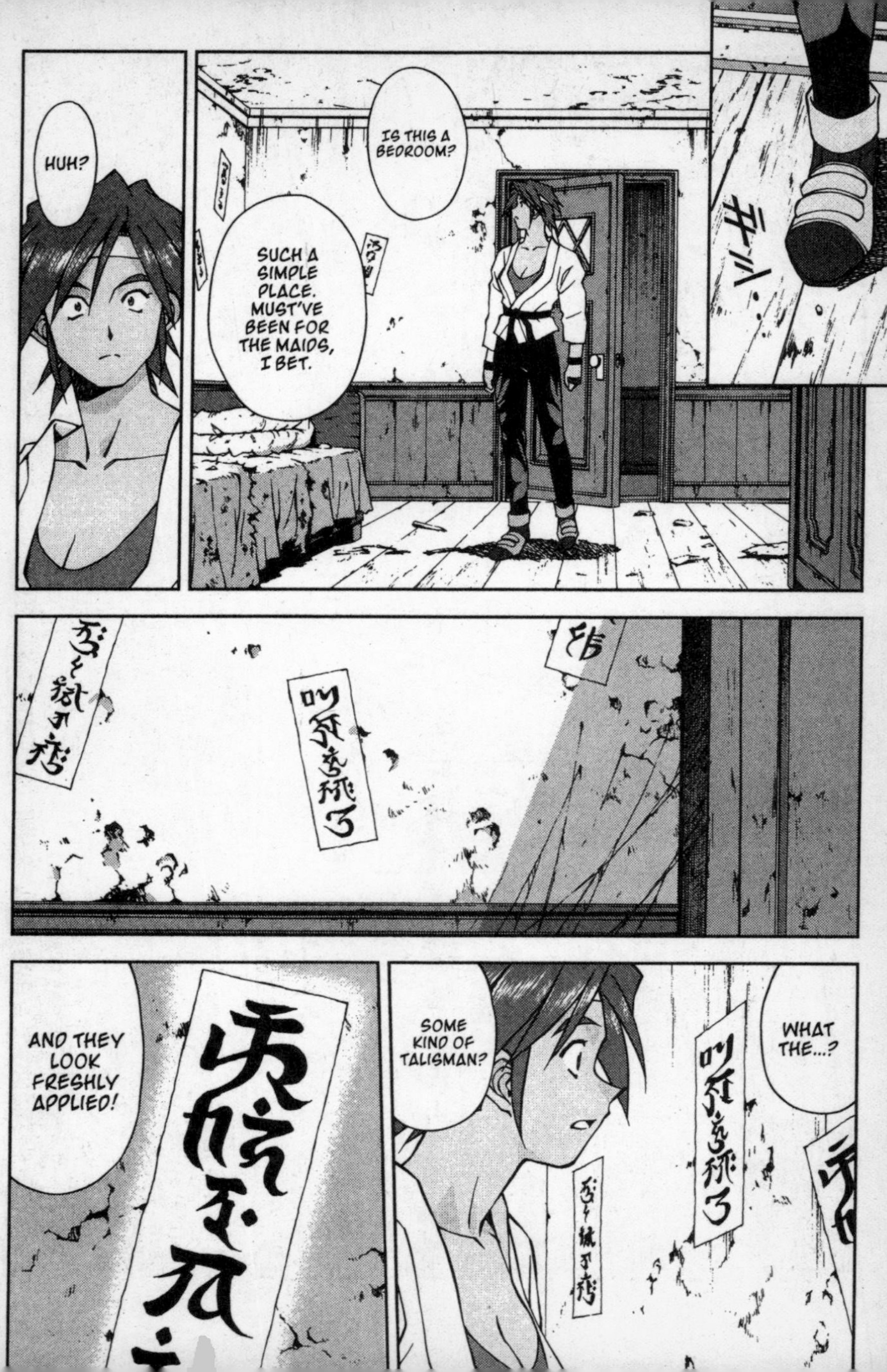
IS THIS A BEDROOM?
SUCH A SIMPLE PLACE. MUST'VE BEEN FOR THE MAIDS, I BET.
HUH?
WHAT THE...?
SOME KIND OF TALISMAN?
AND THEY LOOK FRESHLY APPLIED!

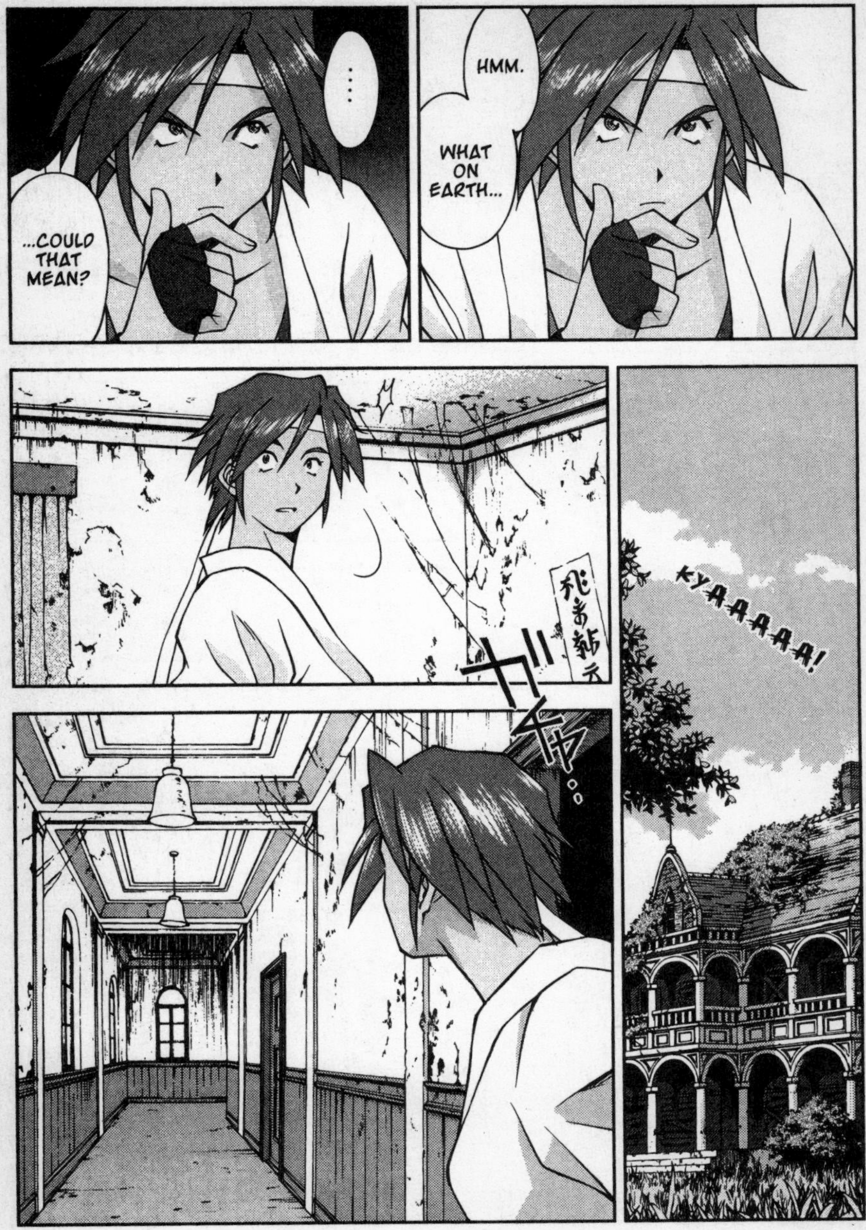
HMM.
WHAT ON EARTH...
....
...COULD THAT MEAN?
KYAAAAAAA!

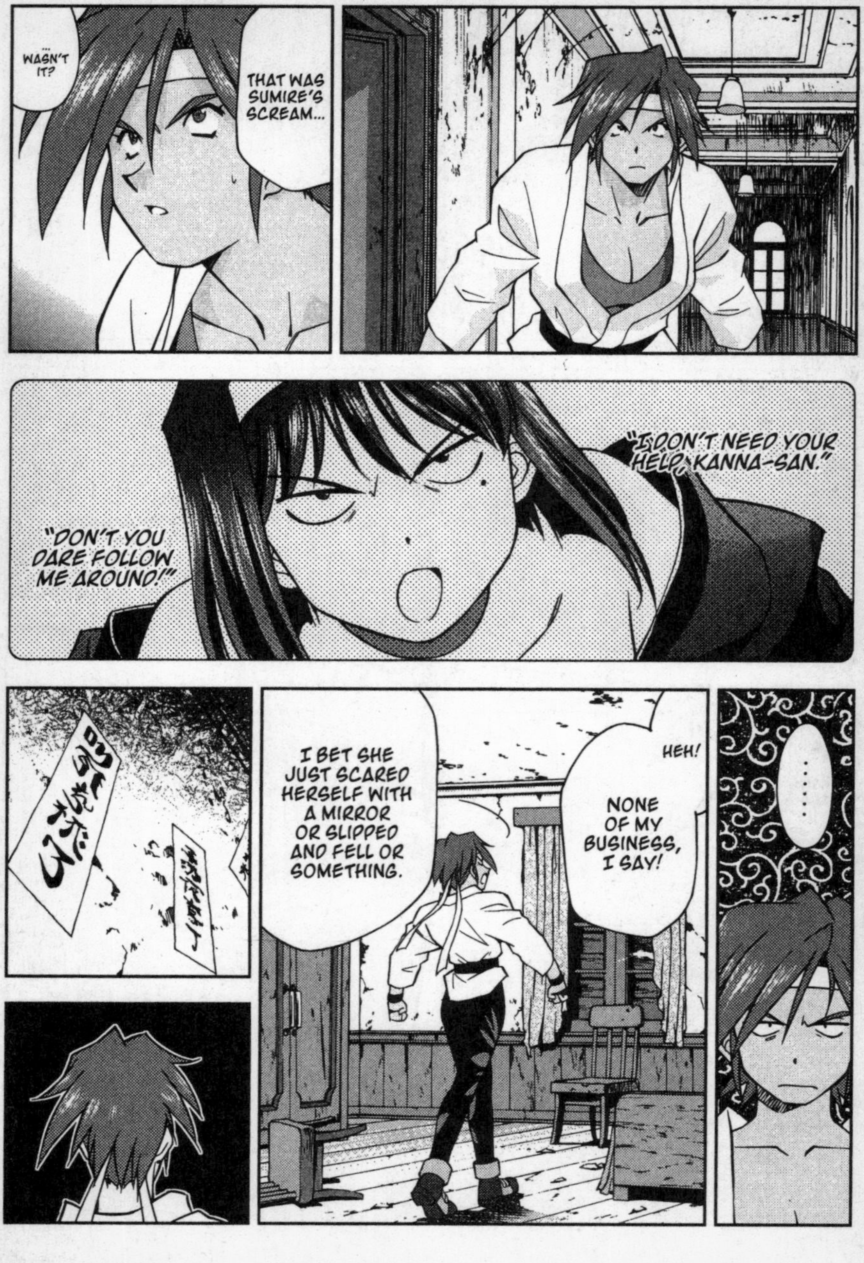
THAT WAS SUMIRE'S SCREAM...
...WASN'T IT?
"I DON'T NEED YOUR HELP, KANNA-SAN."
"DON'T YOU DARE FOLLOW ME AROUND!"
......
HEH!
NONE OF MY BUSINESS, I SAY!
I BET SHE JUST SCARED HERSELF WITH A MIRROR OR SLIPPED AND FELL OR SOMETHING.

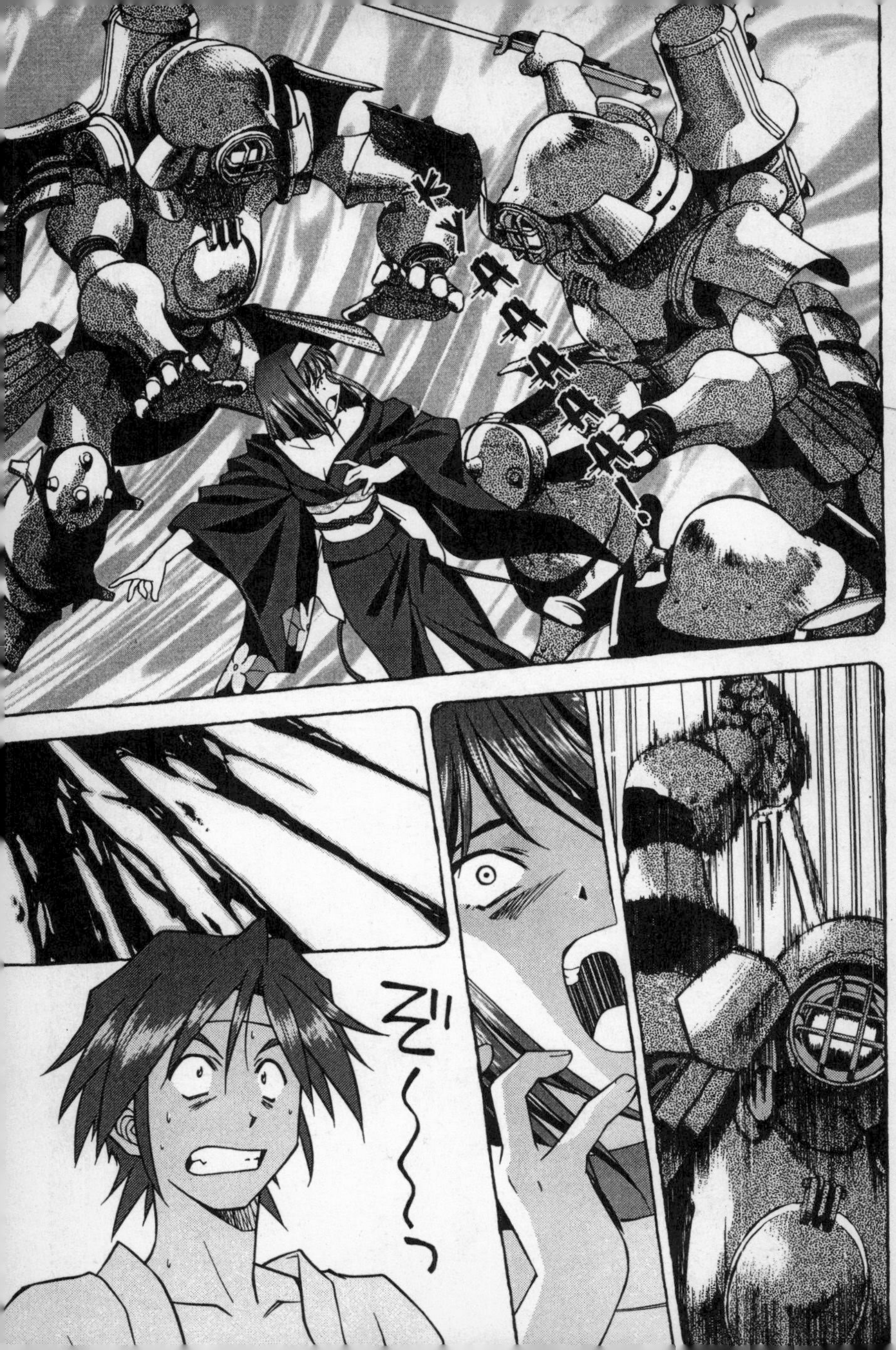
KYAAAAA-!
ぞ〜っ

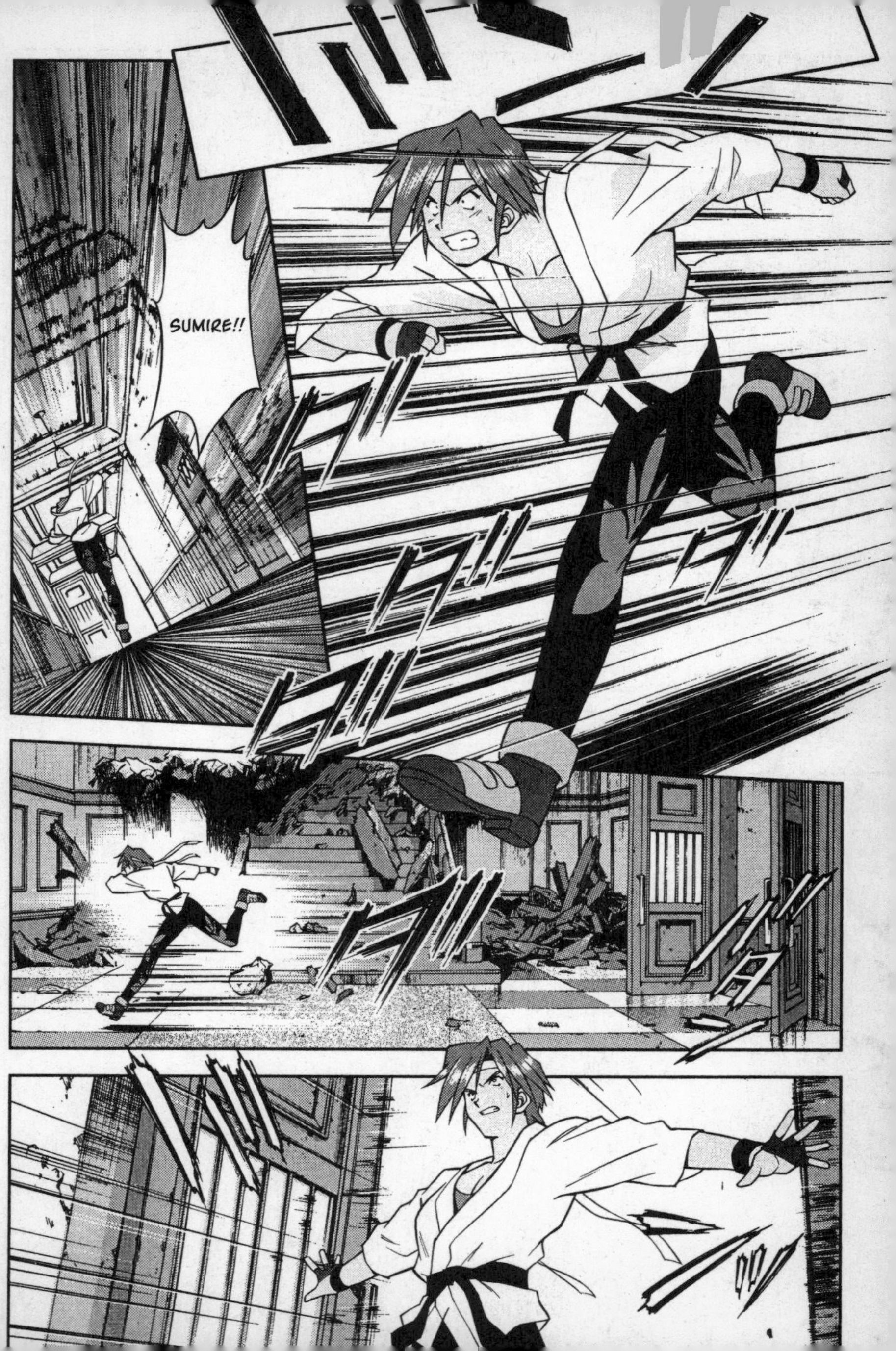
SUMIRE!!

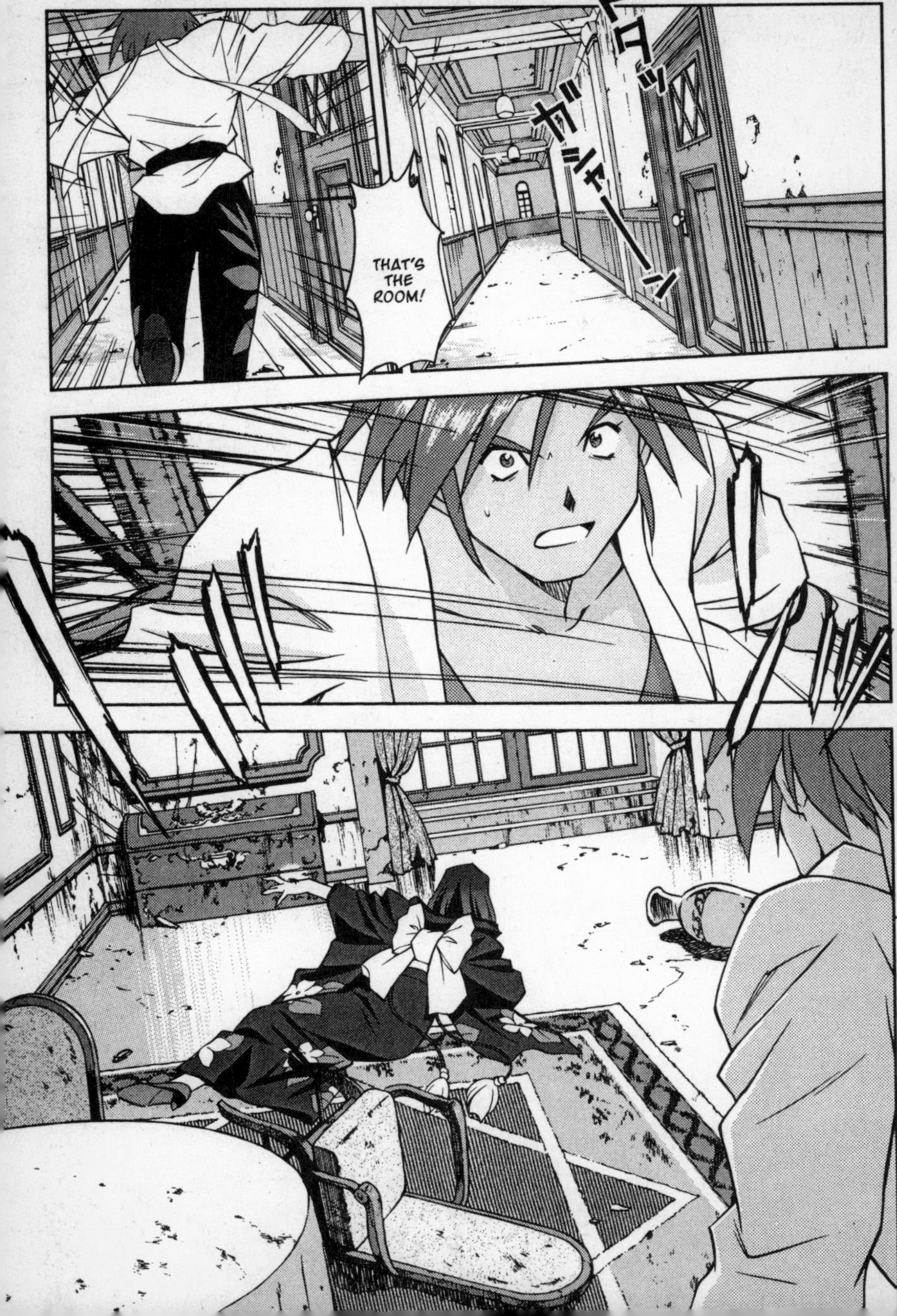
ドタッ
ガシャーン
THAT'S THE ROOM!

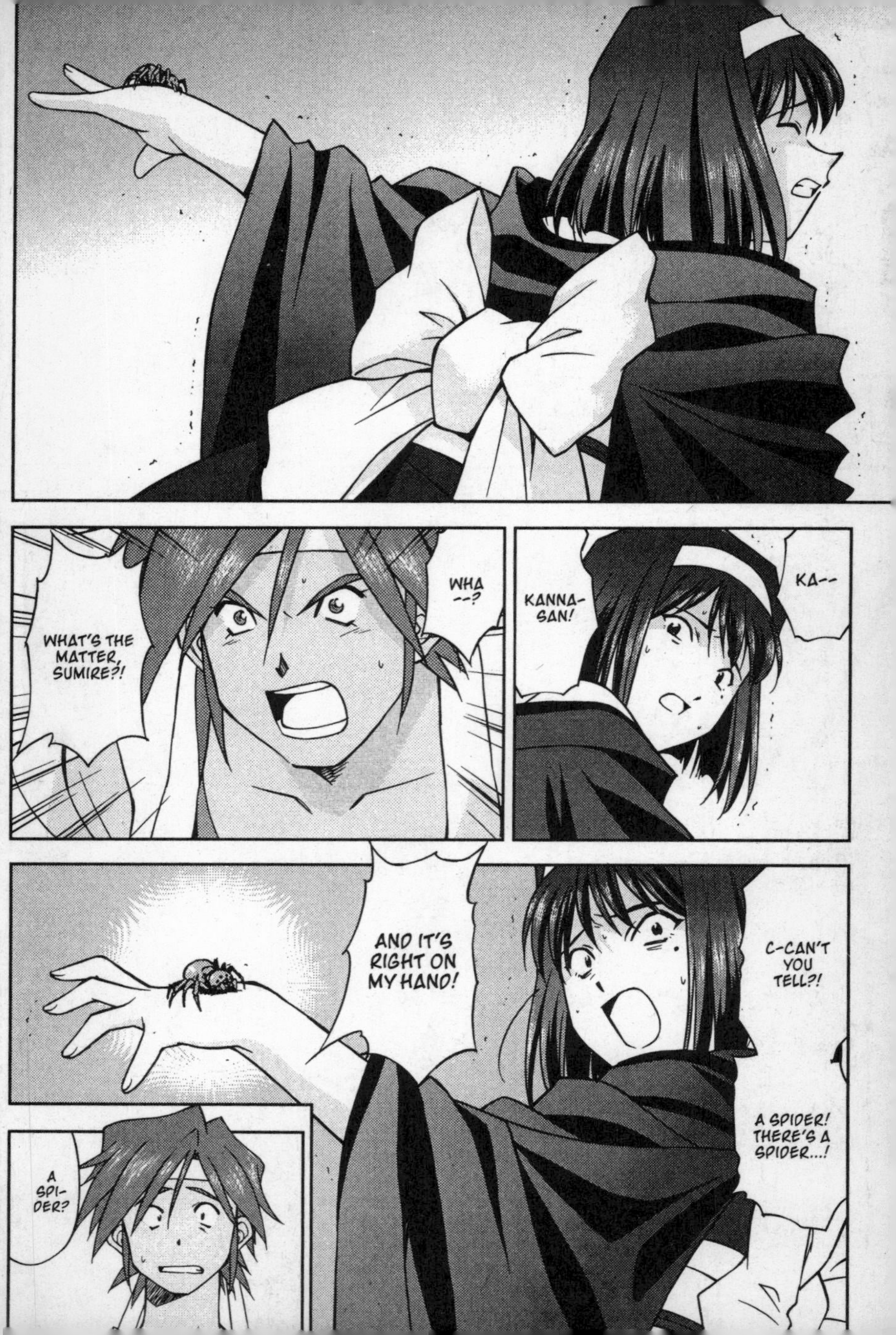
KA--
KANNA-SAN!
WHA--?
WHAT'S THE MATTER, SUMIRE?!
C-CAN'T YOU TELL?!
A SPIDER! THERE'S A SPIDER...!
AND IT'S RIGHT ON MY HAND!
A SPIDER?

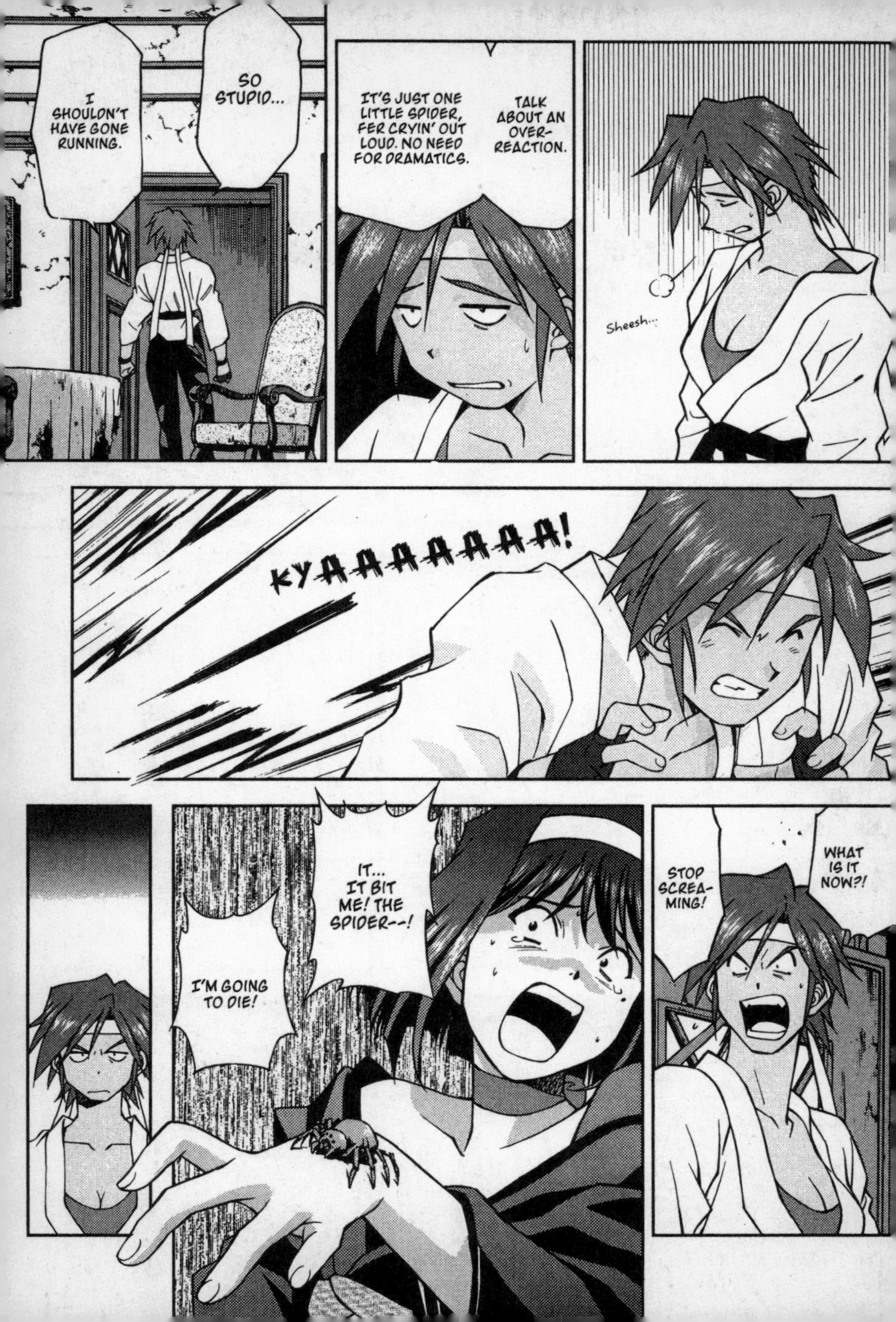
Sheesh...
TALK ABOUT AN OVER-REACTION.
IT'S JUST ONE LITTLE SPIDER, FER CRYIN' OUT LOUD. NO NEED FOR DRAMATICS.
SO STUPID...
I SHOULDN'T HAVE GONE RUNNING.
KYAAAAAAAA!
WHAT IS IT NOW?!
STOP SCREAMING!
IT... IT BIT ME! THE SPIDER--!
I'M GOING TO DIE!

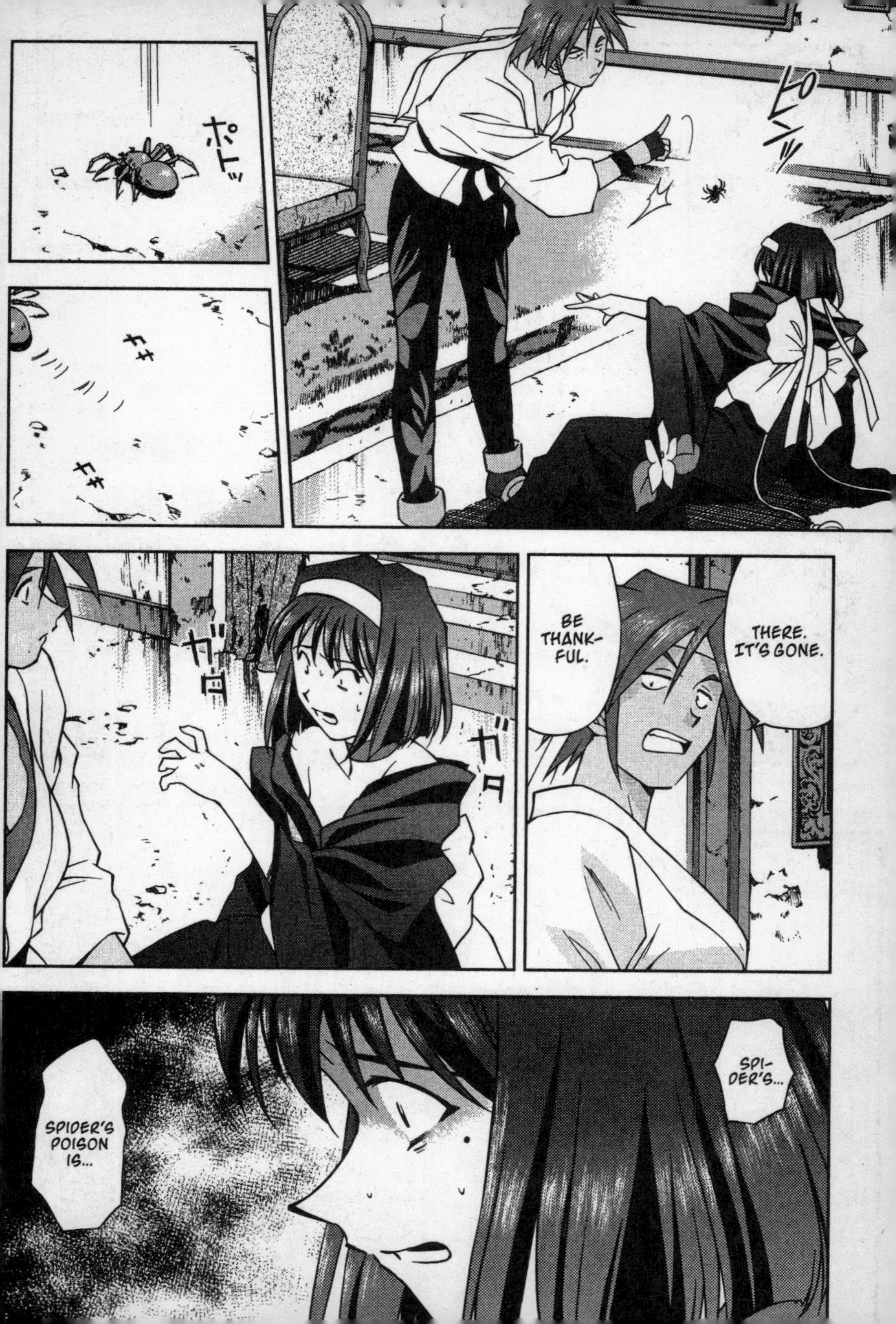
ピンッ
ポトッ
THERE. IT'S GONE.
BE THANKFUL.
ガタ
ガタ
SPI-DER'S...
SPIDER'S POISON IS...

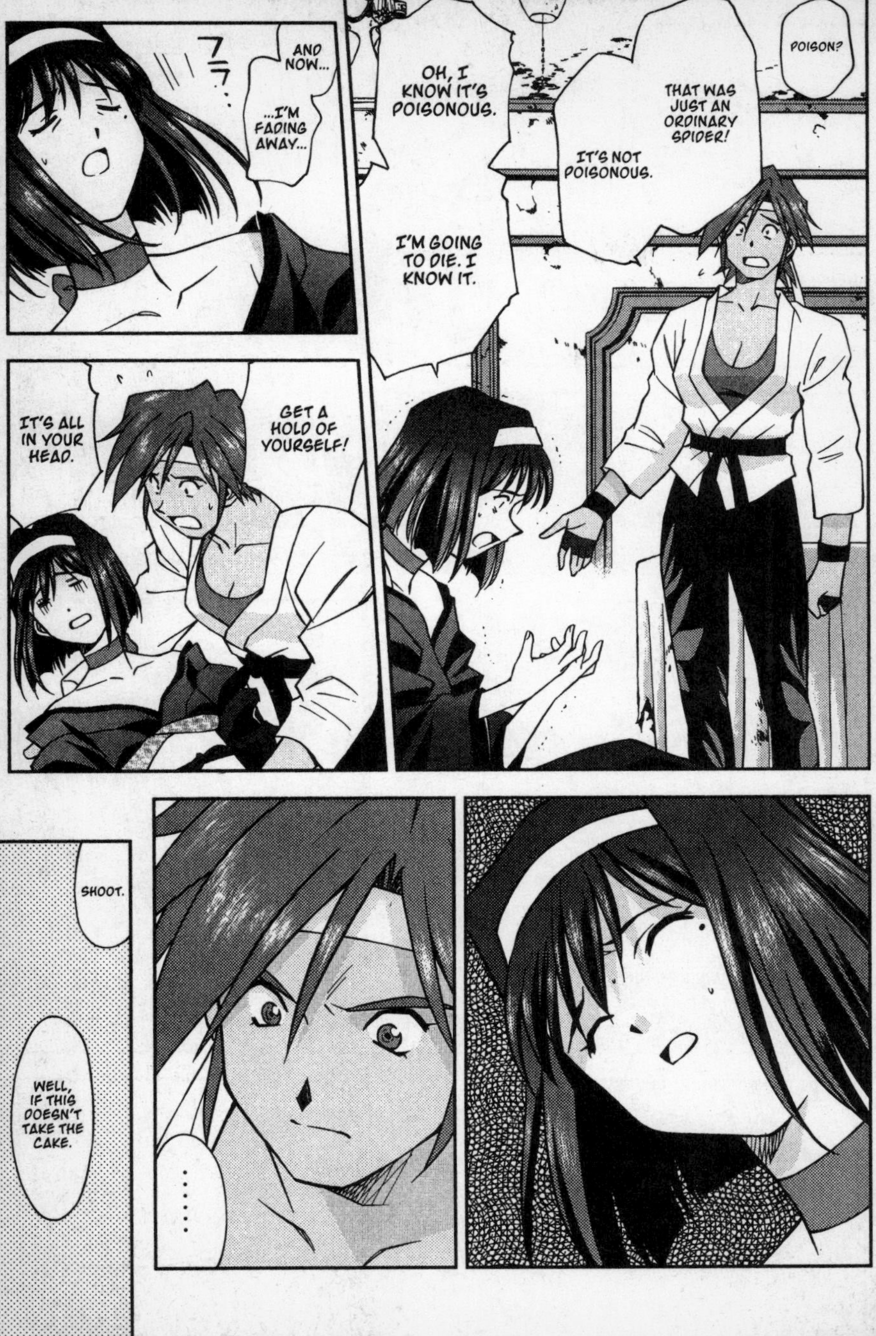
POISON?
THAT WAS JUST AN ORDINARY SPIDER!
IT'S NOT POISONOUS.
OH, I KNOW IT'S POISONOUS.
I'M GOING TO DIE. I KNOW IT.
AND NOW...
...I'M FADING AWAY...
GET A HOLD OF YOURSELF!
IT'S ALL IN YOUR HEAD.
......
SHOOT.
WELL, IF THIS DOESN'T TAKE THE CAKE.

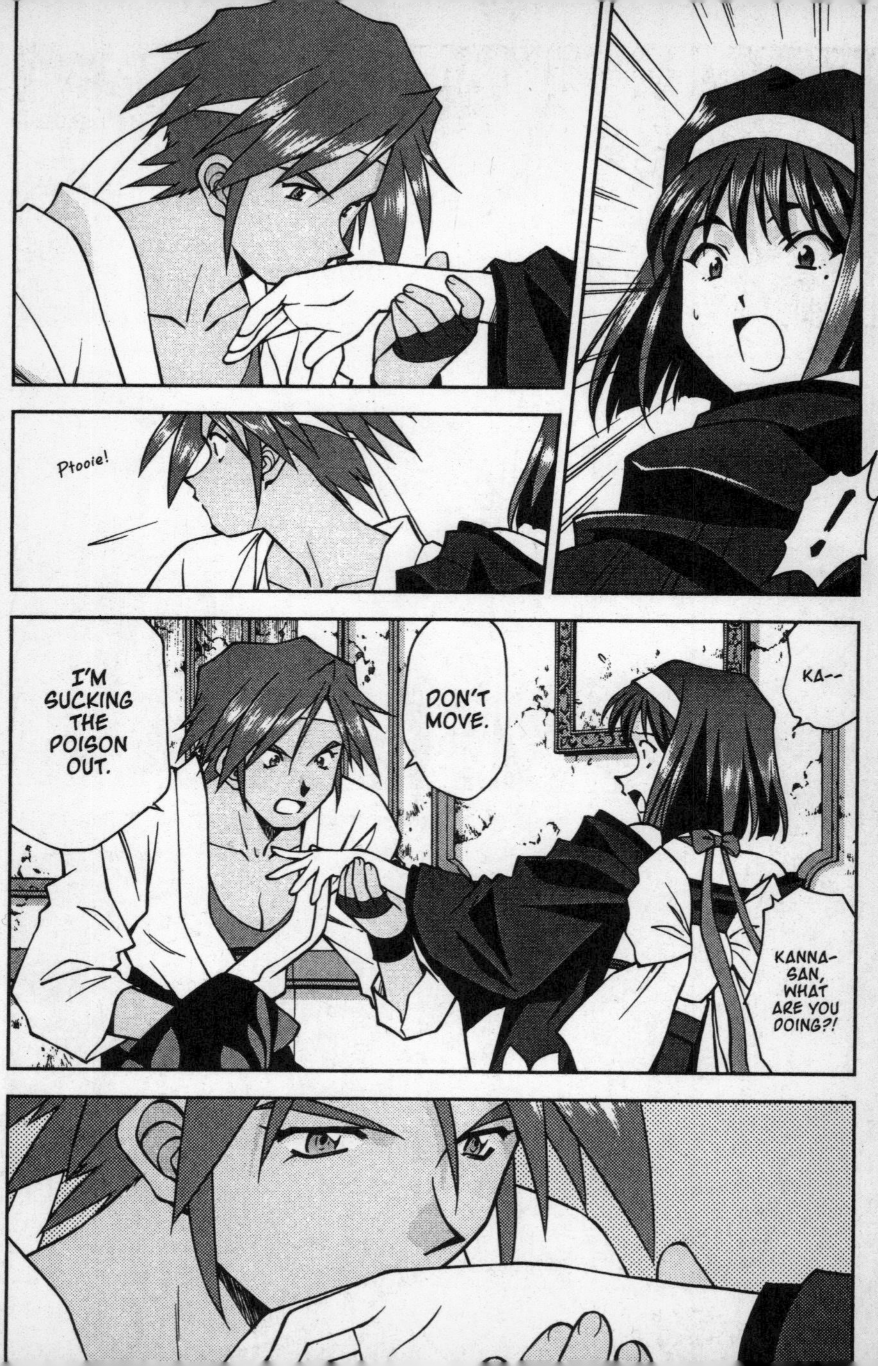
!
Ptooie!
KA--
KANNA-SAN, WHAT ARE YOU DOING?!
DON'T MOVE.
I'M SUCKING THE POISON OUT.

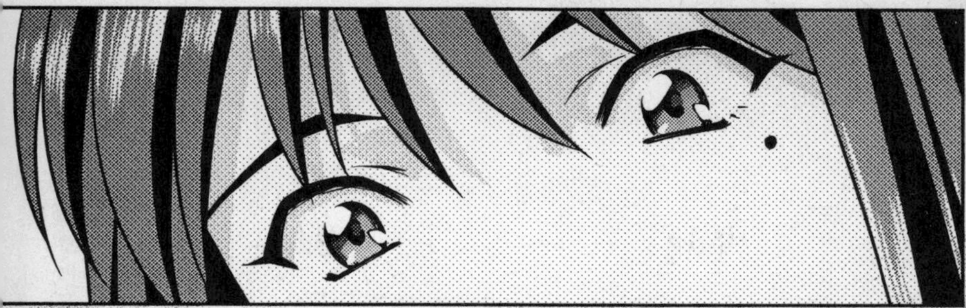
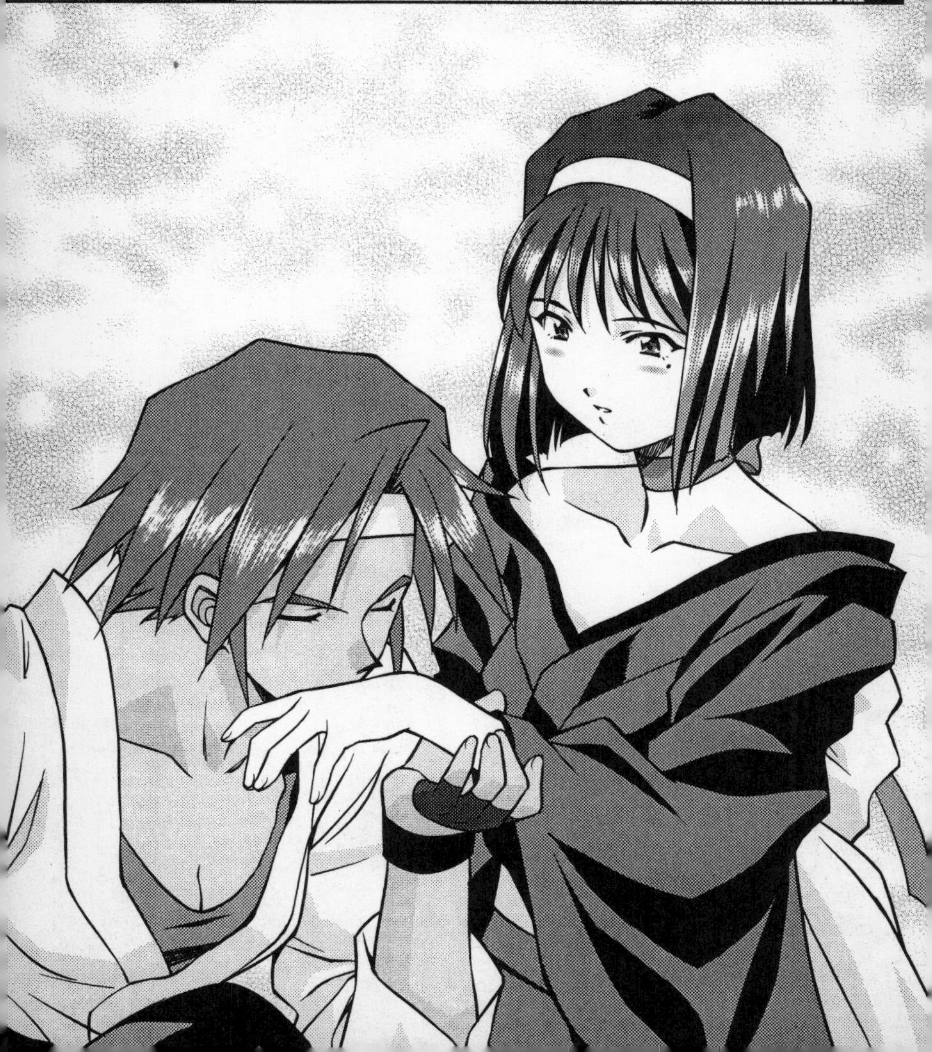

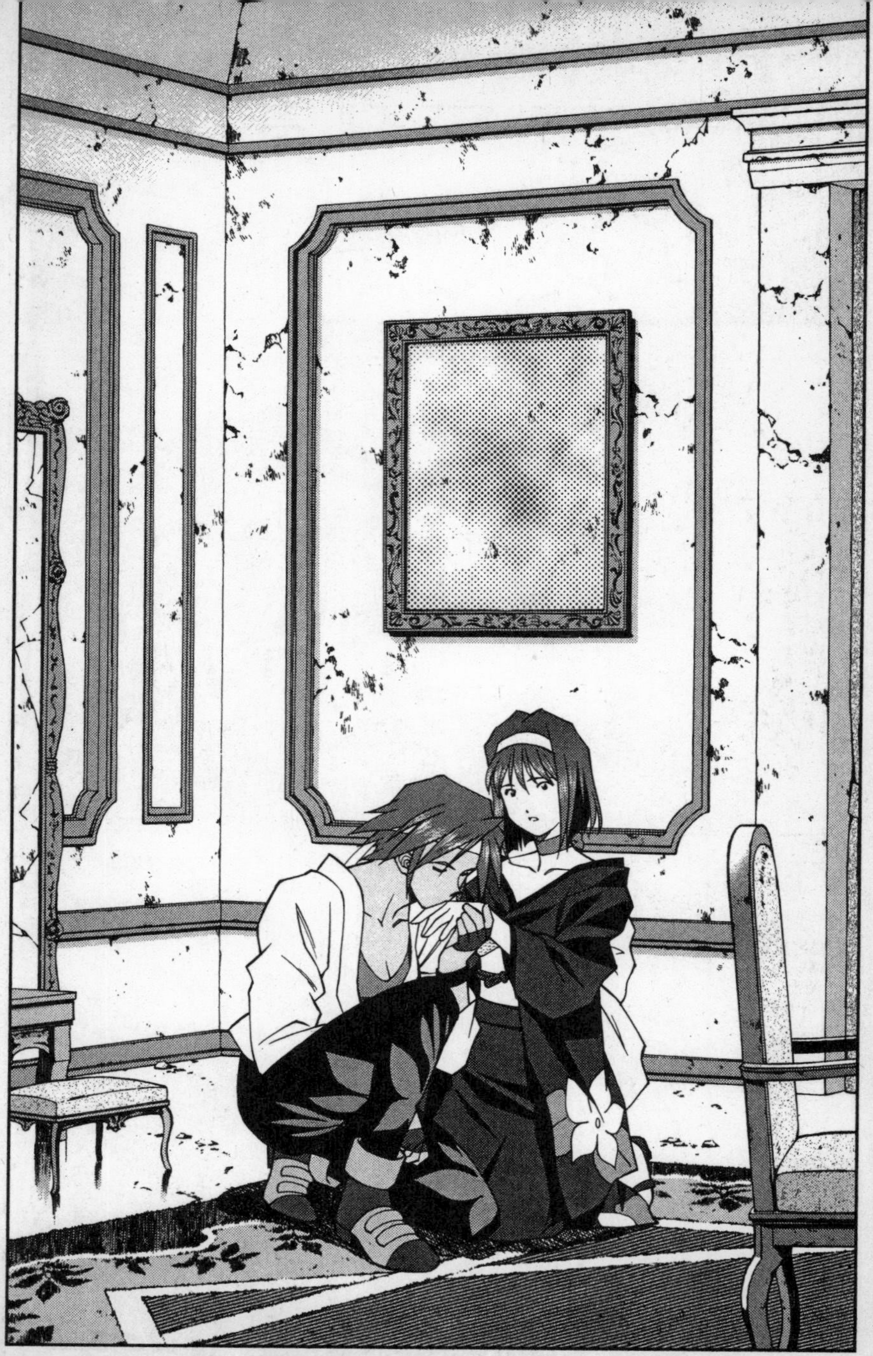

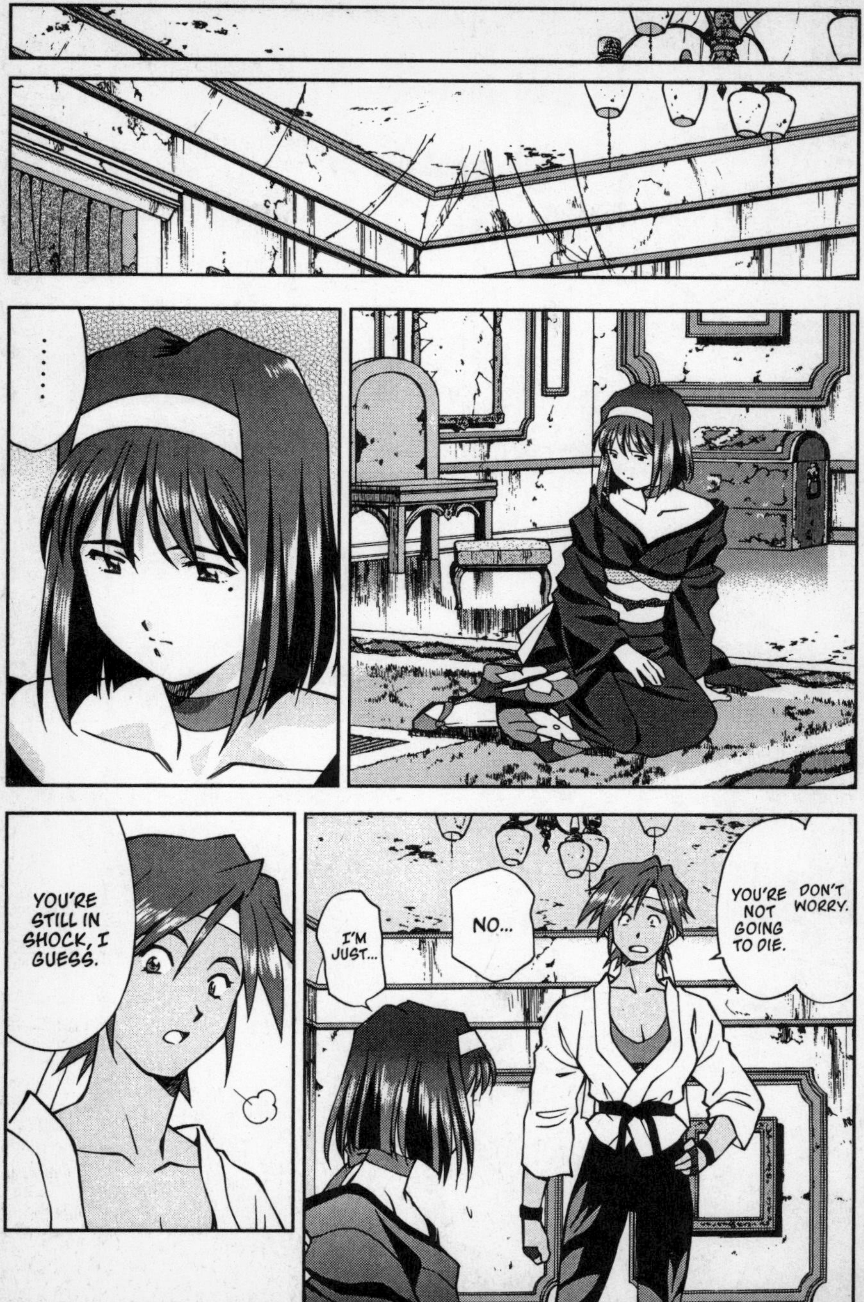
......
DON'T WORRY. YOU'RE NOT GOING TO DIE.
NO...
I'M JUST...
YOU'RE STILL IN SHOCK, I GUESS.

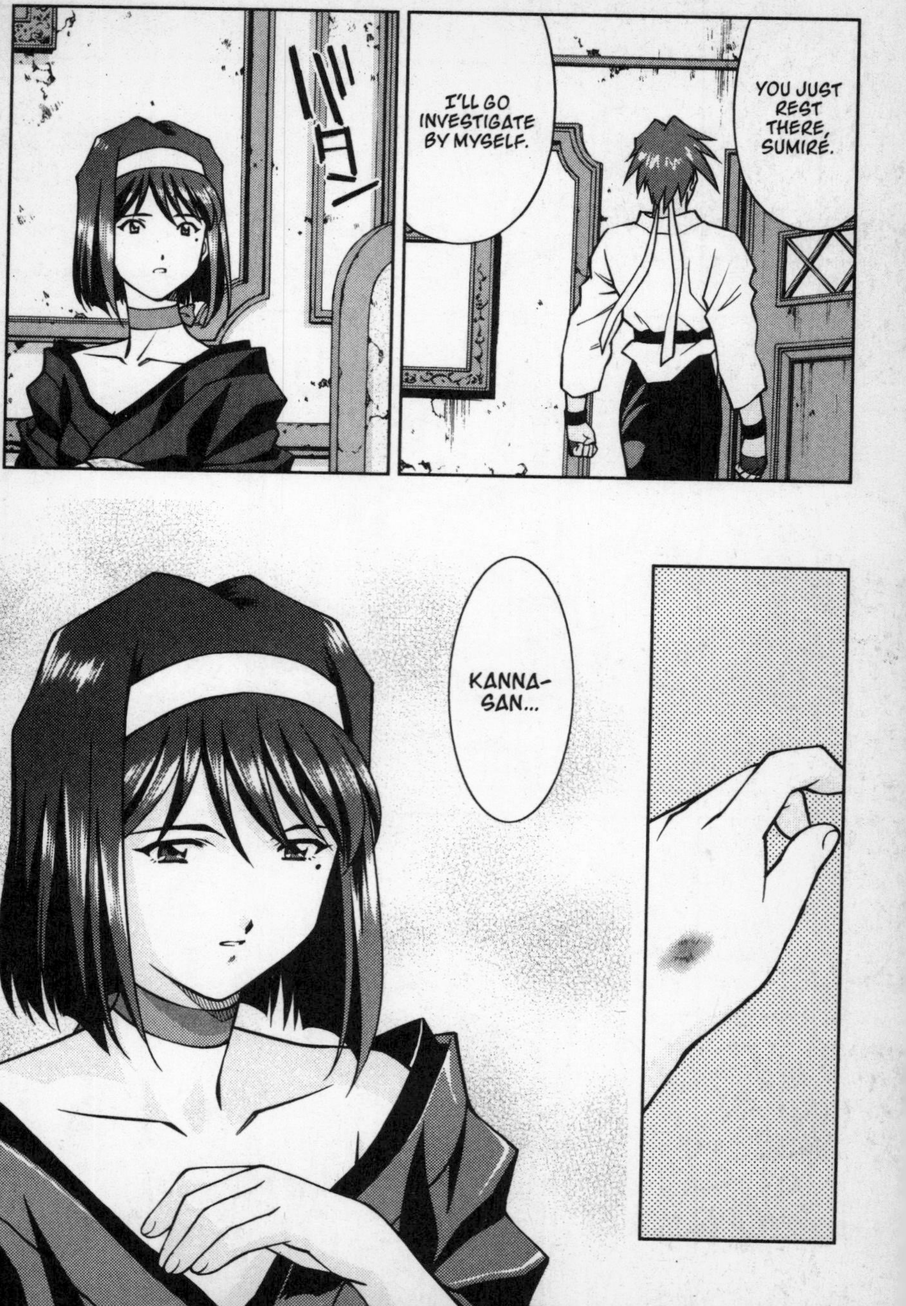
YOU JUST REST THERE, SUMIRÉ.
I'LL GO INVESTIGATE BY MYSELF.
バタン
KANNA-SAN...

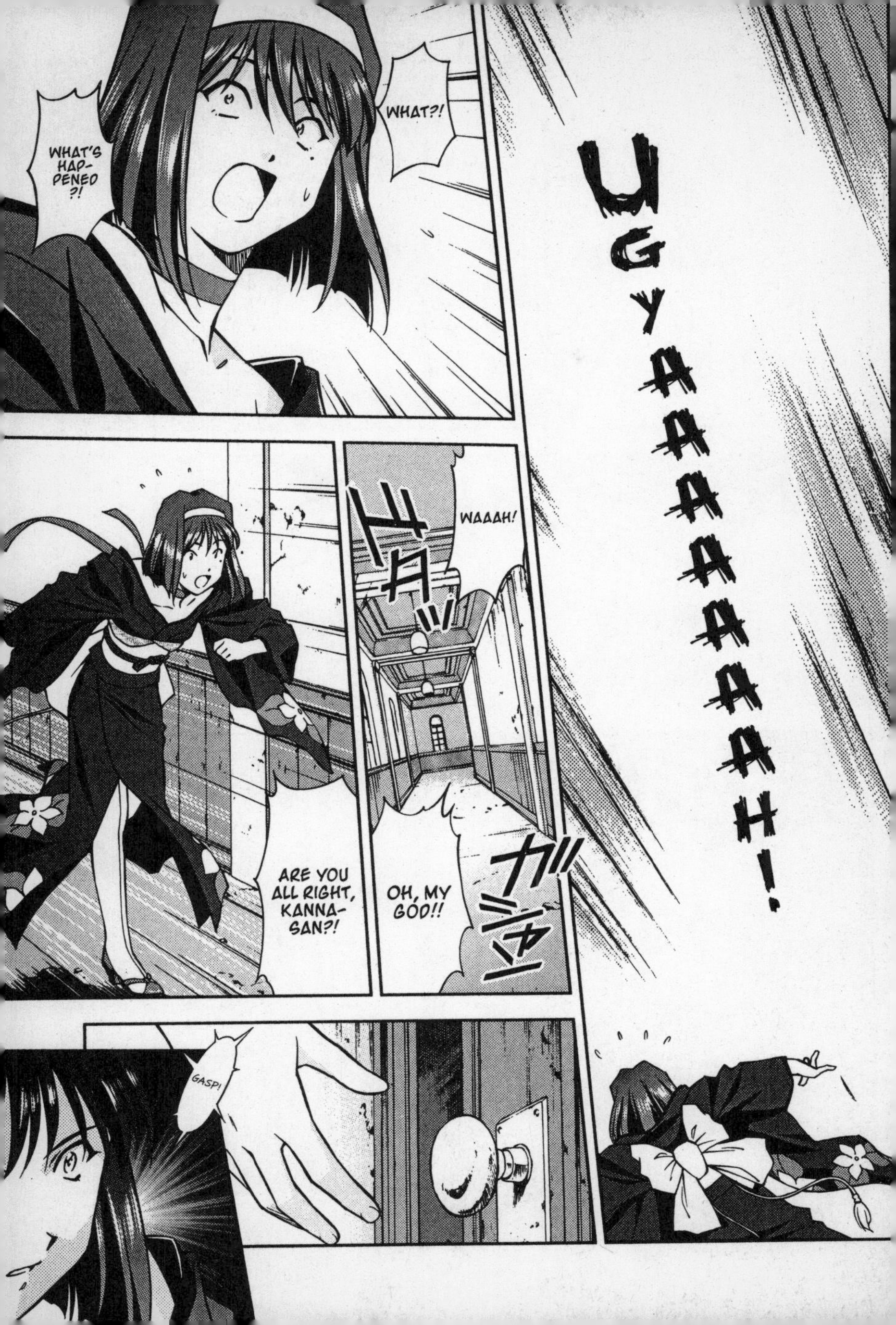
UGYAAAAAAAH!
WHAT?!
WHAT'S HAP-PENED?!
WAAAH!
OH, MY GOD!!
ARE YOU ALL RIGHT, KANNA-SAN?!
GASP!

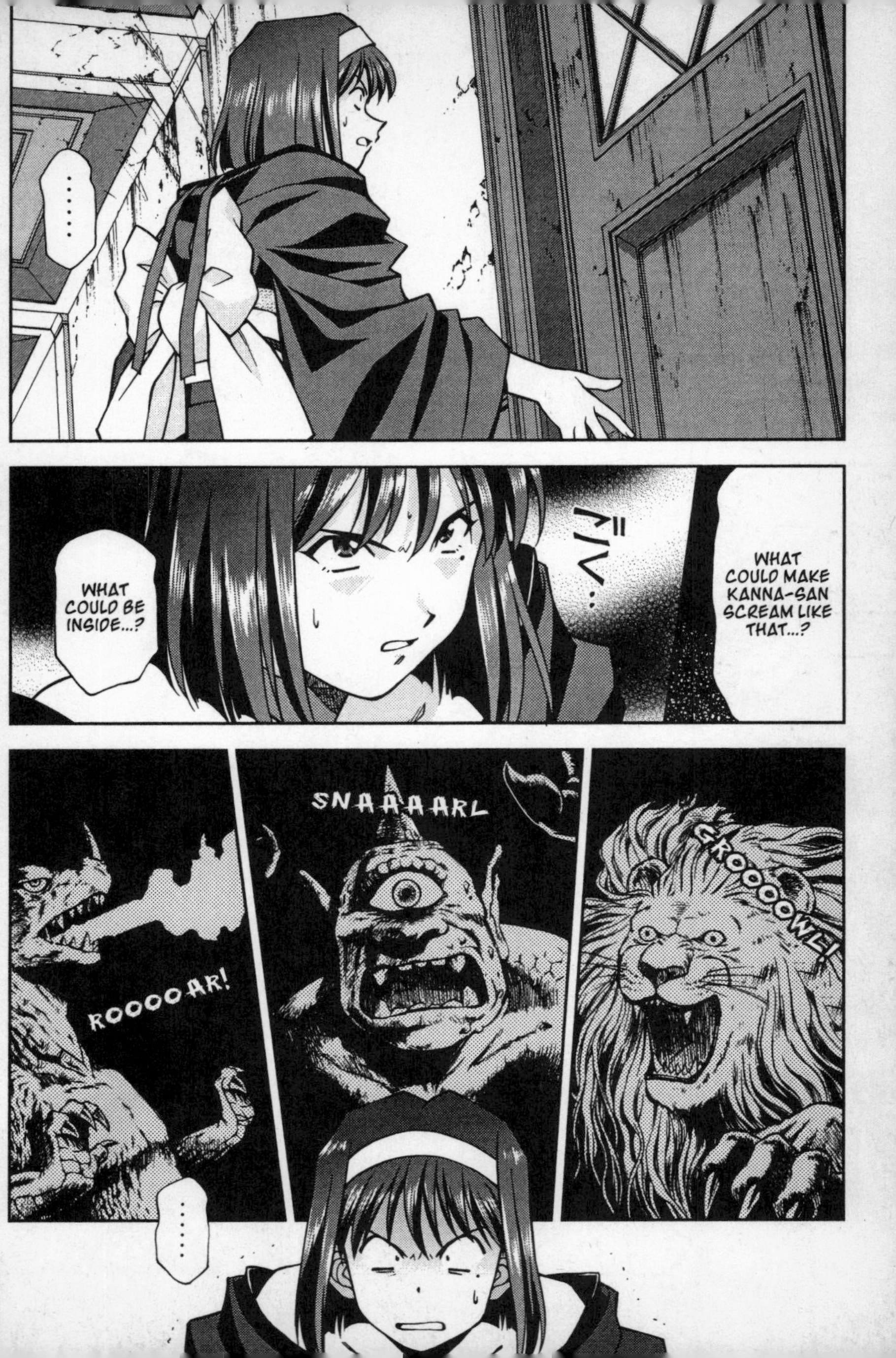
......
WHAT COULD MAKE KANNA-SAN SCREAM LIKE THAT...?
バ...
WHAT COULD BE INSIDE...?
GROOOOWL!
SNAAAAARL
ROOOOAR!
......

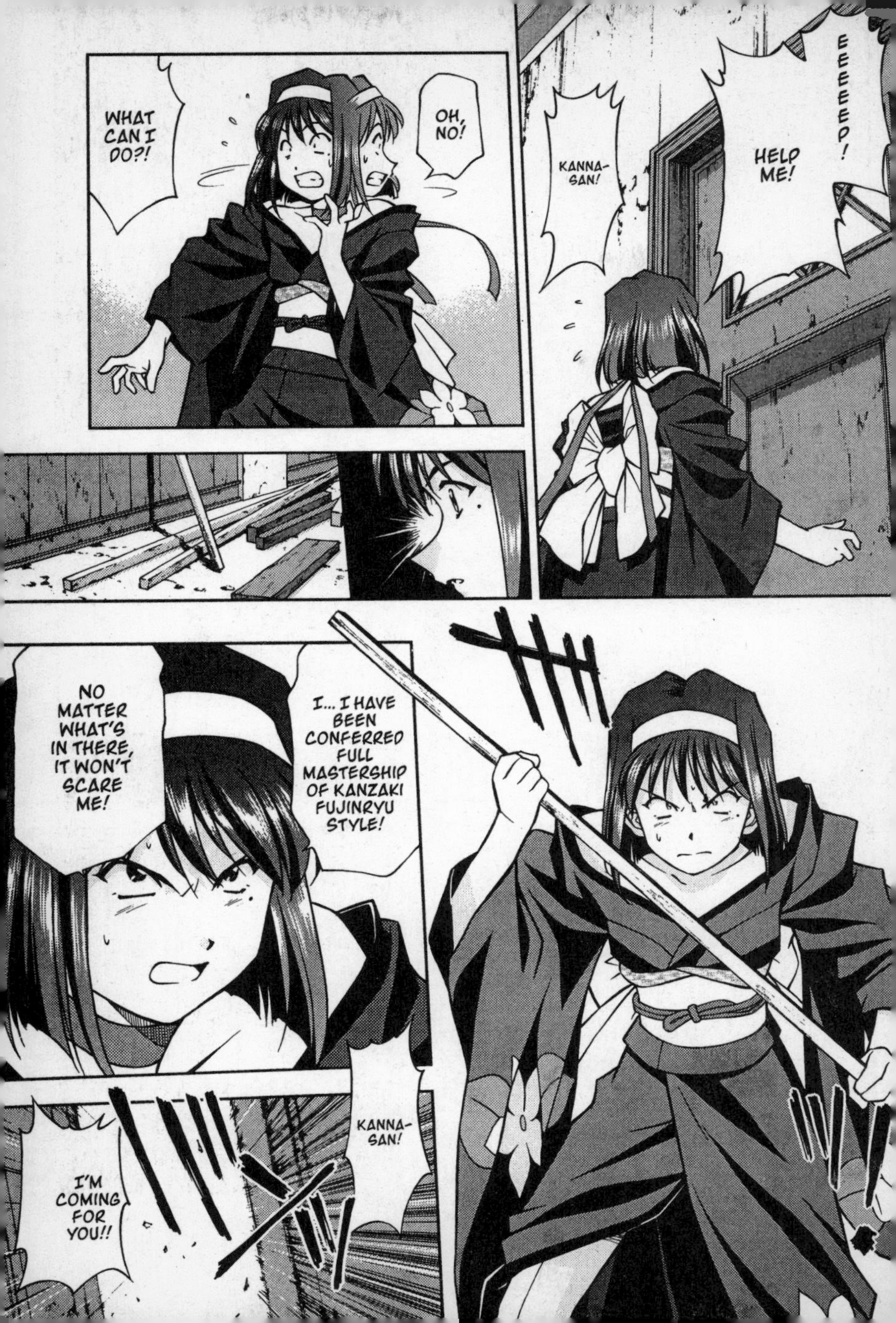
EEEEEEP!
HELP ME!
KANNA-SAN!
OH, NO!
WHAT CAN I DO?!
I... I HAVE BEEN CONFERRED FULL MASTERSHIP OF KANZAKI FUJINRYU STYLE!
NO MATTER WHAT'S IN THERE, IT WON'T SCARE ME!
KANNA-SAN!
I'M COMING FOR YOU!!

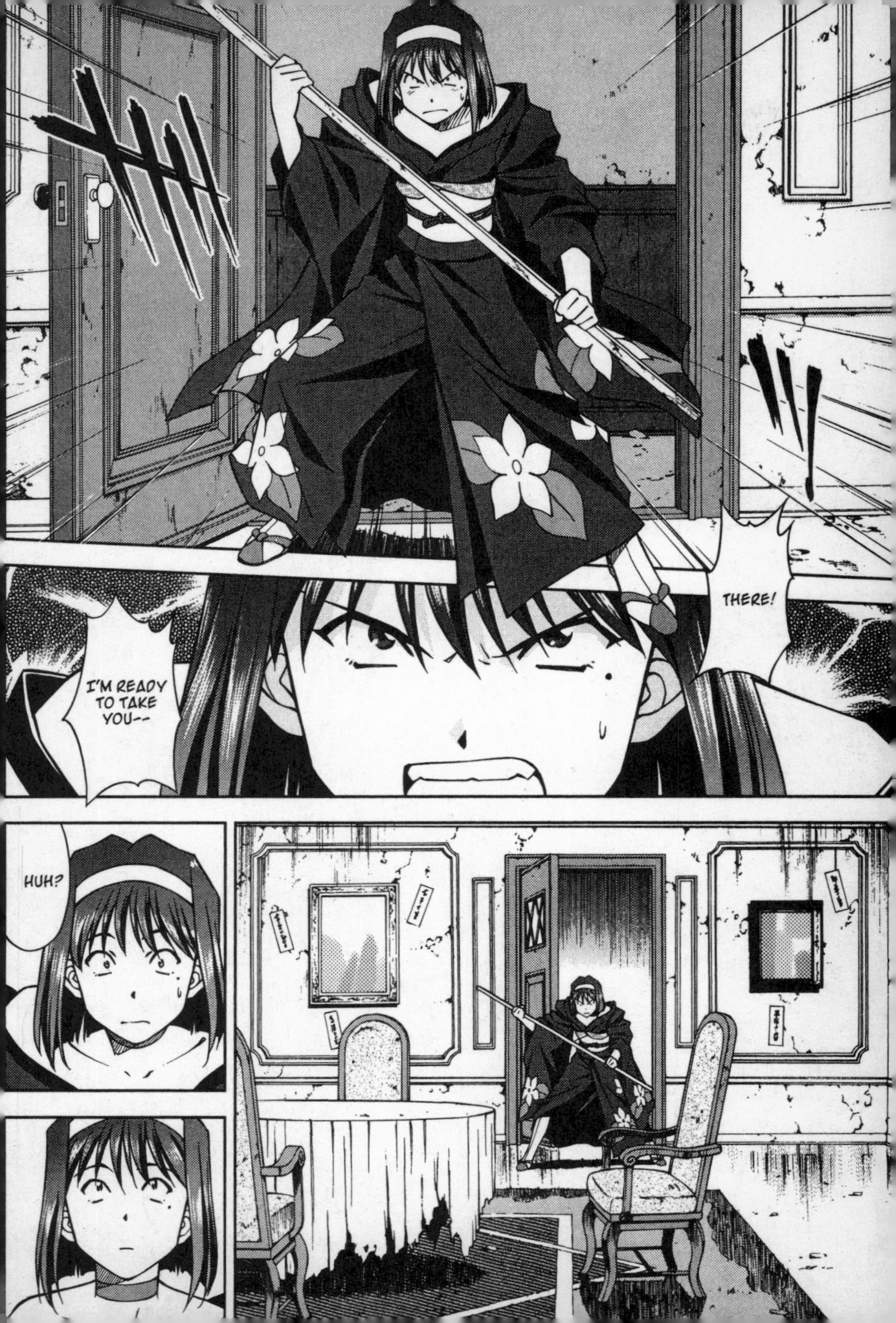
THERE!
I'M READY TO TAKE YOU--
HUH?

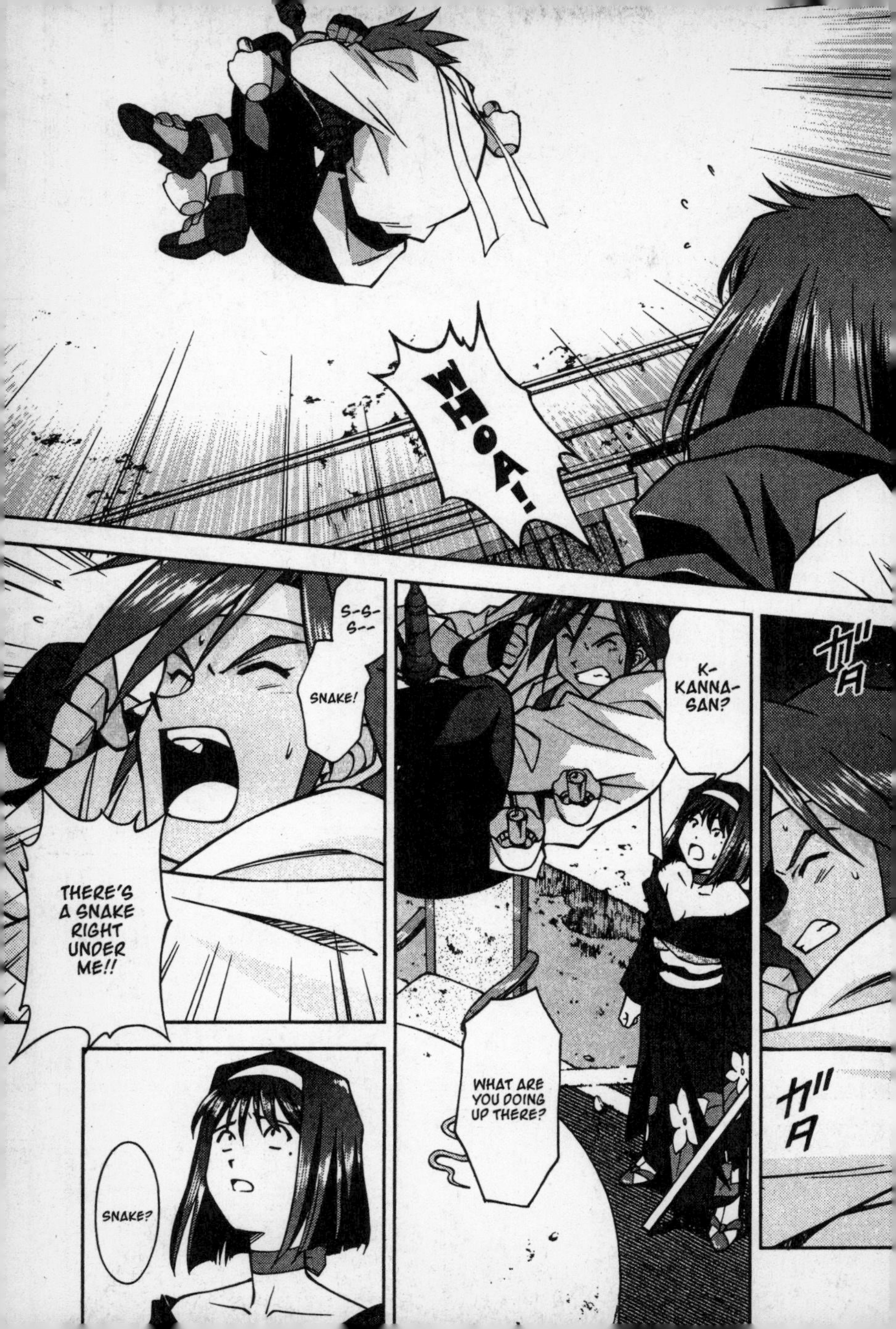
WHOA!!
ガタ
K-KANNA-SAN?
WHAT ARE YOU DOING UP THERE?
S-S-S--
SNAKE!
THERE'S A SNAKE RIGHT UNDER ME!!
ガタ
SNAKE?

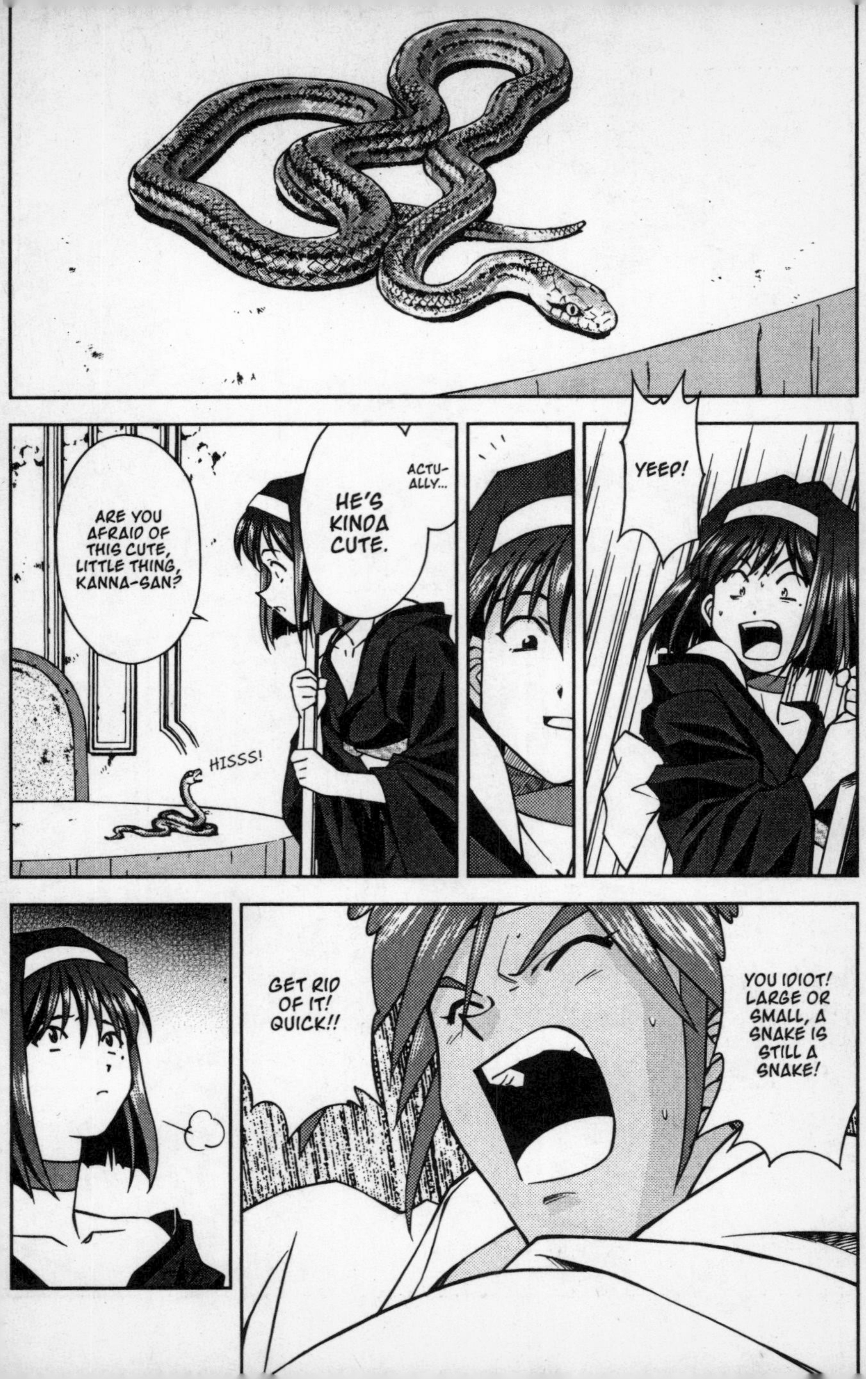
YEEP!
ACTU-ALLY... HE'S KINDA CUTE.
ARE YOU AFRAID OF THIS CUTE, LITTLE THING, KANNA-SAN?
HISSS!
YOU IDIOT! LARGE OR SMALL, A SNAKE IS STILL A SNAKE!
GET RID OF IT! QUICK!!

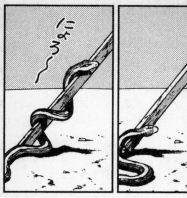

COME HERE NOW.

IF YOU STAY THERE, YOU'LL GET SQUASHED BY KANNA-SAN.

UGH...

OFF YOU GO.

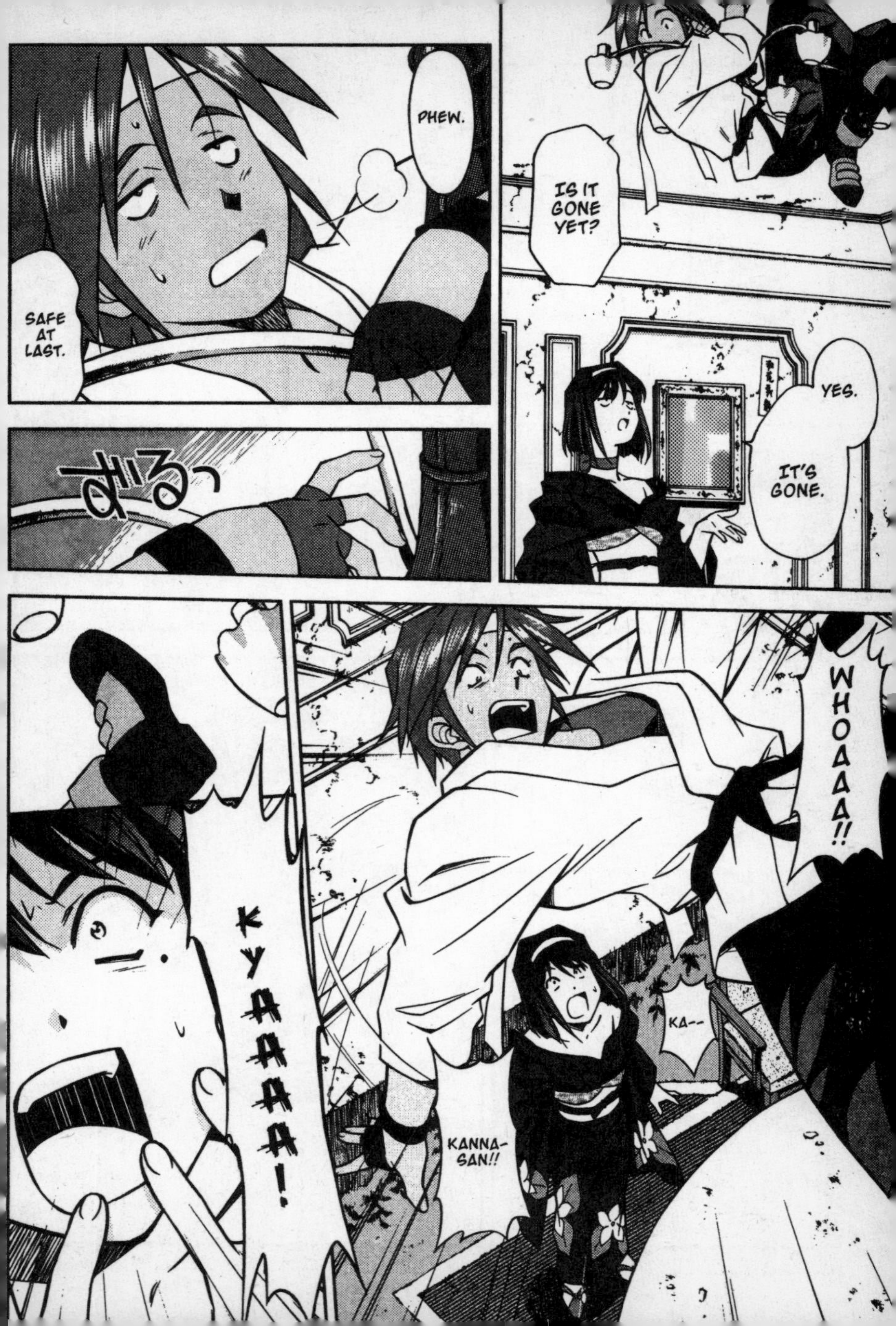
IS IT GONE YET?
YES.
IT'S GONE.
PHEW.
SAFE AT LAST.
ずるっ
WHOAAAA!!
KA--
KANNA-SAN!!
KYAAAAA!

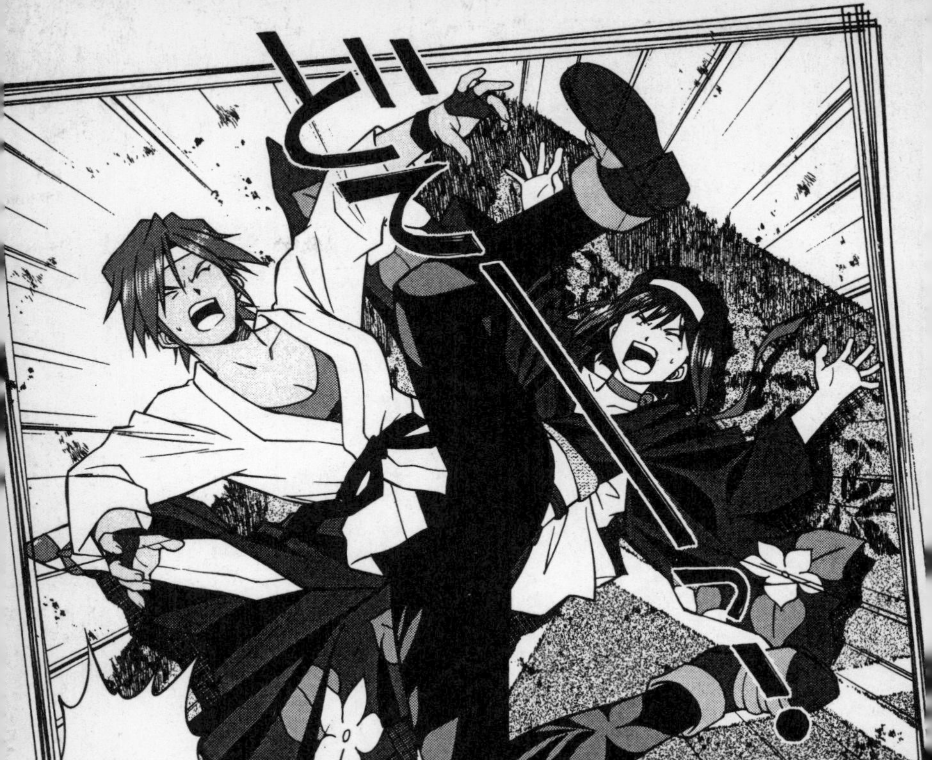
OOF!
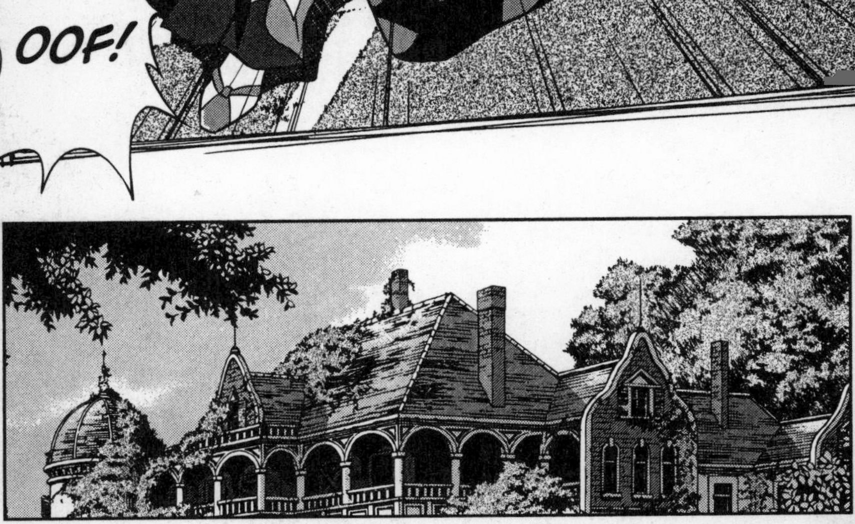

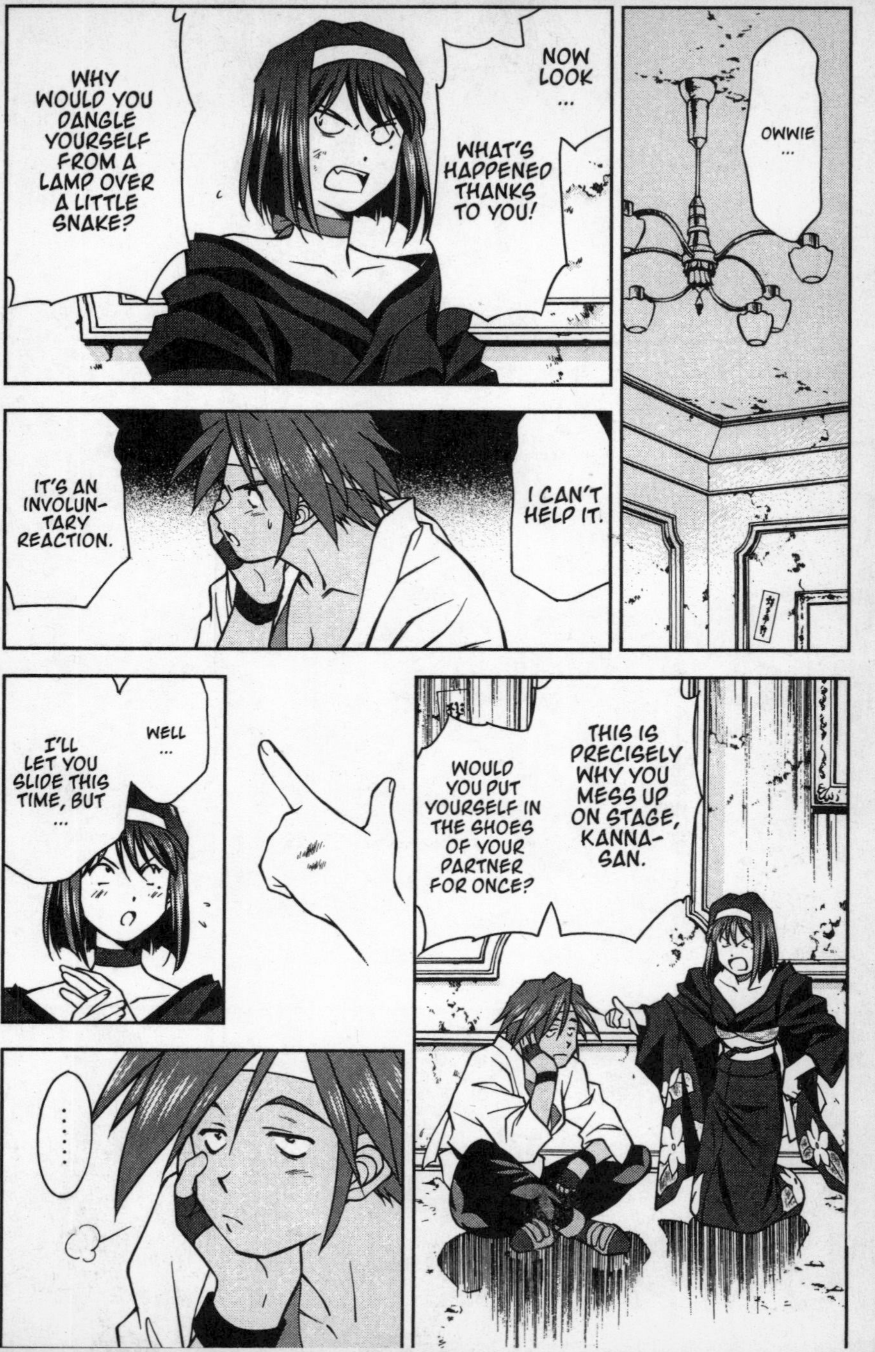
OWWIE ...
NOW LOOK ...
WHAT'S HAPPENED THANKS TO YOU!
WHY WOULD YOU DANGLE YOURSELF FROM A LAMP OVER A LITTLE SNAKE?
I CAN'T HELP IT.
IT'S AN INVOLUNTARY REACTION.
THIS IS PRECISELY WHY YOU MESS UP ON STAGE, KANNA-SAN.
WOULD YOU PUT YOURSELF IN THE SHOES OF YOUR PARTNER FOR ONCE?
WELL ...
I'LL LET YOU SLIDE THIS TIME, BUT ...
......

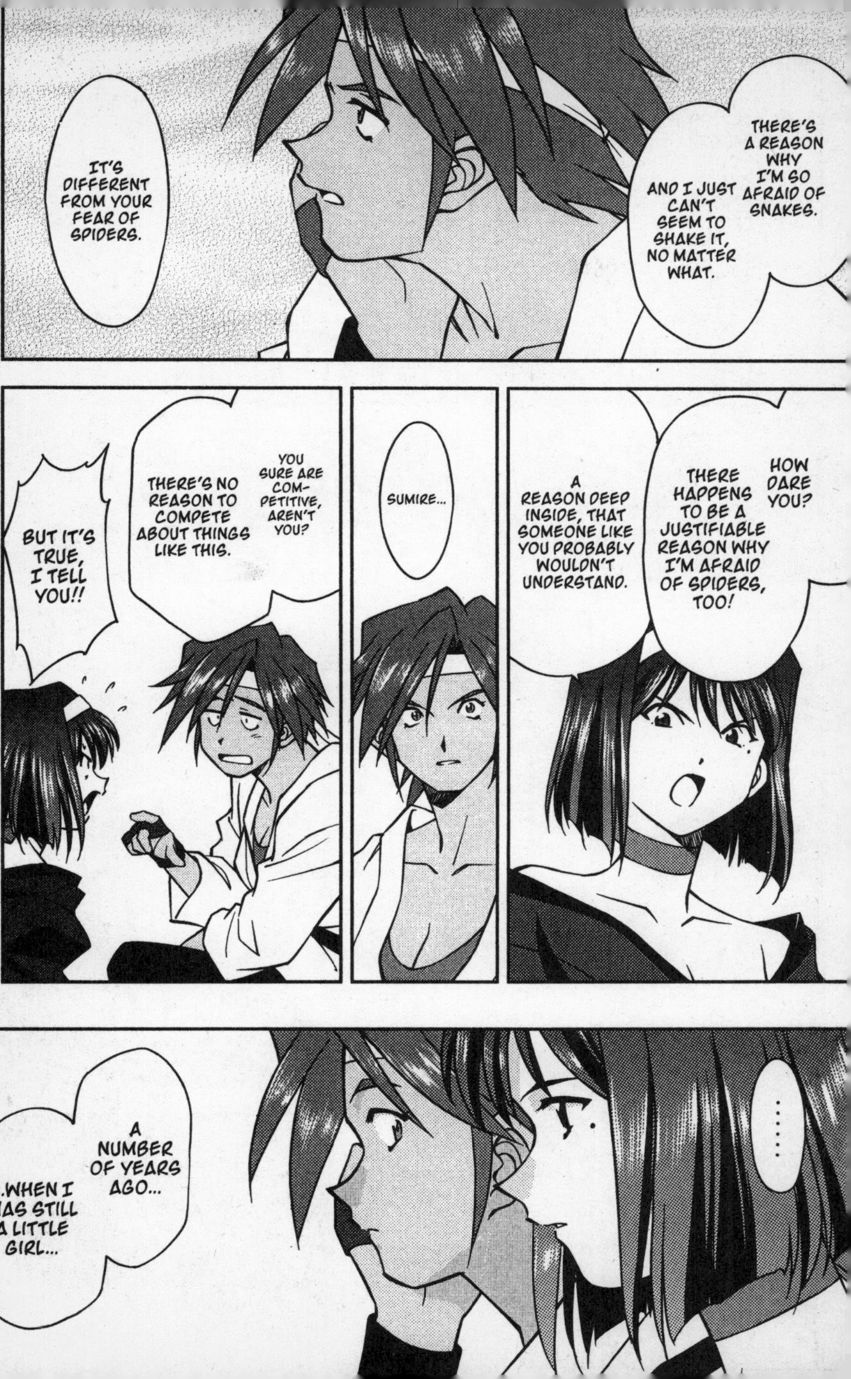
THERE'S A REASON WHY I'M SO AFRAID OF SNAKES.
AND I JUST CAN'T SEEM TO SHAKE IT, NO MATTER WHAT.
IT'S DIFFERENT FROM YOUR FEAR OF SPIDERS.
HOW DARE YOU?
THERE HAPPENS TO BE A JUSTIFIABLE REASON WHY I'M AFRAID OF SPIDERS, TOO!
A REASON DEEP INSIDE, THAT SOMEONE LIKE YOU PROBABLY WOULDN'T UNDERSTAND.
SUMIRE...
YOU SURE ARE COMPETITIVE, AREN'T YOU?
THERE'S NO REASON TO COMPETE ABOUT THINGS LIKE THIS.
BUT IT'S TRUE, I TELL YOU!!
......
A NUMBER OF YEARS AGO...
...WHEN I WAS STILL A LITTLE GIRL...

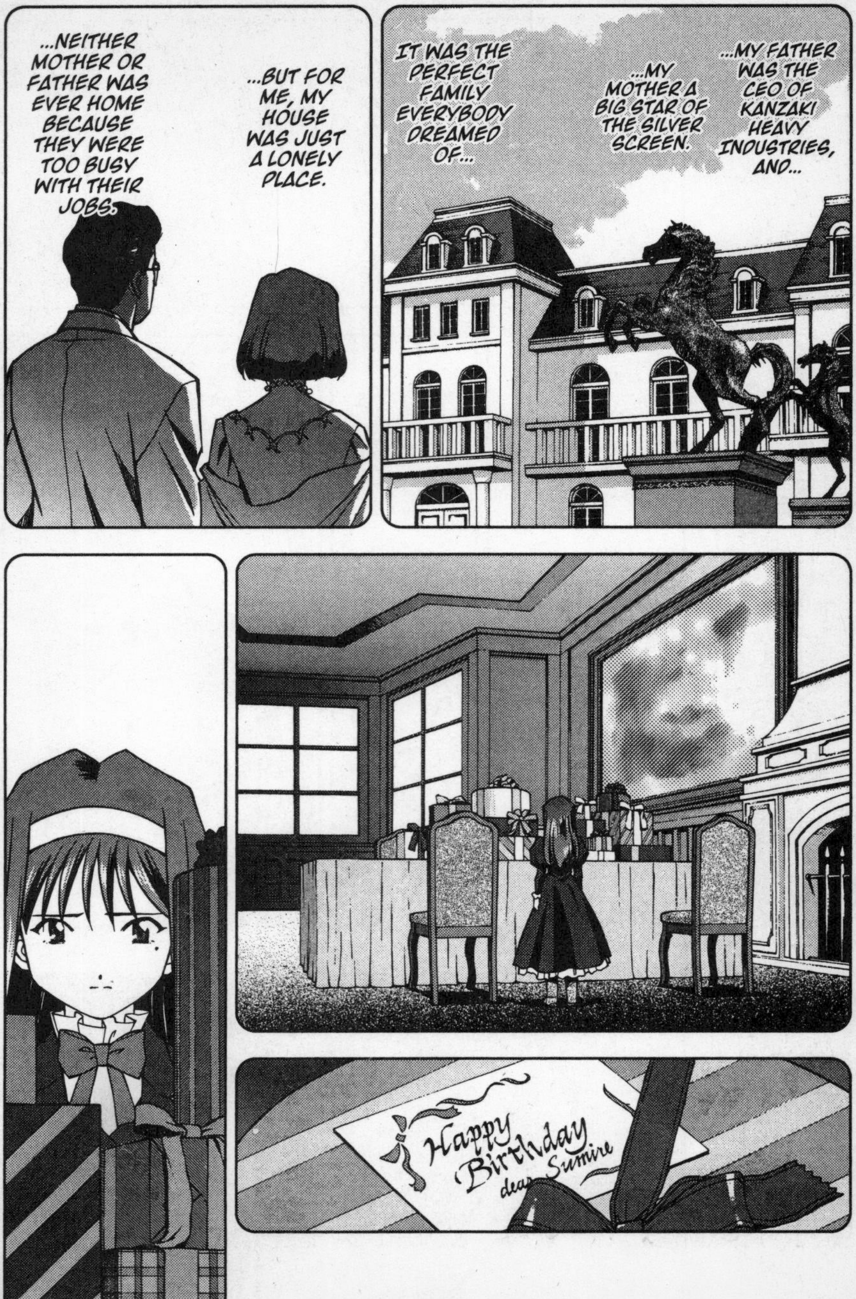
...MY FATHER WAS THE CEO OF KANZAKI HEAVY INDUSTRIES, AND...
...MY MOTHER A BIG STAR OF THE SILVER SCREEN.
IT WAS THE PERFECT FAMILY EVERYBODY DREAMED OF...
...BUT FOR ME, MY HOUSE WAS JUST A LONELY PLACE.
...NEITHER MOTHER OR FATHER WAS EVER HOME BECAUSE THEY WERE TOO BUSY WITH THEIR JOBS.
Happy Birthday dear Sumire

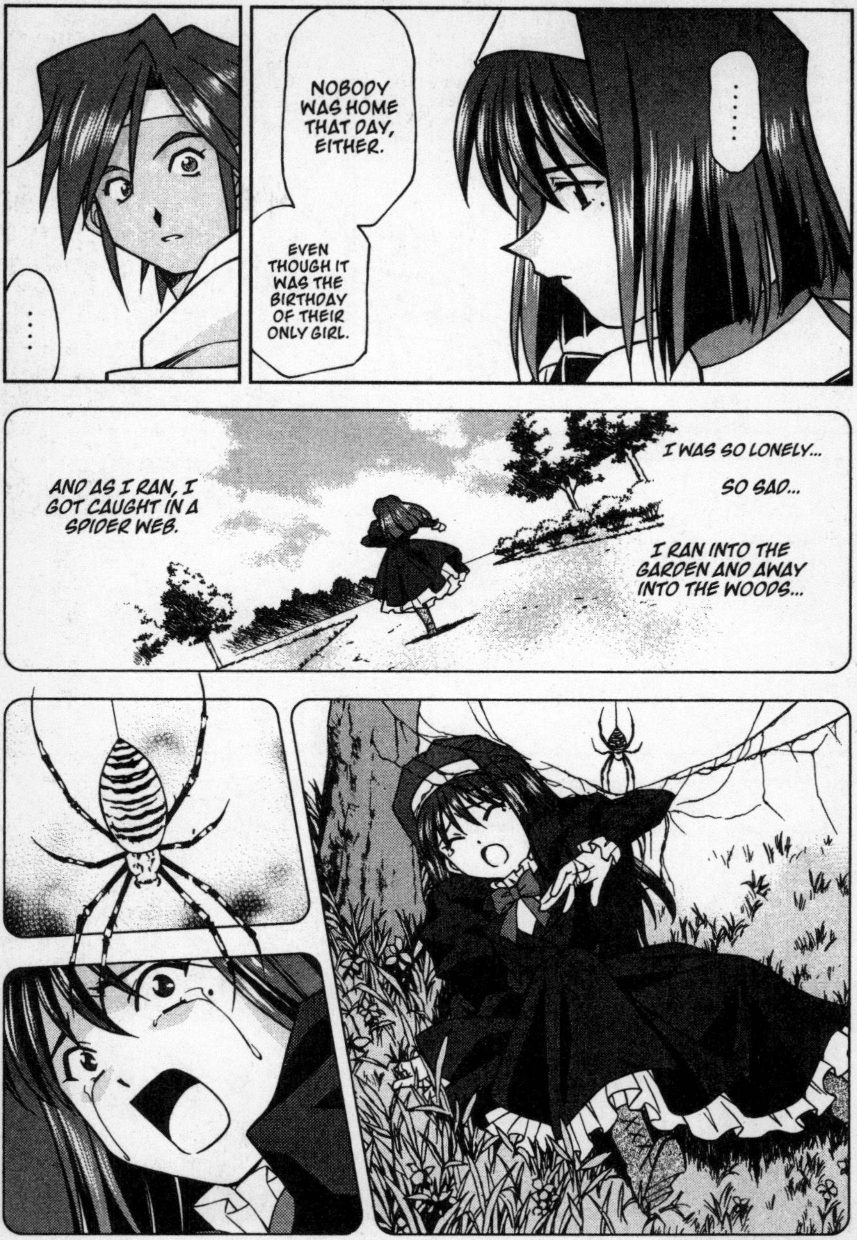
......
NOBODY WAS HOME THAT DAY, EITHER.
EVEN THOUGH IT WAS THE BIRTHDAY OF THEIR ONLY GIRL.
....
I WAS SO LONELY...
SO SAD...
I RAN INTO THE GARDEN AND AWAY INTO THE WOODS...
AND AS I RAN, I GOT CAUGHT IN A SPIDER WEB.

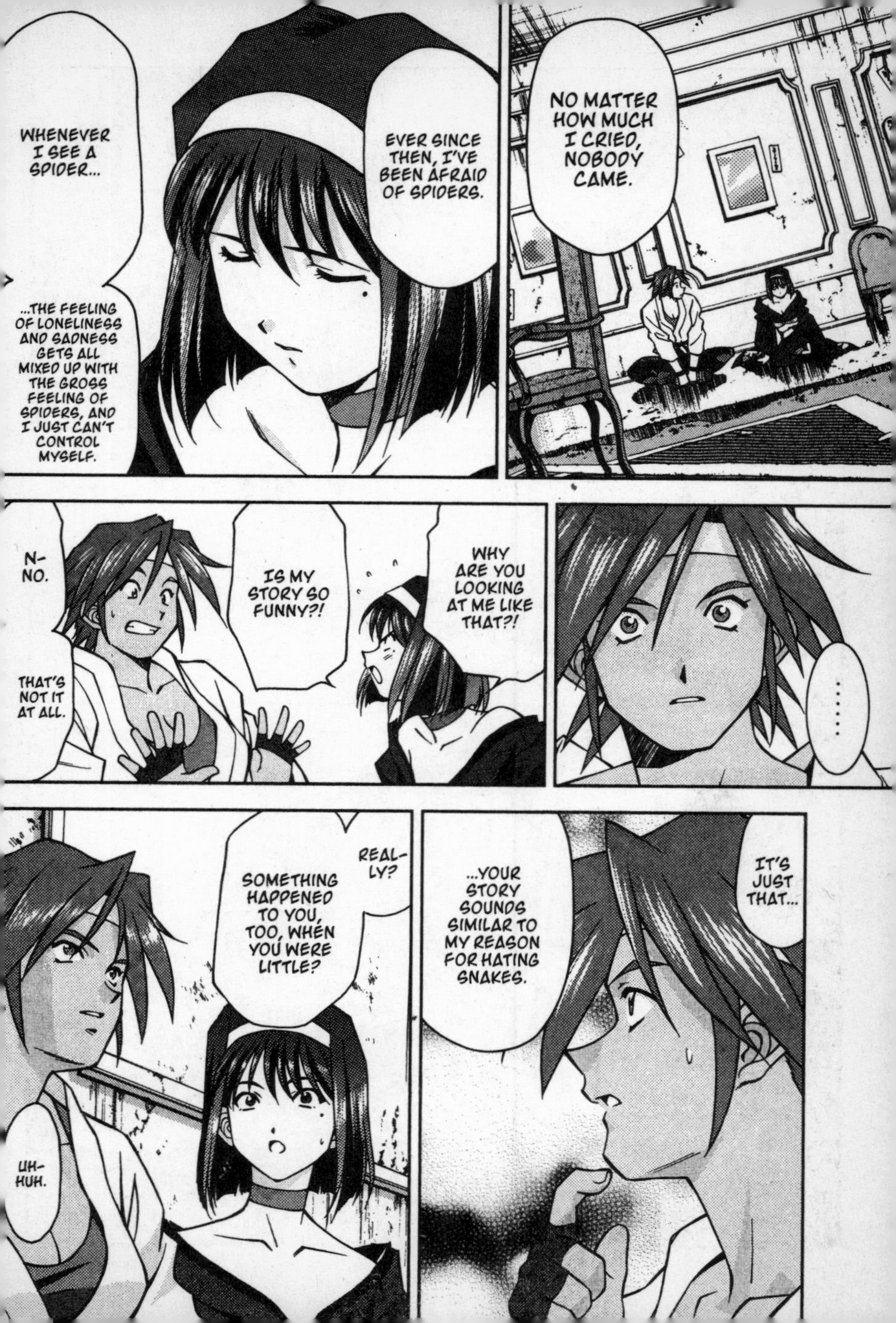
NO MATTER HOW MUCH I CRIED, NOBODY CAME.
EVER SINCE THEN, I'VE BEEN AFRAID OF SPIDERS.
WHENEVER I SEE A SPIDER...
...THE FEELING OF LONELINESS AND SADNESS GETS ALL MIXED UP WITH THE GROSS FEELING OF SPIDERS, AND I JUST CAN'T CONTROL MYSELF.
......
WHY ARE YOU LOOKING AT ME LIKE THAT?!
IS MY STORY SO FUNNY?!
N-NO.
THAT'S NOT IT AT ALL.
IT'S JUST THAT...
...YOUR STORY SOUNDS SIMILAR TO MY REASON FOR HATING SNAKES.
REAL-LY?
SOMETHING HAPPENED TO YOU, TOO, WHEN YOU WERE LITTLE?
UH-HUH.

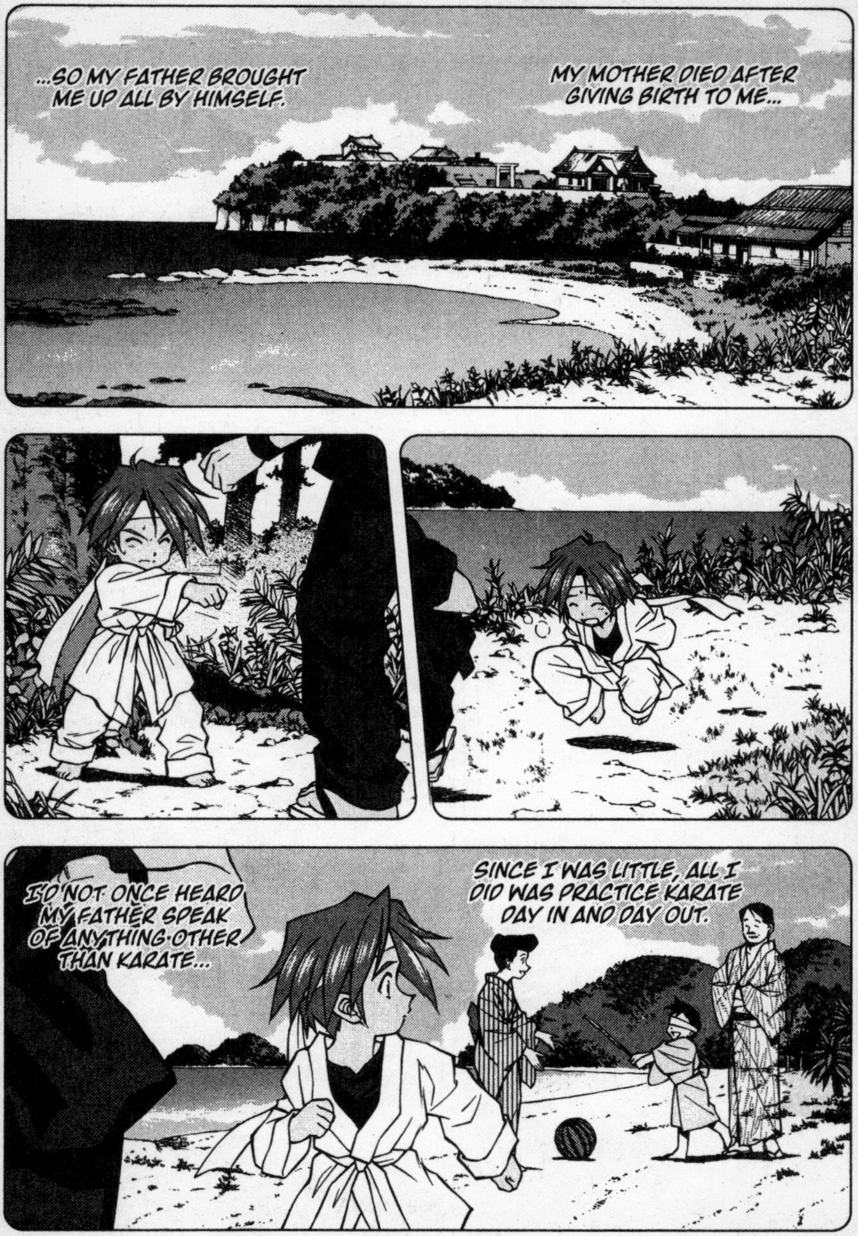
MY MOTHER DIED AFTER GIVING BIRTH TO ME...
...SO MY FATHER BROUGHT ME UP ALL BY HIMSELF.
SINCE I WAS LITTLE, ALL I DID WAS PRACTICE KARATE DAY IN AND DAY OUT.
I'D NOT ONCE HEARD MY FATHER SPEAK OF ANYTHING OTHER THAN KARATE...

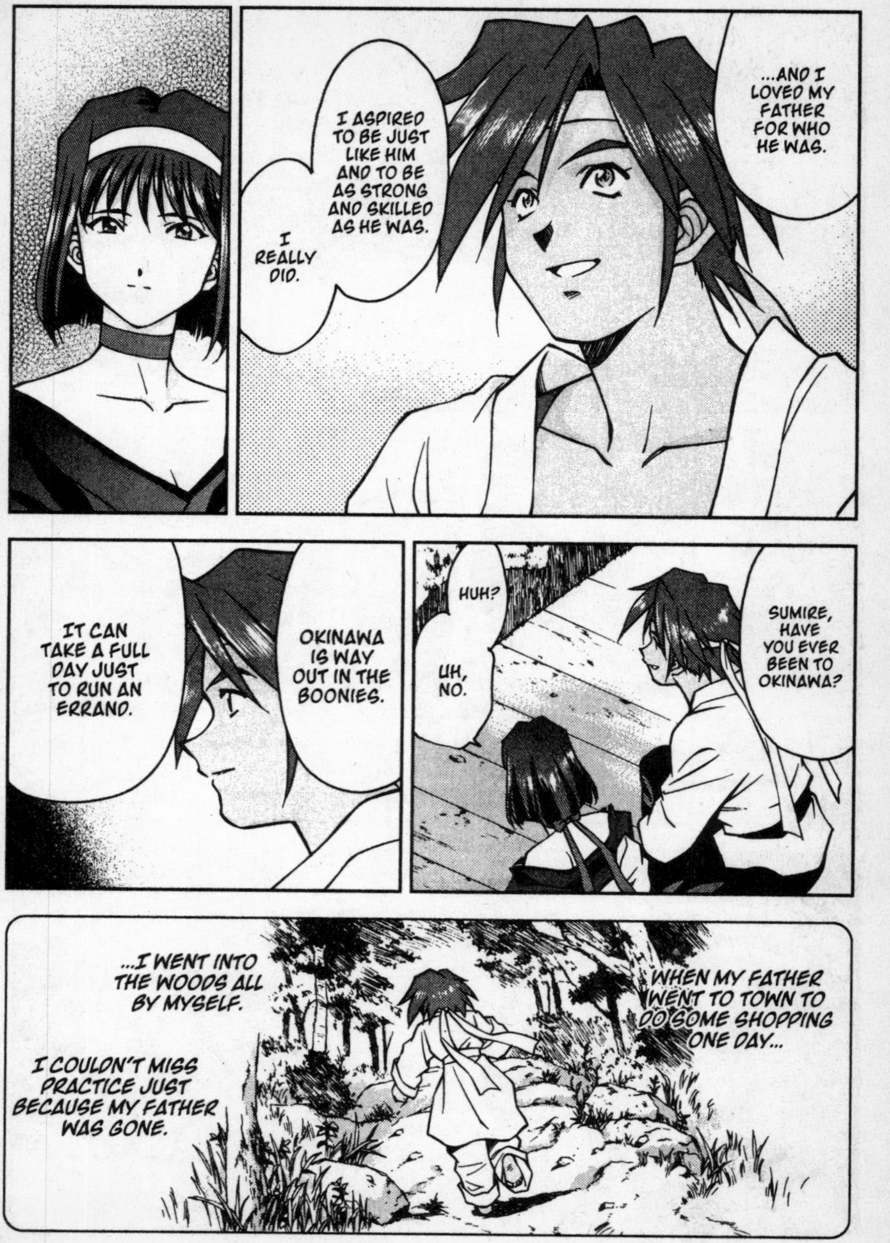
...AND I LOVED MY FATHER FOR WHO HE WAS.
I ASPIRED TO BE JUST LIKE HIM AND TO BE AS STRONG AND SKILLED AS HE WAS.
I REALLY DID.
SUMIRE, HAVE YOU EVER BEEN TO OKINAWA?
HUH?
UH, NO.
OKINAWA IS WAY OUT IN THE BOONIES.
IT CAN TAKE A FULL DAY JUST TO RUN AN ERRAND.
WHEN MY FATHER WENT TO TOWN TO DO SOME SHOPPING ONE DAY...
...I WENT INTO THE WOODS ALL BY MYSELF.
I COULDN'T MISS PRACTICE JUST BECAUSE MY FATHER WAS GONE.

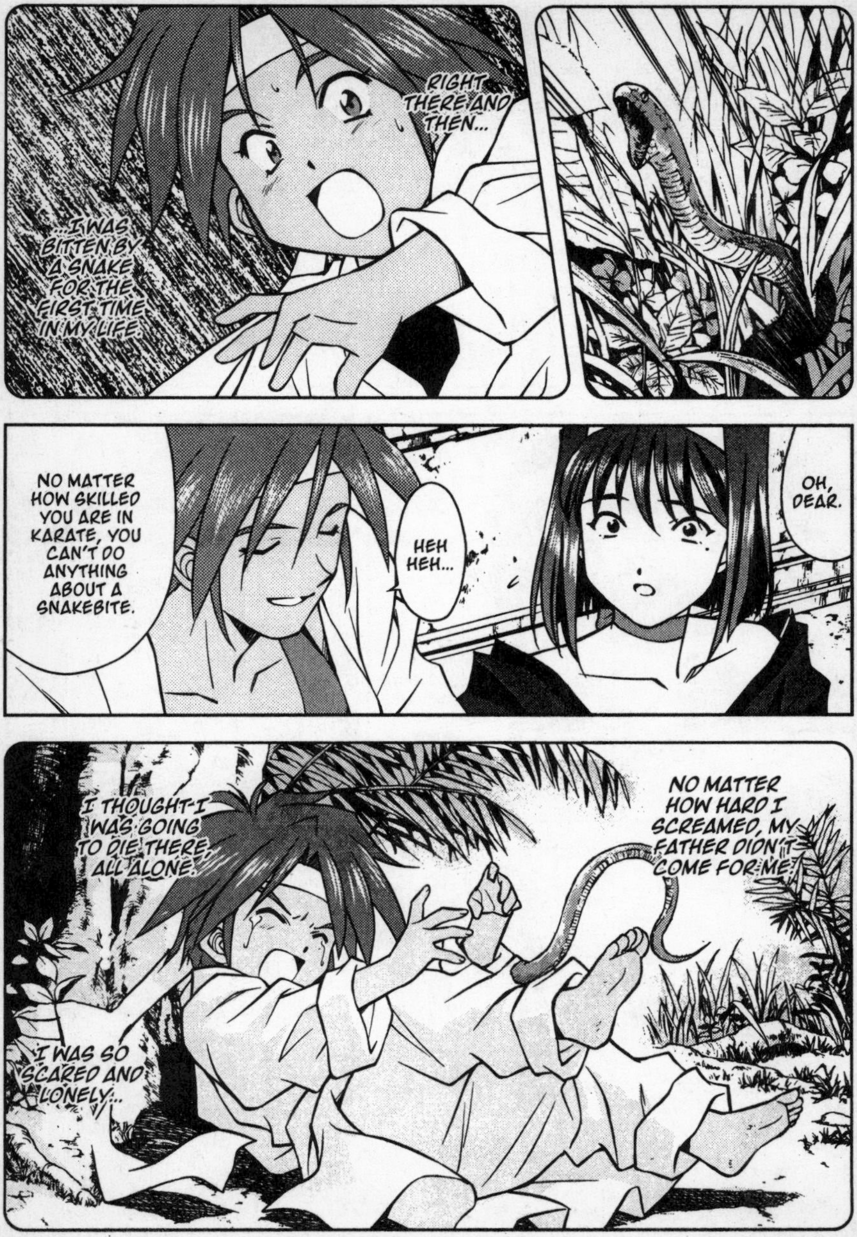
RIGHT THERE AND THEN...
...I WAS BITTEN BY A SNAKE FOR THE FIRST TIME IN MY LIFE.
OH, DEAR.
HEH HEH...
NO MATTER HOW SKILLED YOU ARE IN KARATE, YOU CAN'T DO ANYTHING ABOUT A SNAKEBITE.
NO MATTER HOW HARD I SCREAMED, MY FATHER DIDN'T COME FOR ME.
I THOUGHT I WAS GOING TO DIE THERE, ALL ALONE.
I WAS SO SCARED AND LONELY...

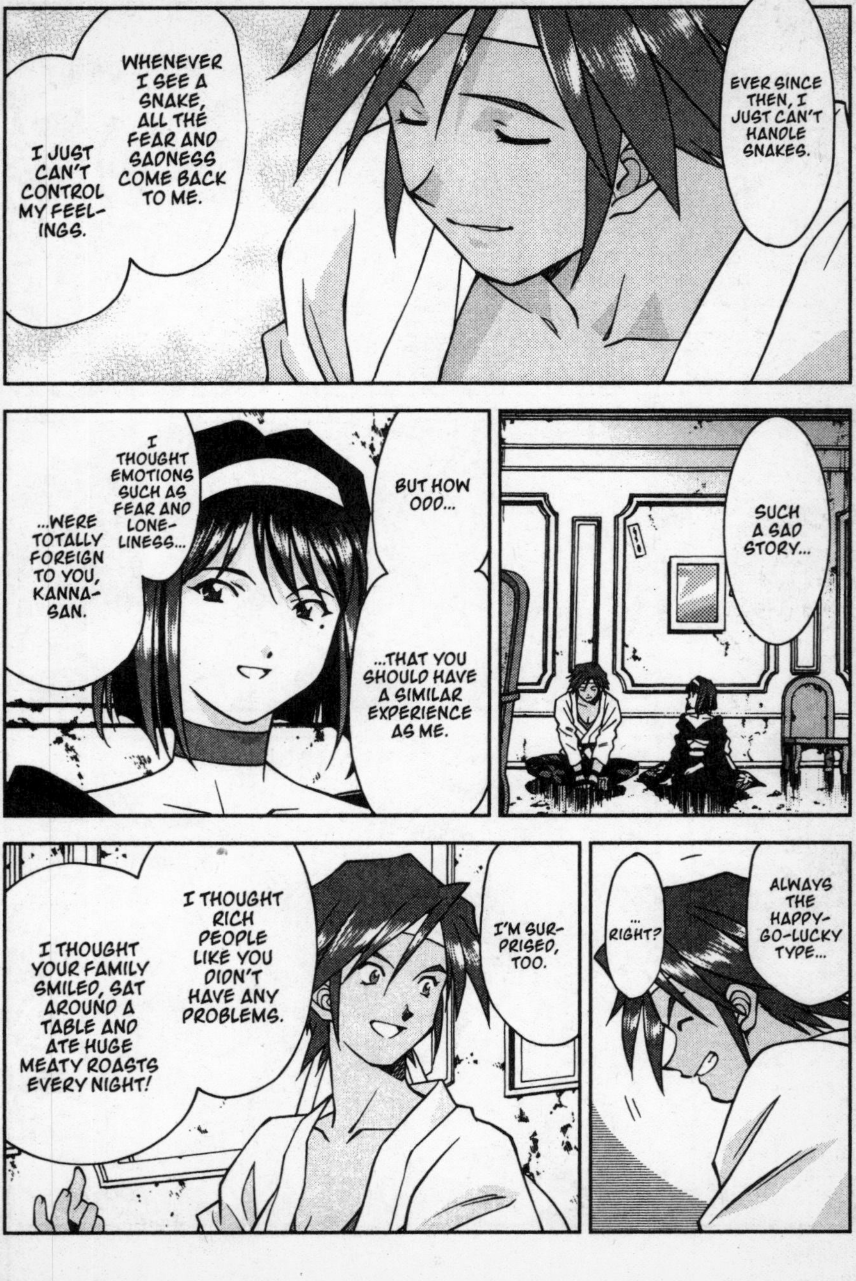
EVER SINCE THEN, I JUST CAN'T HANDLE SNAKES.
WHENEVER I SEE A SNAKE, ALL THE FEAR AND SADNESS COME BACK TO ME.
I JUST CAN'T CONTROL MY FEEL-INGS.
SUCH A SAD STORY...
I THOUGHT EMOTIONS SUCH AS FEAR AND LONE-LINESS...
...WERE TOTALLY FOREIGN TO YOU, KANNA-SAN.
BUT HOW ODD...
...THAT YOU SHOULD HAVE A SIMILAR EXPERIENCE AS ME.
ALWAYS THE HAPPY-GO-LUCKY TYPE...
...RIGHT?
I'M SUR-PRISED, TOO.
I THOUGHT RICH PEOPLE LIKE YOU DIDN'T HAVE ANY PROBLEMS.
I THOUGHT YOUR FAMILY SMILED, SAT AROUND A TABLE AND ATE HUGE MEATY ROASTS EVERY NIGHT!

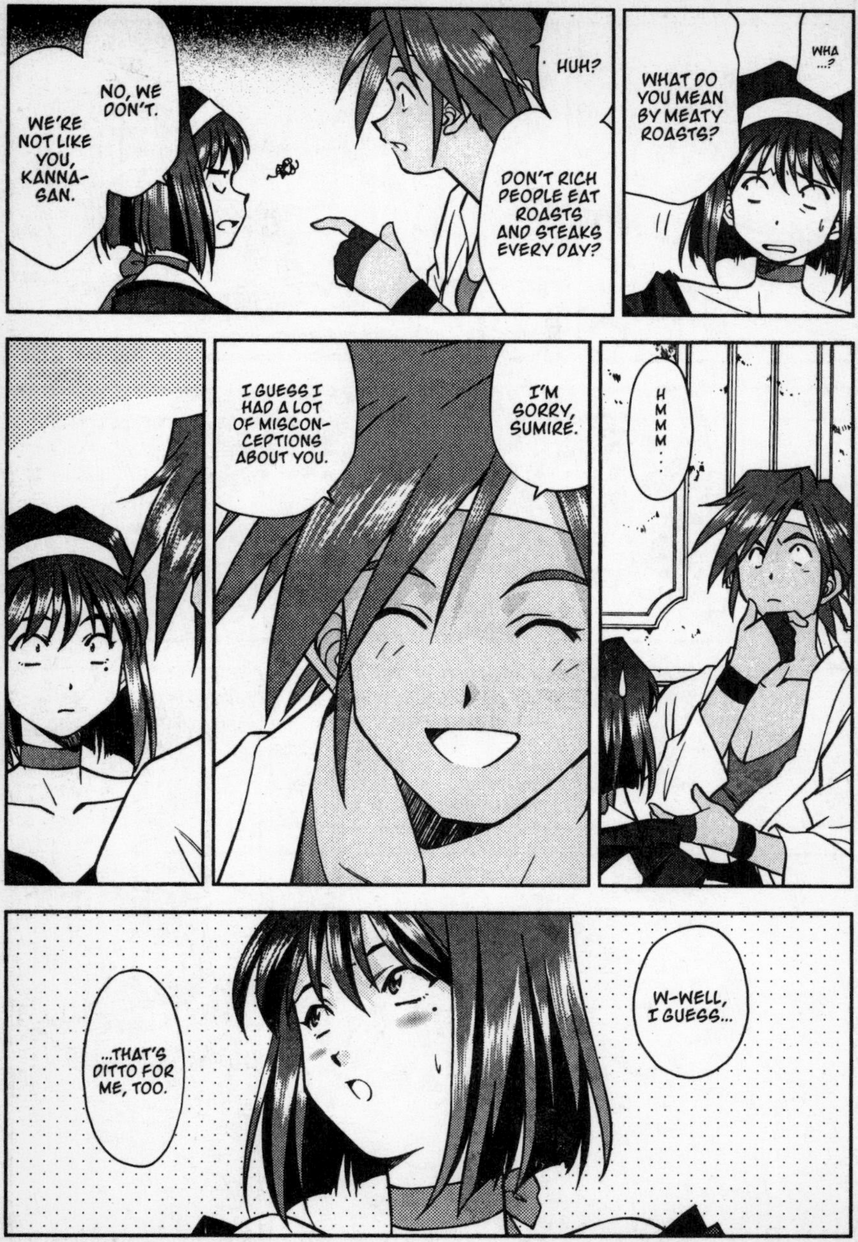
WHA ...?
WHAT DO YOU MEAN BY MEATY ROASTS?
HUH?
DON'T RICH PEOPLE EAT ROASTS AND STEAKS EVERY DAY?
NO, WE DON'T.
WE'RE NOT LIKE YOU, KANNA-SAN.
HMMM...
I'M SORRY, SUMIRE.
I GUESS I HAD A LOT OF MISCONCEPTIONS ABOUT YOU.
W-WELL, I GUESS...
...THAT'S DITTO FOR ME, TOO.

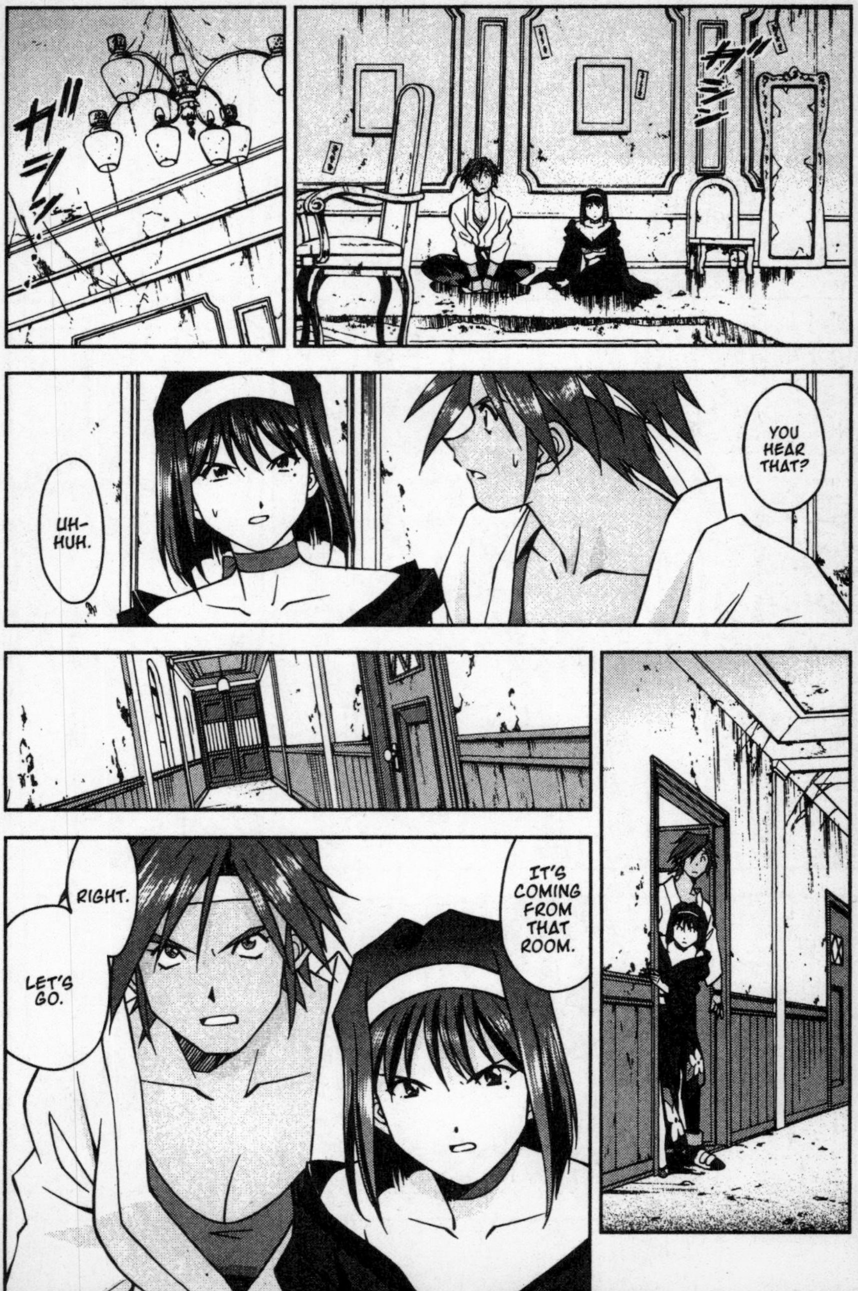
YOU HEAR THAT?
UH-HUH.
IT'S COMING FROM THAT ROOM.
RIGHT.
LET'S GO.

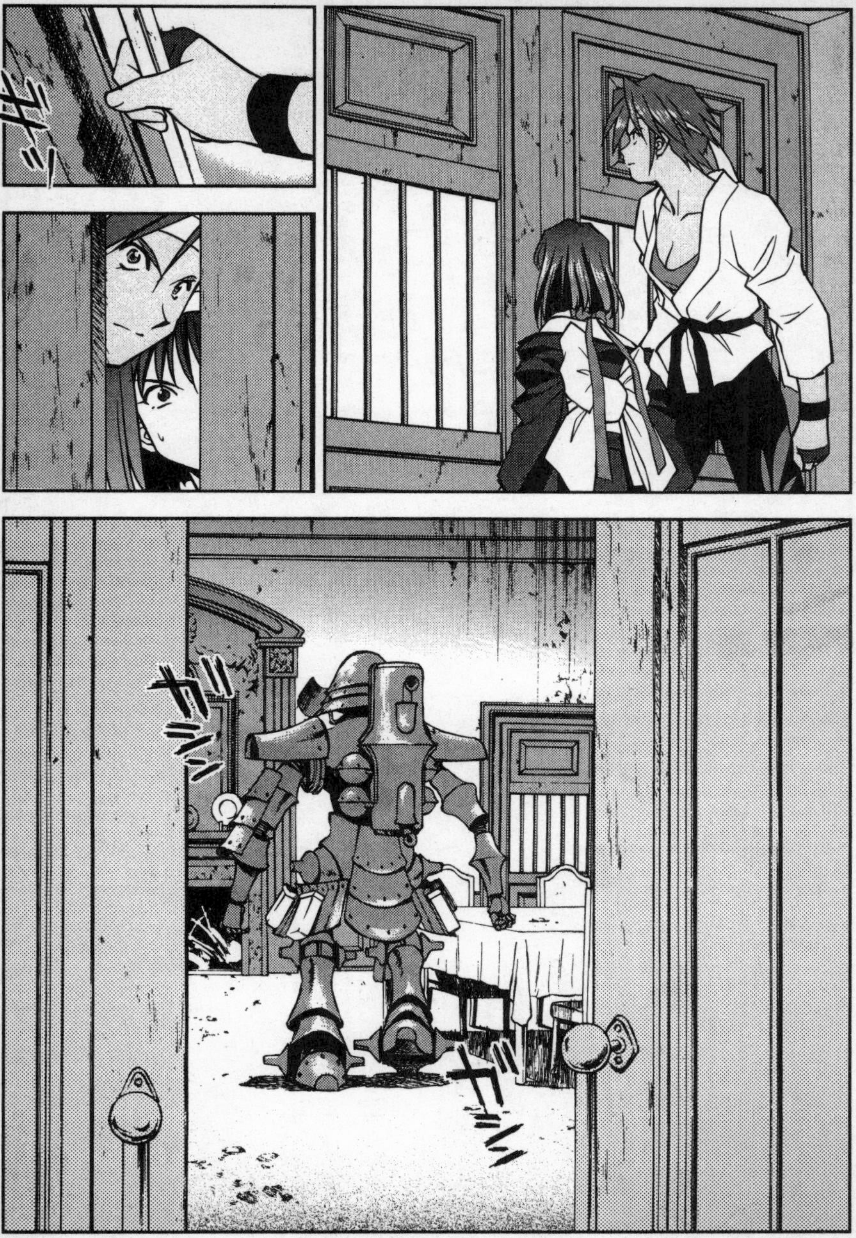

Birds of a Feather?--End of Act

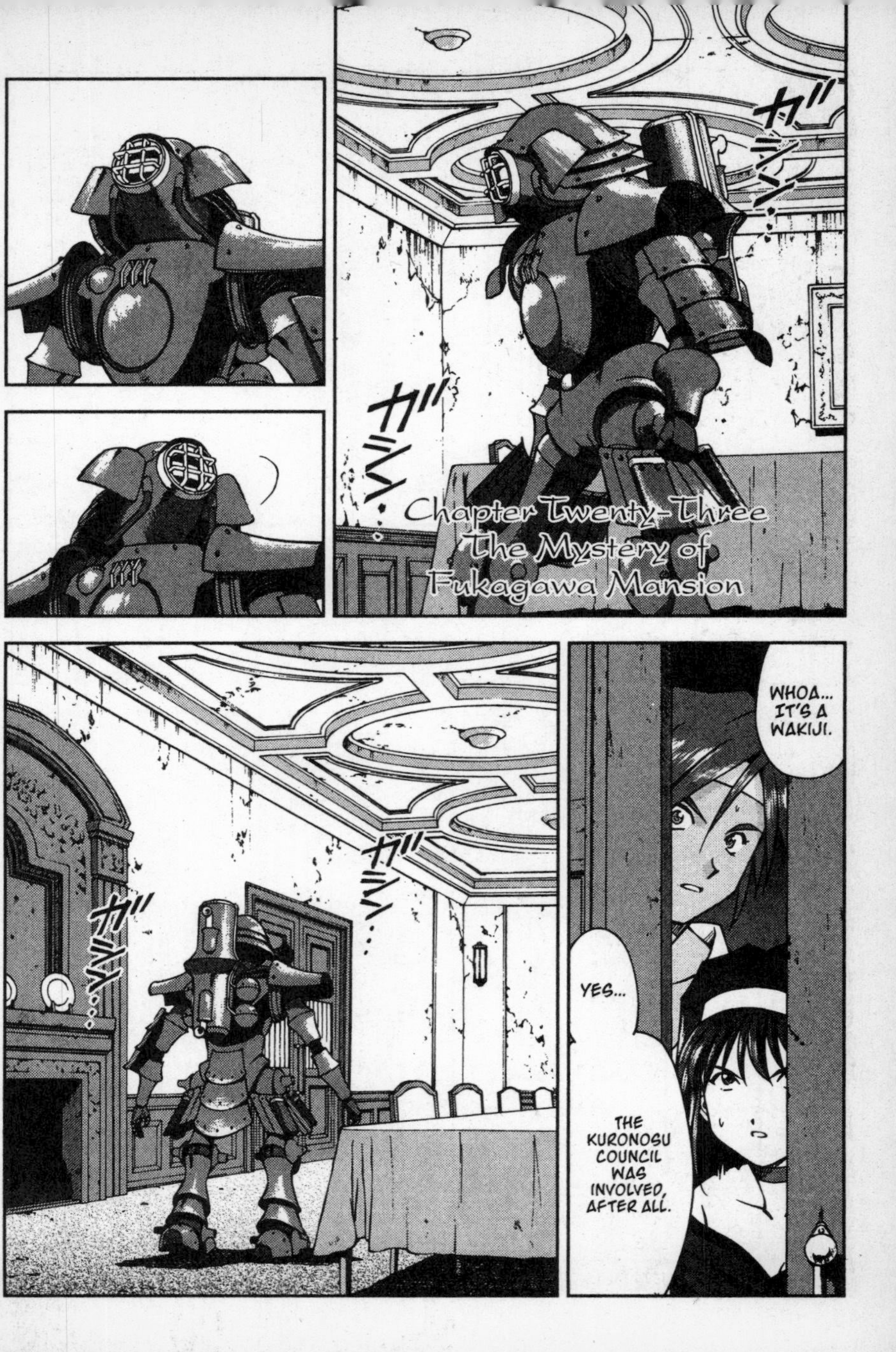
Chapter Twenty-Three
The Mystery of
Fukagawa Mansion
WHOA... IT'S A WAKIJI.
YES...
THE KURONOSU COUNCIL WAS INVOLVED, AFTER ALL.

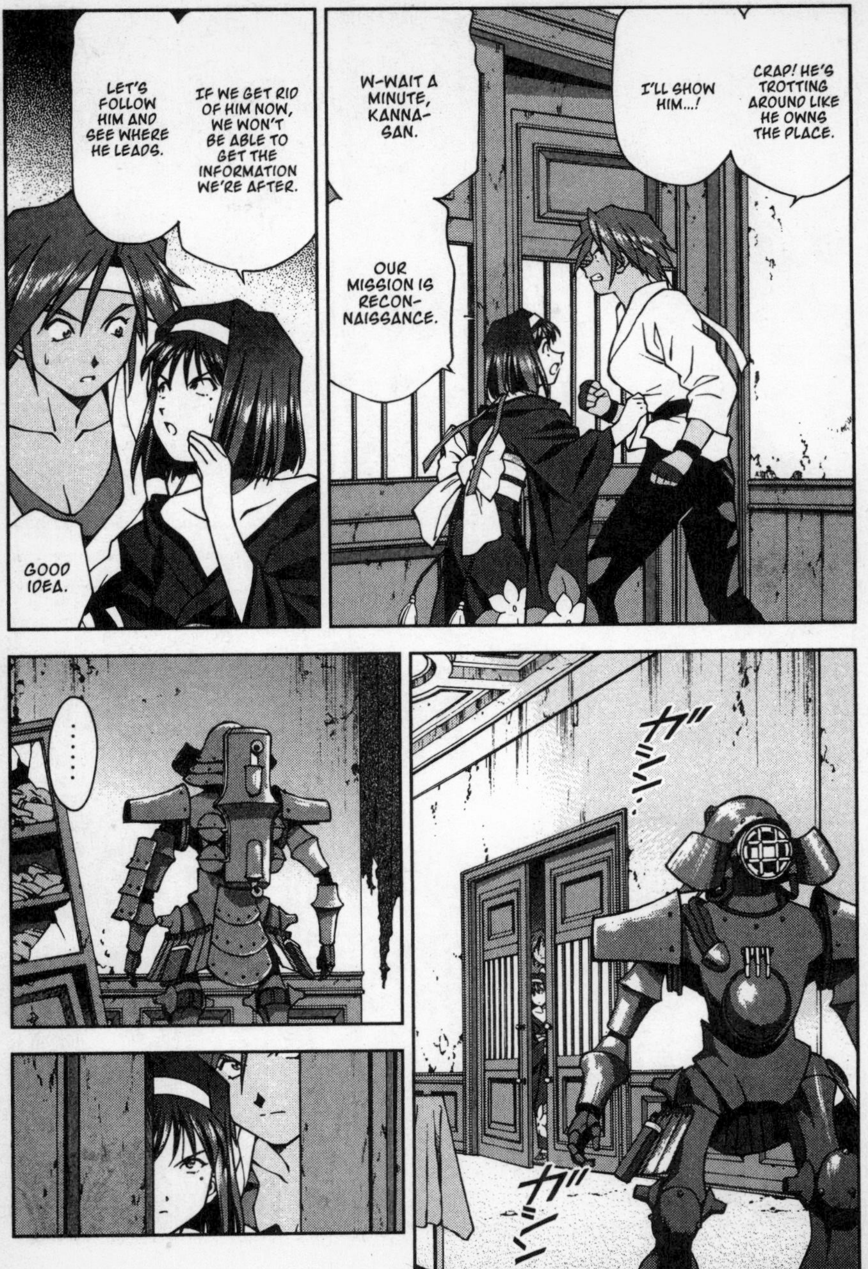
CRAP! HE'S TROTTING AROUND LIKE HE OWNS THE PLACE.
I'LL SHOW HIM...!
W-WAIT A MINUTE, KANNA-SAN.
OUR MISSION IS RECONNAISSANCE.
IF WE GET RID OF HIM NOW, WE WON'T BE ABLE TO GET THE INFORMATION WE'RE AFTER.
LET'S FOLLOW HIM AND SEE WHERE HE LEADS.
GOOD IDEA.
ガシン…
ガシン…
……

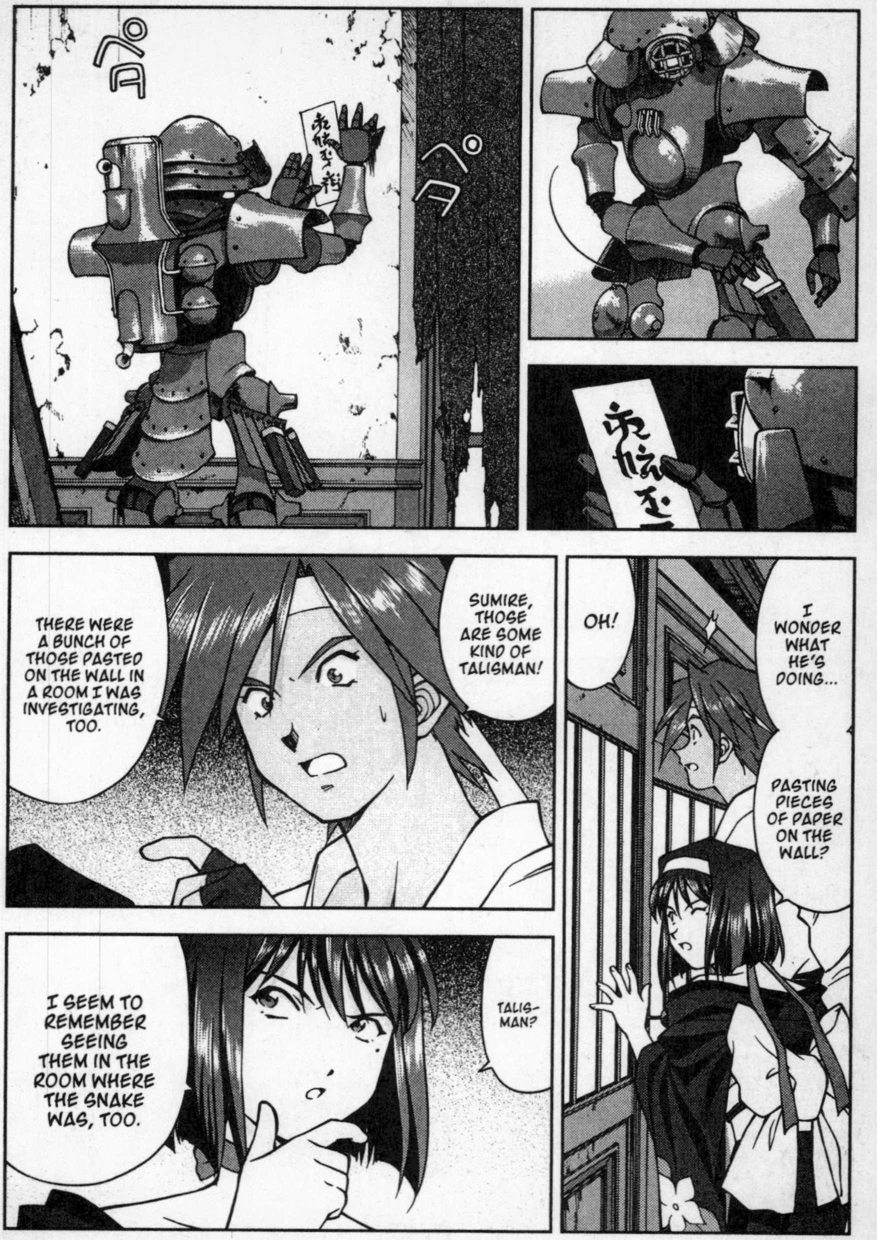
ペタ
ペタ
I WONDER WHAT HE'S DOING...
OH!
PASTING PIECES OF PAPER ON THE WALL?
SUMIRE, THOSE ARE SOME KIND OF TALISMAN!
THERE WERE A BUNCH OF THOSE PASTED ON THE WALL IN A ROOM I WAS INVESTIGATING, TOO.
TALIS-MAN?
I SEEM TO REMEMBER SEEING THEM IN THE ROOM WHERE THE SNAKE WAS, TOO.

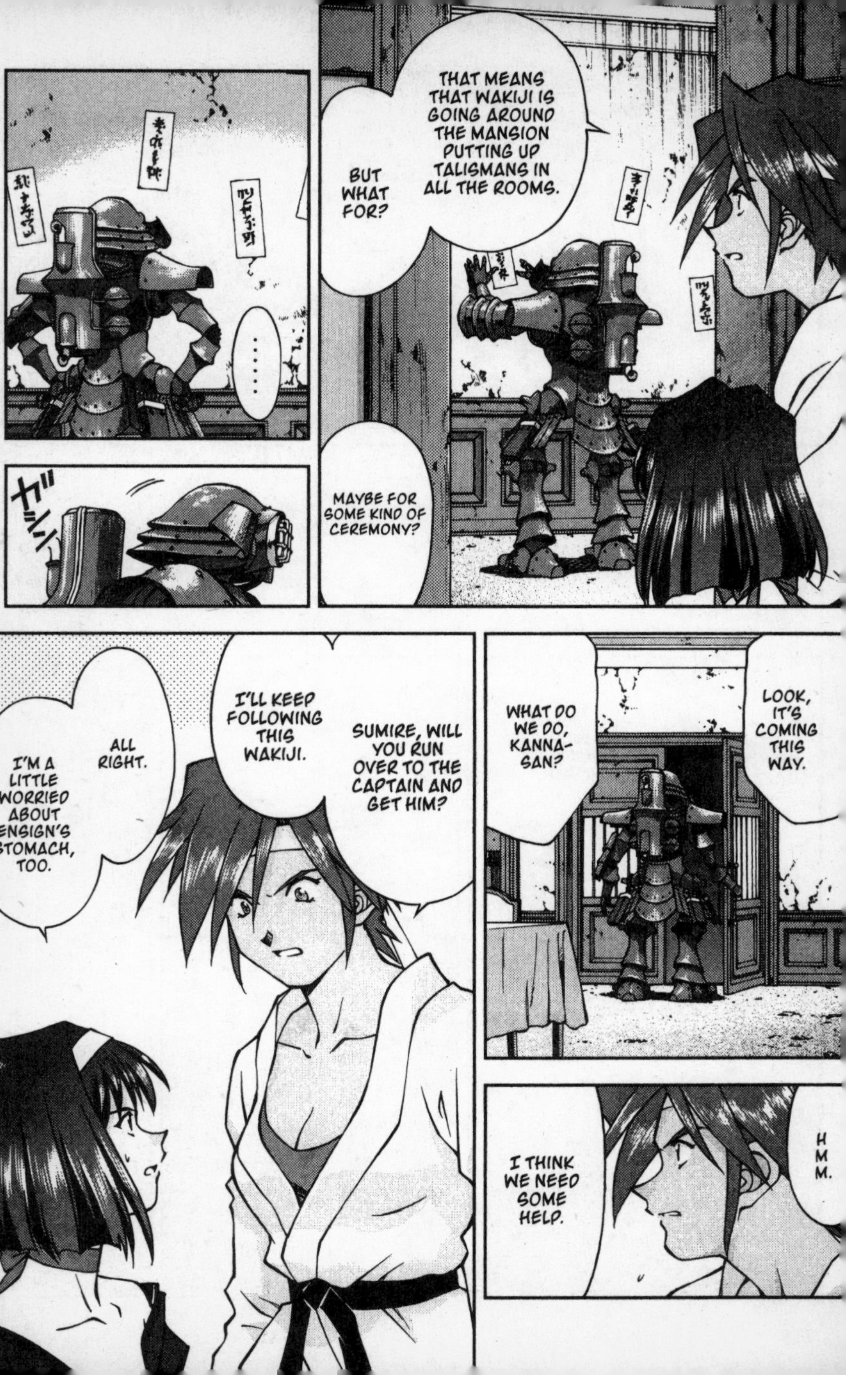
THAT MEANS THAT WAKIJI IS GOING AROUND THE MANSION PUTTING UP TALISMANS IN ALL THE ROOMS.
BUT WHAT FOR?
MAYBE FOR SOME KIND OF CEREMONY?
......
ガシン
LOOK, IT'S COMING THIS WAY.
WHAT DO WE DO, KANNA-SAN?
HMM.
I THINK WE NEED SOME HELP.
I'LL KEEP FOLLOWING THIS WAKIJI.
SUMIRE, WILL YOU RUN OVER TO THE CAPTAIN AND GET HIM?
ALL RIGHT.
I'M A LITTLE WORRIED ABOUT ENSIGN'S STOMACH, TOO.

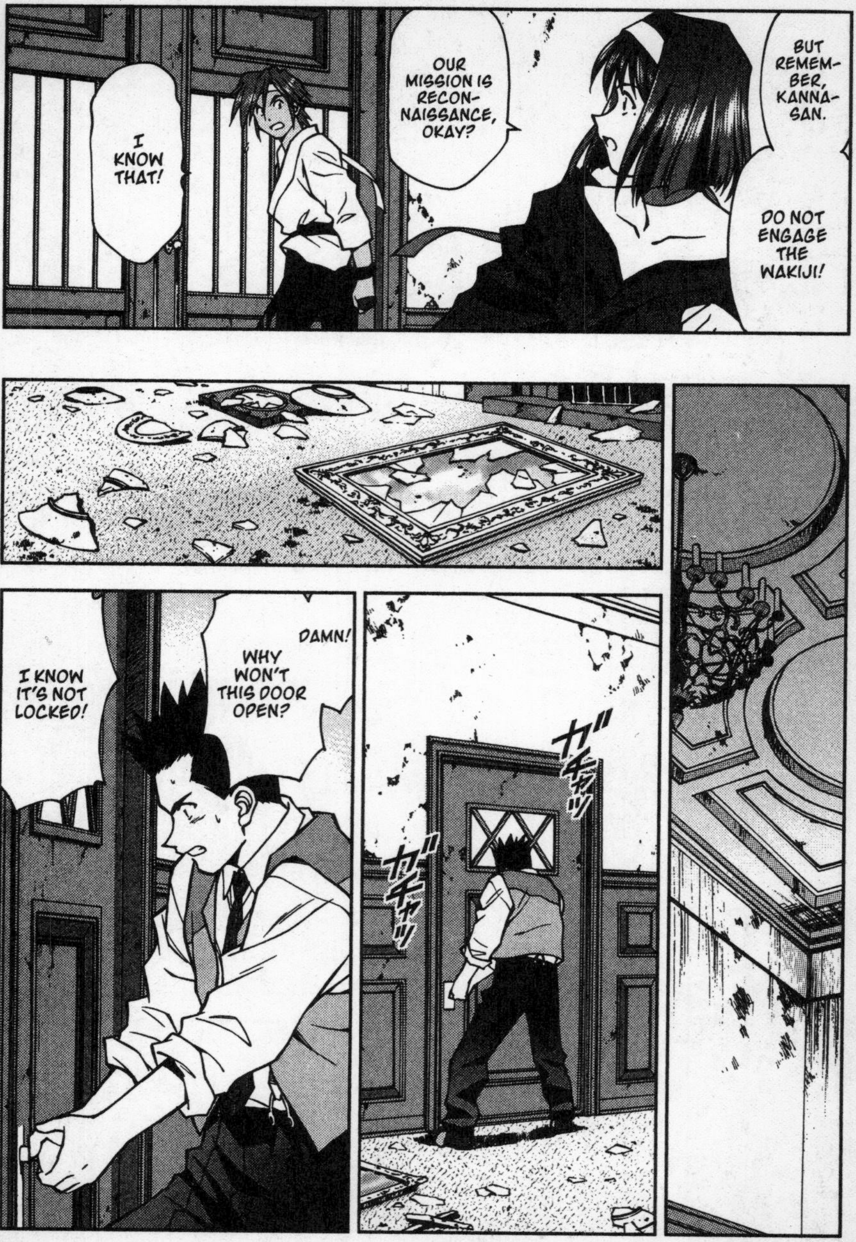
BUT REMEMBER, KANNA-SAN.
DO NOT ENGAGE THE WAKIJI!
OUR MISSION IS RECONNAISSANCE, OKAY?
I KNOW THAT!
ガチャッ
ガチャッ
DAMN!
WHY WON'T THIS DOOR OPEN?
I KNOW IT'S NOT LOCKED!

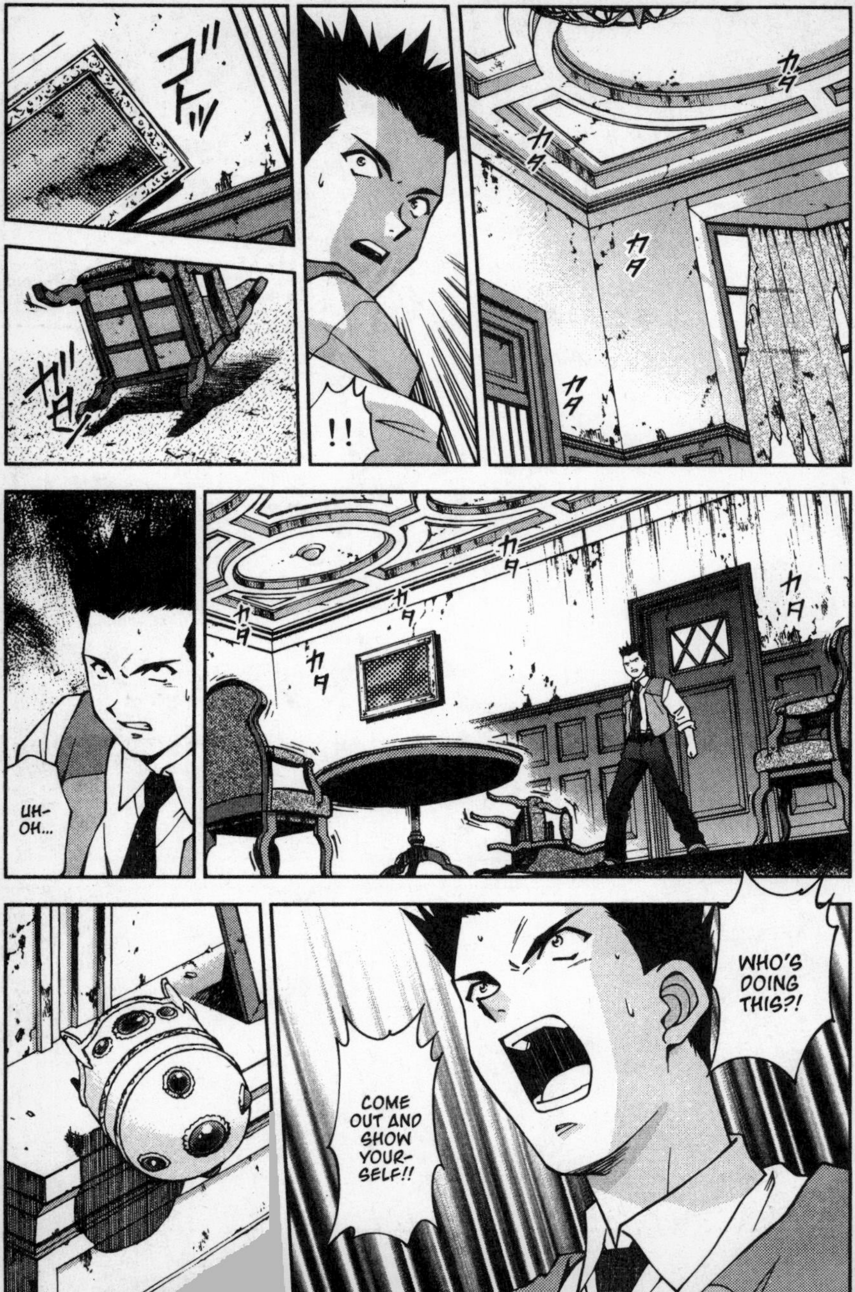

カタ
カタ
カタ
カタ
!!
ゴトッ
ガタン
カタ
カタ
カタ
カタ
カタ
UH-OH...
WHO'S DOING THIS?!
COME OUT AND SHOW YOUR-SELF!!

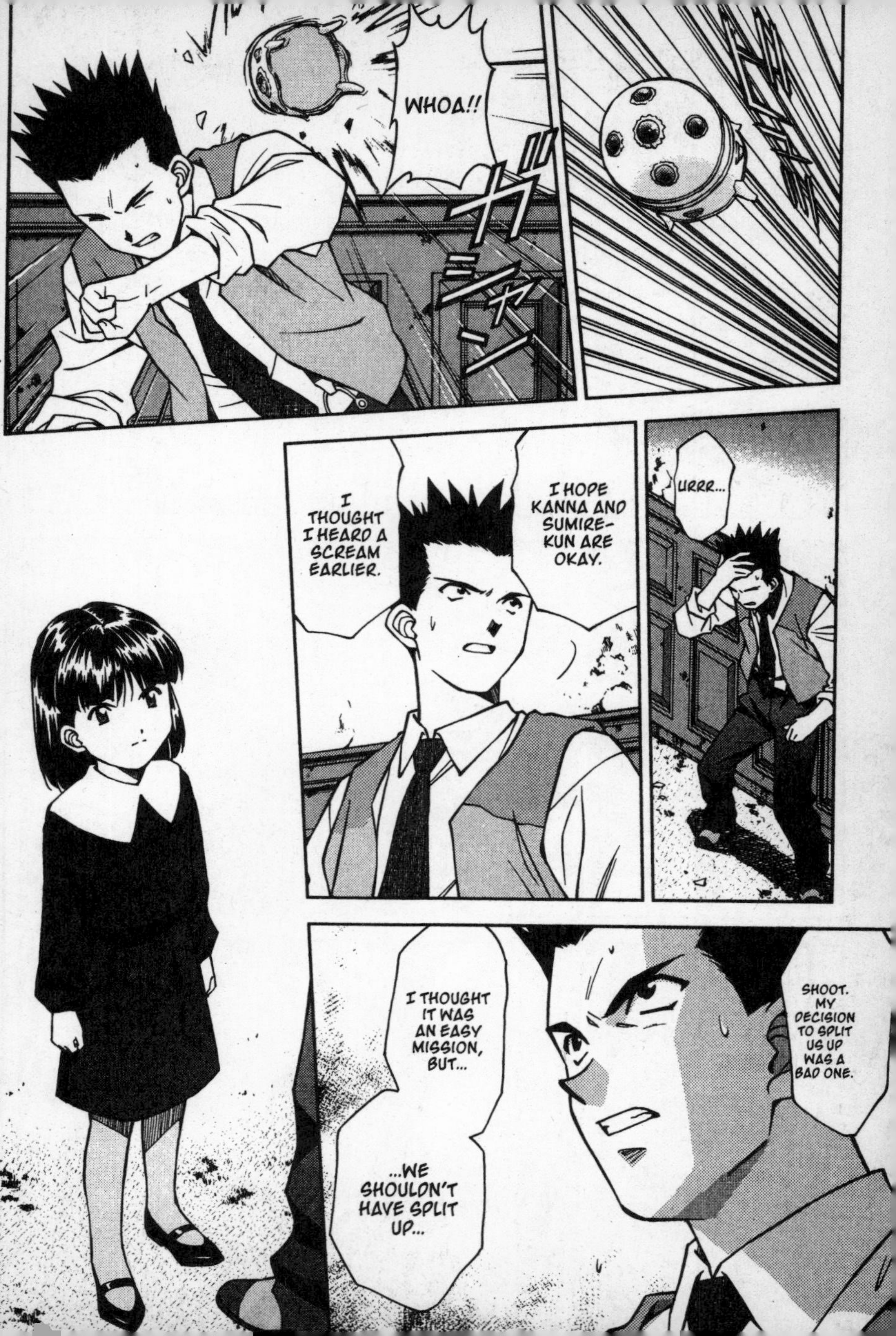
WHOA!!
URRR...
I HOPE KANNA AND SUMIRE-KUN ARE OKAY.
I THOUGHT I HEARD A SCREAM EARLIER.
SHOOT. MY DECISION TO SPLIT US UP WAS A BAD ONE.
I THOUGHT IT WAS AN EASY MISSION, BUT...
...WE SHOULDN'T HAVE SPLIT UP...

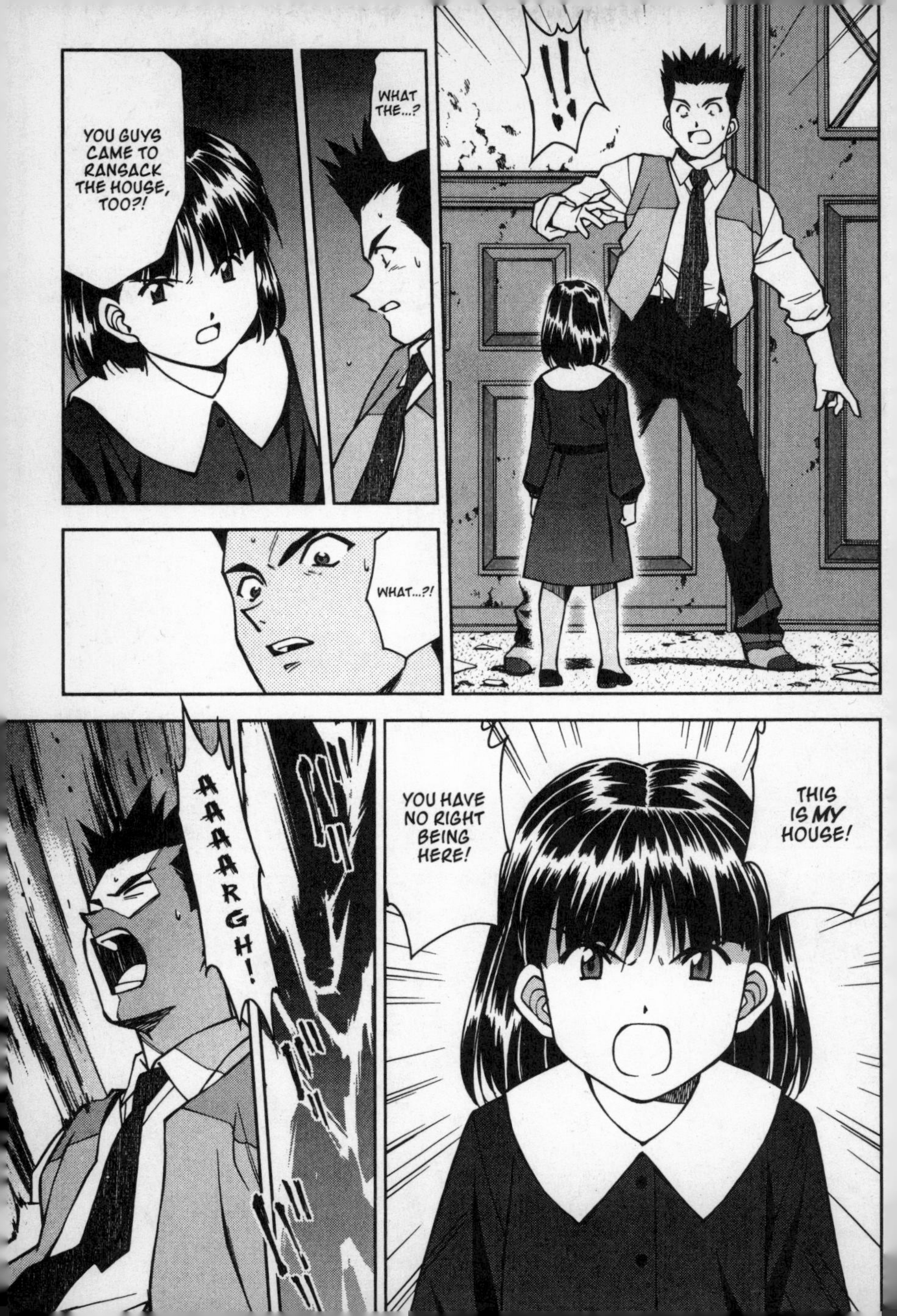
!!
WHAT THE...?
YOU GUYS CAME TO RANSACK THE HOUSE, TOO?!
WHAT...?!
THIS IS MY HOUSE!
YOU HAVE NO RIGHT BEING HERE!
AAAAARGH!

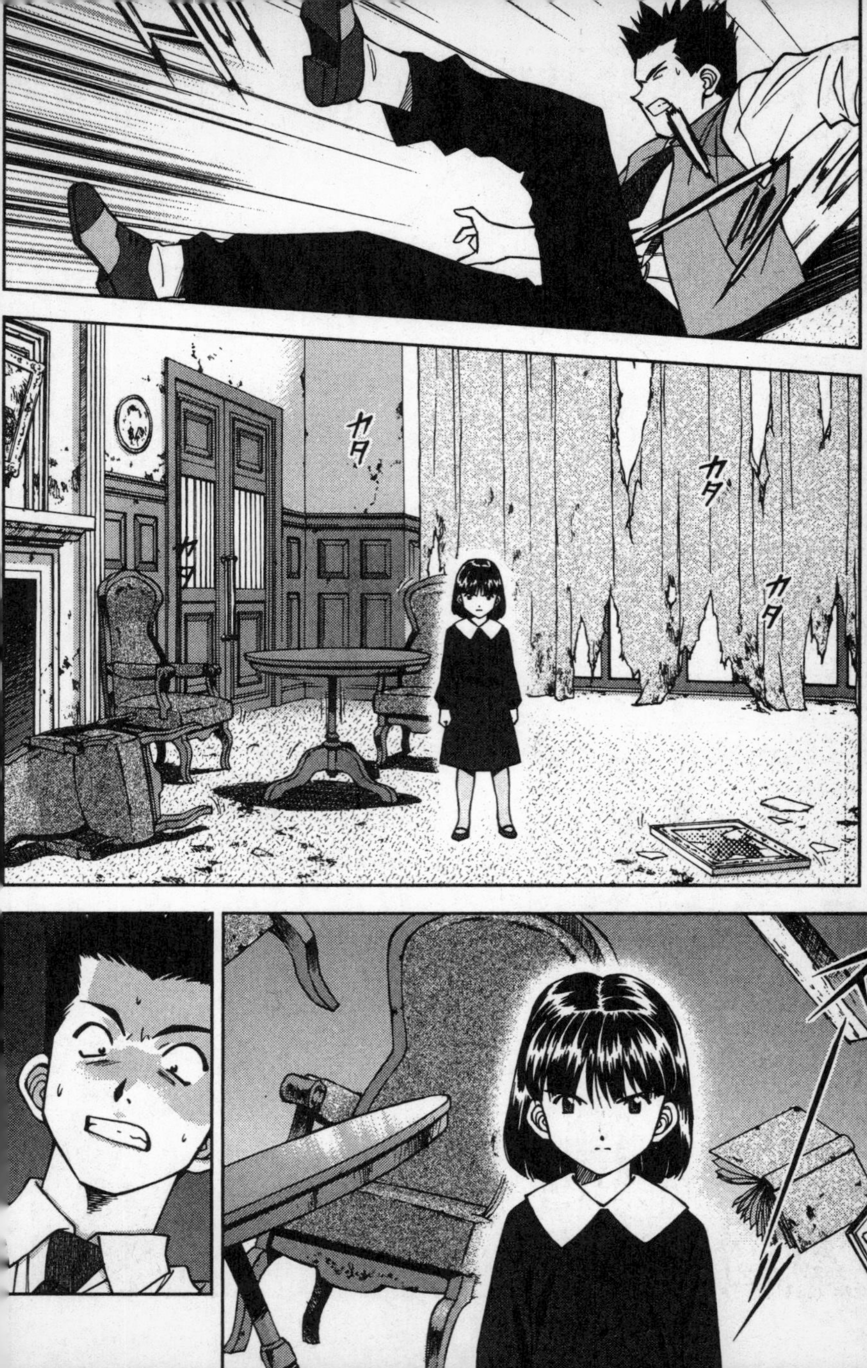
カタ
カタ
カタ
カタ

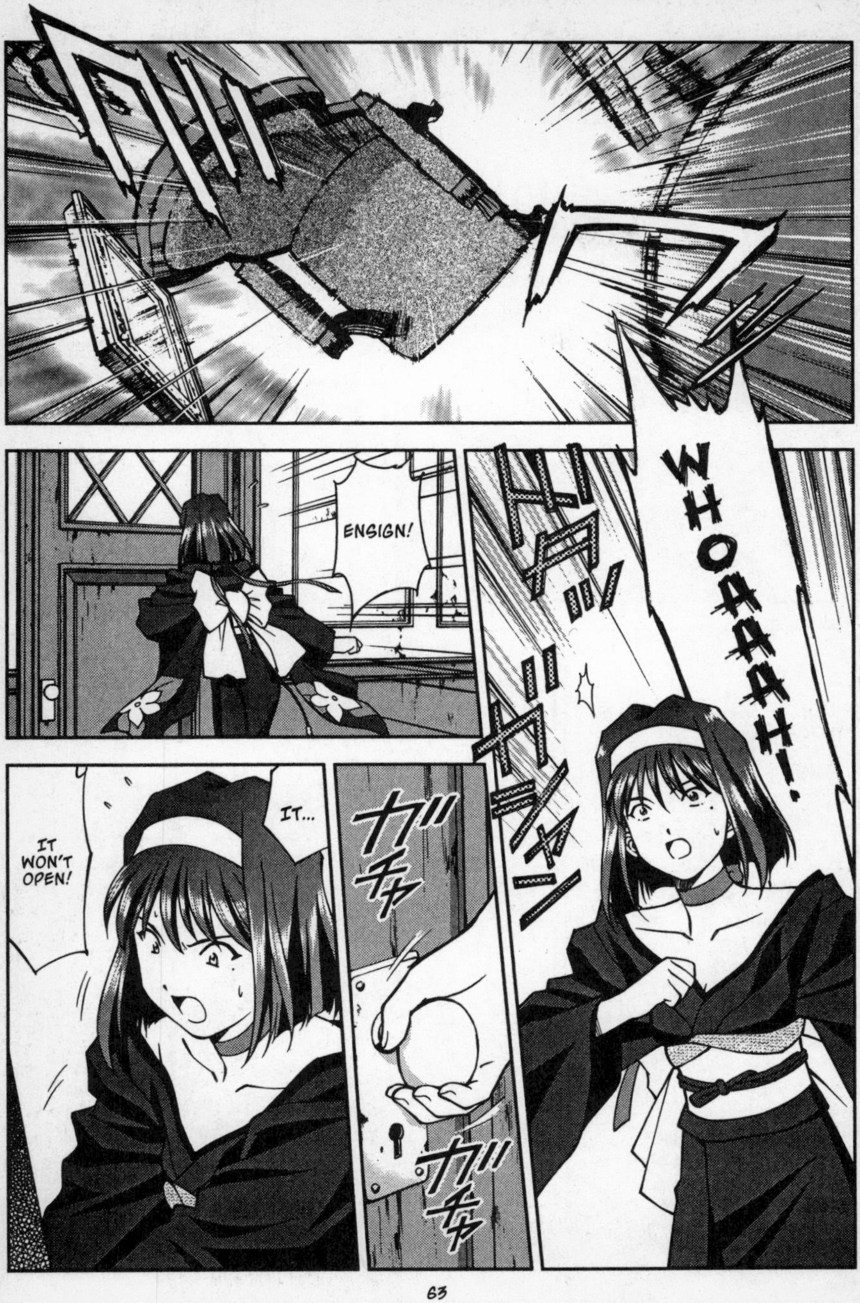
WHOAAAAH!
ENSIGN!
ガチャ
ガチャ
IT...
IT WON'T OPEN!

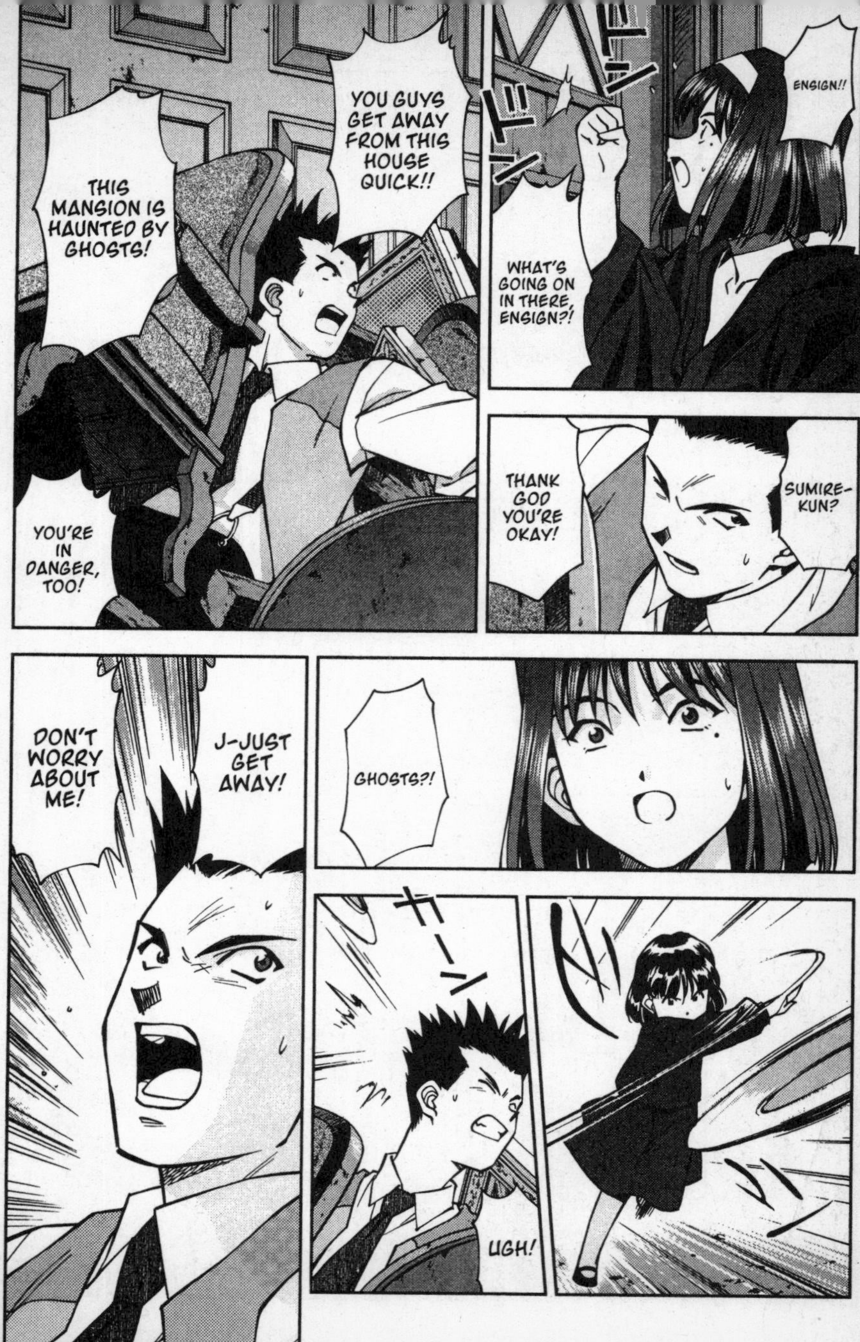
ENSIGN!!
WHAT'S GOING ON IN THERE, ENSIGN?!
SUMIRE-KUN?
THANK GOD YOU'RE OKAY!
YOU GUYS GET AWAY FROM THIS HOUSE QUICK!!
THIS MANSION IS HAUNTED BY GHOSTS!
YOU'RE IN DANGER, TOO!
GHOSTS?!
UGH!
J-JUST GET AWAY!
DON'T WORRY ABOUT ME!

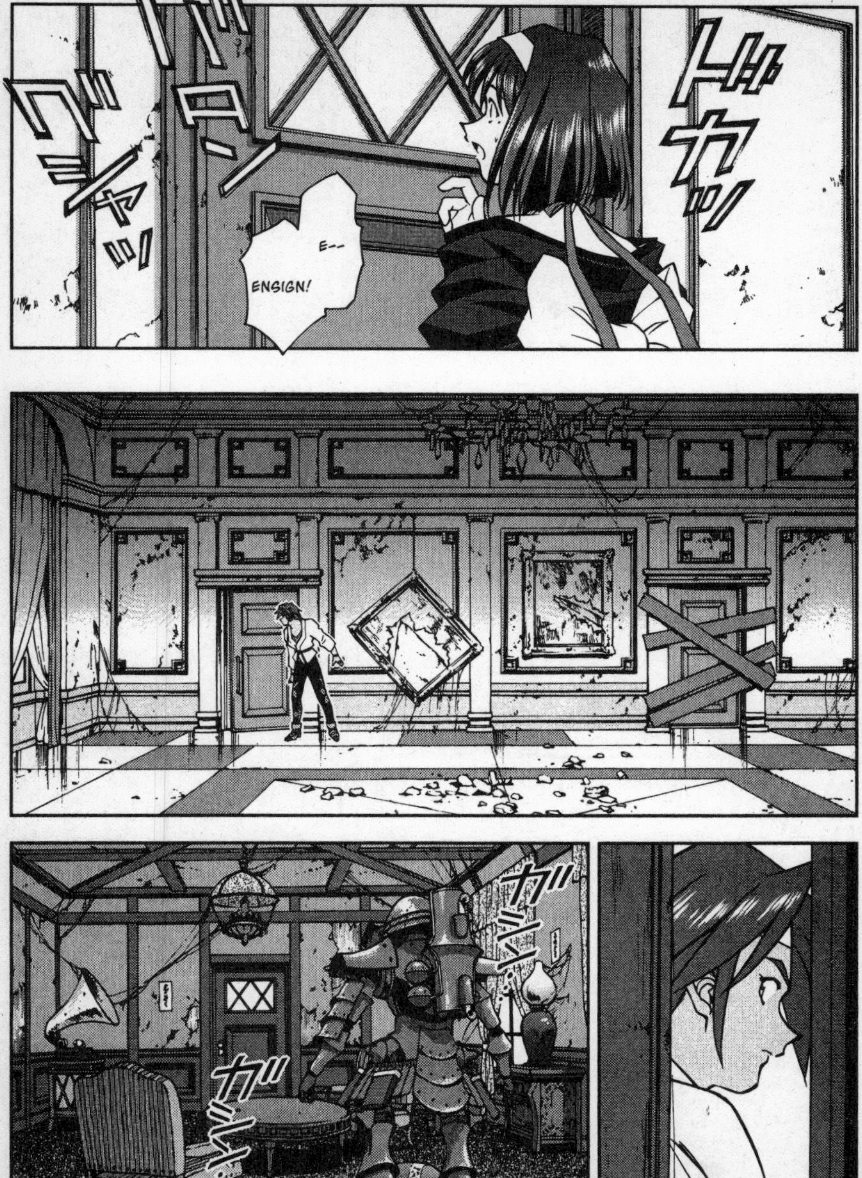
E-- ENSIGN!

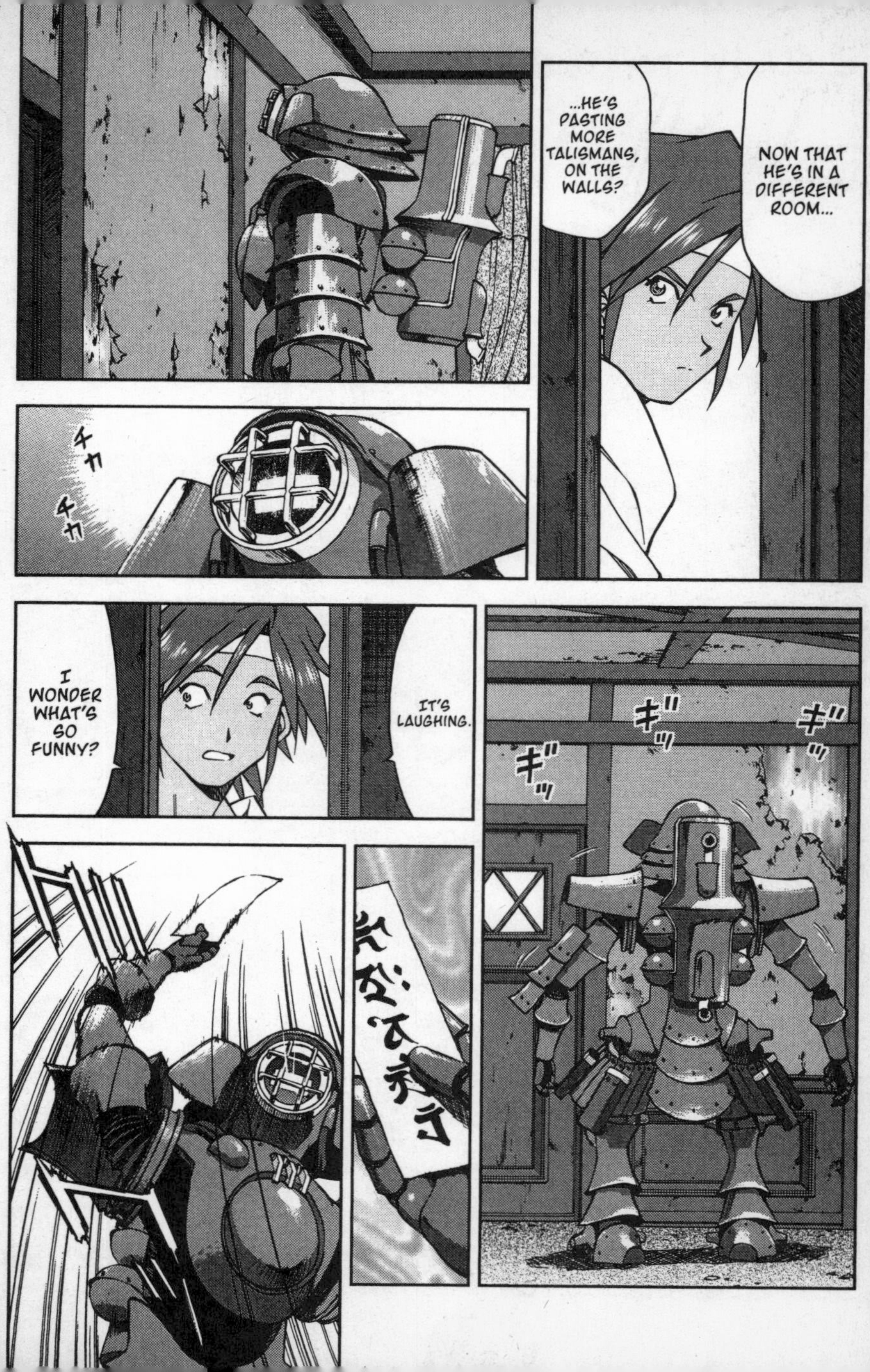
NOW THAT HE'S IN A DIFFERENT ROOM...
...HE'S PASTING MORE TALISMANS, ON THE WALLS?
チカ
チカ
ギッ
ギッ
ギッ
IT'S LAUGHING.
I WONDER WHAT'S SO FUNNY?

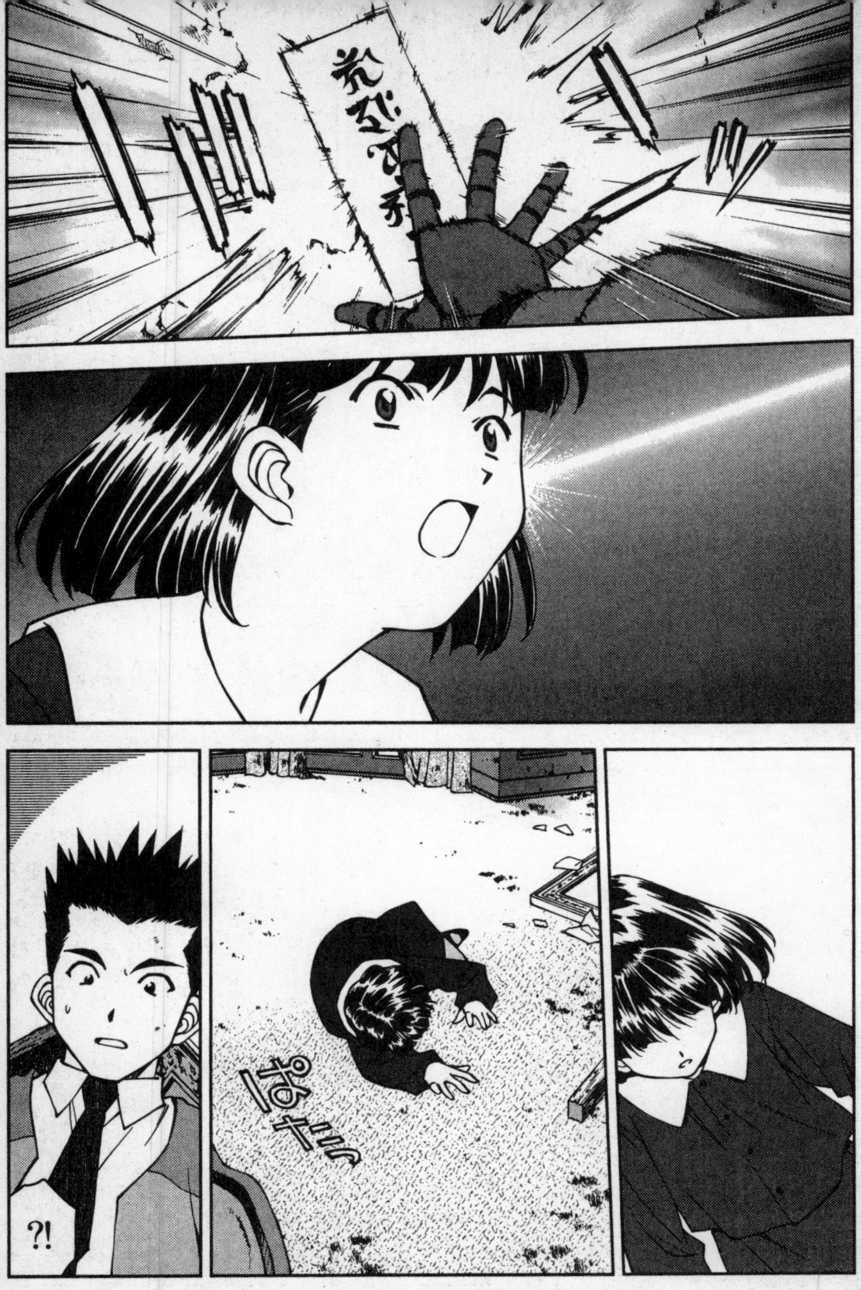
ぱさっ
?!

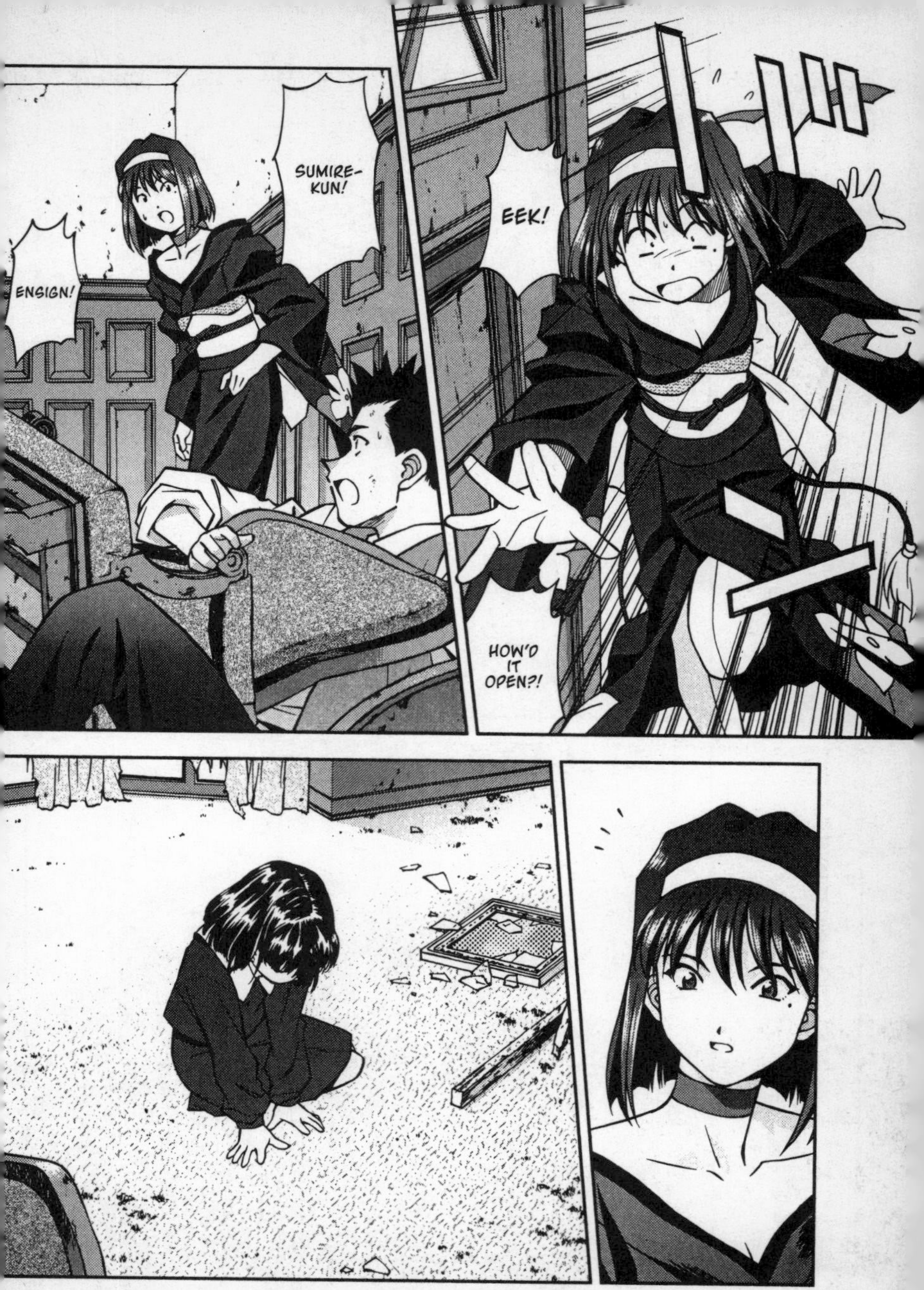
EEK!
HOW'D IT OPEN?!
SUMIRE-KUN!
ENSIGN!

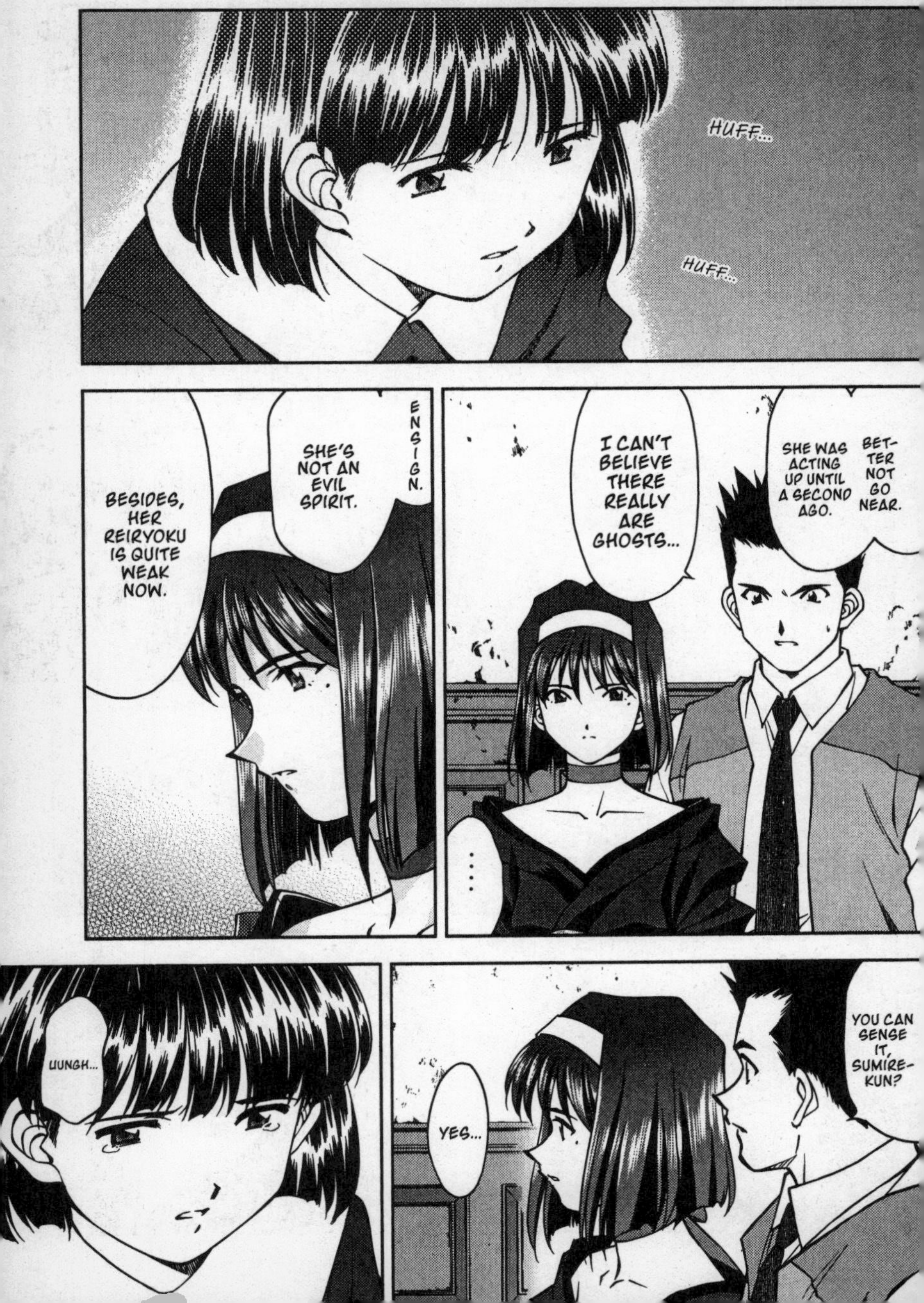
HUFF...
HUFF...
BET-TER NOT GO NEAR.
SHE WAS ACTING UP UNTIL A SECOND AGO.
I CAN'T BELIEVE THERE REALLY ARE GHOSTS...
....
ENSIGN.
SHE'S NOT AN EVIL SPIRIT.
BESIDES, HER REIRYOKU IS QUITE WEAK NOW.
YOU CAN SENSE IT, SUMIRE-KUN?
YES...
UUNGH...

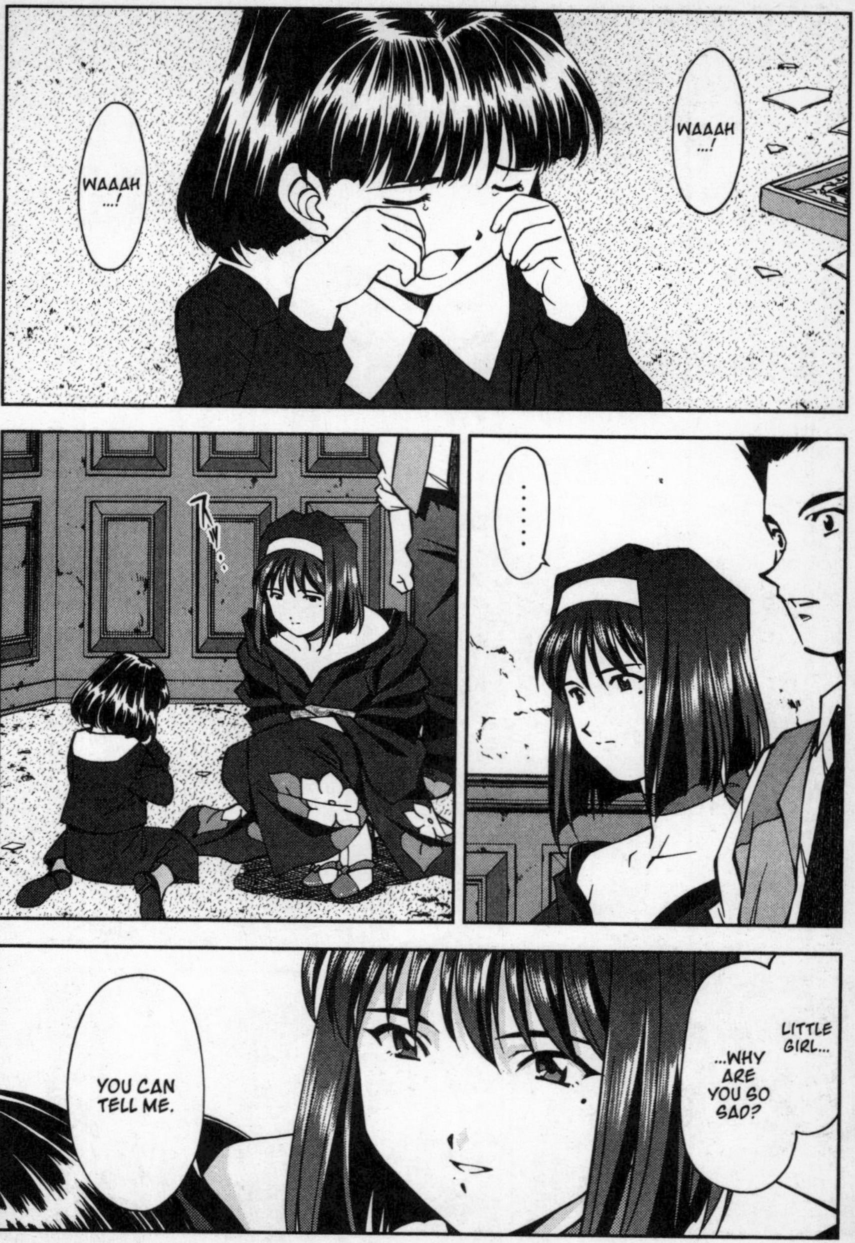
WAAAH ...!
WAAAH ...!
......
LITTLE GIRL...
...WHY ARE YOU SO SAD?
YOU CAN TELL ME.

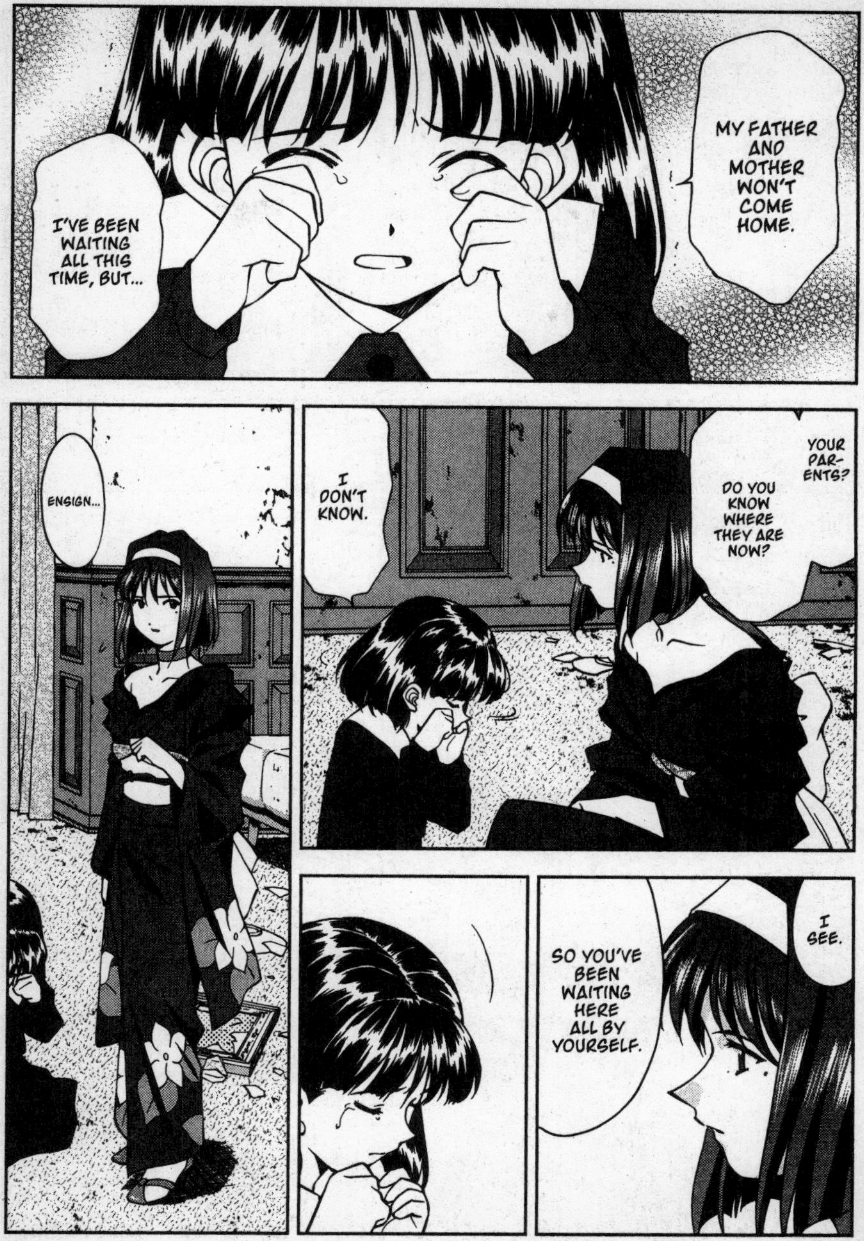
MY FATHER AND MOTHER WON'T COME HOME.
I'VE BEEN WAITING ALL THIS TIME, BUT...
YOUR PAR-ENTS?
DO YOU KNOW WHERE THEY ARE NOW?
I DON'T KNOW.
I SEE.
SO YOU'VE BEEN WAITING HERE ALL BY YOURSELF.
ENSIGN...

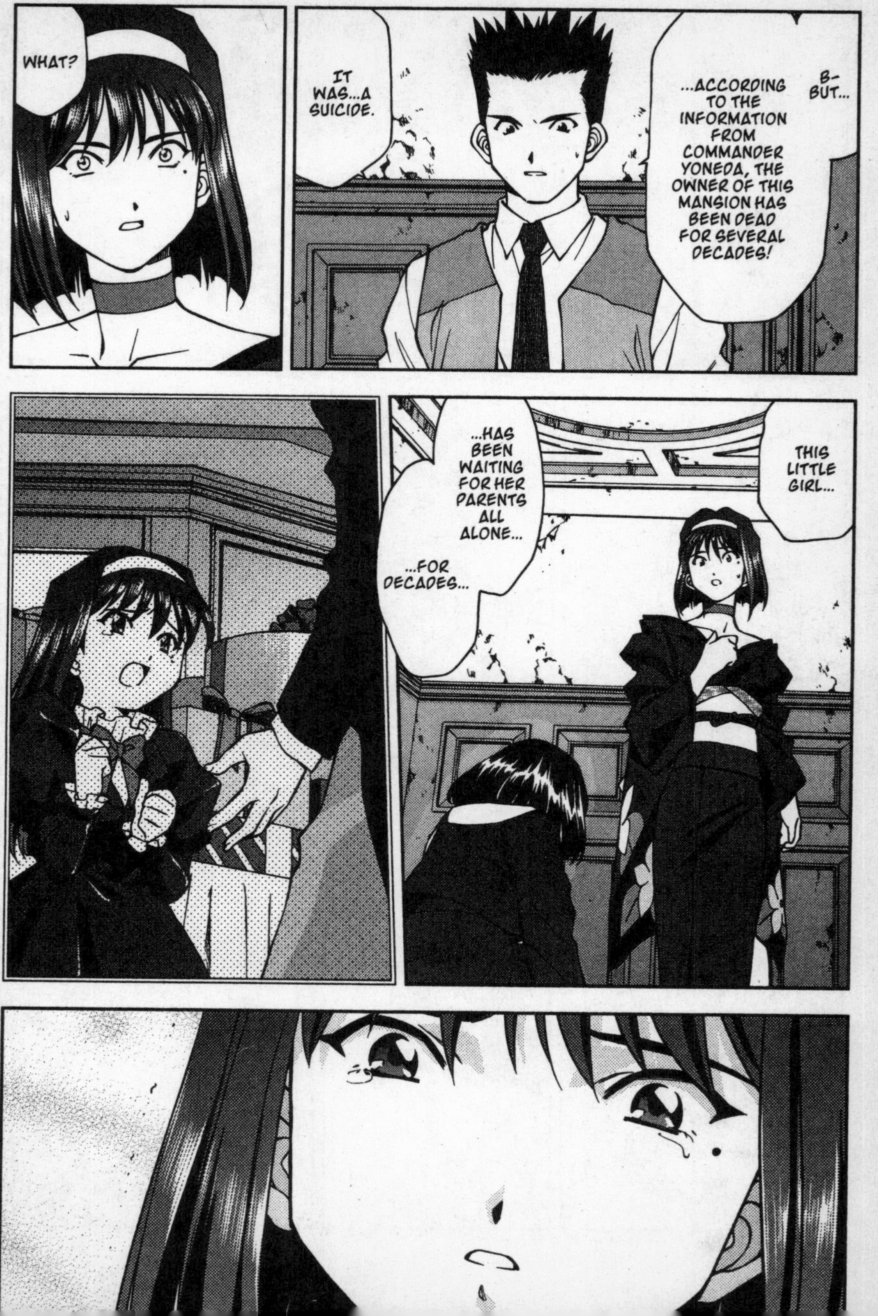
B-BUT...
...ACCORDING TO THE INFORMATION FROM COMMANDER YONEDA, THE OWNER OF THIS MANSION HAS BEEN DEAD FOR SEVERAL DECADES!
IT WAS...A SUICIDE.
WHAT?
THIS LITTLE GIRL...
...HAS BEEN WAITING FOR HER PARENTS ALL ALONE...
...FOR DECADES...

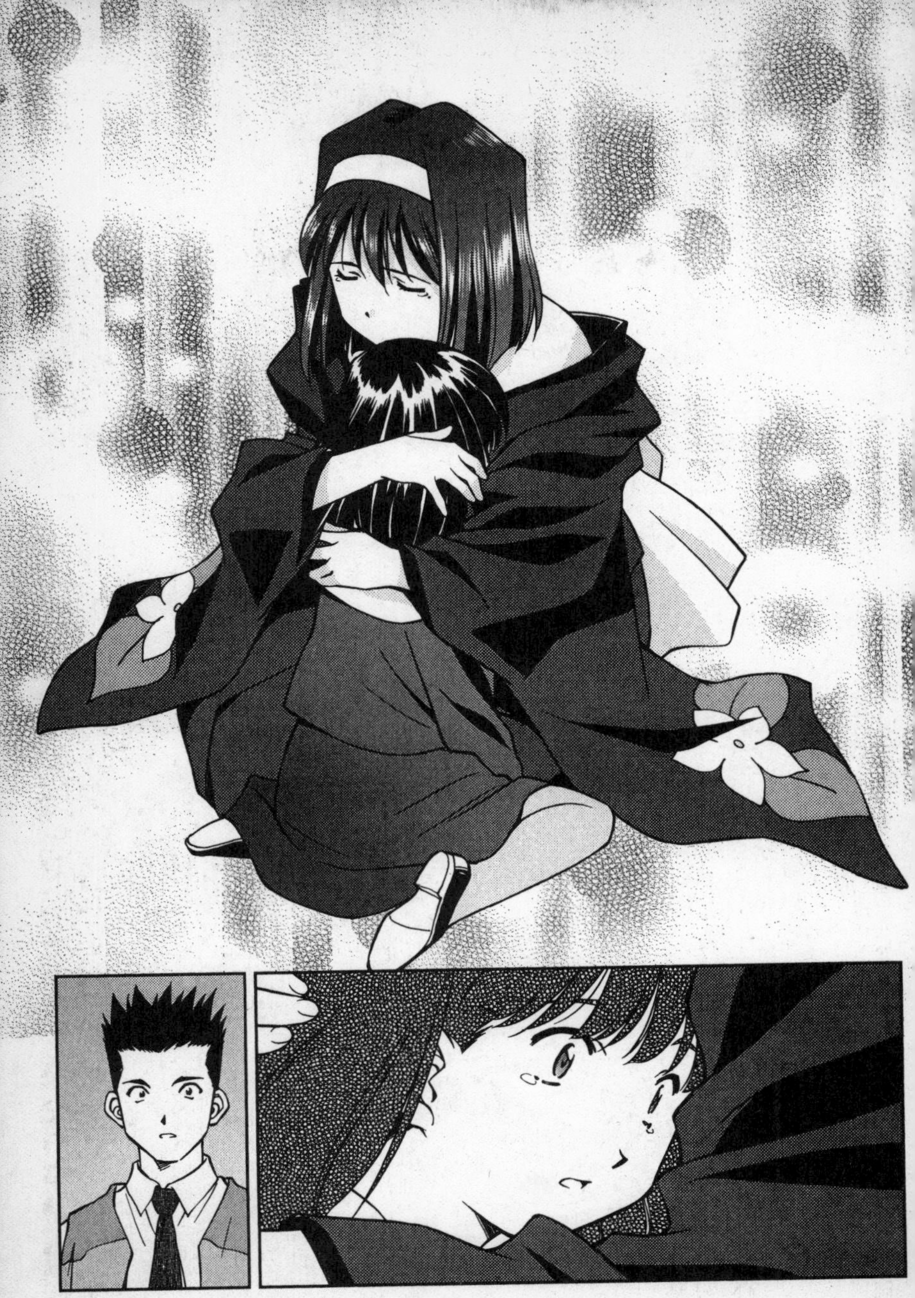

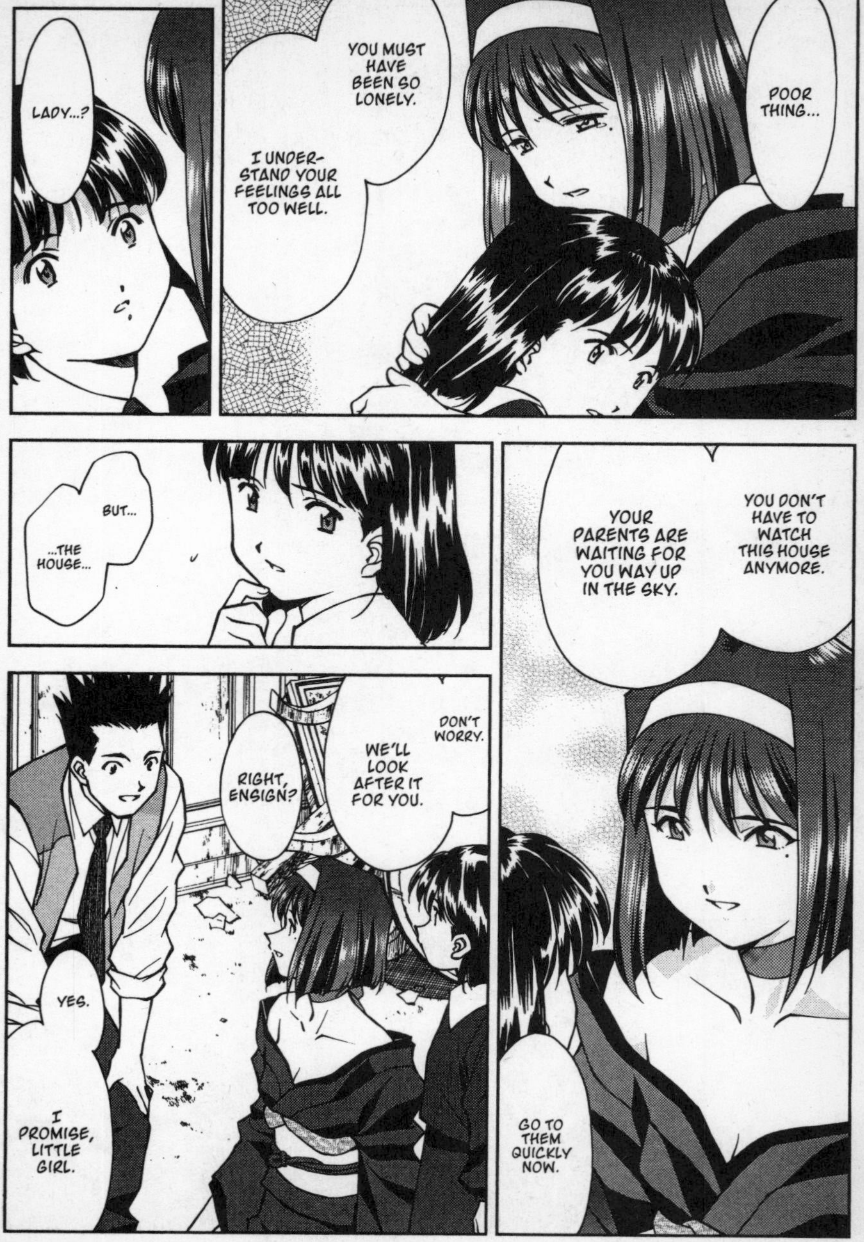
POOR THING...
YOU MUST HAVE BEEN SO LONELY.
I UNDER-STAND YOUR FEELINGS ALL TOO WELL.
LADY...?
YOU DON'T HAVE TO WATCH THIS HOUSE ANYMORE.
YOUR PARENTS ARE WAITING FOR YOU WAY UP IN THE SKY.
BUT...
...THE HOUSE...
DON'T WORRY.
WE'LL LOOK AFTER IT FOR YOU.
RIGHT, ENSIGN?
YES.
I PROMISE, LITTLE GIRL.
GO TO THEM QUICKLY NOW.

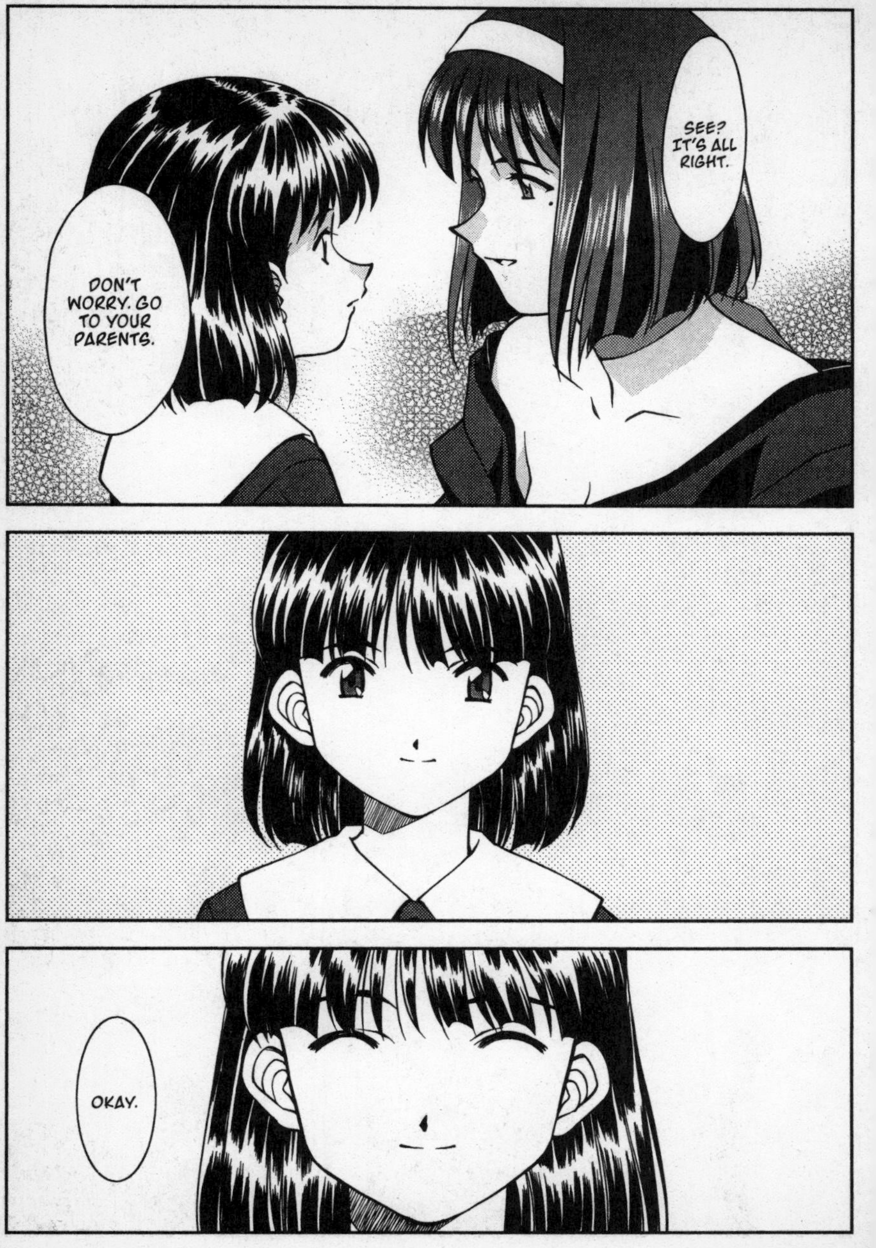
SEE? IT'S ALL RIGHT.
DON'T WORRY. GO TO YOUR PARENTS.
OKAY.

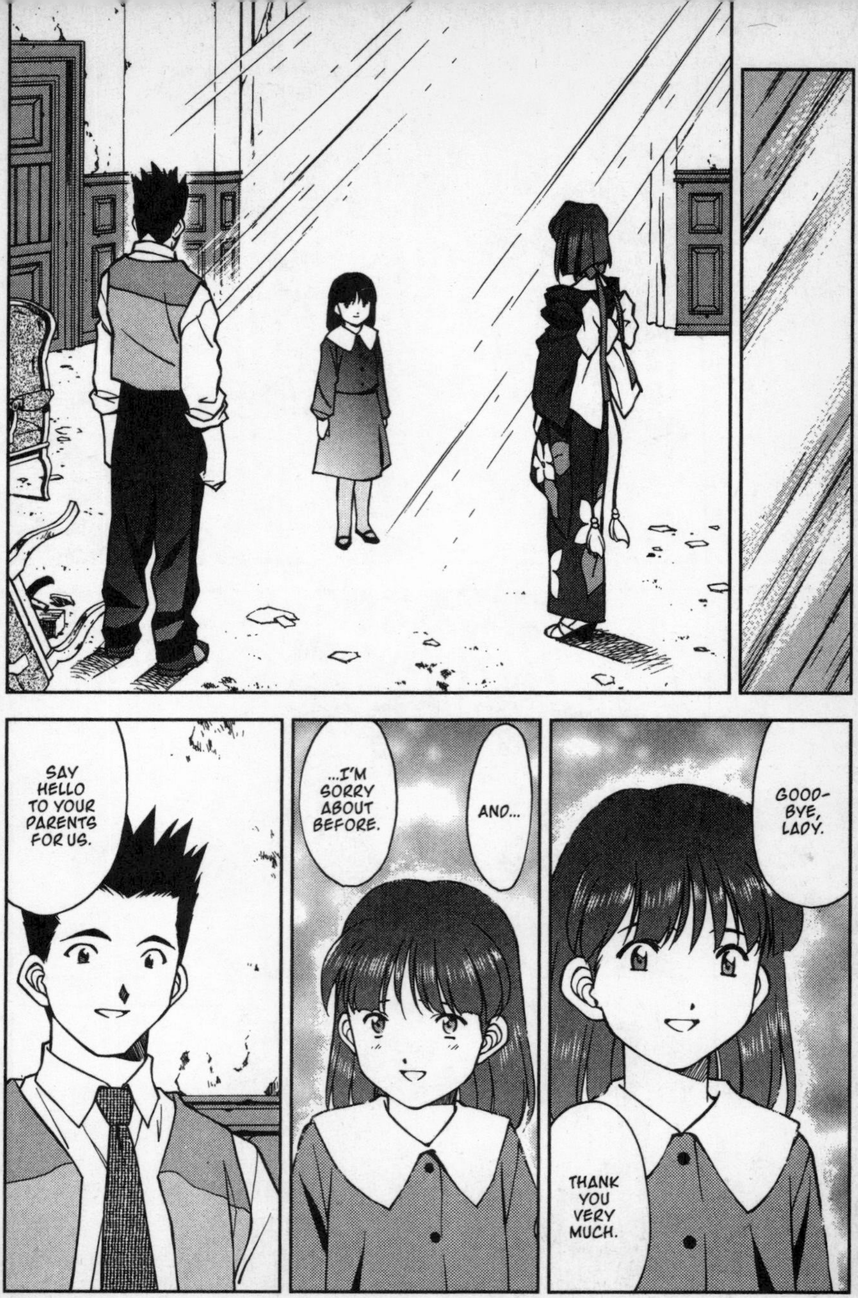
GOOD-BYE, LADY.
THANK YOU VERY MUCH.
AND...
...I'M SORRY ABOUT BEFORE.
SAY HELLO TO YOUR PARENTS FOR US.

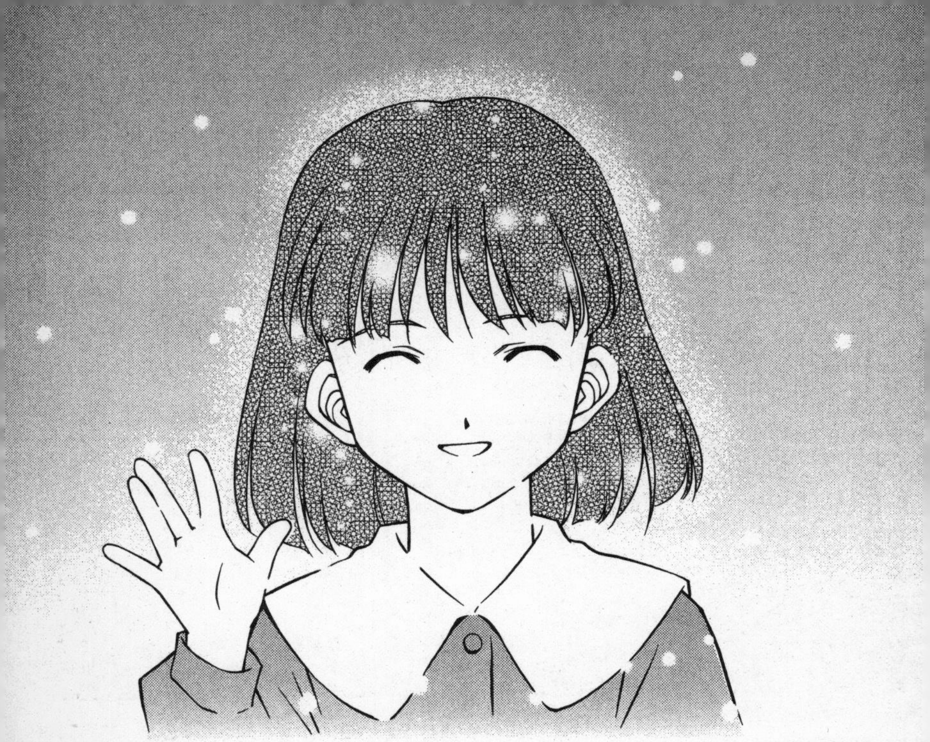
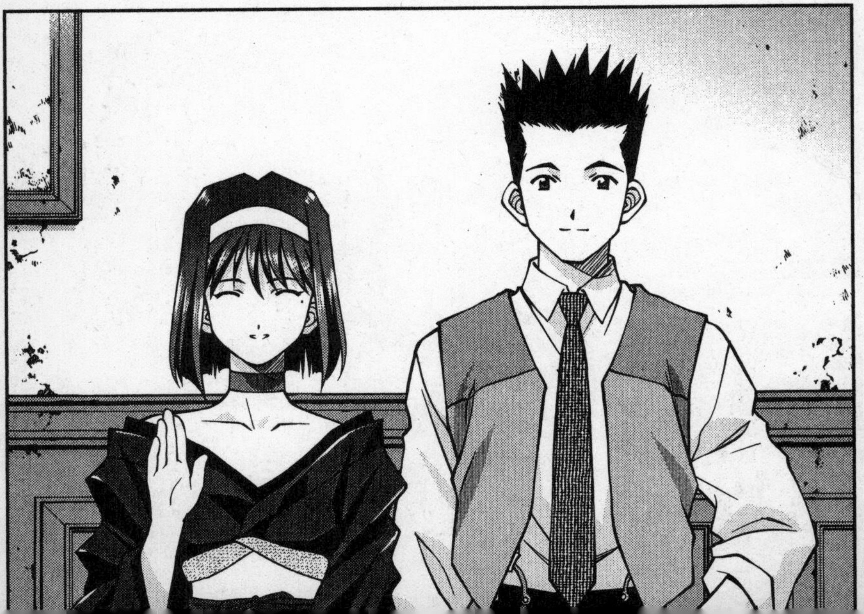

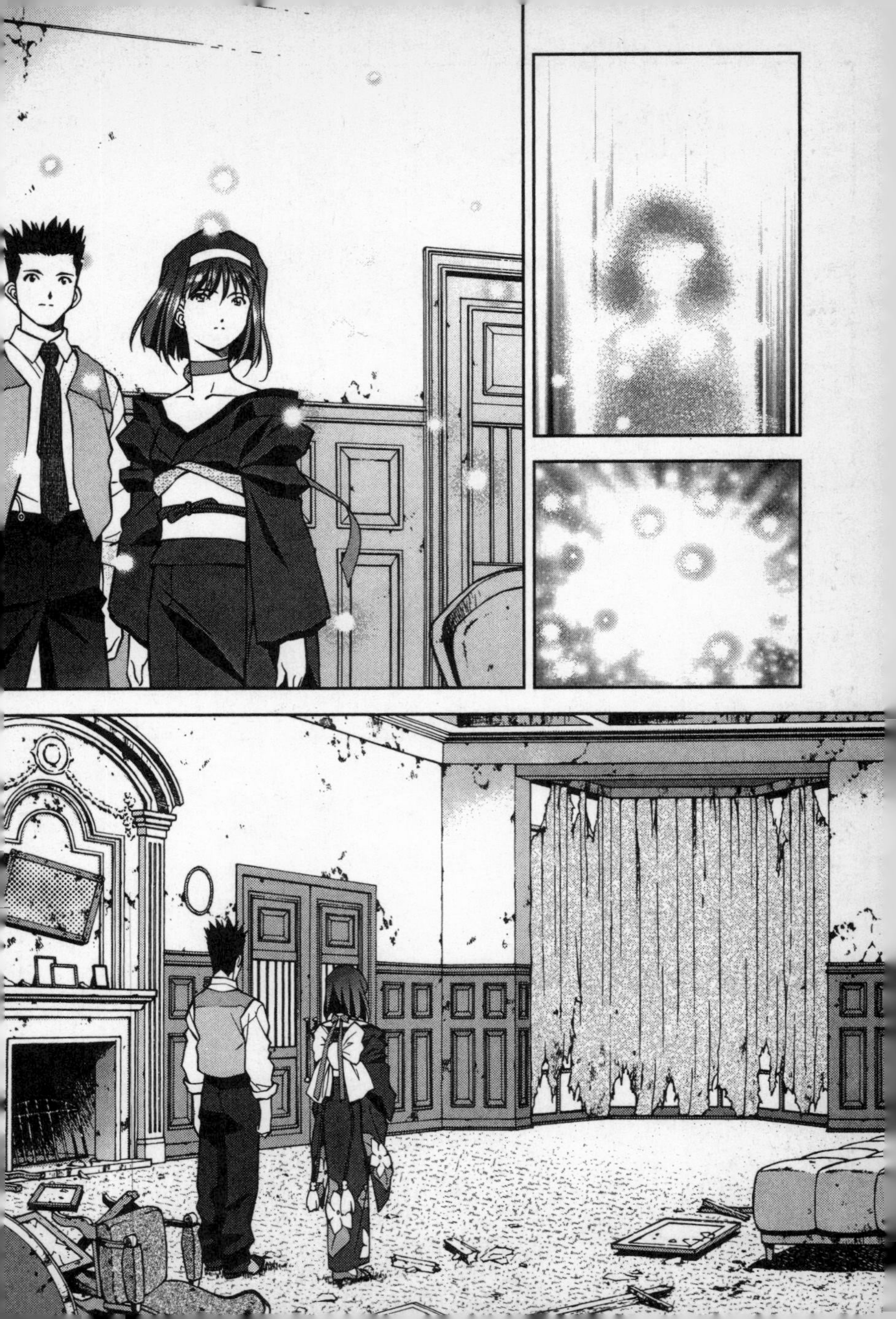

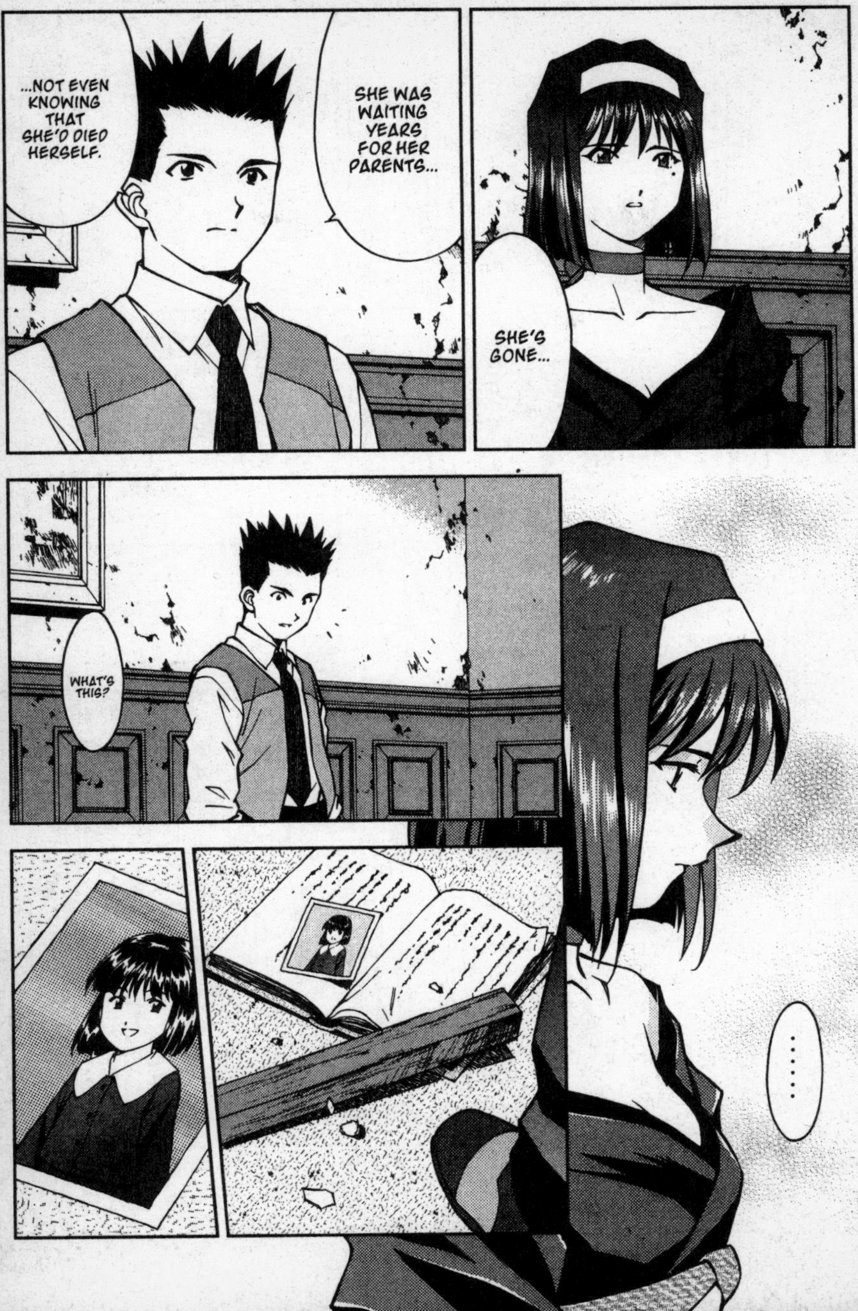
SHE'S GONE...
SHE WAS WAITING YEARS FOR HER PARENTS...
...NOT EVEN KNOWING THAT SHE'D DIED HERSELF.
WHAT'S THIS?
......

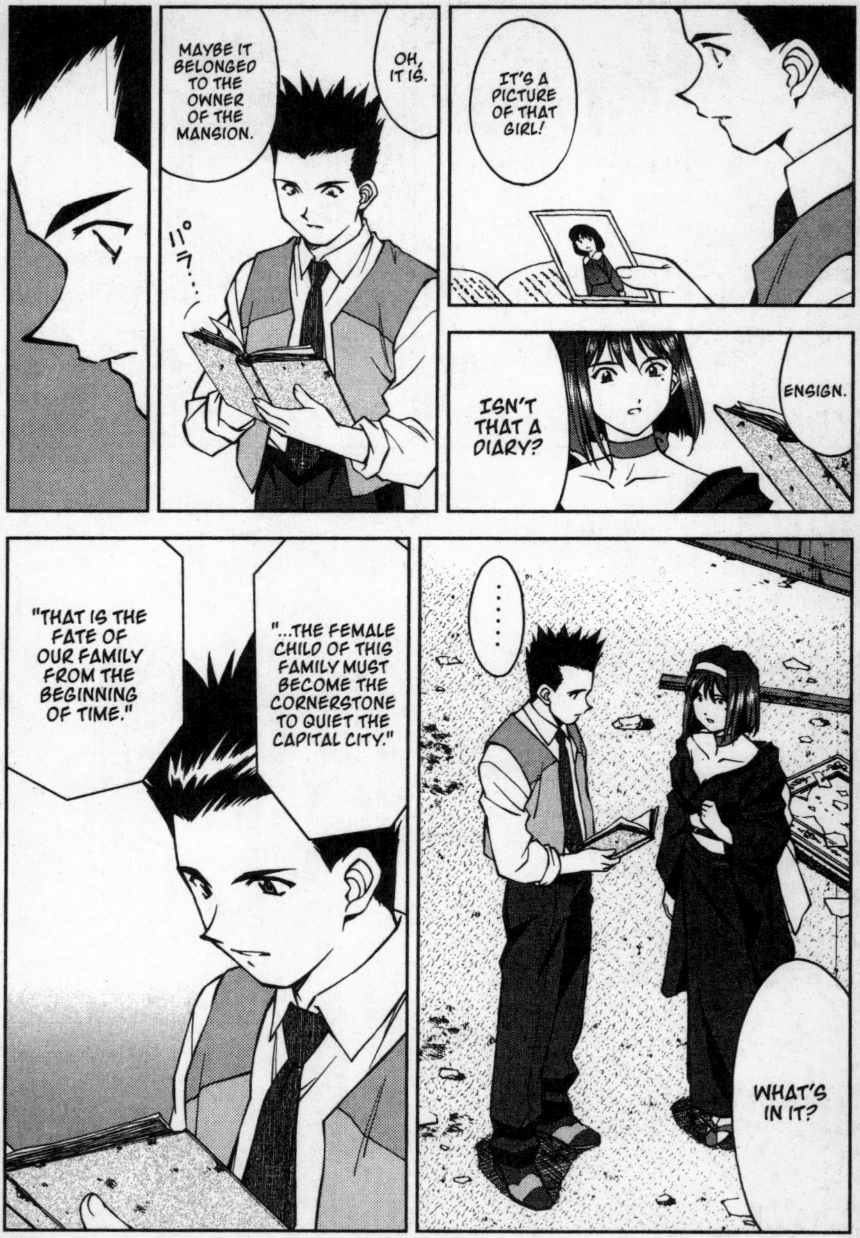
IT'S A PICTURE OF THAT GIRL!
ENSIGN.
ISN'T THAT A DIARY?
OH, IT IS.
MAYBE IT BELONGED TO THE OWNER OF THE MANSION.
パラ…
WHAT'S IN IT?
......
"...THE FEMALE CHILD OF THIS FAMILY MUST BECOME THE CORNERSTONE TO QUIET THE CAPITAL CITY."
"THAT IS THE FATE OF OUR FAMILY FROM THE BEGINNING OF TIME."

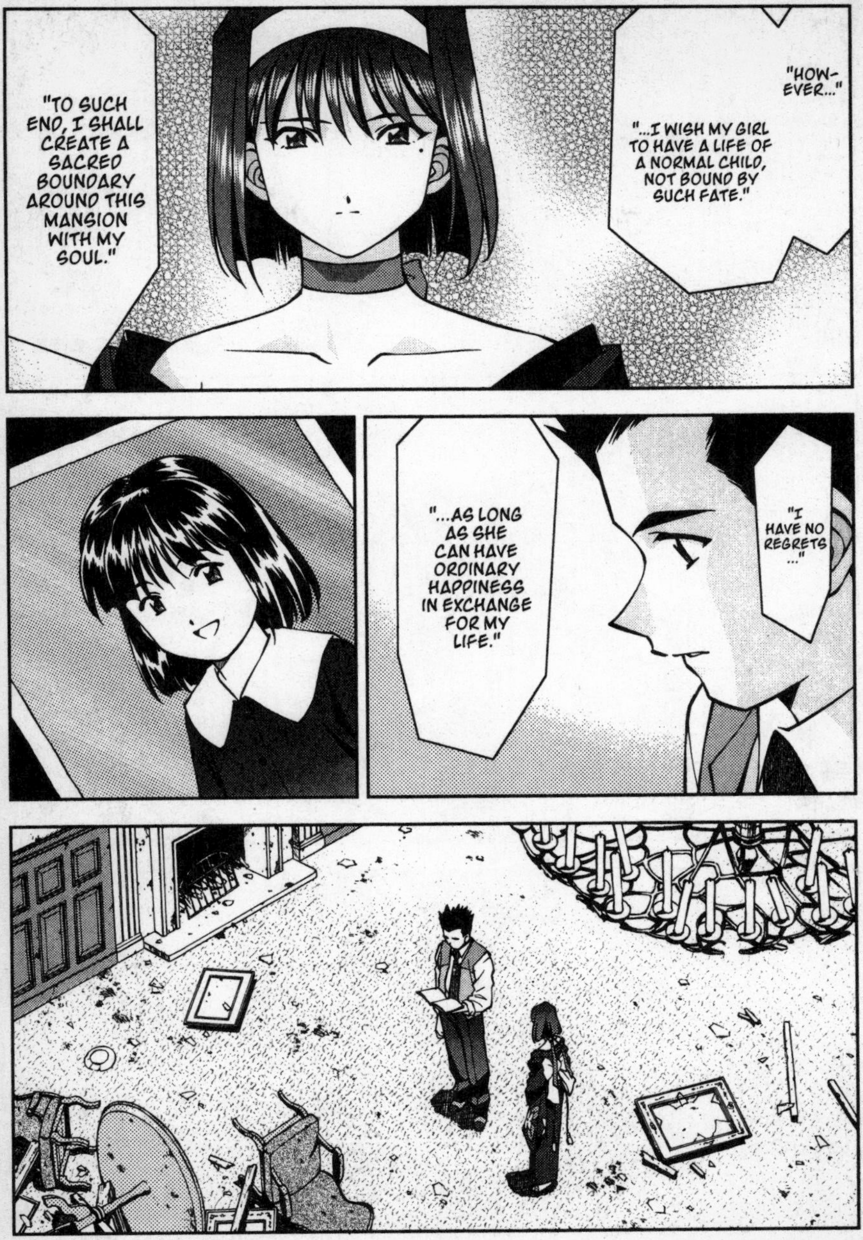
"HOW-EVER..."
"...I WISH MY GIRL TO HAVE A LIFE OF A NORMAL CHILD, NOT BOUND BY SUCH FATE."
"TO SUCH END, I SHALL CREATE A SACRED BOUNDARY AROUND THIS MANSION WITH MY SOUL."
"I HAVE NO REGRETS..."
"...AS LONG AS SHE CAN HAVE ORDINARY HAPPINESS IN EXCHANGE FOR MY LIFE."

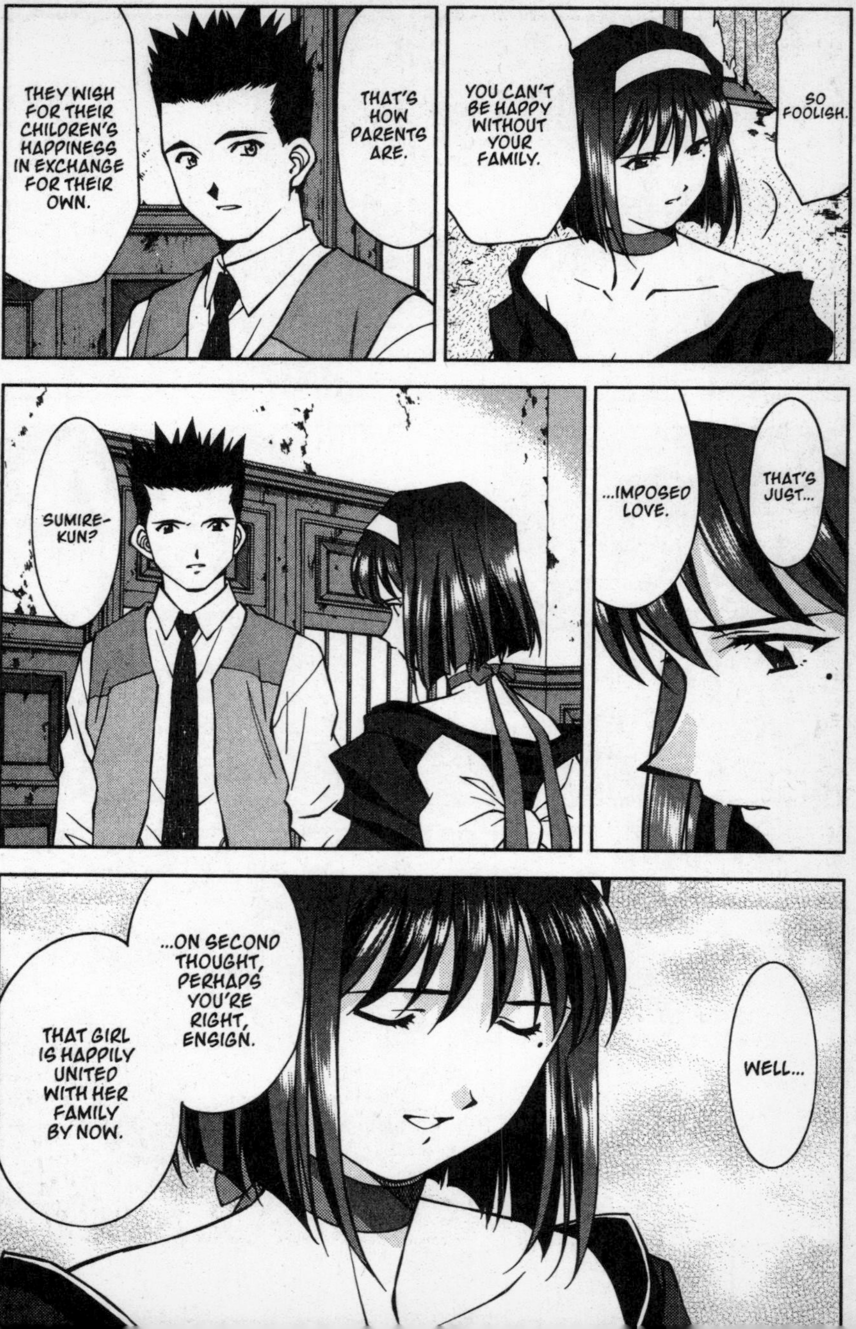
YOU CAN'T BE HAPPY WITHOUT YOUR FAMILY.
SO FOOLISH.
THAT'S HOW PARENTS ARE.
THEY WISH FOR THEIR CHILDREN'S HAPPINESS IN EXCHANGE FOR THEIR OWN.
THAT'S JUST...
...IMPOSED LOVE.
SUMIRE-KUN?
WELL...
...ON SECOND THOUGHT, PERHAPS YOU'RE RIGHT, ENSIGN.
THAT GIRL IS HAPPILY UNITED WITH HER FAMILY BY NOW.

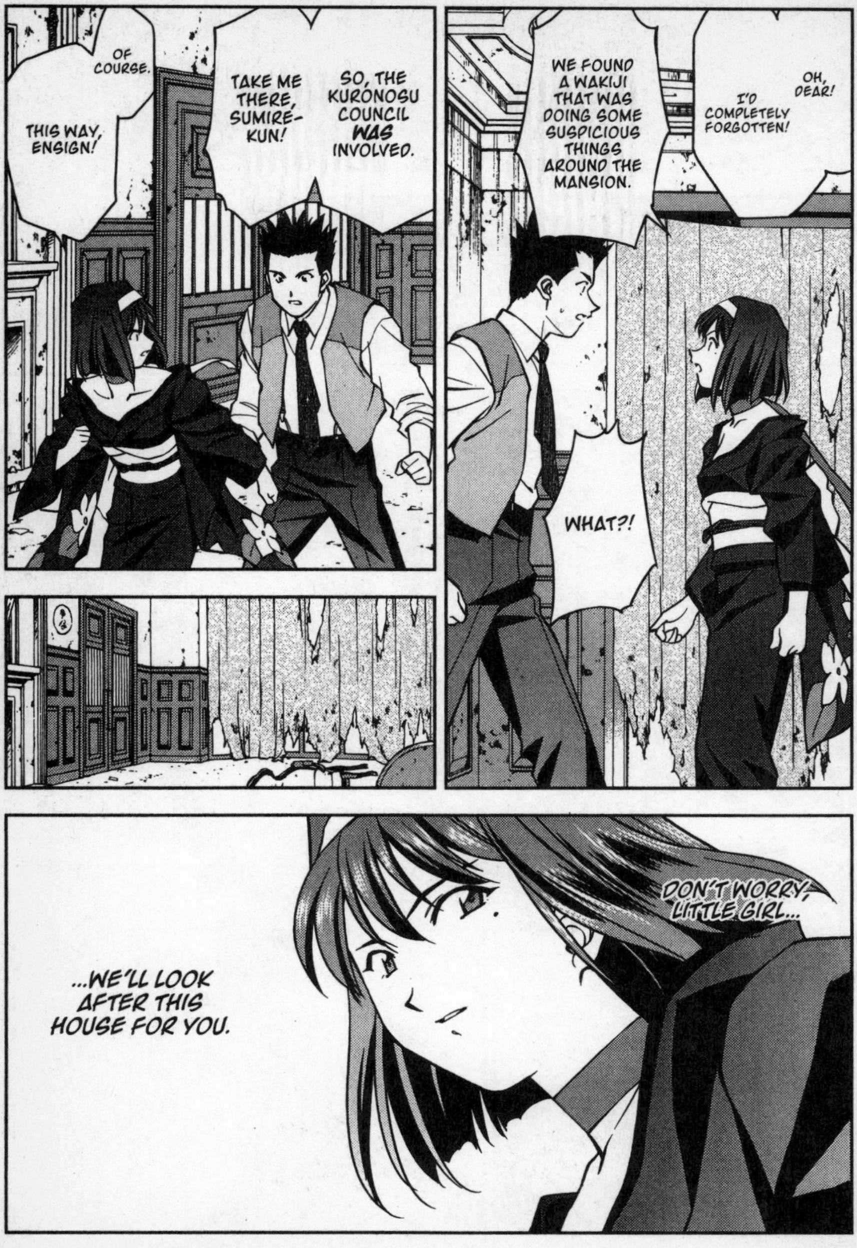
OH, DEAR!
I'D COMPLETELY FORGOTTEN!
WE FOUND A WAKIJI THAT WAS DOING SOME SUSPICIOUS THINGS AROUND THE MANSION.
WHAT?!
SO, THE KURONOSU COUNCIL WAS INVOLVED.
TAKE ME THERE, SUMIRE-KUN!
OF COURSE.
THIS WAY, ENSIGN!
DON'T WORRY, LITTLE GIRL...
...WE'LL LOOK AFTER THIS HOUSE FOR YOU.

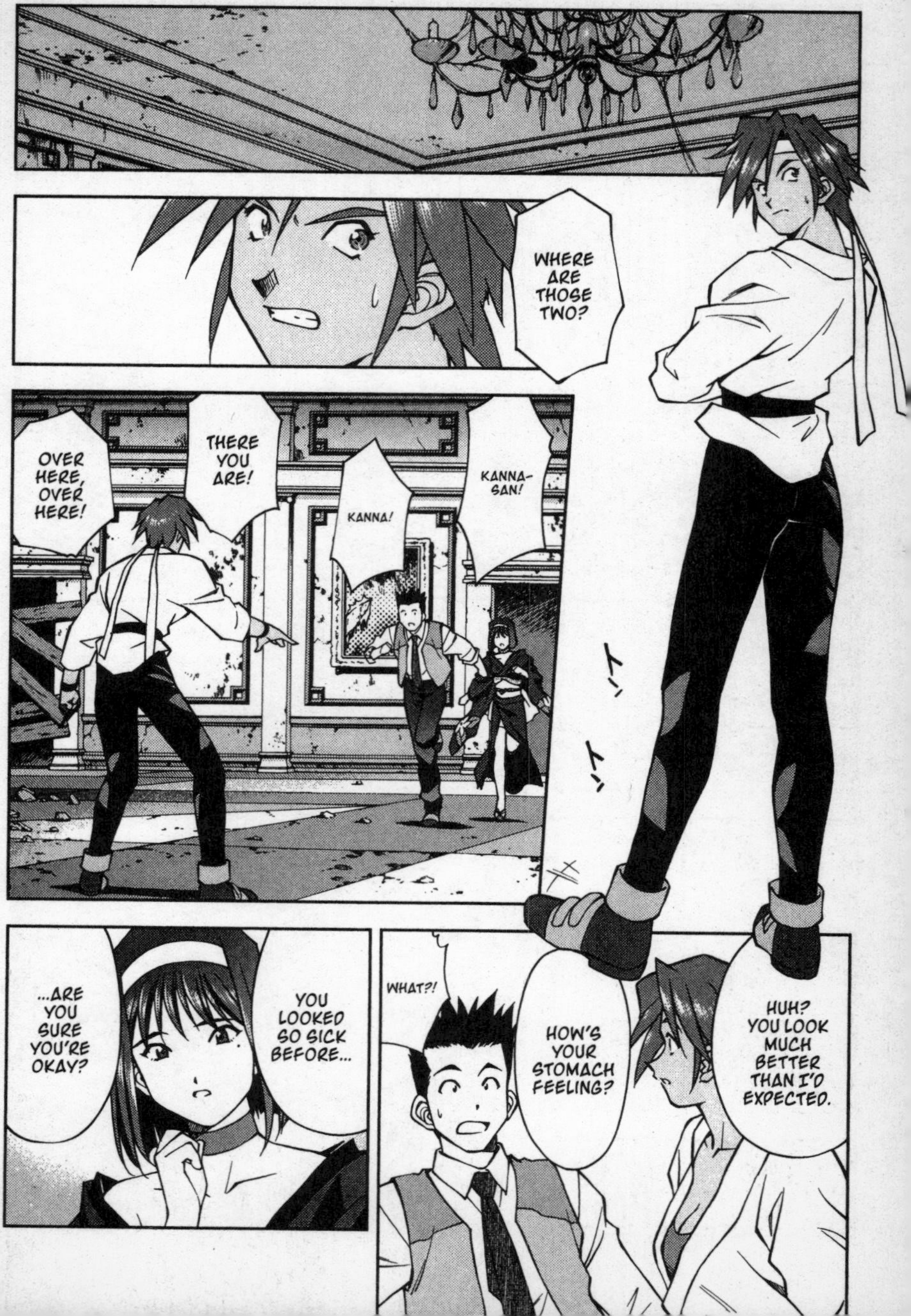
WHERE ARE THOSE TWO?
KANNA-SAN!
KANNA!
THERE YOU ARE!
OVER HERE, OVER HERE!
HUH? YOU LOOK MUCH BETTER THAN I'D EXPECTED.
HOW'S YOUR STOMACH FEELING?
WHAT?!
YOU LOOKED SO SICK BEFORE...
...ARE YOU SURE YOU'RE OKAY?

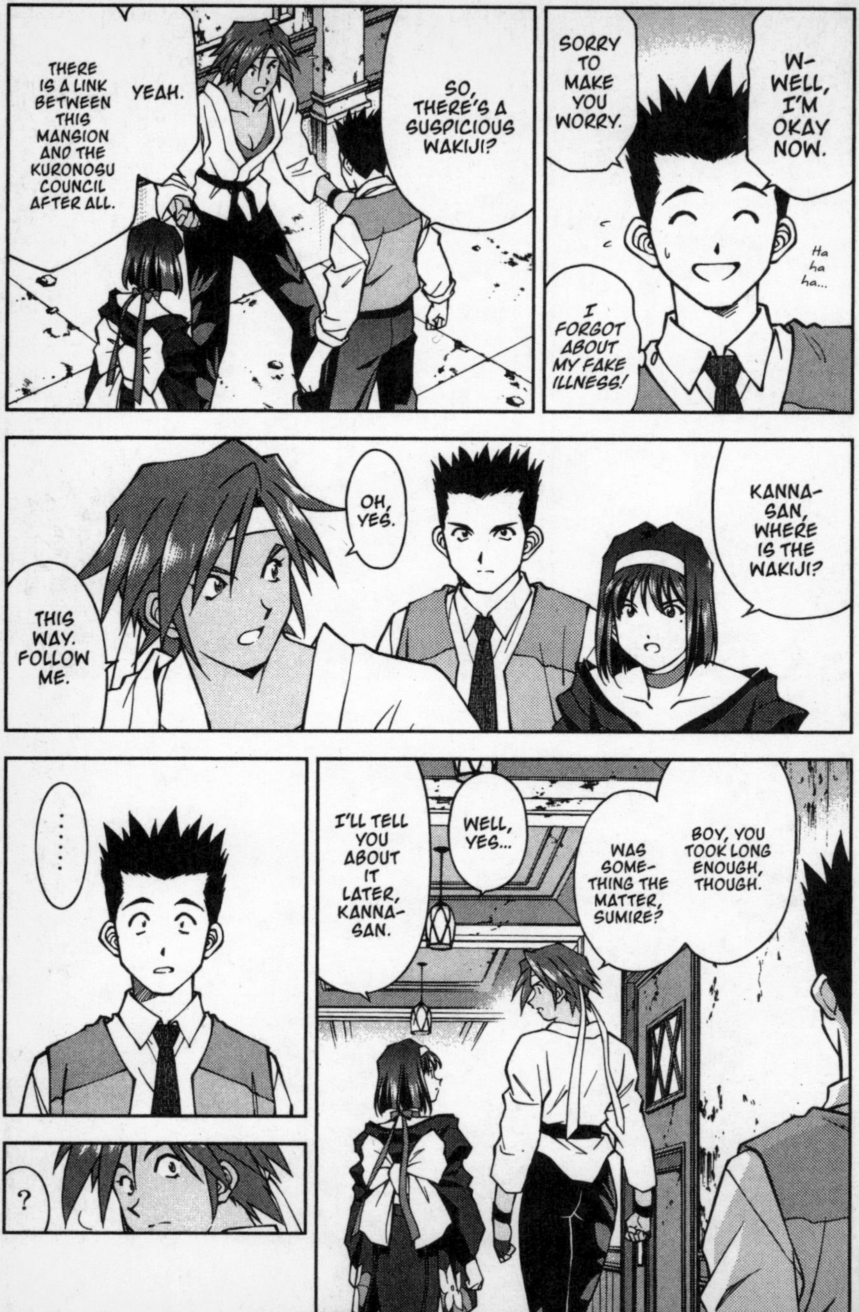
W-WELL, I'M OKAY NOW.
SORRY TO MAKE YOU WORRY.
Ha ha ha...
I FORGOT ABOUT MY FAKE ILLNESS!
SO, THERE'S A SUSPICIOUS WAKIJI?
YEAH.
THERE IS A LINK BETWEEN THIS MANSION AND THE KURONOSU COUNCIL AFTER ALL.
KANNA-SAN, WHERE IS THE WAKIJI?
OH, YES.
THIS WAY. FOLLOW ME.
BOY, YOU TOOK LONG ENOUGH, THOUGH.
WAS SOMETHING THE MATTER, SUMIRE?
WELL, YES...
I'LL TELL YOU ABOUT IT LATER, KANNA-SAN.
......
?

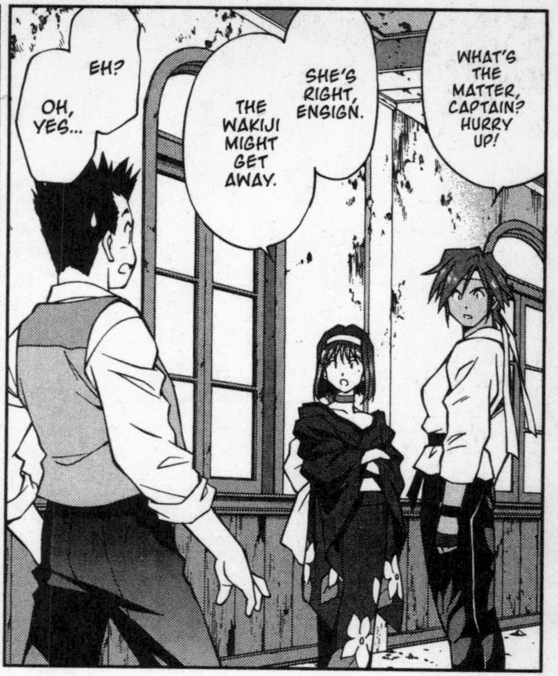
WHAT'S THE MATTER, CAPTAIN? HURRY UP!
SHE'S RIGHT, ENSIGN. THE WAKIJI MIGHT GET AWAY.
EH?
OH, YES...
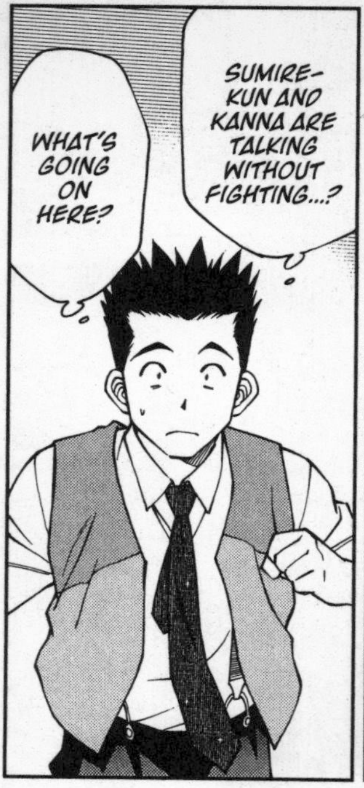
SUMIRE-KUN AND KANNA ARE TALKING WITHOUT FIGHTING...?
WHAT'S GOING ON HERE?
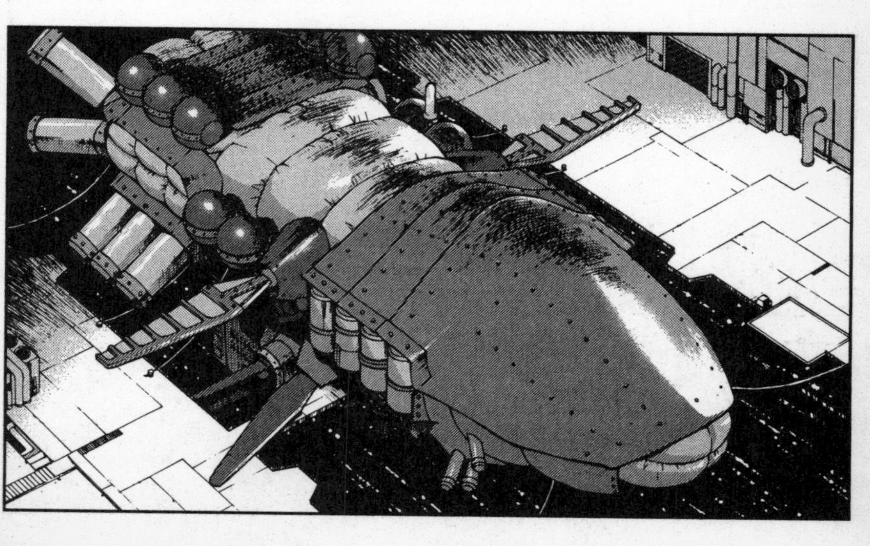

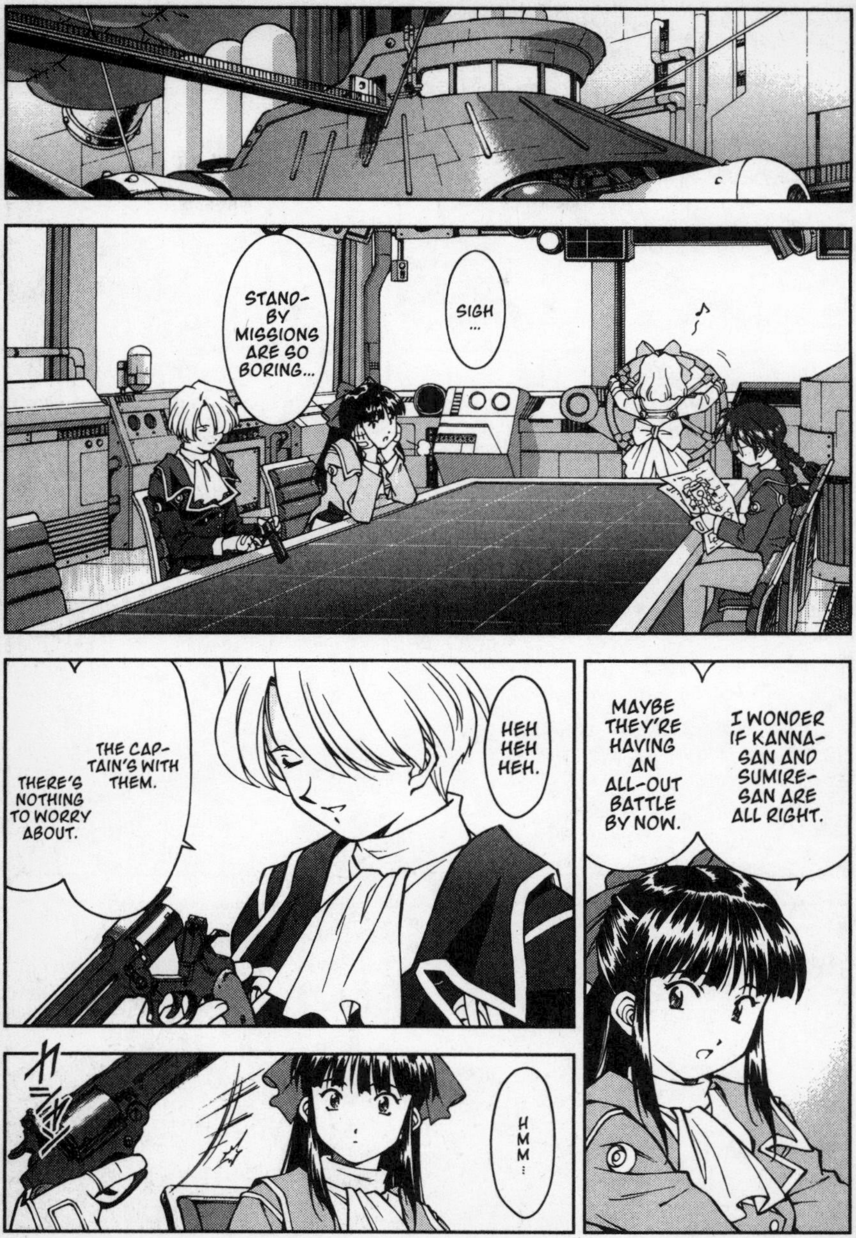
STAND-BY MISSIONS ARE SO BORING...
SIGH...
I WONDER IF KANNA-SAN AND SUMIRE-SAN ARE ALL RIGHT.
MAYBE THEY'RE HAVING AN ALL-OUT BATTLE BY NOW.
HEH HEH HEH.
THE CAPTAIN'S WITH THEM.
THERE'S NOTHING TO WORRY ABOUT.
HMM...

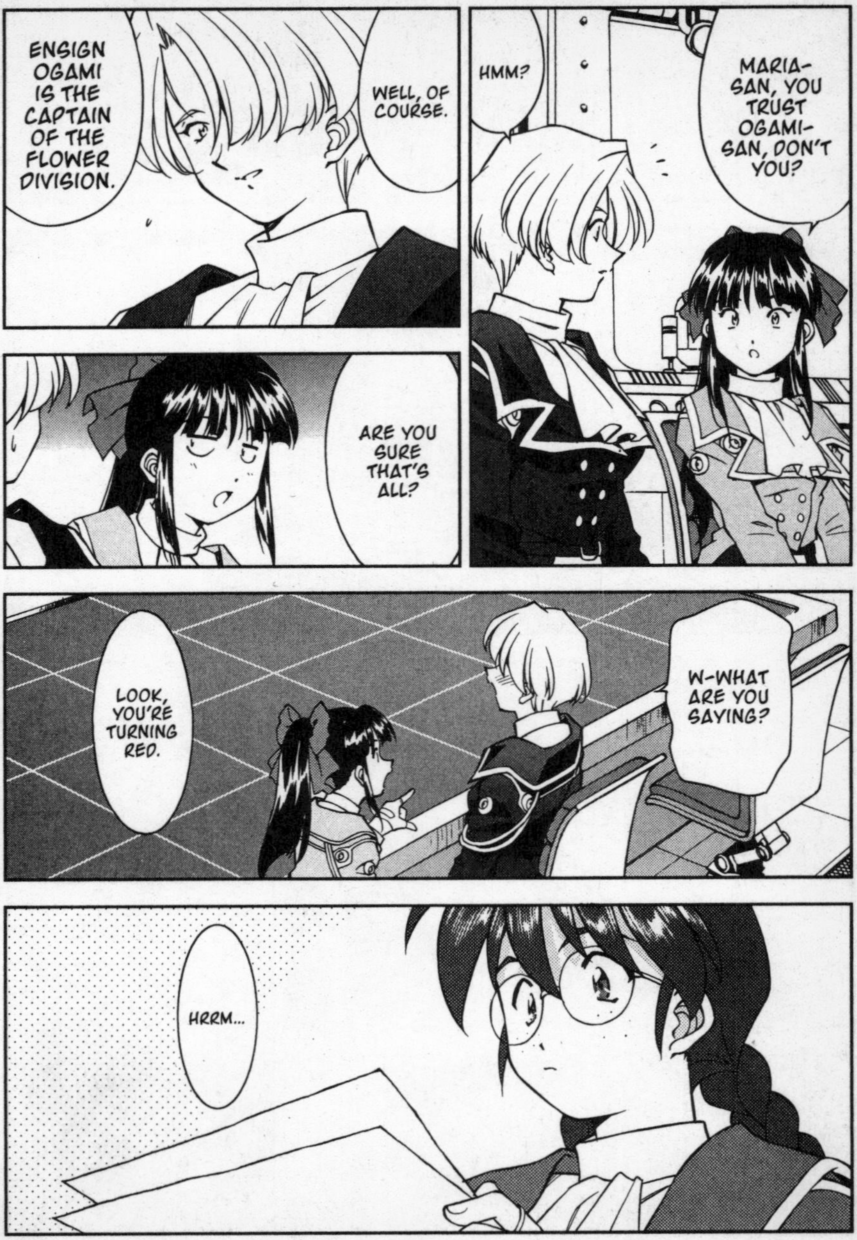
MARIA-SAN, YOU TRUST OGAMI-SAN, DON'T YOU?
HMM?
WELL, OF COURSE.
ENSIGN OGAMI IS THE CAPTAIN OF THE FLOWER DIVISION.
ARE YOU SURE THAT'S ALL?
W-WHAT ARE YOU SAYING?
LOOK, YOU'RE TURNING RED.
HRRM...

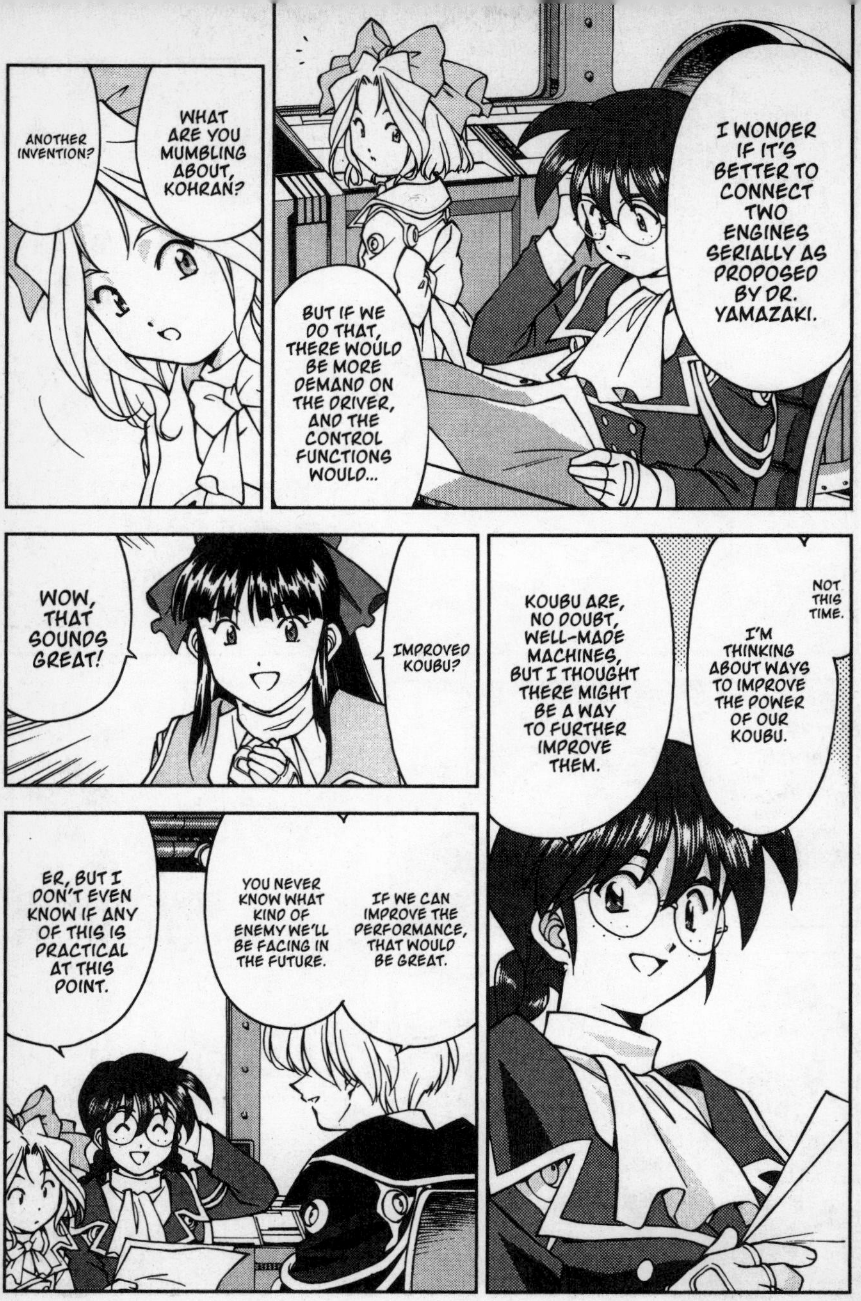
I WONDER IF IT'S BETTER TO CONNECT TWO ENGINES SERIALLY AS PROPOSED BY DR. YAMAZAKI.
BUT IF WE DO THAT, THERE WOULD BE MORE DEMAND ON THE DRIVER, AND THE CONTROL FUNCTIONS WOULD...
WHAT ARE YOU MUMBLING ABOUT, KOHRAN?
ANOTHER INVENTION?
NOT THIS TIME.
I'M THINKING ABOUT WAYS TO IMPROVE THE POWER OF OUR KOUBU.
KOUBU ARE, NO DOUBT, WELL-MADE MACHINES, BUT I THOUGHT THERE MIGHT BE A WAY TO FURTHER IMPROVE THEM.
IMPROVED KOUBU?
WOW, THAT SOUNDS GREAT!
IF WE CAN IMPROVE THE PERFORMANCE, THAT WOULD BE GREAT.
YOU NEVER KNOW WHAT KIND OF ENEMY WE'LL BE FACING IN THE FUTURE.
ER, BUT I DON'T EVEN KNOW IF ANY OF THIS IS PRACTICAL AT THIS POINT.

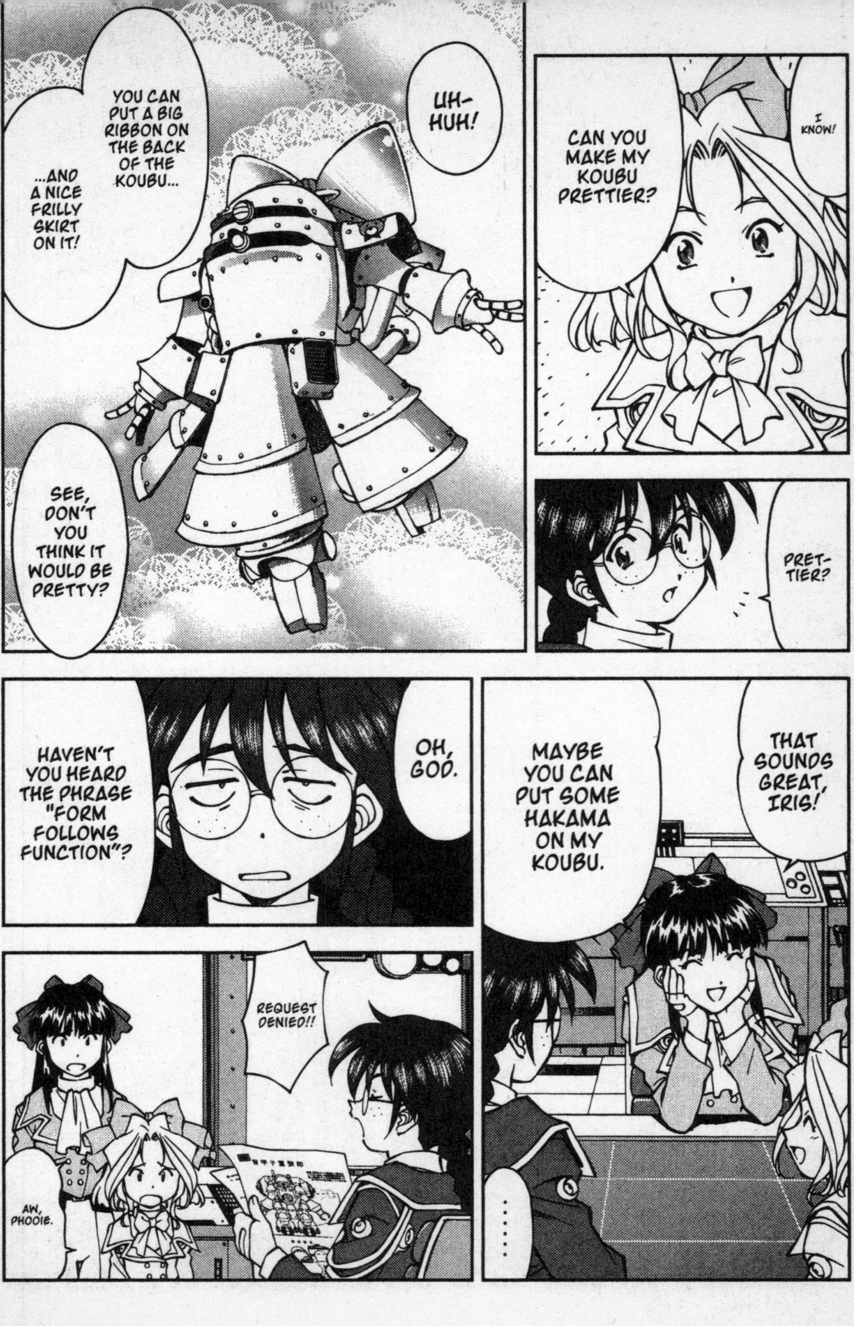
I KNOW!
CAN YOU MAKE MY KOUBU PRETTIER?
PRET-TIER?
UH-HUH!
YOU CAN PUT A BIG RIBBON ON THE BACK OF THE KOUBU...
...AND A NICE FRILLY SKIRT ON IT!
SEE, DON'T YOU THINK IT WOULD BE PRETTY?
THAT SOUNDS GREAT, IRIS!
MAYBE YOU CAN PUT SOME HAKAMA ON MY KOUBU.
......
OH, GOD.
HAVEN'T YOU HEARD THE PHRASE "FORM FOLLOWS FUNCTION"?
REQUEST DENIED!!
AW, PHOOIE.

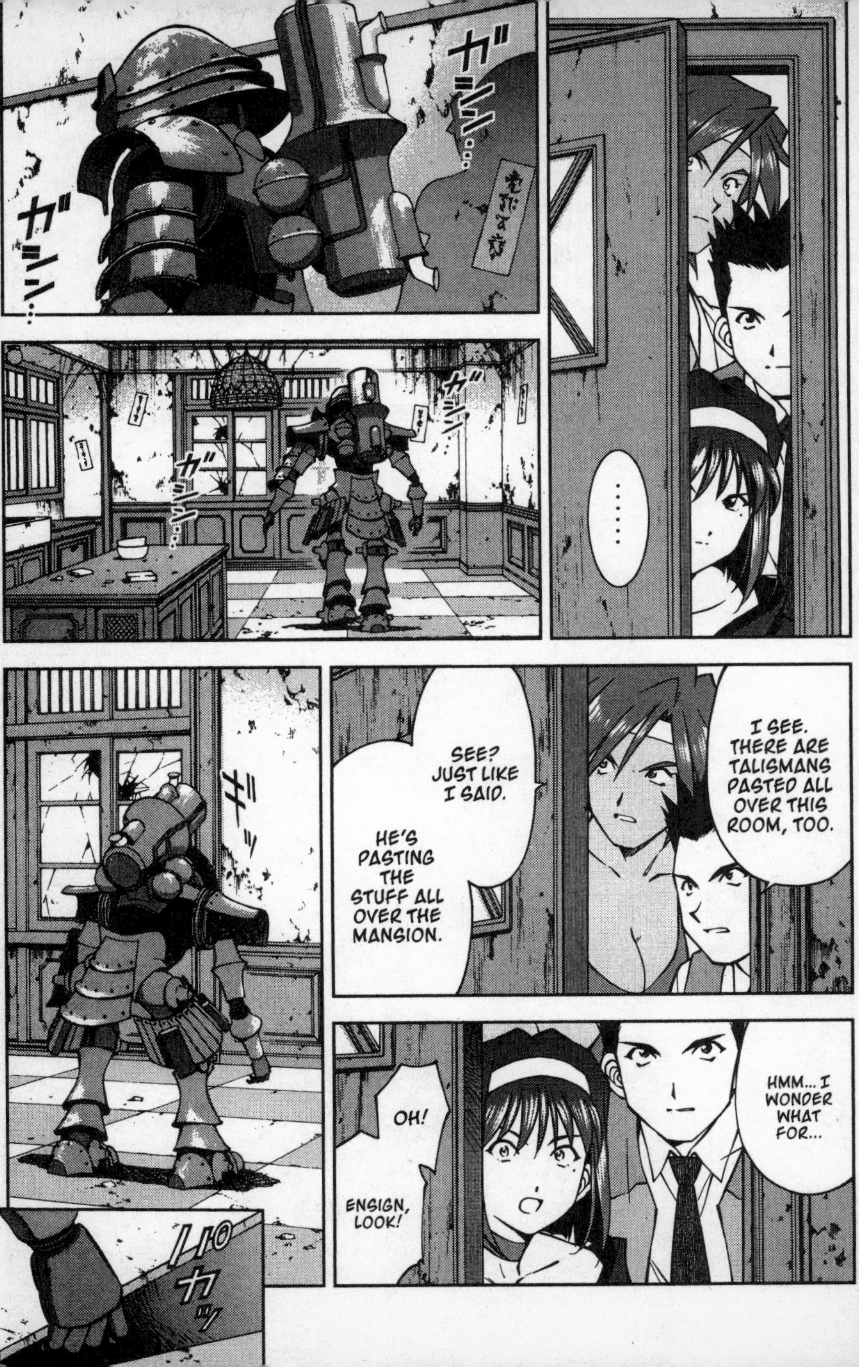
......
ガシン...
ガシン...
ガシン
ガシン...
I SEE. THERE ARE TALISMANS PASTED ALL OVER THIS ROOM, TOO.
SEE? JUST LIKE I SAID.
HE'S PASTING THE STUFF ALL OVER THE MANSION.
HMM... I WONDER WHAT FOR...
OH!
ENSIGN, LOOK!
ギッ
パカッ

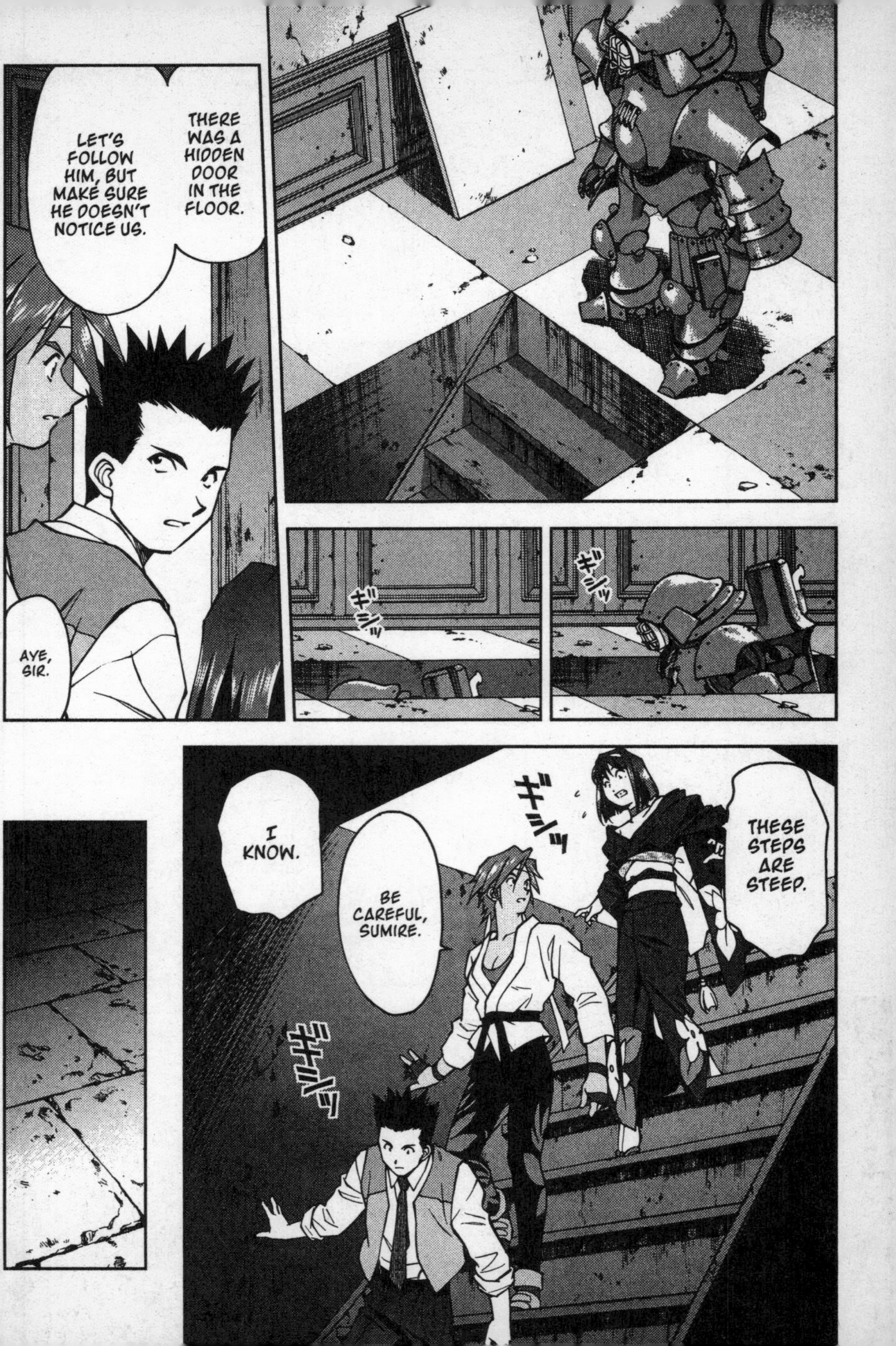
THERE WAS A HIDDEN DOOR IN THE FLOOR.
LET'S FOLLOW HIM, BUT MAKE SURE HE DOESN'T NOTICE US.
AYE, SIR.
ギシッ
ギシッ
THESE STEPS ARE STEEP.
ギシッ
BE CAREFUL, SUMIRE.
I KNOW.
ギシッ

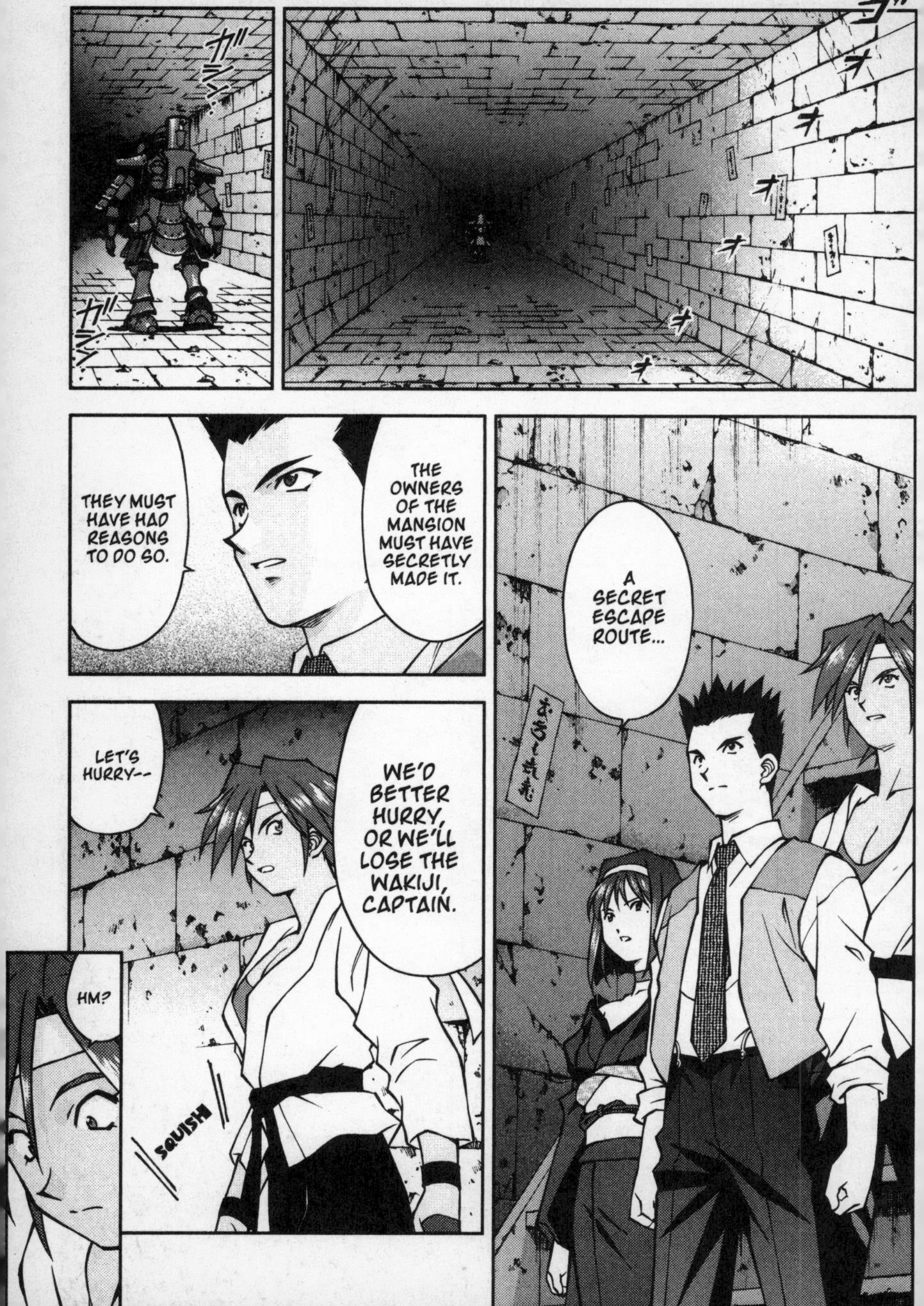
A SECRET ESCAPE ROUTE...
THE OWNERS OF THE MANSION MUST HAVE SECRETLY MADE IT.
THEY MUST HAVE HAD REASONS TO DO SO.
WE'D BETTER HURRY, OR WE'LL LOSE THE WAKIJI, CAPTAIN.
LET'S HURRY--
SQUISH
HM?

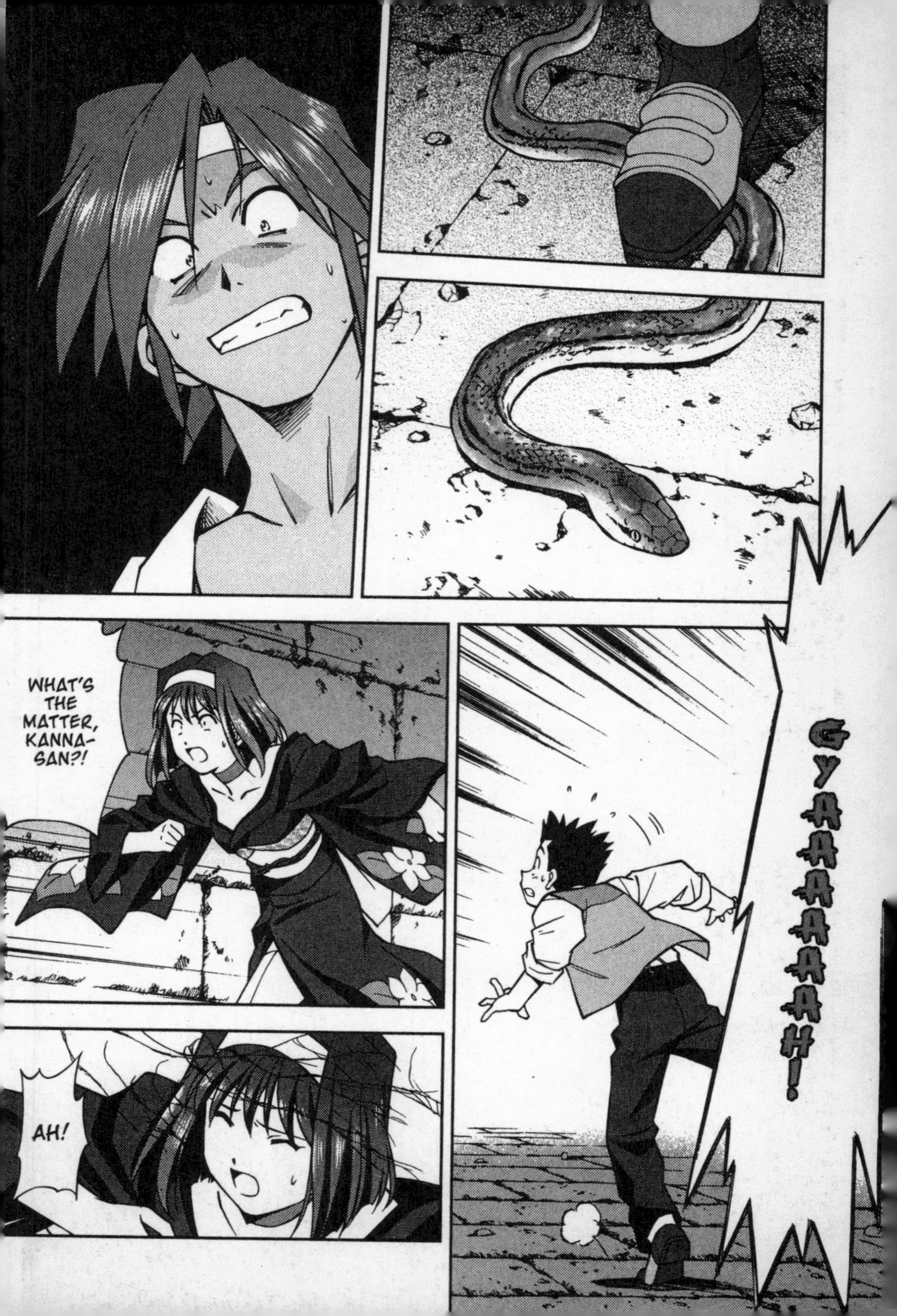
GYAAAAAAAH!
WHAT'S THE MATTER, KANNA-SAN?!
AH!

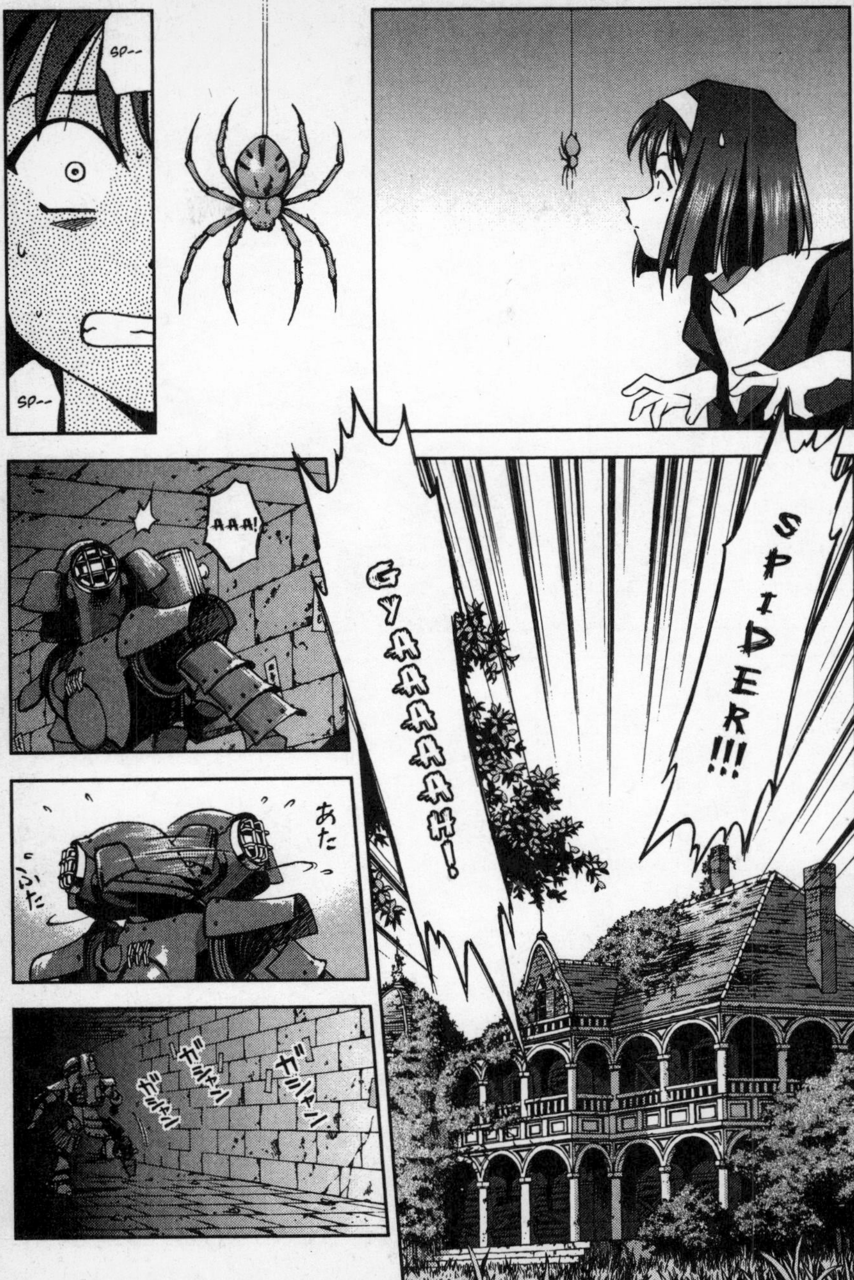
SP--
SP--
SPIDER!!!
GYAAAAAH!
AAA!
あた
ふた
ガシャン
ガシャン
ガシャン

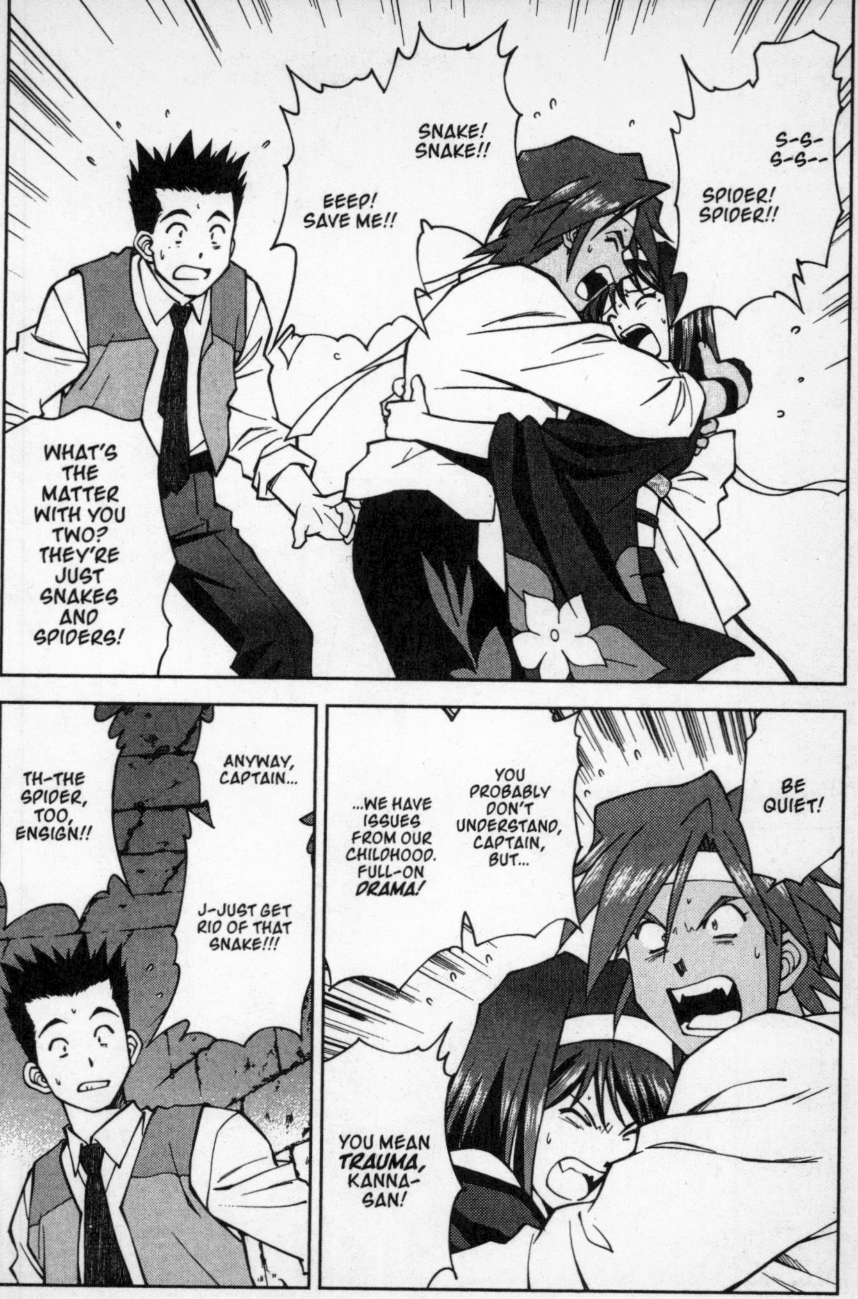
S-S-S-S--
SPIDER! SPIDER!!
SNAKE! SNAKE!!
EEEP! SAVE ME!!
WHAT'S THE MATTER WITH YOU TWO? THEY'RE JUST SNAKES AND SPIDERS!
BE QUIET!
YOU PROBABLY DON'T UNDERSTAND, CAPTAIN, BUT...
...WE HAVE ISSUES FROM OUR CHILDHOOD. FULL-ON *DRAMA!*
YOU MEAN *TRAUMA,* KANNA-SAN!
ANYWAY, CAPTAIN...
TH-THE SPIDER, TOO, ENSIGN!!
J-JUST GET RID OF THAT SNAKE!!!

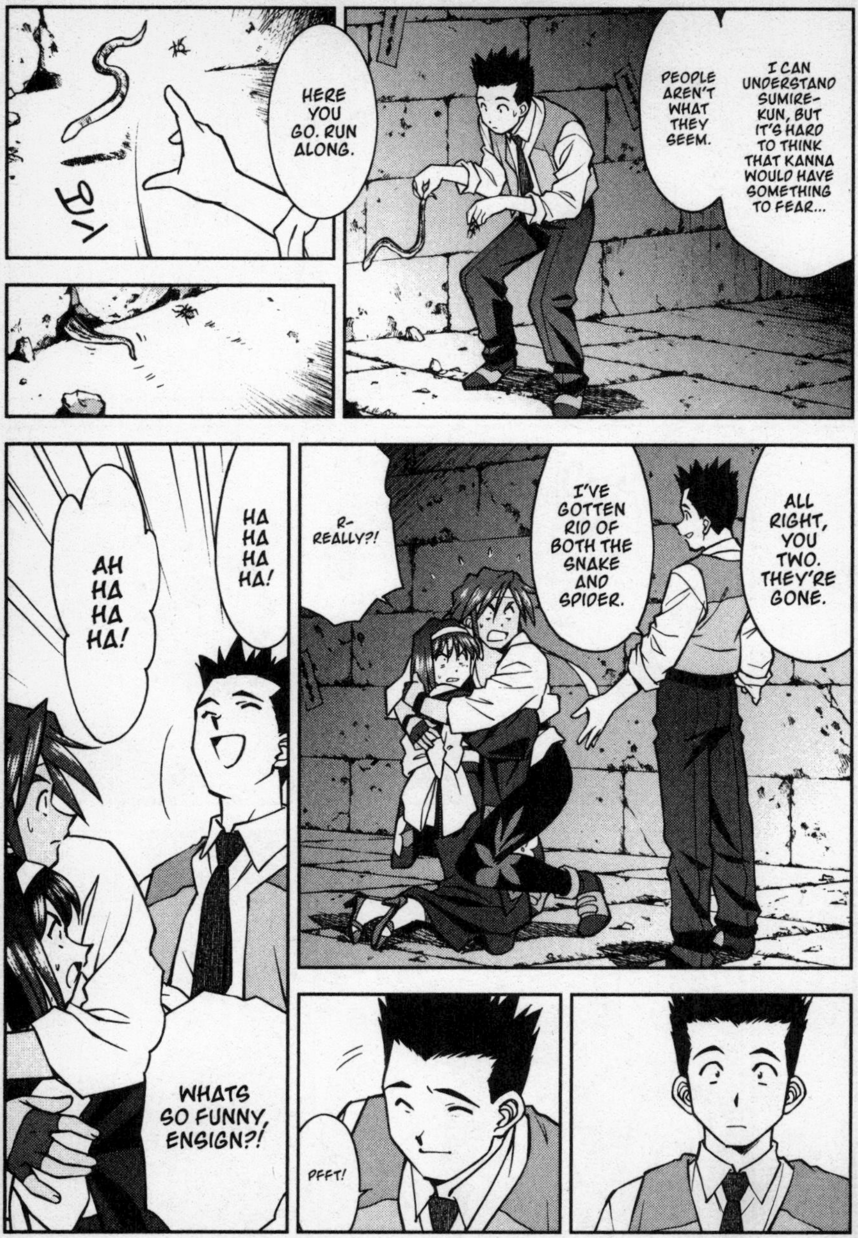
I CAN UNDERSTAND SUMIRE-KUN, BUT IT'S HARD TO THINK THAT KANNA WOULD HAVE SOMETHING TO FEAR...
PEOPLE AREN'T WHAT THEY SEEM.
HERE YOU GO. RUN ALONG.
ALL RIGHT, YOU TWO. THEY'RE GONE.
I'VE GOTTEN RID OF BOTH THE SNAKE AND SPIDER.
R-REALLY?!
PFFT!
HA HA HA HA!
AH HA HA HA!
WHATS SO FUNNY, ENSIGN?!

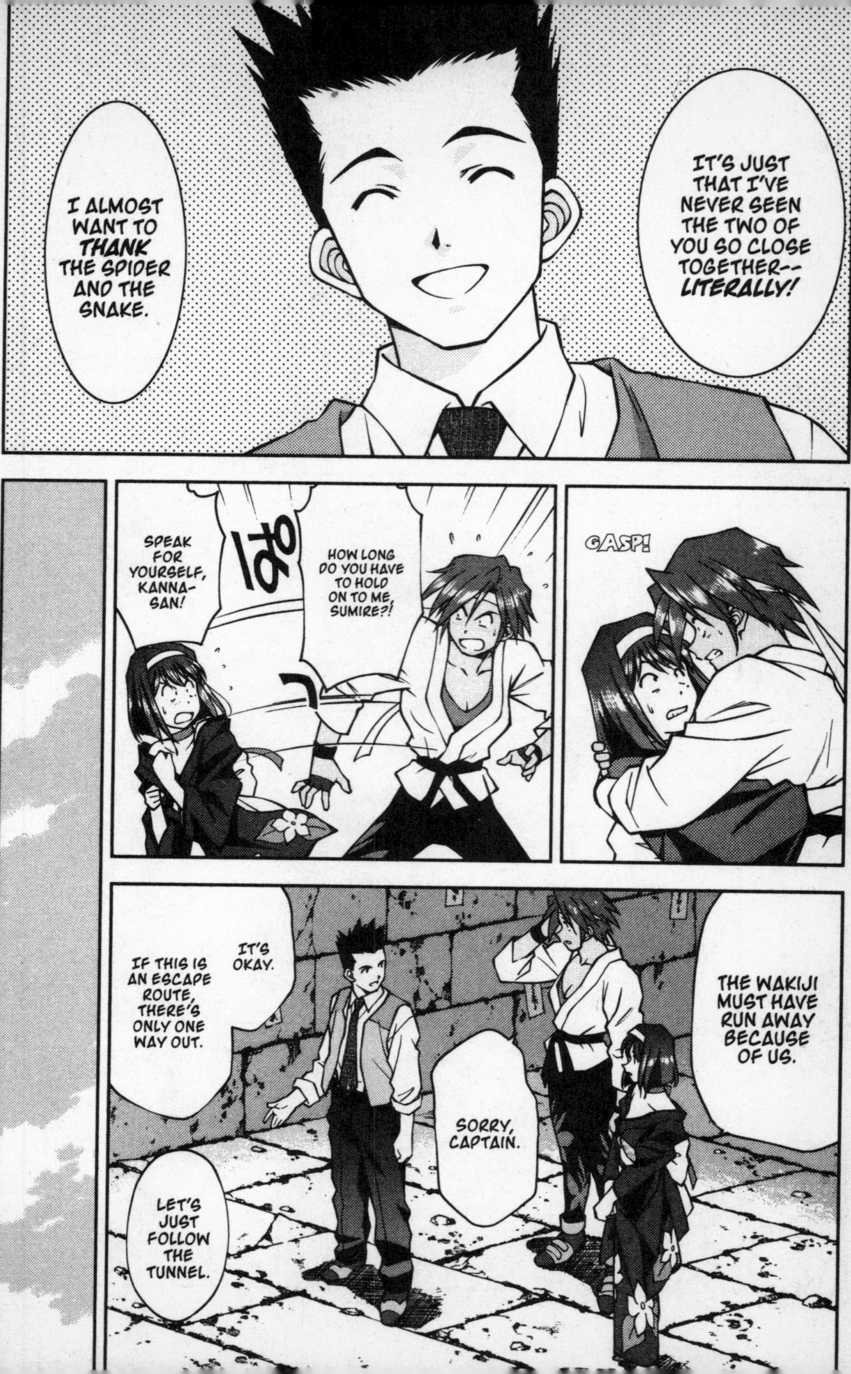
IT'S JUST THAT I'VE NEVER SEEN THE TWO OF YOU SO CLOSE TOGETHER--LITERALLY!
I ALMOST WANT TO THANK THE SPIDER AND THE SNAKE.
GASP!
HOW LONG DO YOU HAVE TO HOLD ON TO ME, SUMIRE?!
ぱっ
SPEAK FOR YOURSELF, KANNA-SAN!
THE WAKIJI MUST HAVE RUN AWAY BECAUSE OF US.
SORRY, CAPTAIN.
IT'S OKAY.
IF THIS IS AN ESCAPE ROUTE, THERE'S ONLY ONE WAY OUT.
LET'S JUST FOLLOW THE TUNNEL.

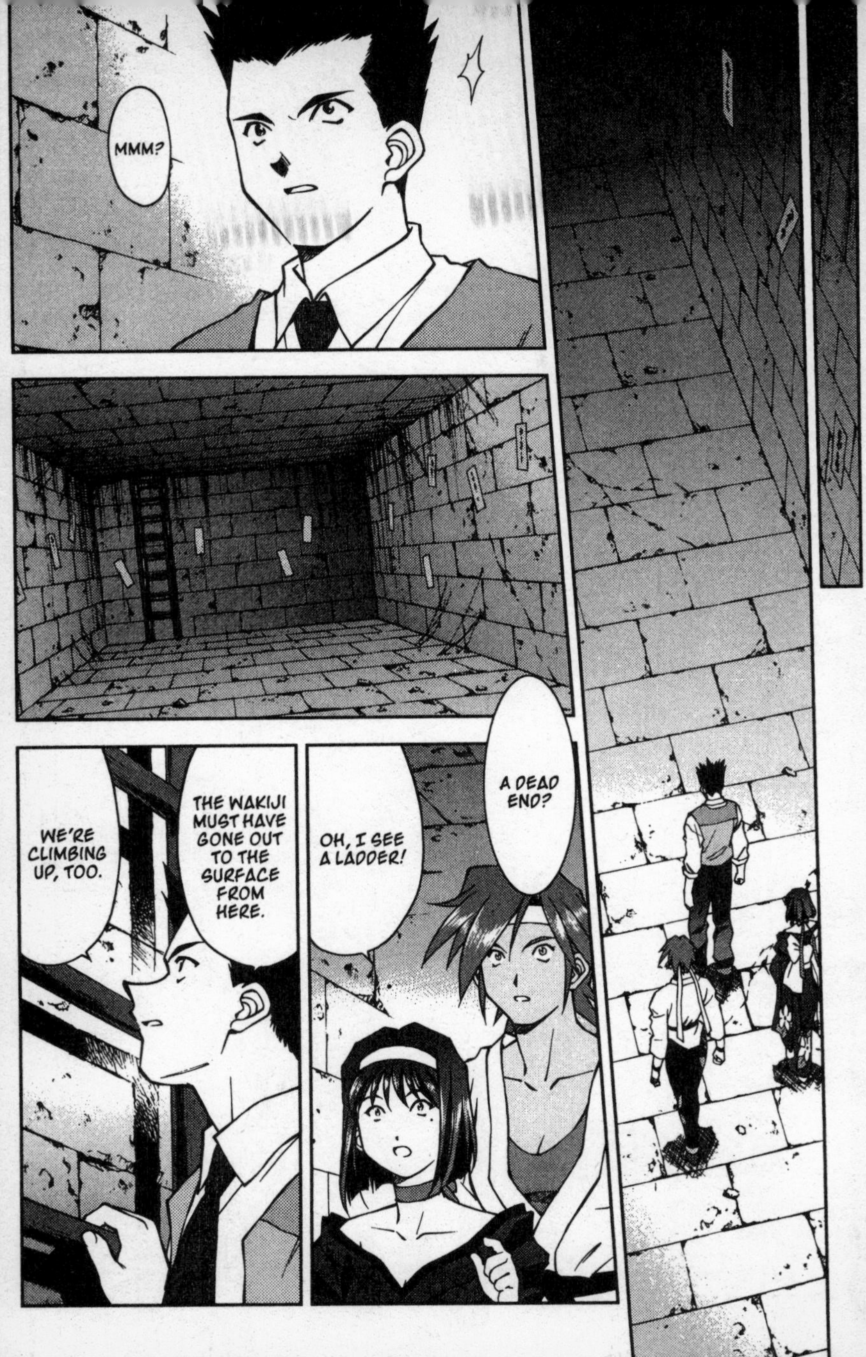
MMM?
A DEAD END?
OH, I SEE A LADDER!
THE WAKIJI MUST HAVE GONE OUT TO THE SURFACE FROM HERE.
WE'RE CLIMBING UP, TOO.

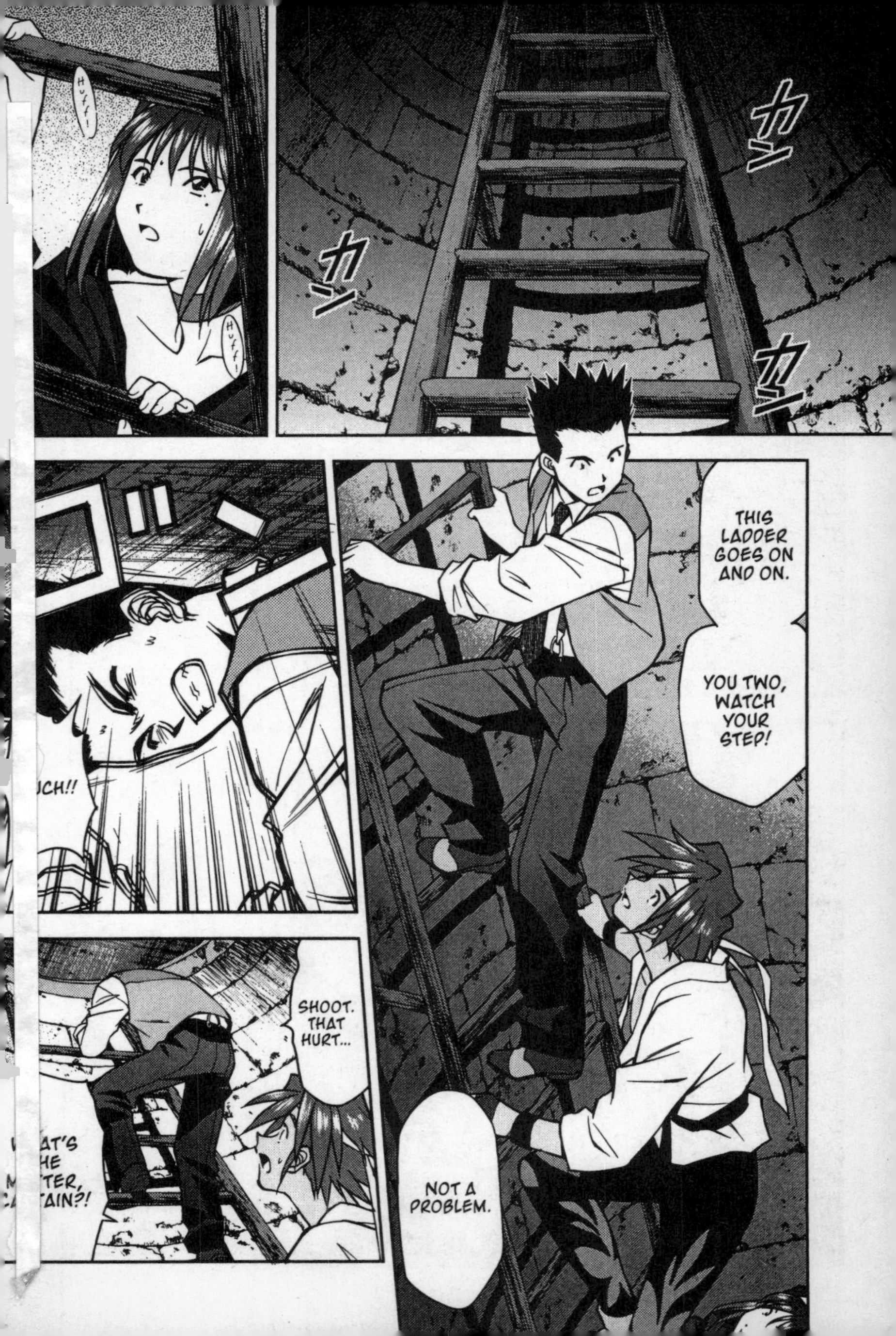
カン
カン
カン
Huff!
Huff!
THIS LADDER GOES ON AND ON.
YOU TWO, WATCH YOUR STEP!
NOT A PROBLEM.
UCH!!
SHOOT. THAT HURT...

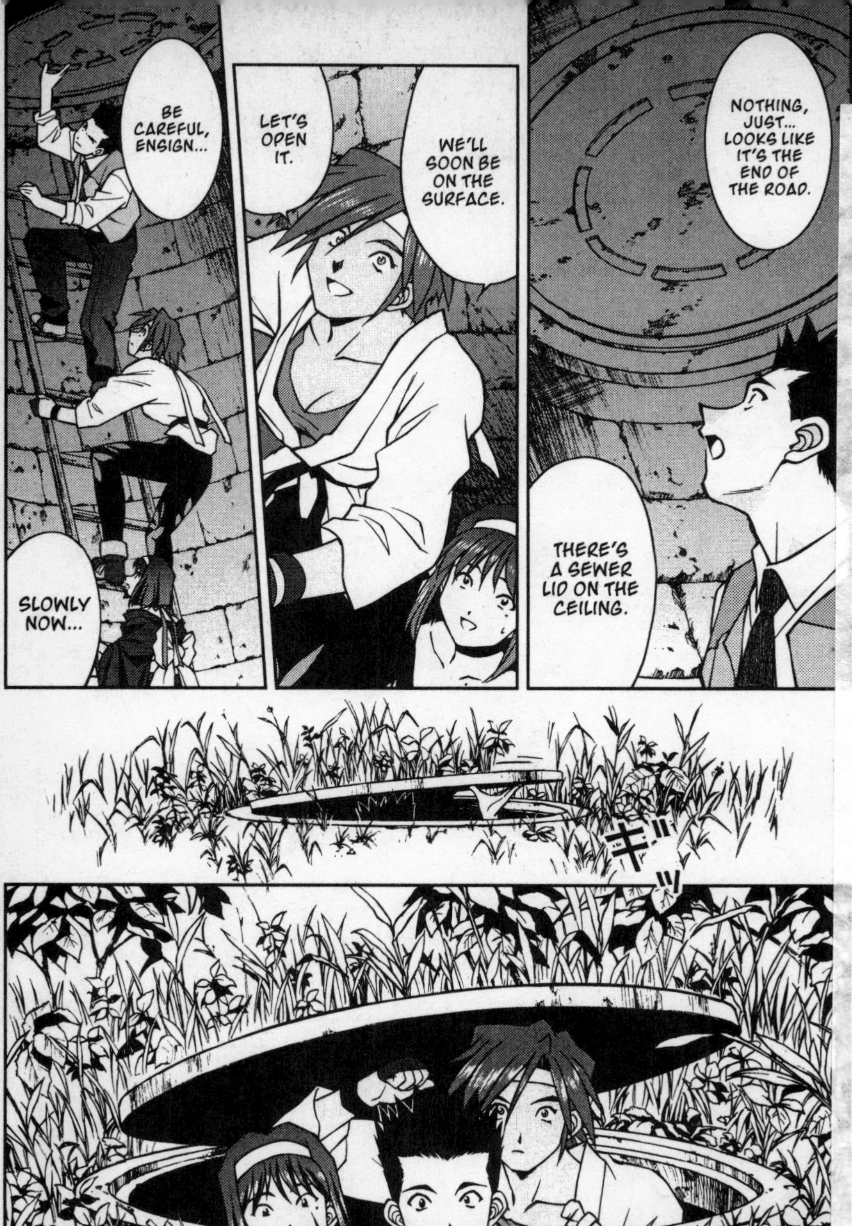
NOTHING, JUST... LOOKS LIKE IT'S THE END OF THE ROAD.
THERE'S A SEWER LID ON THE CEILING.
WE'LL SOON BE ON THE SURFACE.
LET'S OPEN IT.
BE CAREFUL, ENSIGN...
SLOWLY NOW...
ギッ

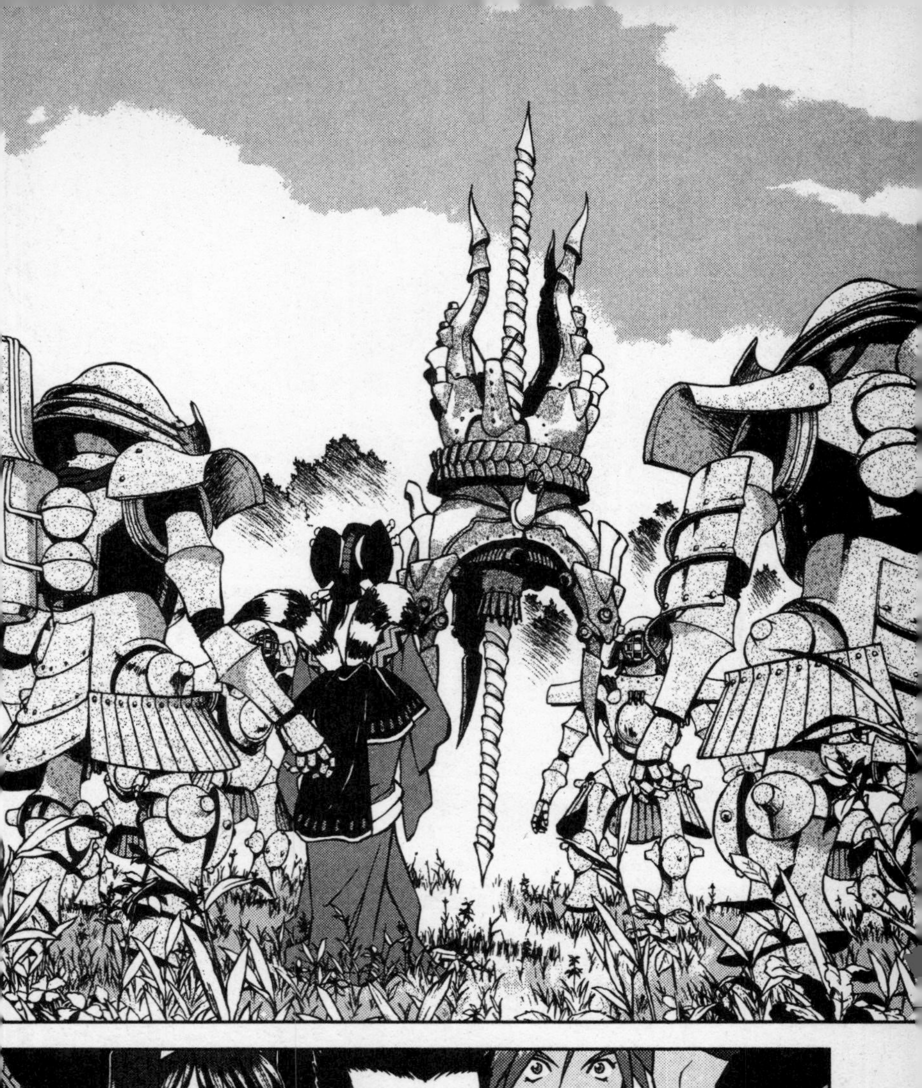

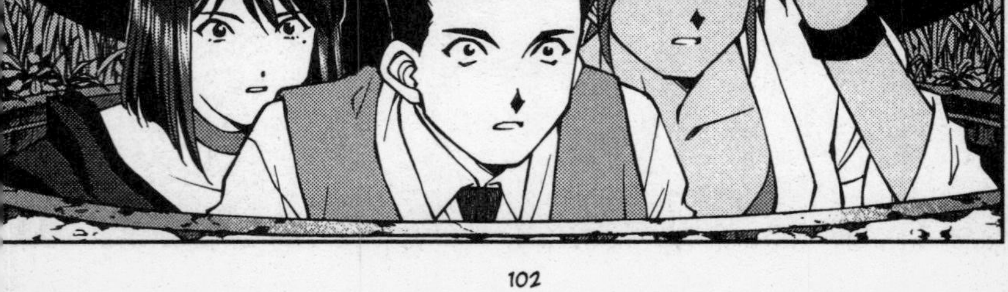

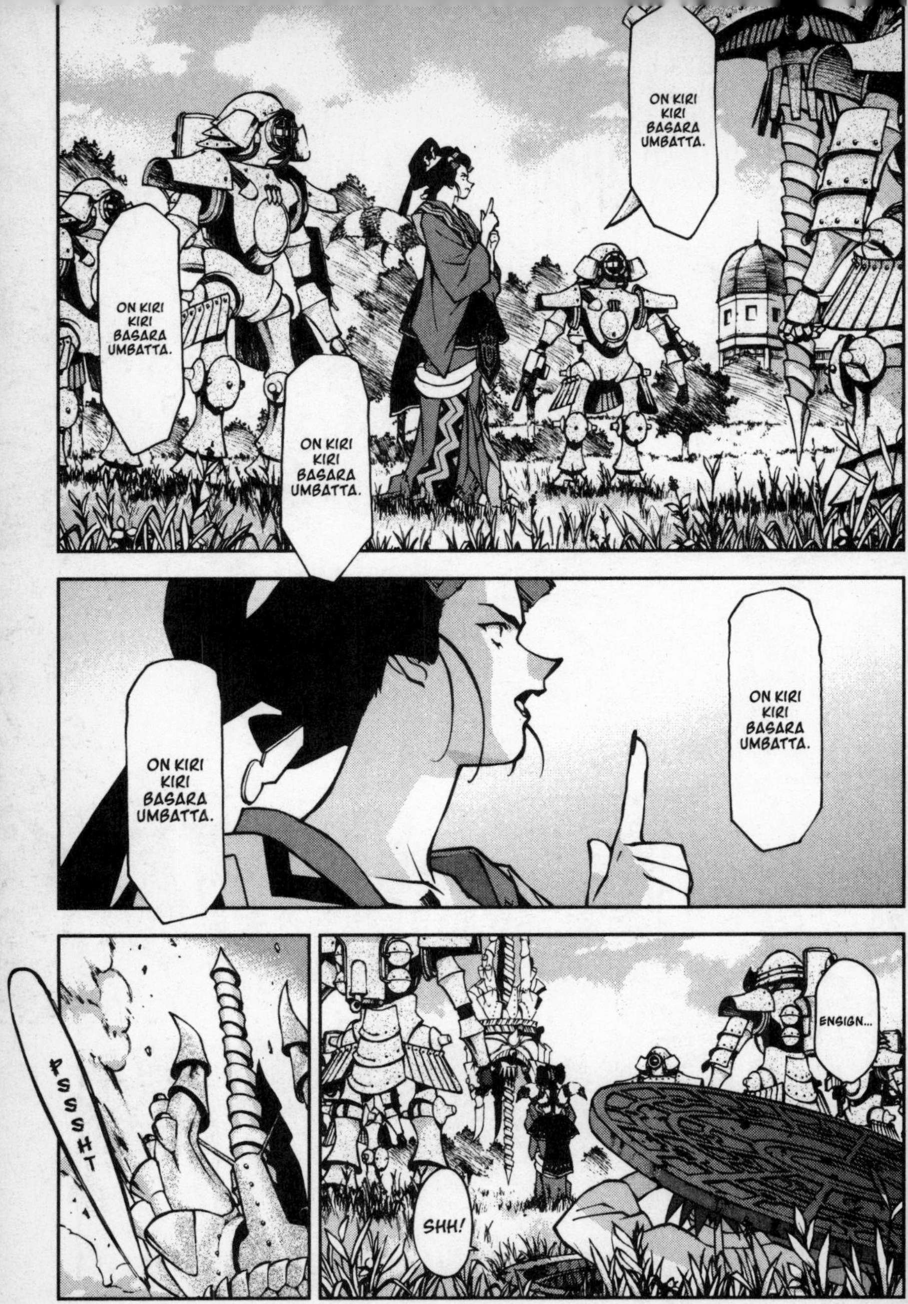
ON KIRI KIRI BASARA UMBATTA.
ON KIRI KIRI BASARA UMBATTA.
ON KIRI KIRI BASARA UMBATTA.
ON KIRI KIRI BASARA UMBATTA.
ON KIRI KIRI BASARA UMBATTA.
ENSIGN...
SHH!
PSSSHT

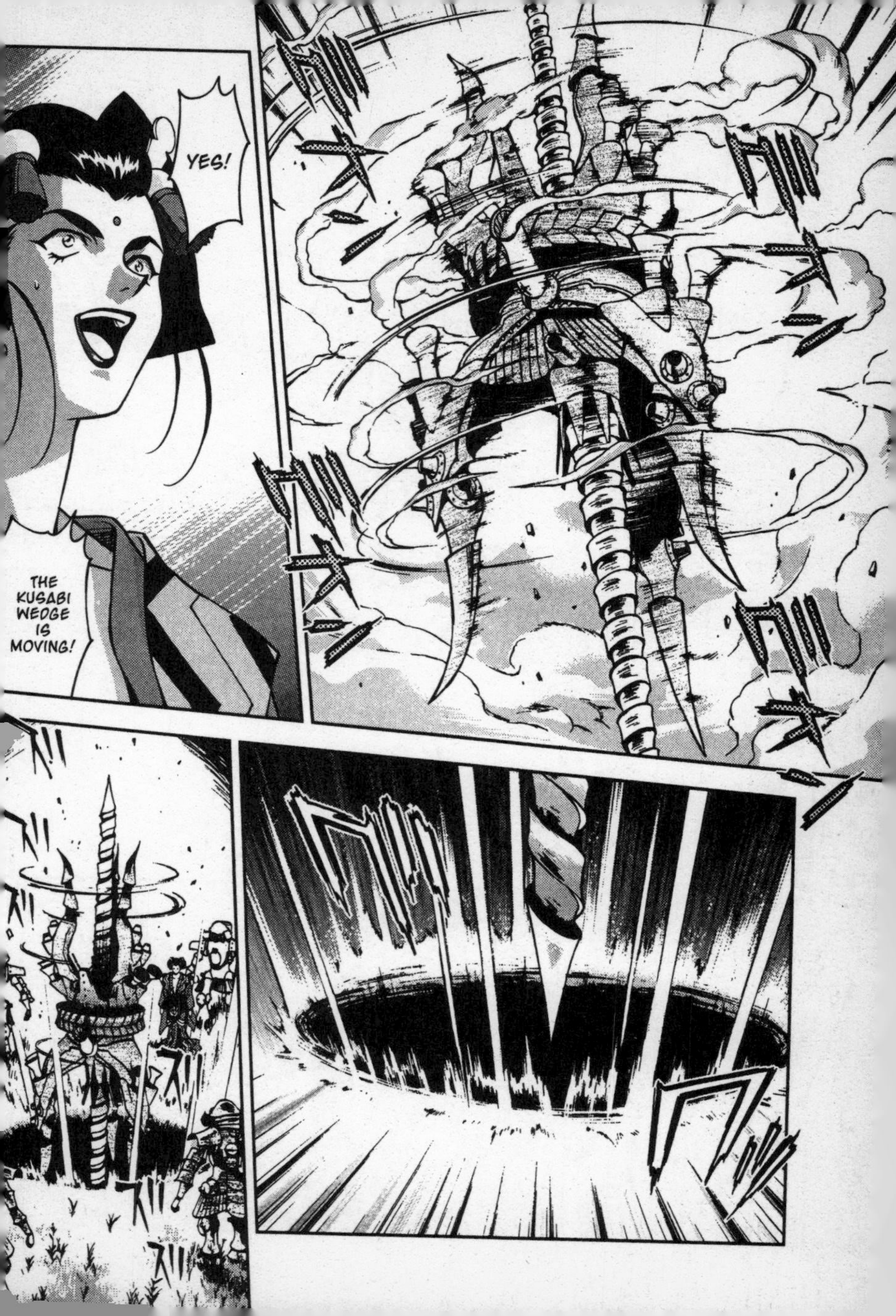
YES!
THE KUSABI WEDGE IS MOVING!

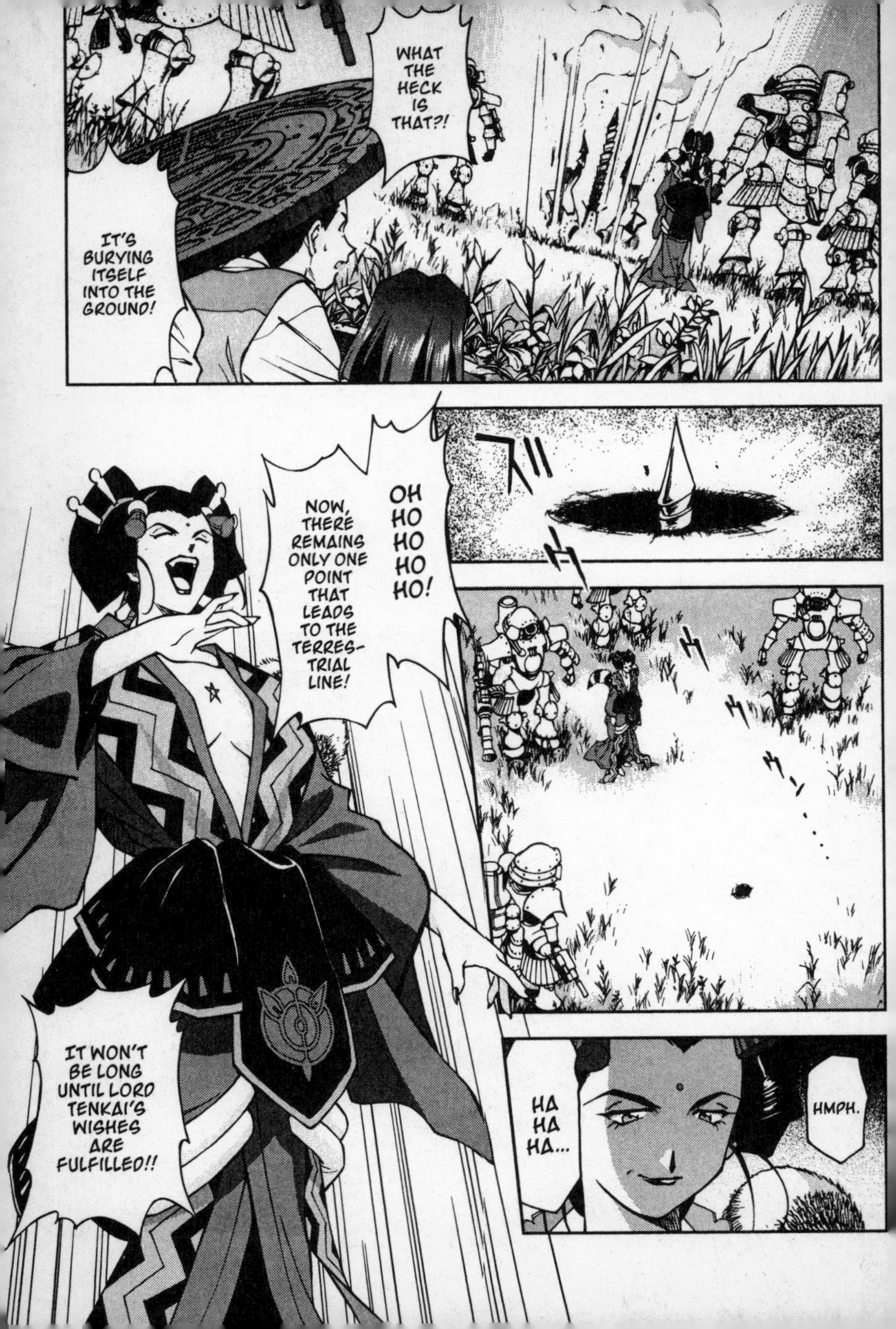
WHAT THE HECK IS THAT?!
IT'S BURYING ITSELF INTO THE GROUND!
HMPH.
HA HA HA...
OH HO HO HO HO!
NOW, THERE REMAINS ONLY ONE POINT THAT LEADS TO THE TERRES-TRIAL LINE!
IT WON'T BE LONG UNTIL LORD TENKAI'S WISHES ARE FULFILLED!!

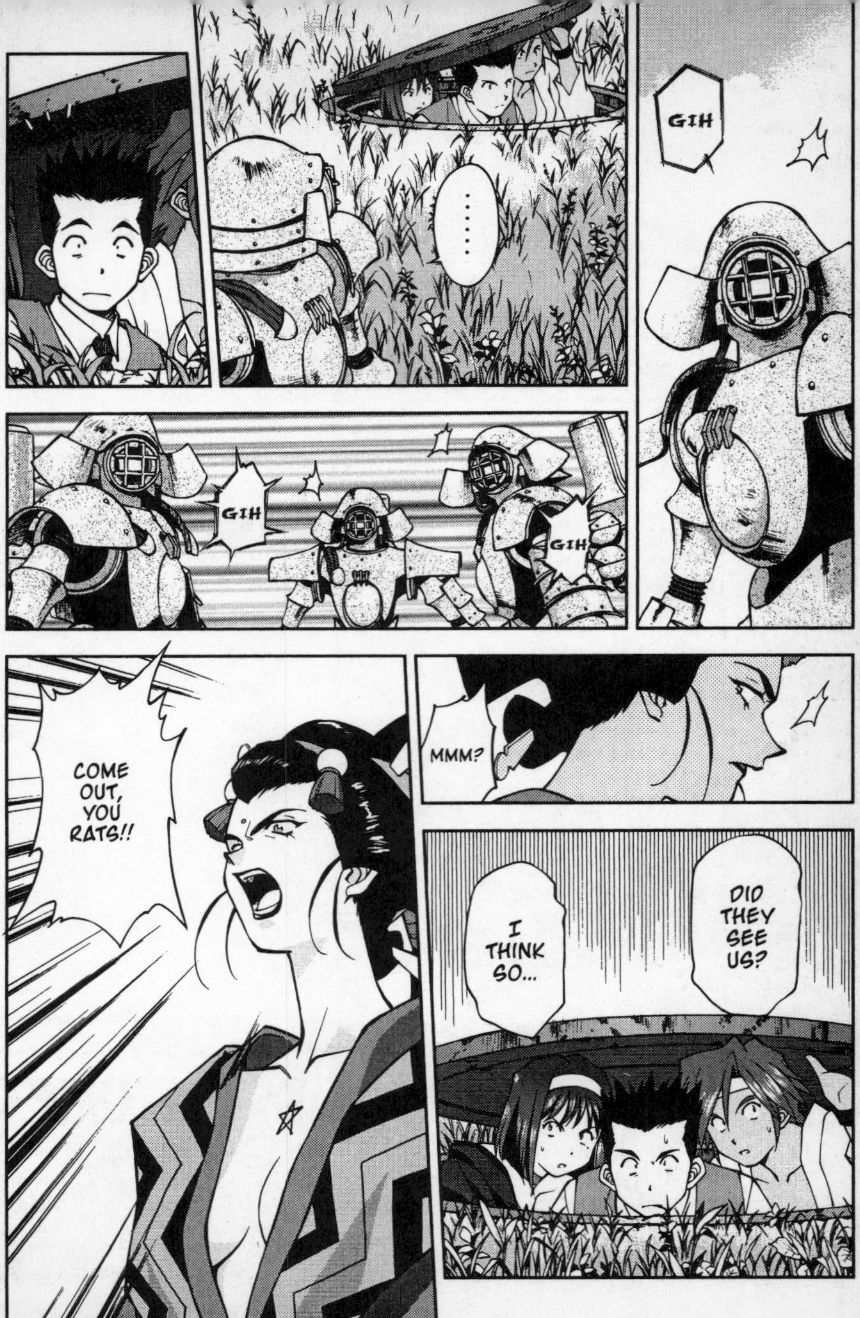
GIH
......
GIH
GIH
MMM?
DID THEY SEE US?
I THINK SO...
COME OUT, YOU RATS!!

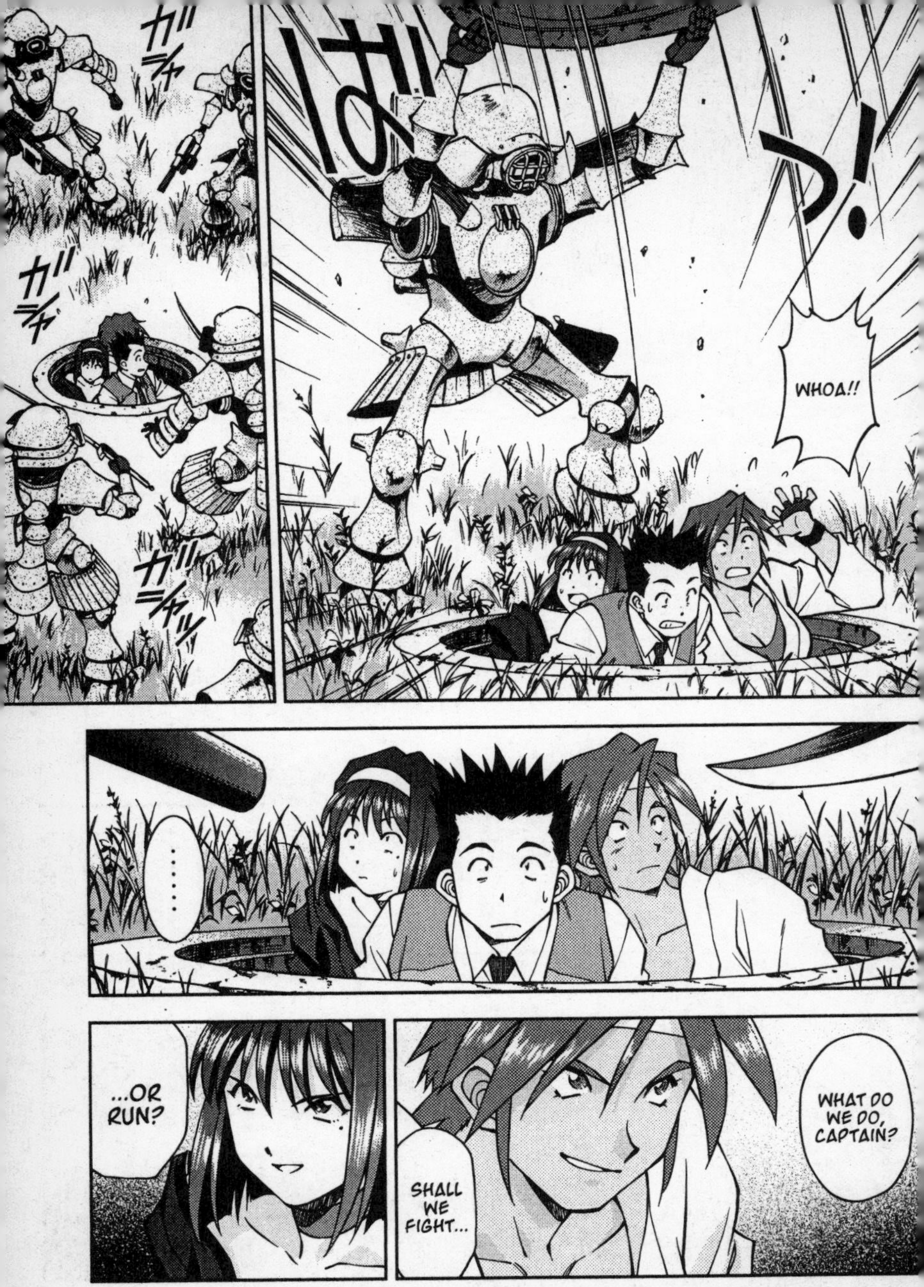
WHOA!!
......
WHAT DO WE DO, CAPTAIN?
SHALL WE FIGHT...
...OR RUN?

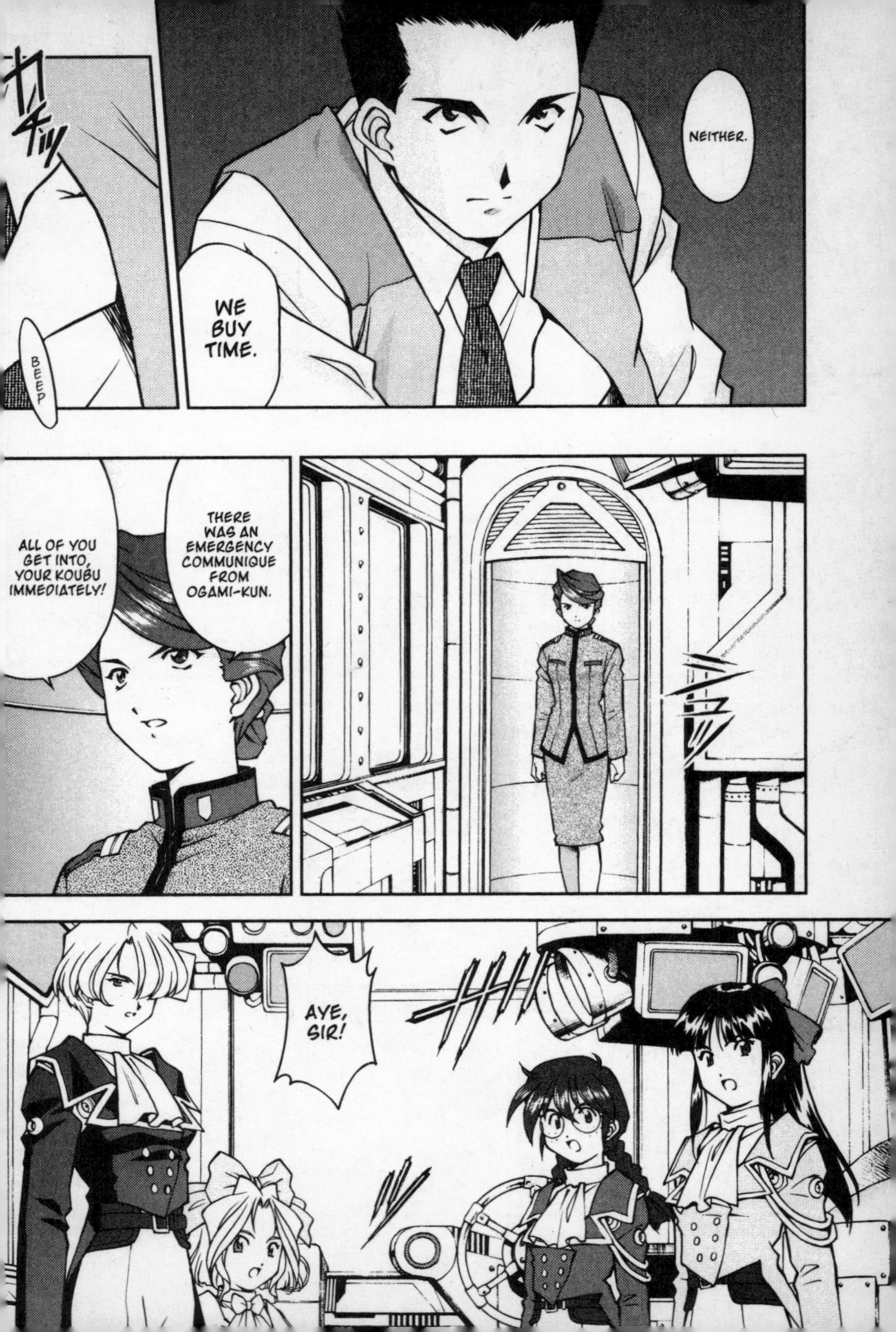
NEITHER.
WE BUY TIME.
BEEP
THERE WAS AN EMERGENCY COMMUNIQUE FROM OGAMI-KUN.
ALL OF YOU GET INTO, YOUR KOUBU IMMEDIATELY!
AYE, SIR!

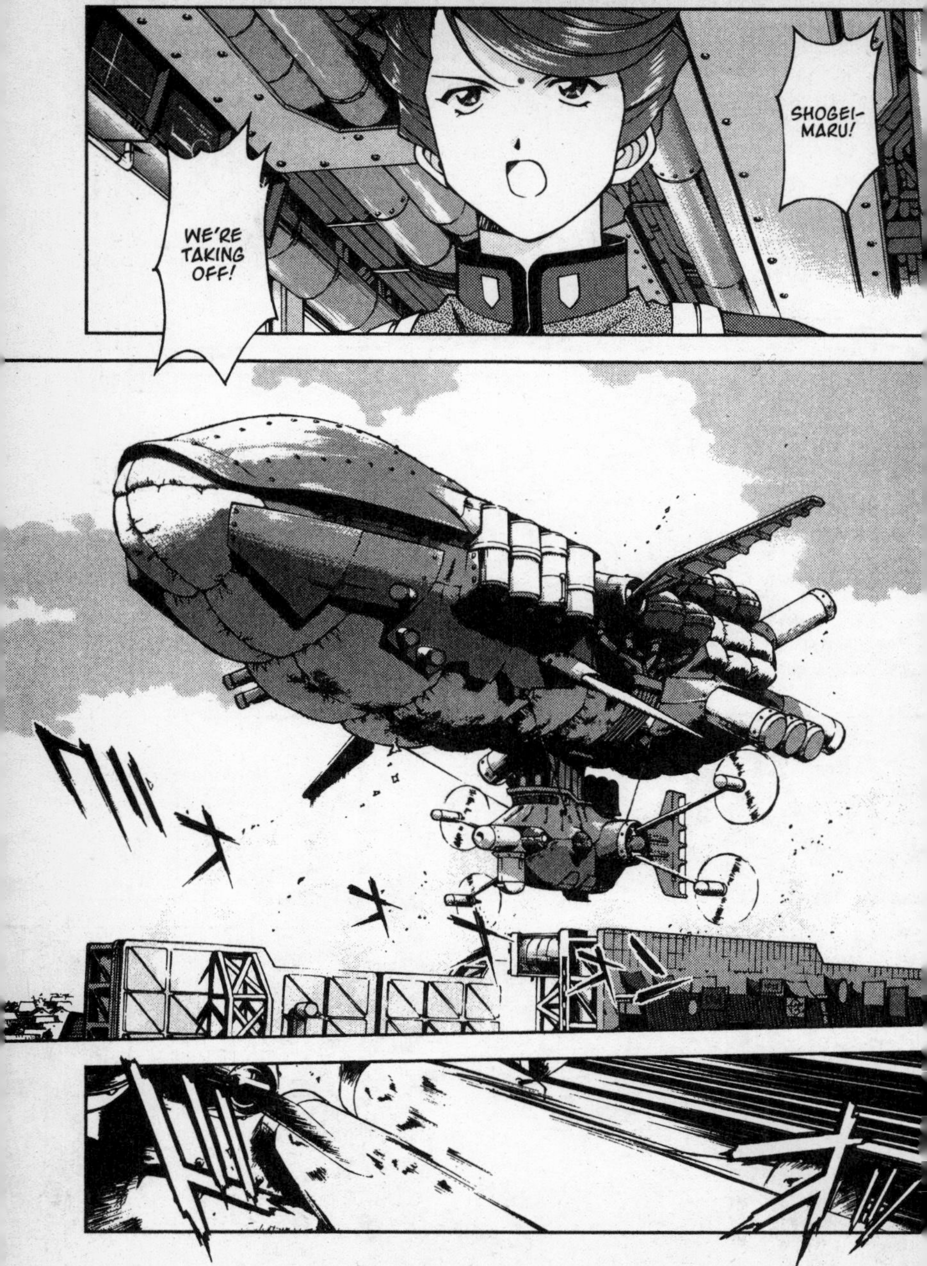
SHOGEI-MARU!
WE'RE TAKING OFF!

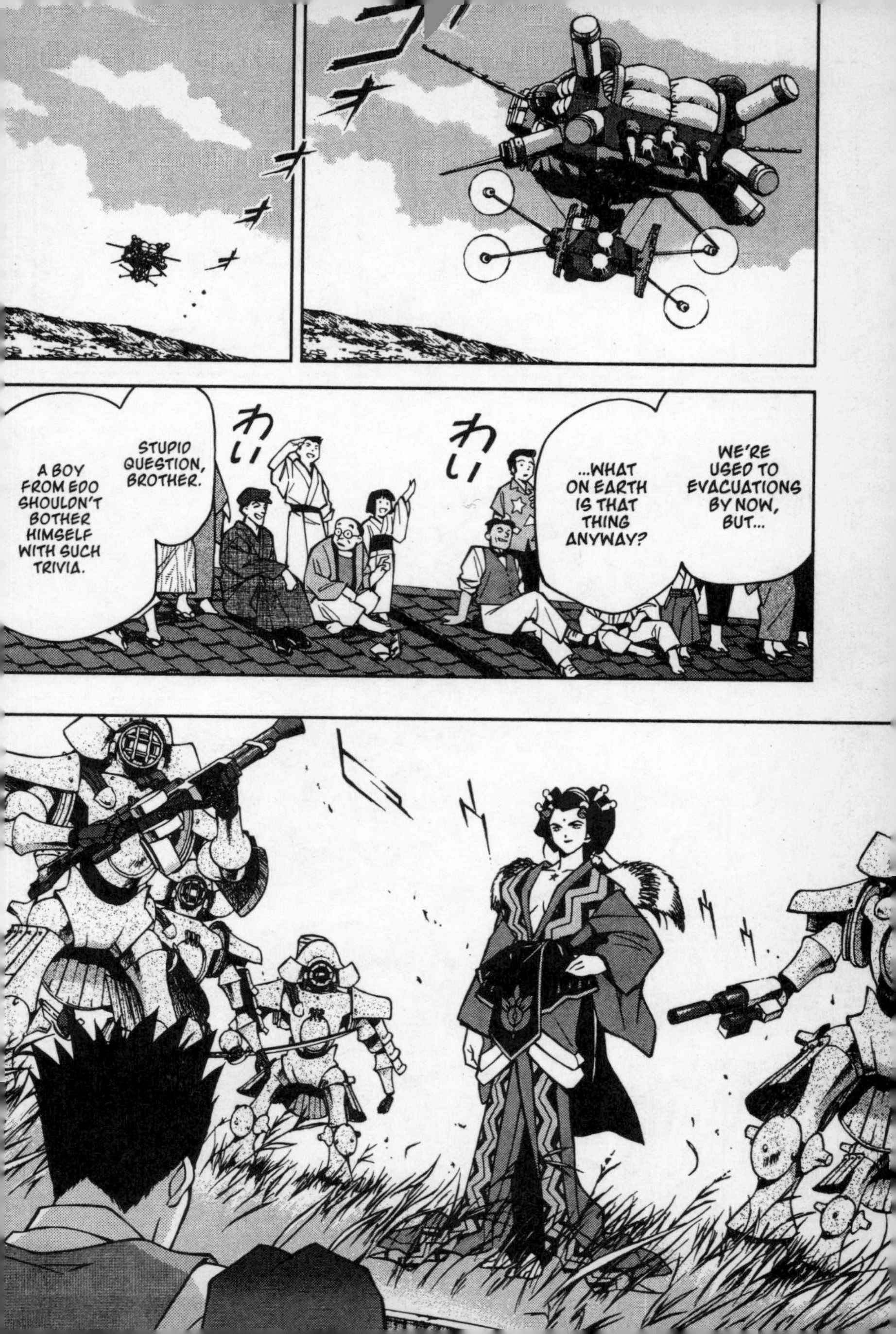
WE'RE USED TO EVACUATIONS BY NOW, BUT...
...WHAT ON EARTH IS THAT THING ANYWAY?
わい
わい
STUPID QUESTION, BROTHER.
A BOY FROM EDO SHOULDN'T BOTHER HIMSELF WITH SUCH TRIVIA.

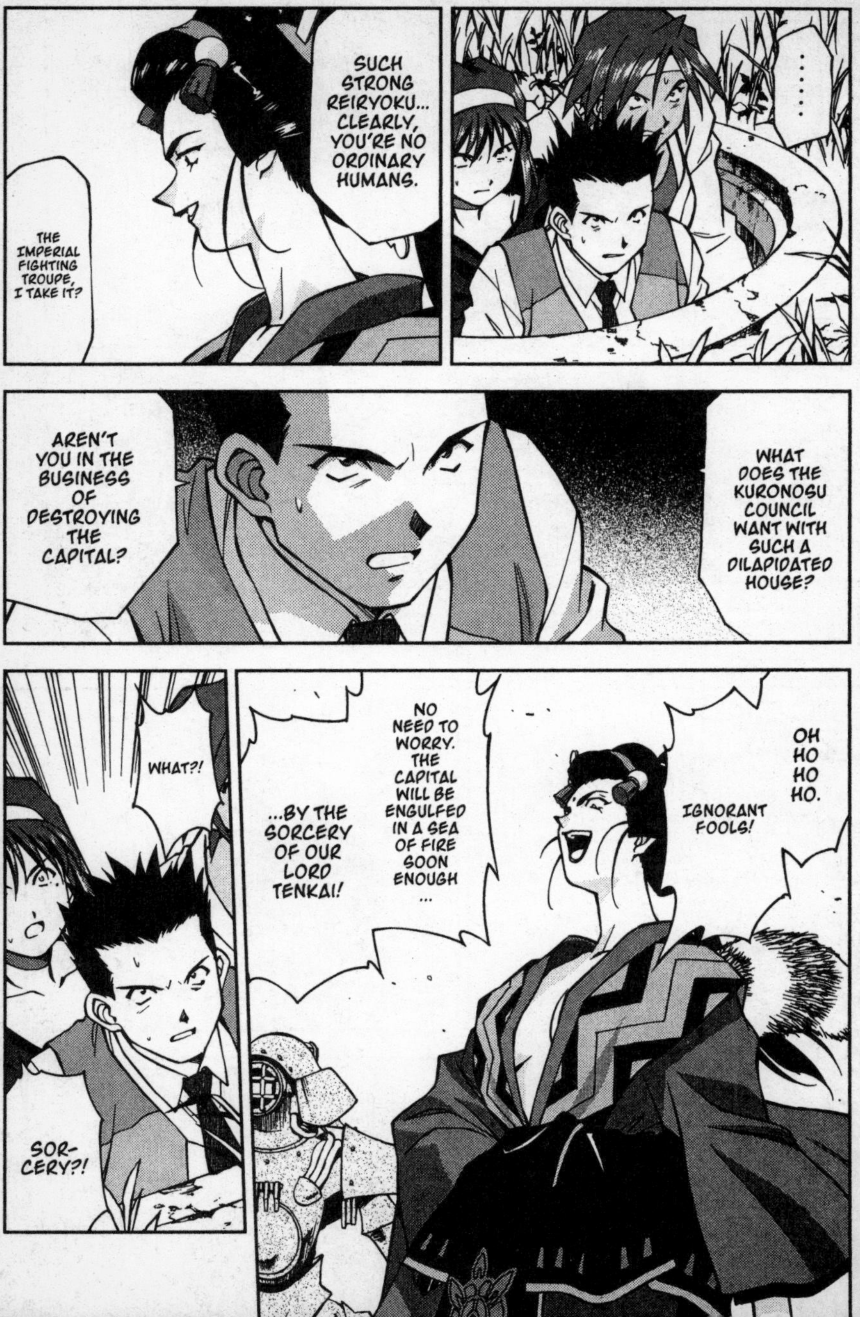
......
SUCH STRONG REIRYOKU... CLEARLY, YOU'RE NO ORDINARY HUMANS.
THE IMPERIAL FIGHTING TROUPE, I TAKE IT?
WHAT DOES THE KURONOSU COUNCIL WANT WITH SUCH A DILAPIDATED HOUSE?
AREN'T YOU IN THE BUSINESS OF DESTROYING THE CAPITAL?
OH HO HO HO.
IGNORANT FOOLS!
NO NEED TO WORRY. THE CAPITAL WILL BE ENGULFED IN A SEA OF FIRE SOON ENOUGH ...
...BY THE SORCERY OF OUR LORD TENKAI!
WHAT?!
SOR-CERY?!

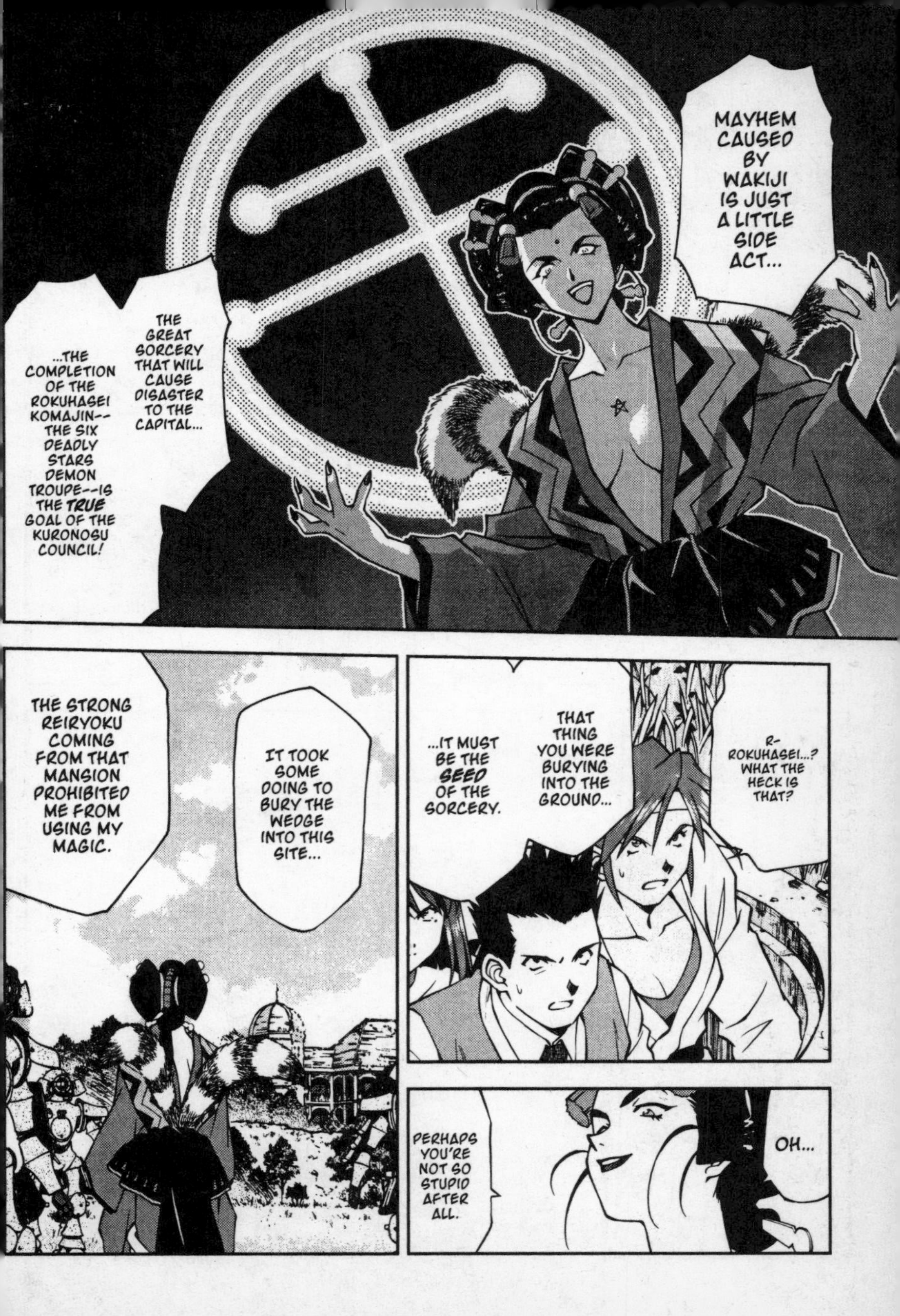
MAYHEM CAUSED BY WAKIJI IS JUST A LITTLE SIDE ACT...
THE GREAT SORCERY THAT WILL CAUSE DISASTER TO THE CAPITAL...
...THE COMPLETION OF THE ROKUHASEI KOMAJIN--THE SIX DEADLY STARS DEMON TROUPE--IS THE **TRUE** GOAL OF THE KURONOSU COUNCIL!
R-ROKUHASEI...? WHAT THE HECK IS THAT?
THAT THING YOU WERE BURYING INTO THE GROUND...
...IT MUST BE THE **SEED** OF THE SORCERY.
OH...
PERHAPS YOU'RE NOT SO STUPID AFTER ALL.
IT TOOK SOME DOING TO BURY THE WEDGE INTO THIS SITE...
THE STRONG REIRYOKU COMING FROM THAT MANSION PROHIBITED ME FROM USING MY MAGIC.

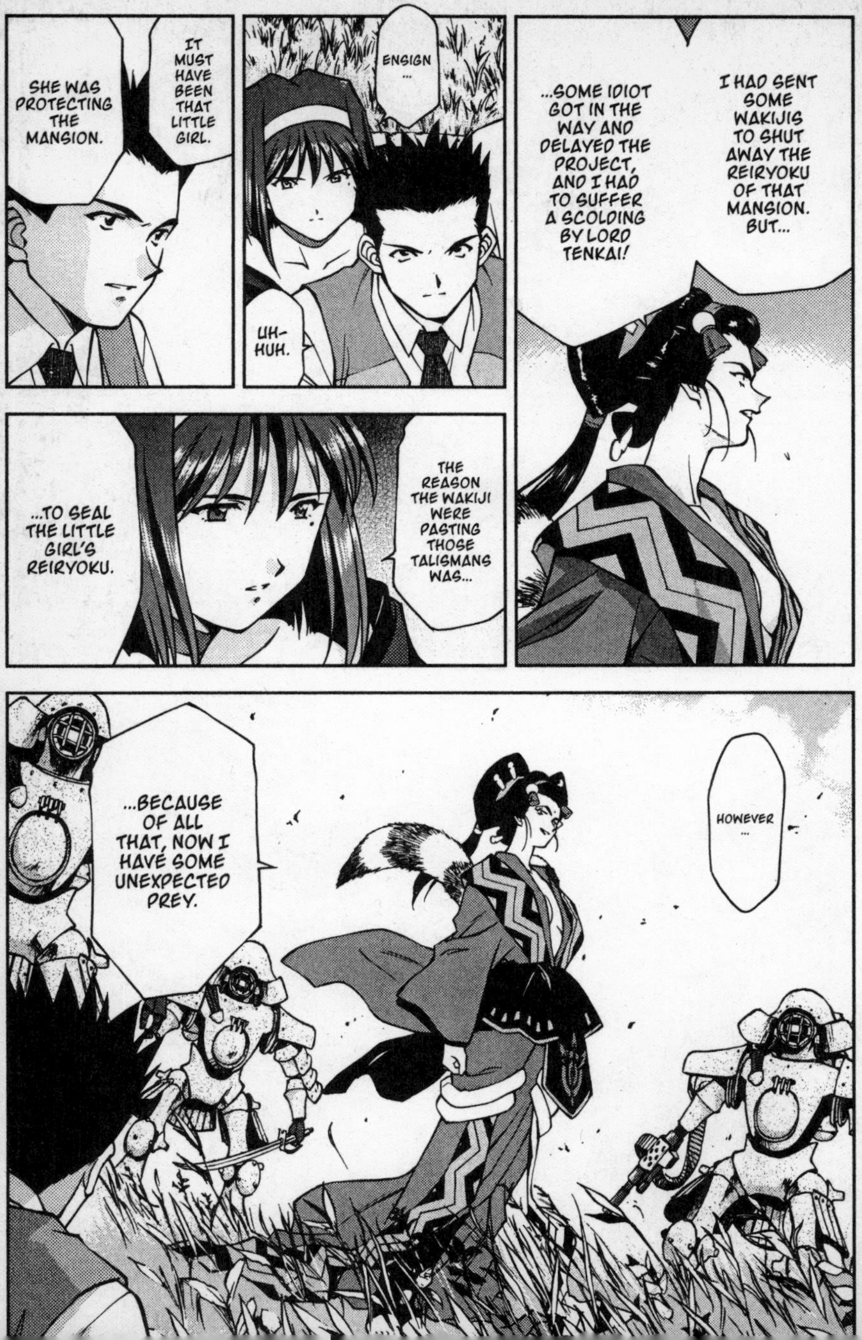
I HAD SENT SOME WAKIJIS TO SHUT AWAY THE REIRYOKU OF THAT MANSION. BUT...
...SOME IDIOT GOT IN THE WAY AND DELAYED THE PROJECT, AND I HAD TO SUFFER A SCOLDING BY LORD TENKAI!
ENSIGN...
UH-HUH.
IT MUST HAVE BEEN THAT LITTLE GIRL.
SHE WAS PROTECTING THE MANSION.
THE REASON THE WAKIJI WERE PASTING THOSE TALISMANS WAS...
...TO SEAL THE LITTLE GIRL'S REIRYOKU.
HOWEVER...
...BECAUSE OF ALL THAT, NOW I HAVE SOME UNEXPECTED PREY.

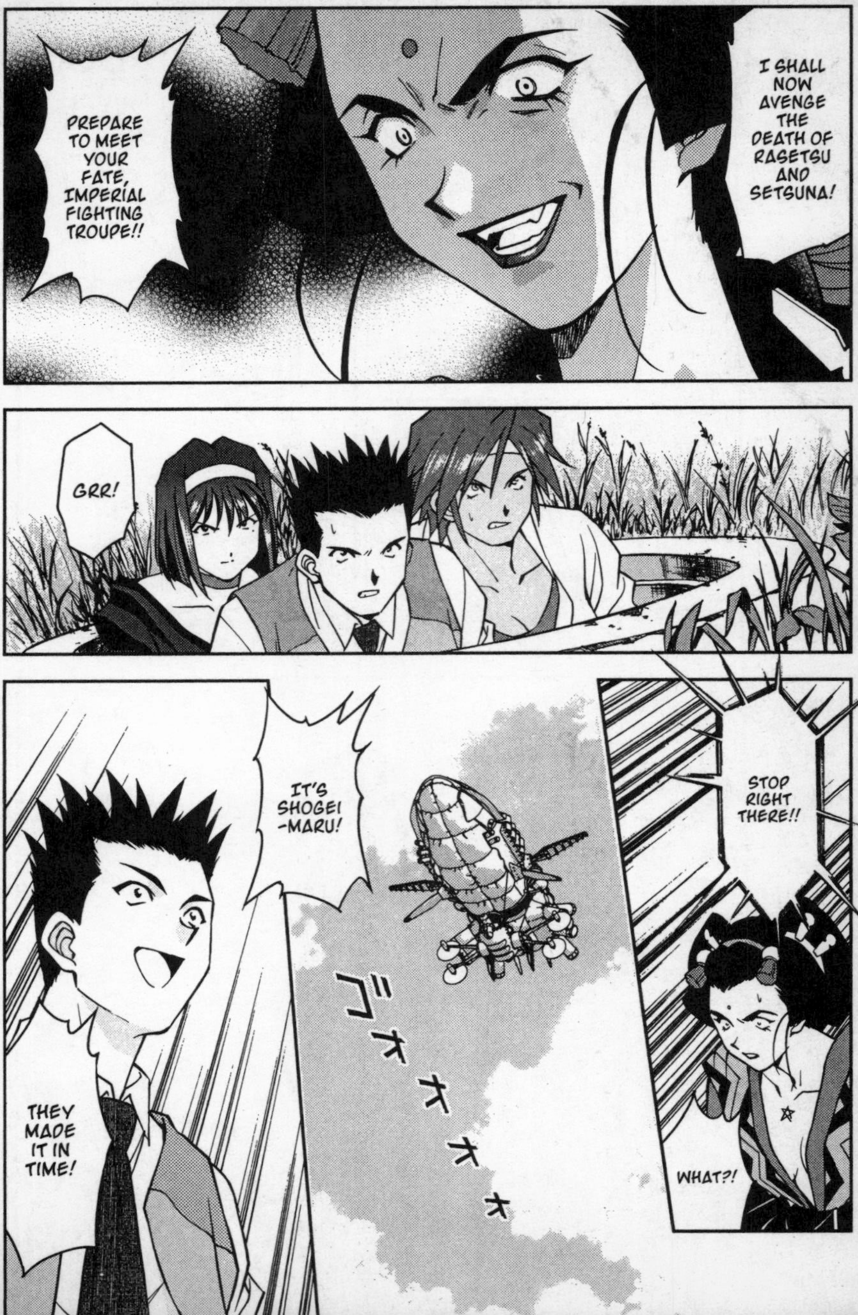
I SHALL NOW AVENGE THE DEATH OF RASETSU AND SETSUNA!
PREPARE TO MEET YOUR FATE, IMPERIAL FIGHTING TROUPE!!
GRR!
STOP RIGHT THERE!!
WHAT?!
IT'S SHOGEI-MARU!
ゴオオォォ
THEY MADE IT IN TIME!

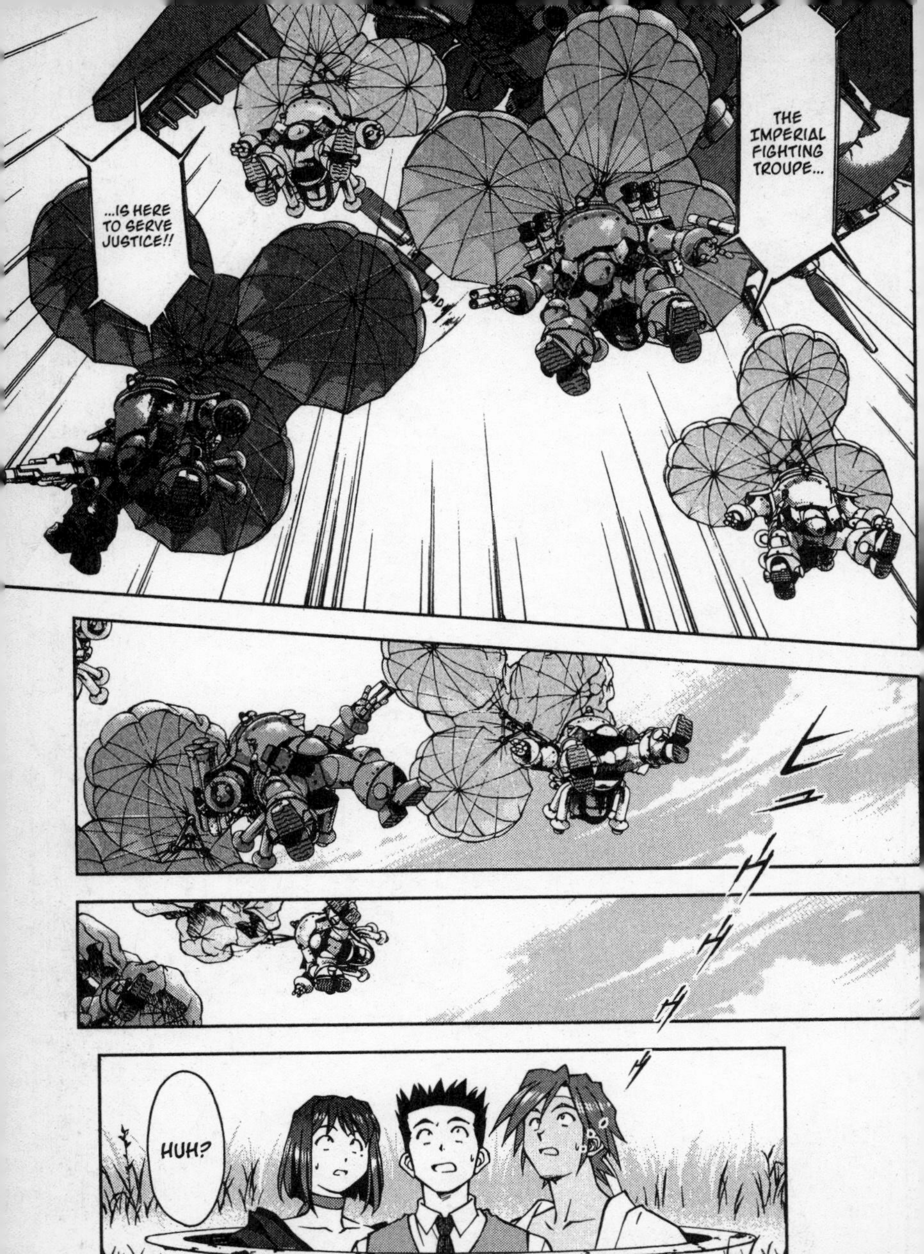
THE IMPERIAL FIGHTING TROUPE...
...IS HERE TO SERVE JUSTICE!!
HUH?

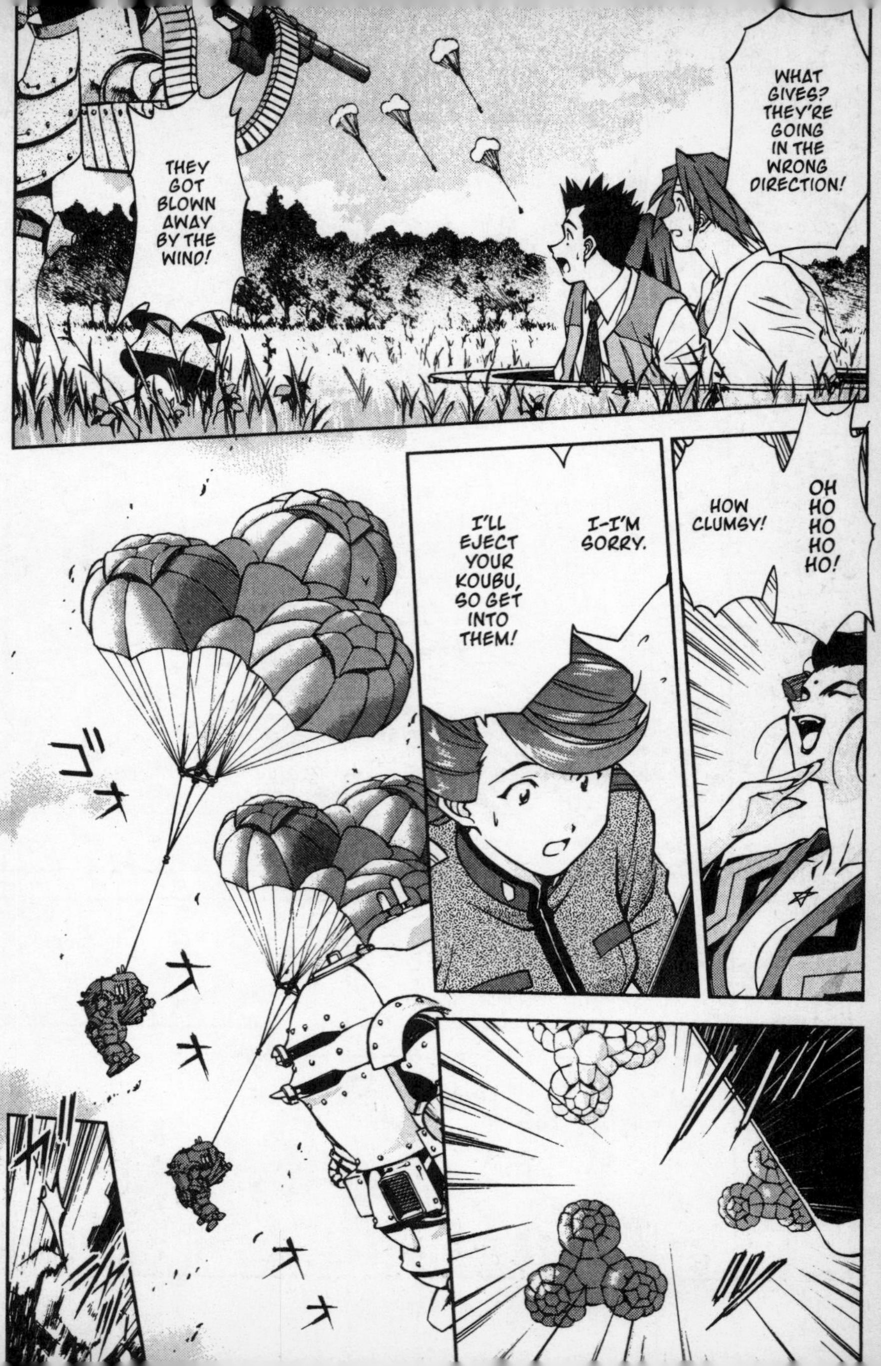
WHAT GIVES? THEY'RE GOING IN THE WRONG DIRECTION!
THEY GOT BLOWN AWAY BY THE WIND!
OH HO HO HO HO!
HOW CLUMSY!
I-I'M SORRY.
I'LL EJECT YOUR KOUBU, SO GET INTO THEM!

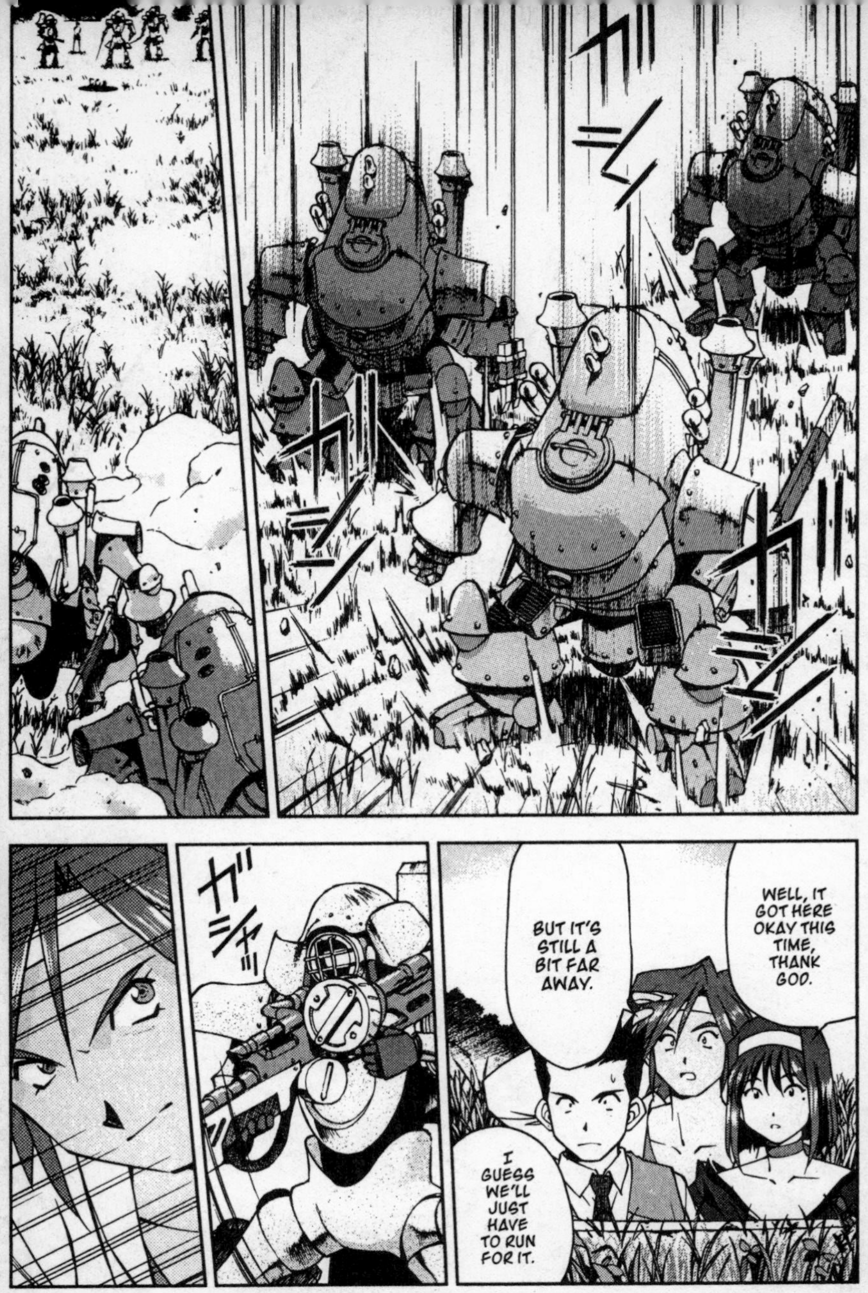
WELL, IT GOT HERE OKAY THIS TIME, THANK GOD.
BUT IT'S STILL A BIT FAR AWAY.
I GUESS WE'LL JUST HAVE TO RUN FOR IT.

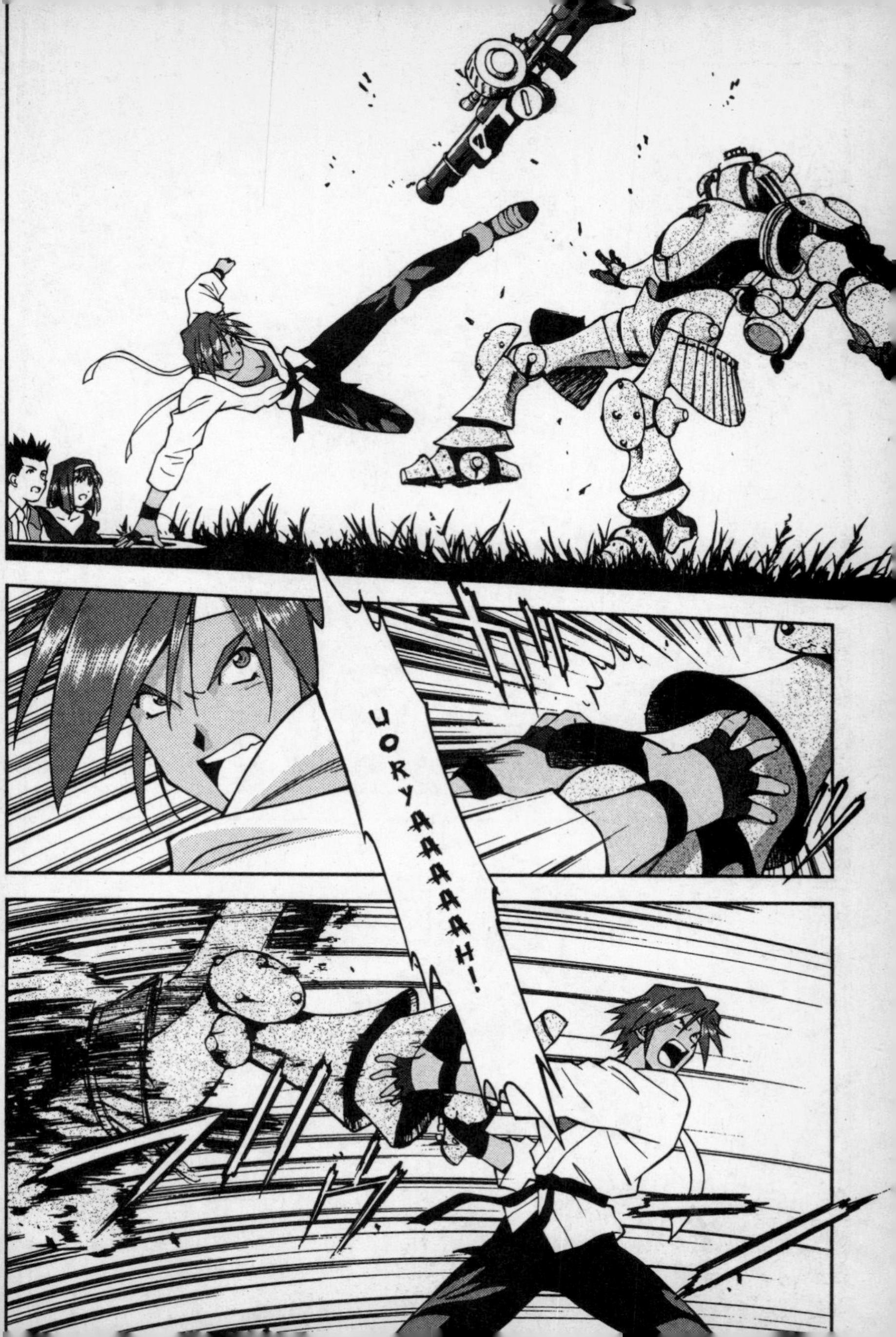

UORYAAAAAAH!

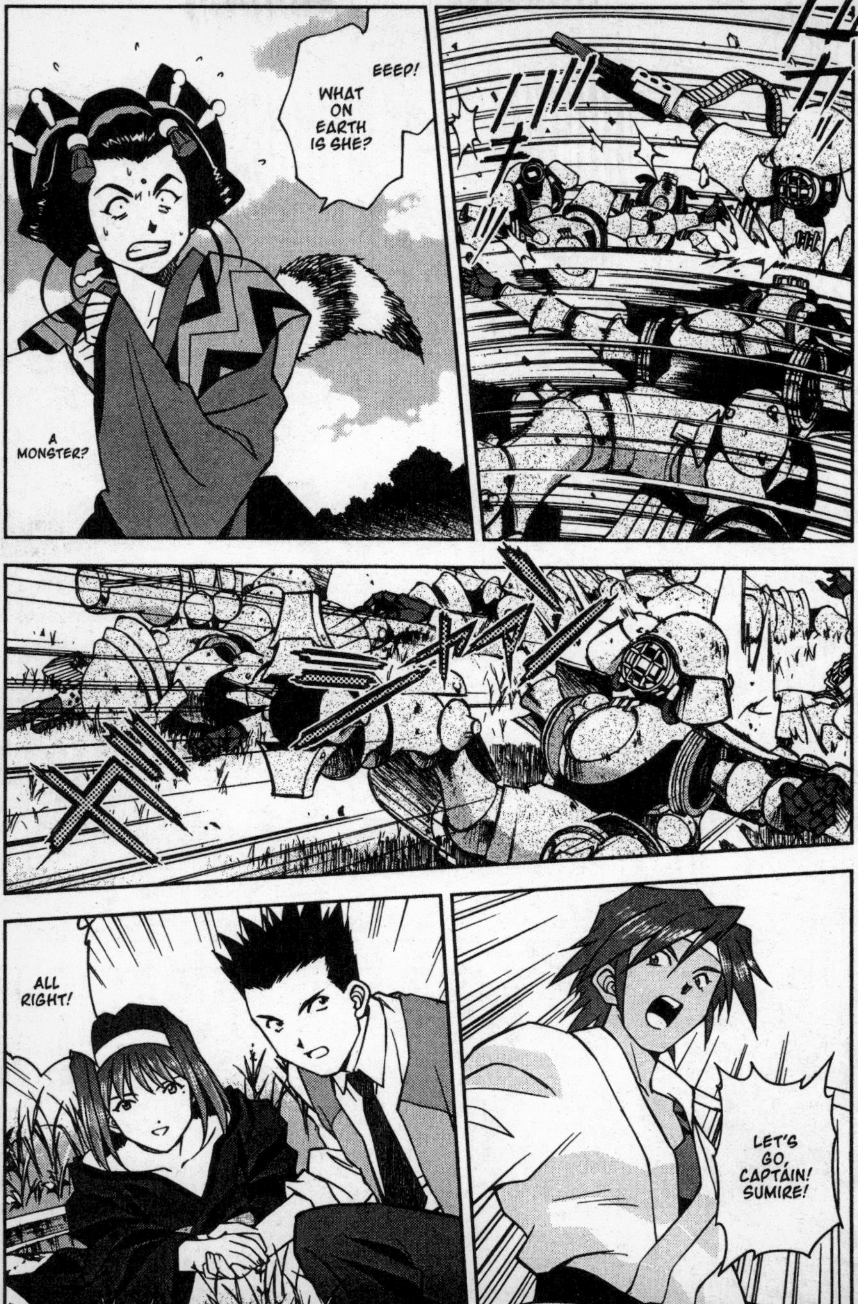
EEEP!
WHAT ON EARTH IS SHE?
A MONSTER?
LET'S GO, CAPTAIN! SUMIRE!
ALL RIGHT!

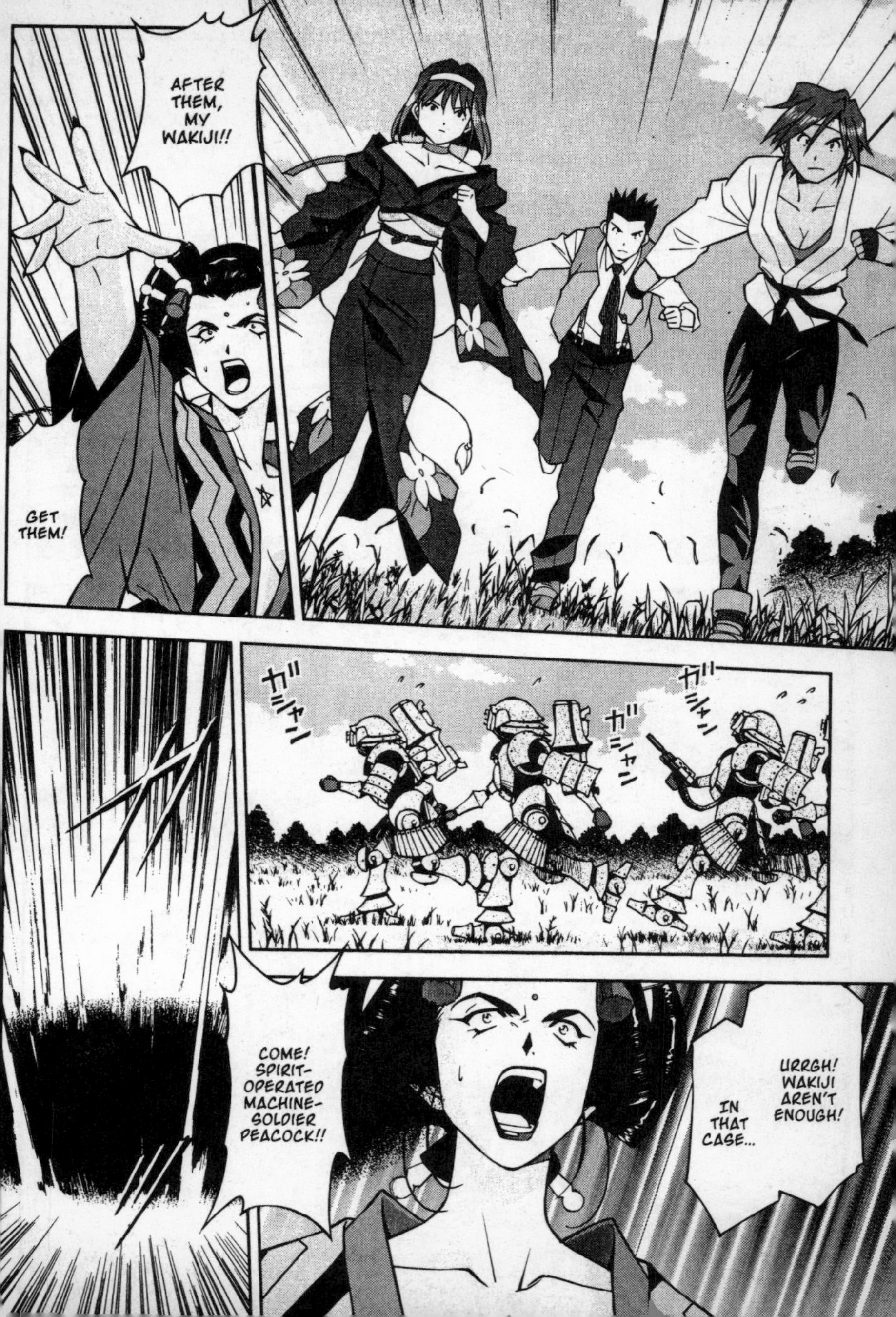
AFTER THEM, MY WAKIJI!!
GET THEM!
ガシャン
ガシャン
ガシャン
URRGH! WAKIJI AREN'T ENOUGH!
IN THAT CASE...
COME! SPIRIT-OPERATED MACHINE-SOLDIER PEACOCK!!

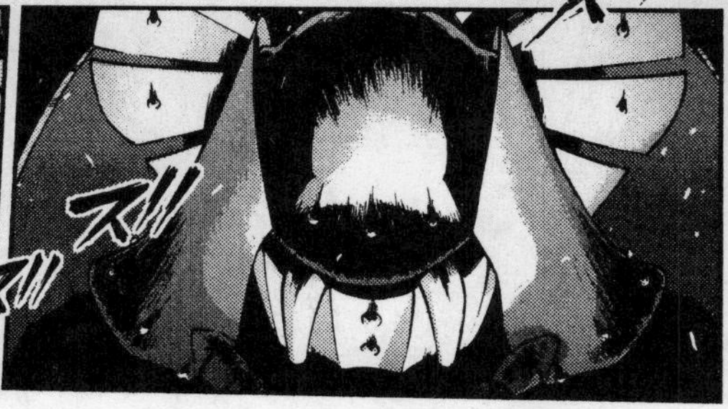
ズ
ズ
ズ
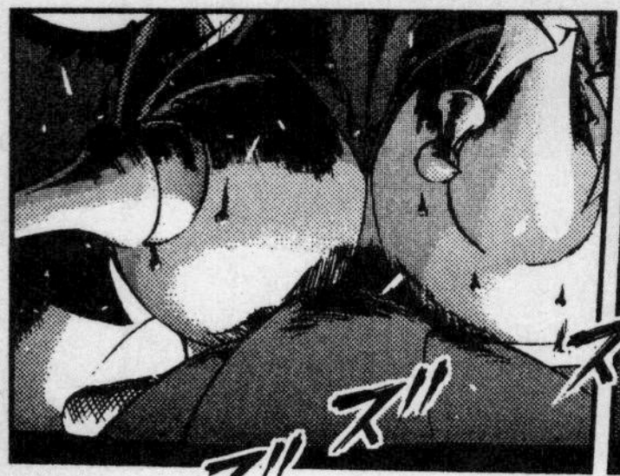
ズ
ズ
ズ
ズ
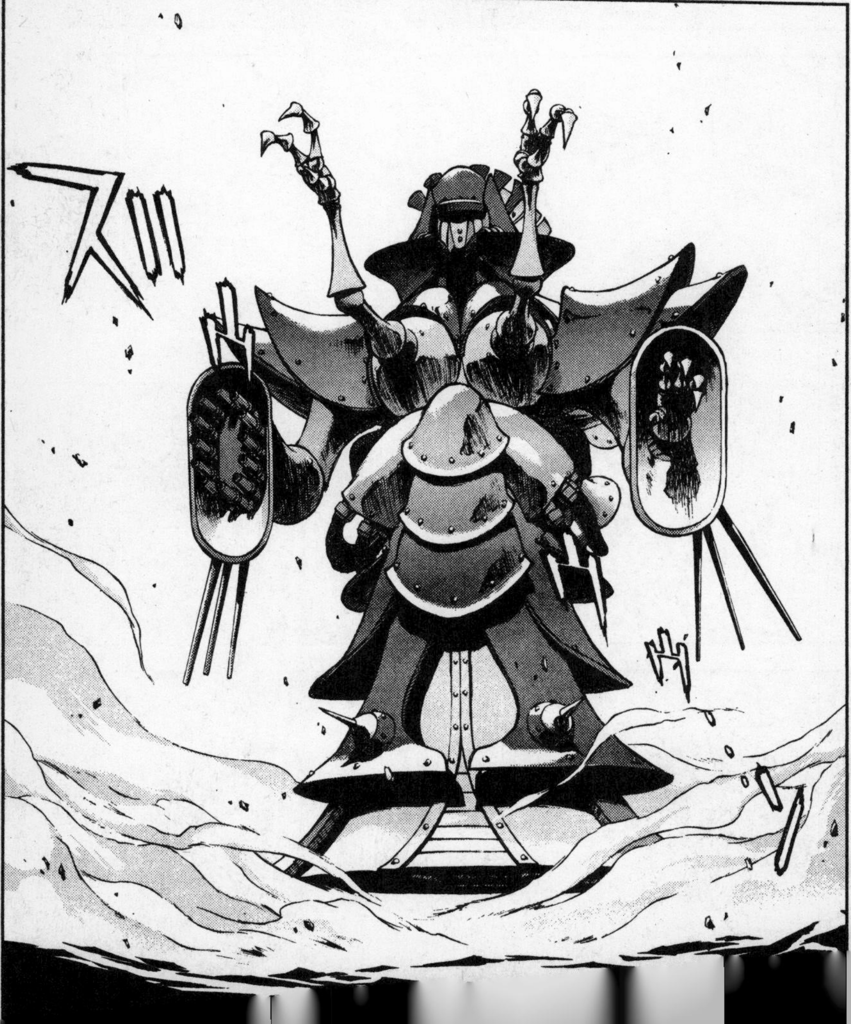
ズ
ガ

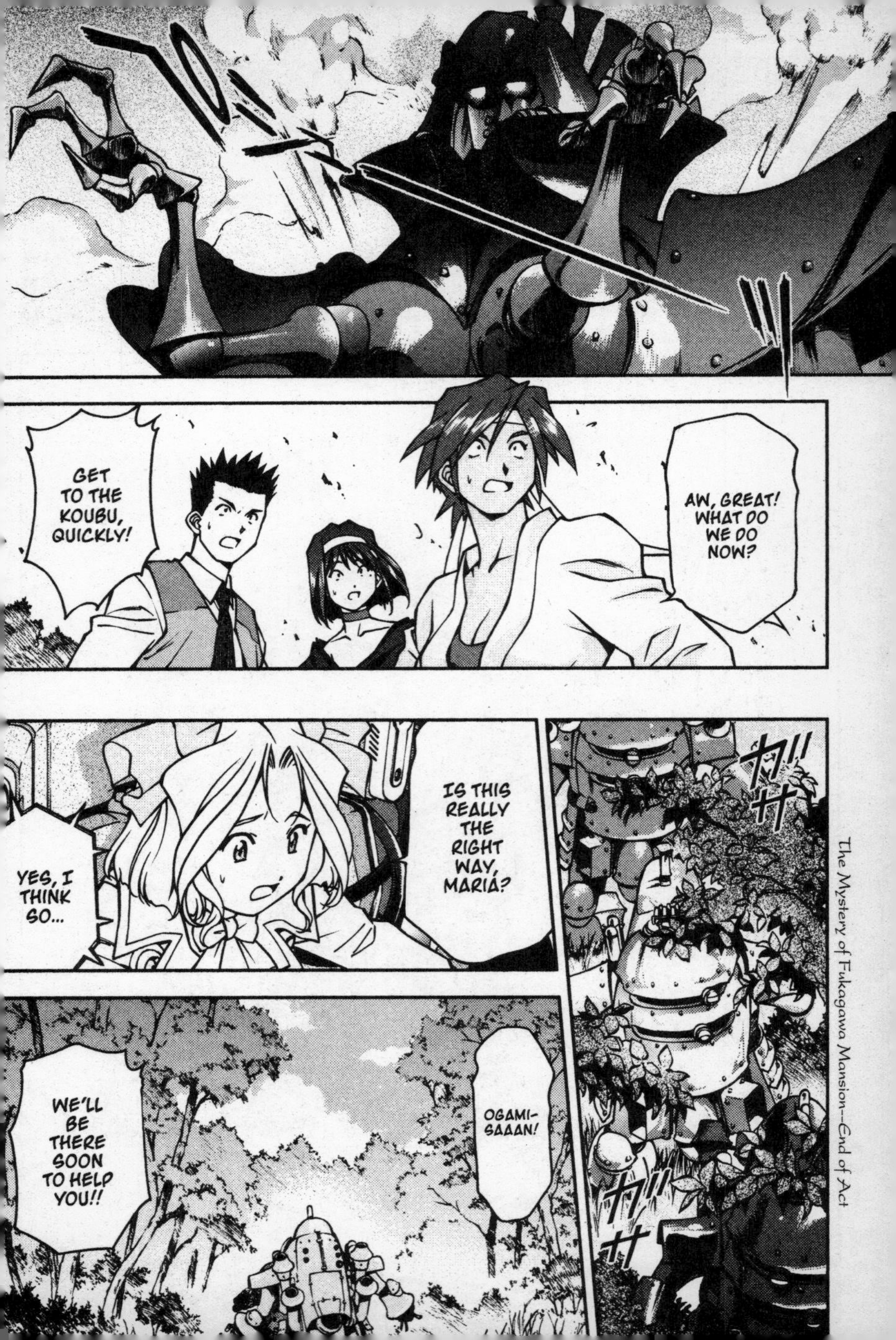
AW, GREAT! WHAT DO WE DO NOW?
GET TO THE KOUBU, QUICKLY!
IS THIS REALLY THE RIGHT WAY, MARIA?
YES, I THINK SO...
OGAMI-SAAAN!
WE'LL BE THERE SOON TO HELP YOU!!

The Mystery of Fukagawa Mansion--End of Act

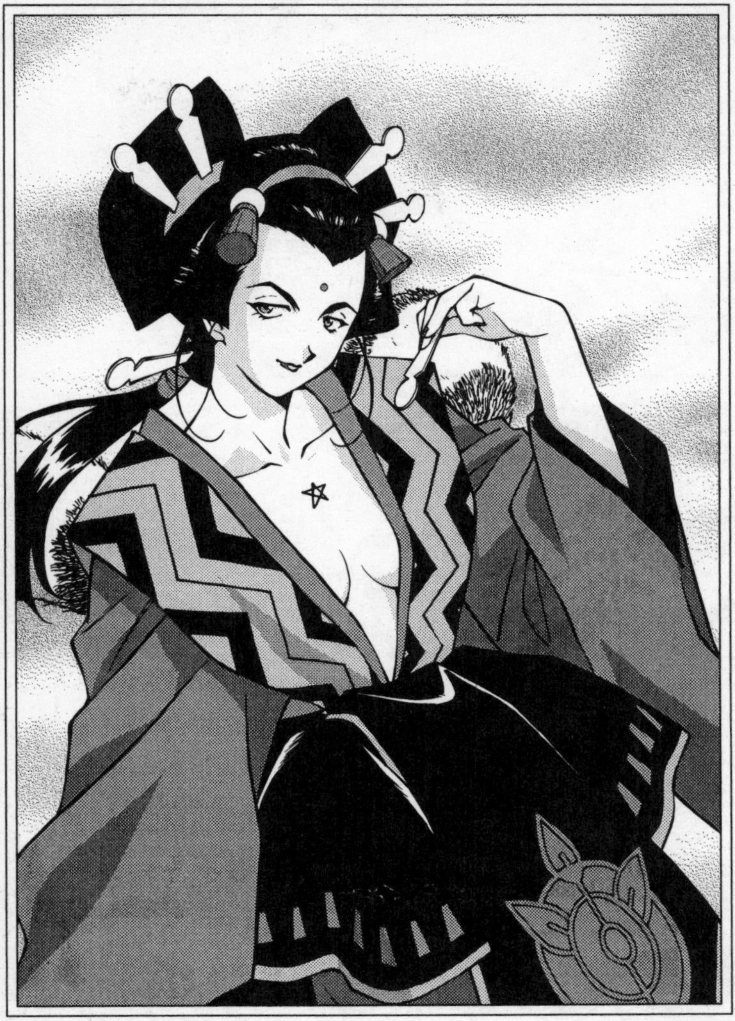

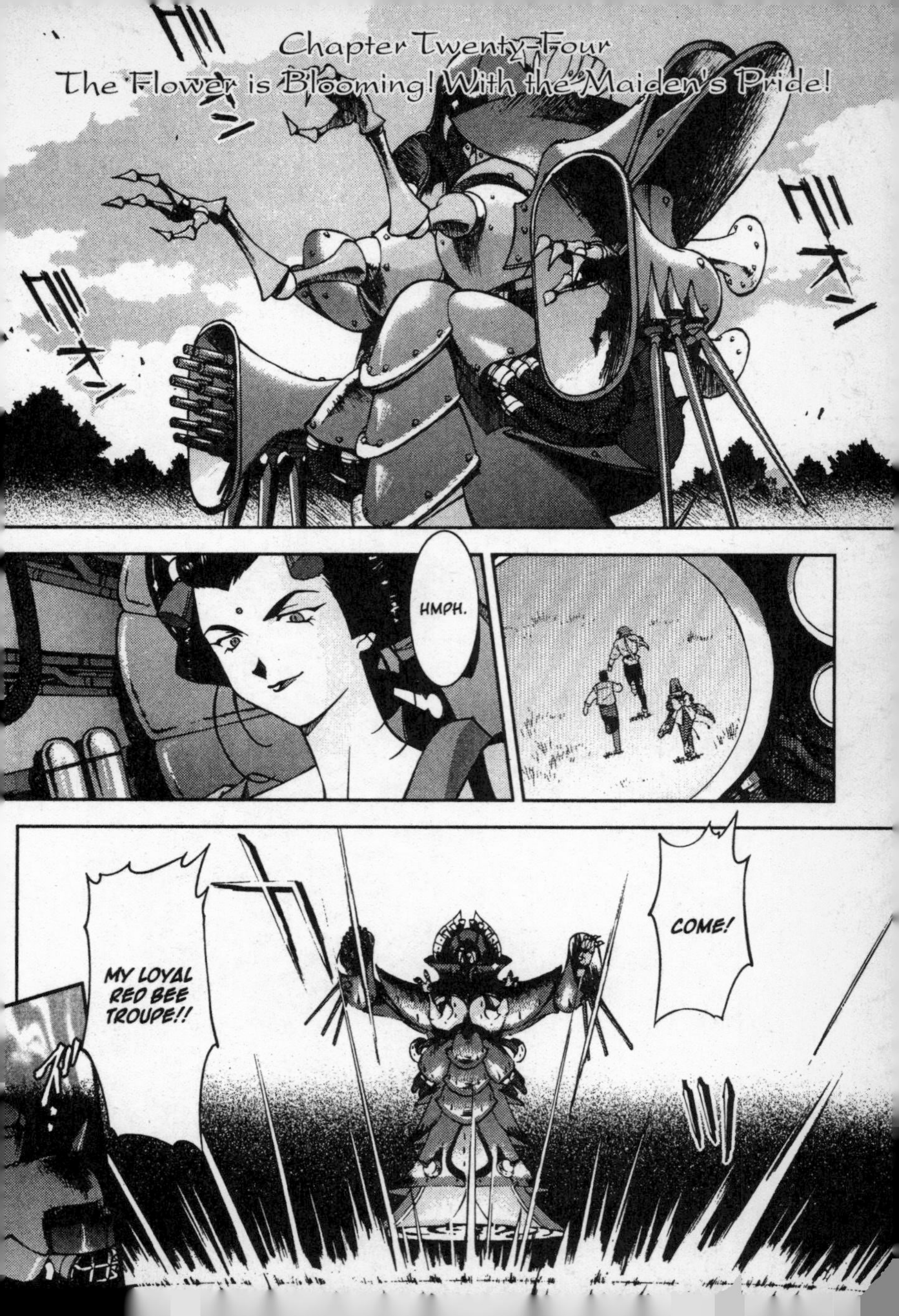
Chapter Twenty-Four
The Flower is Blooming! With the Maiden's Pride!
HMPH.
COME!
MY LOYAL RED BEE TROUPE!!

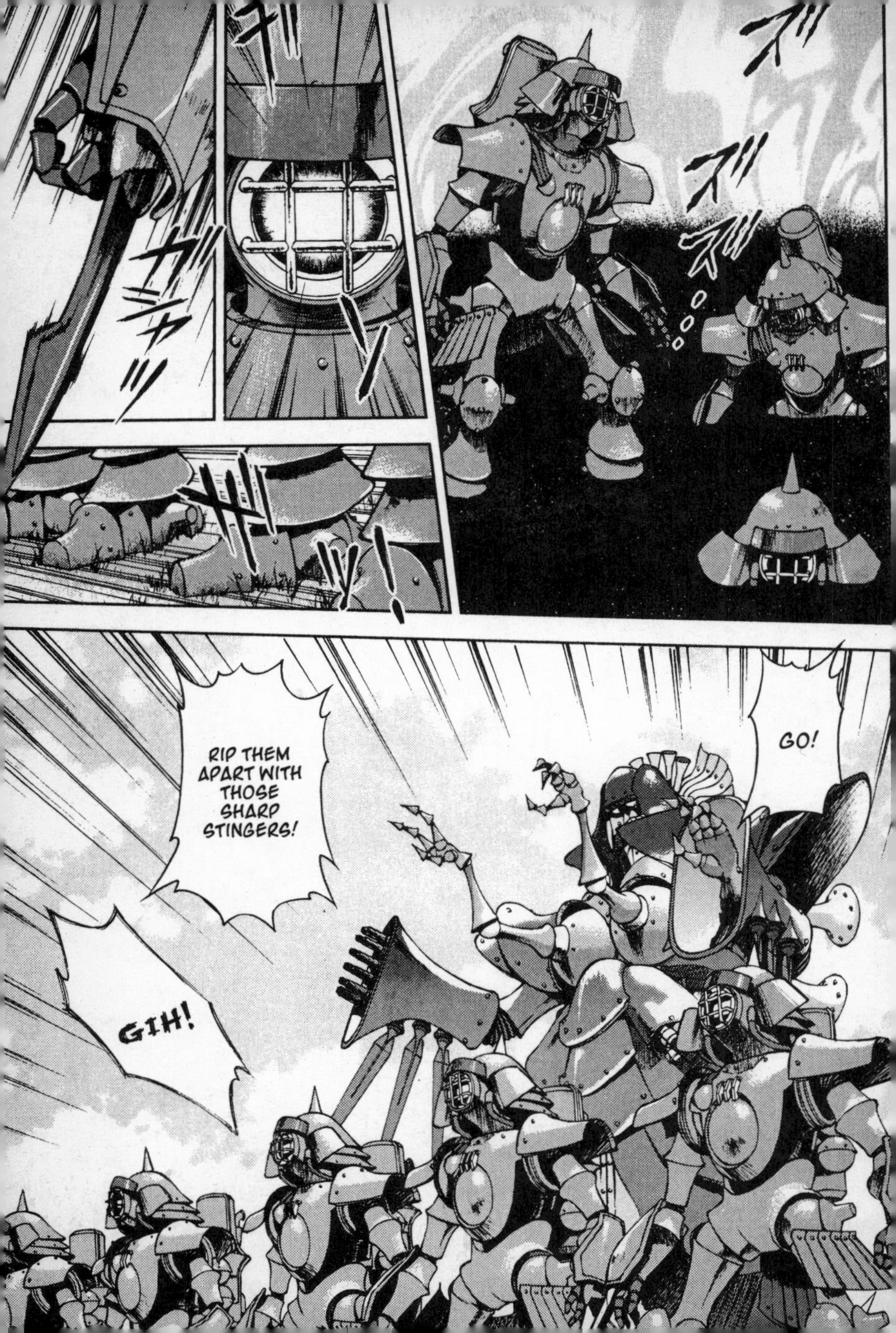
GO!
RIP THEM APART WITH THOSE SHARP STINGERS!
GIH!

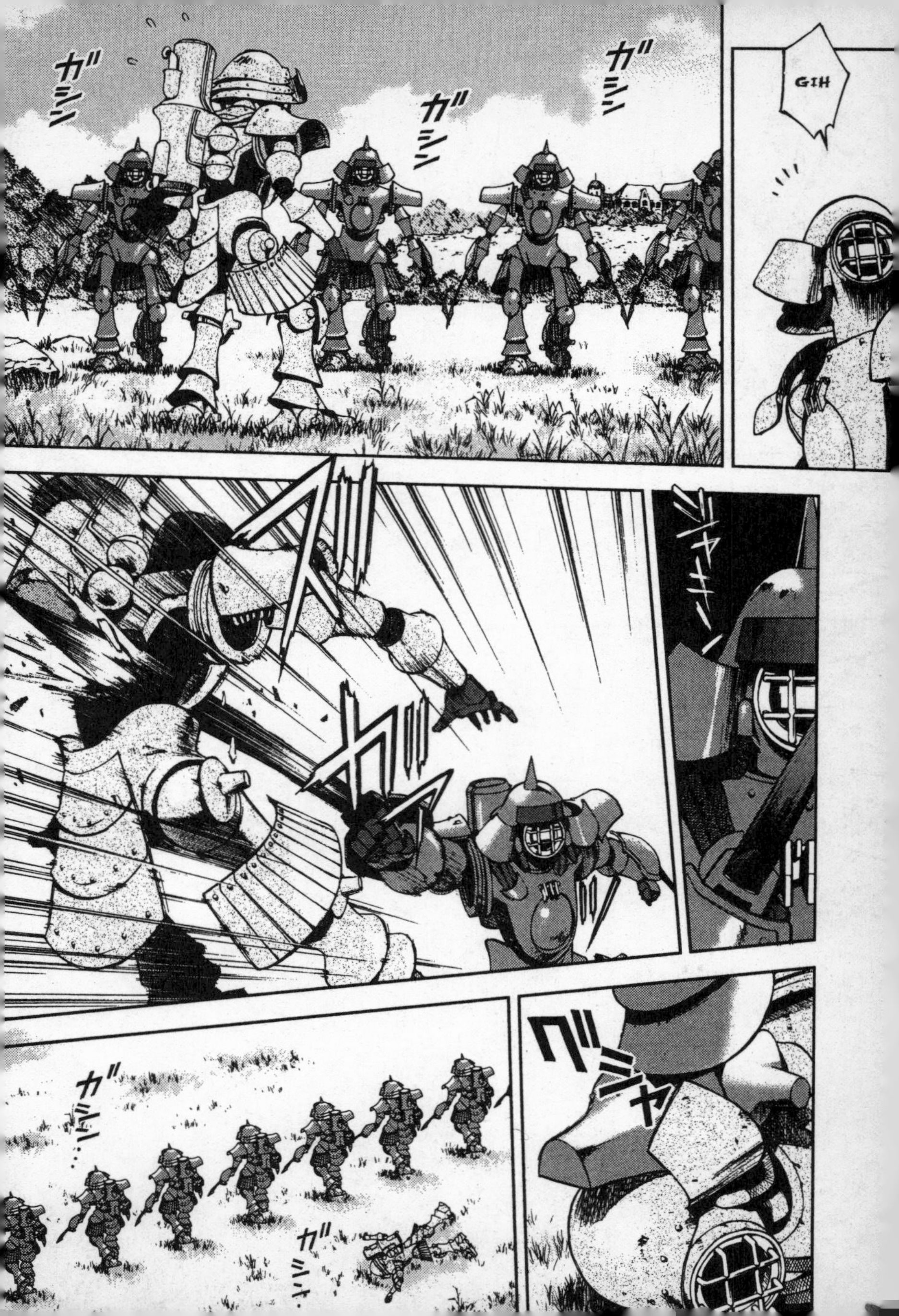
GIH
ガシン
ガシン
ガシン
ジャキン
グシャ
ガシン…
ガシン

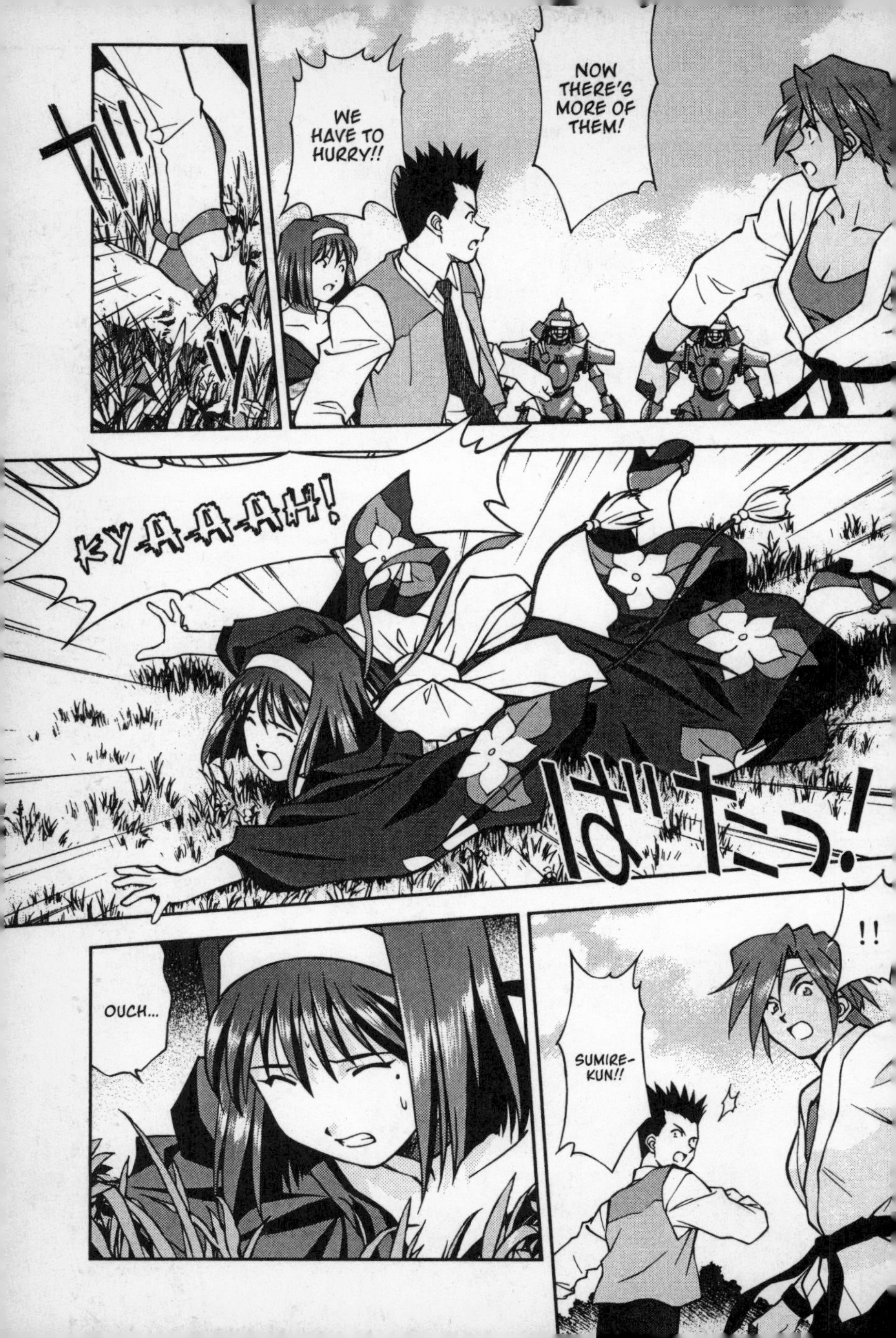
NOW THERE'S MORE OF THEM!
WE HAVE TO HURRY!!
KYA-A-A-AH!
ばたっ!
!!
SUMIRE-KUN!!
OUCH...

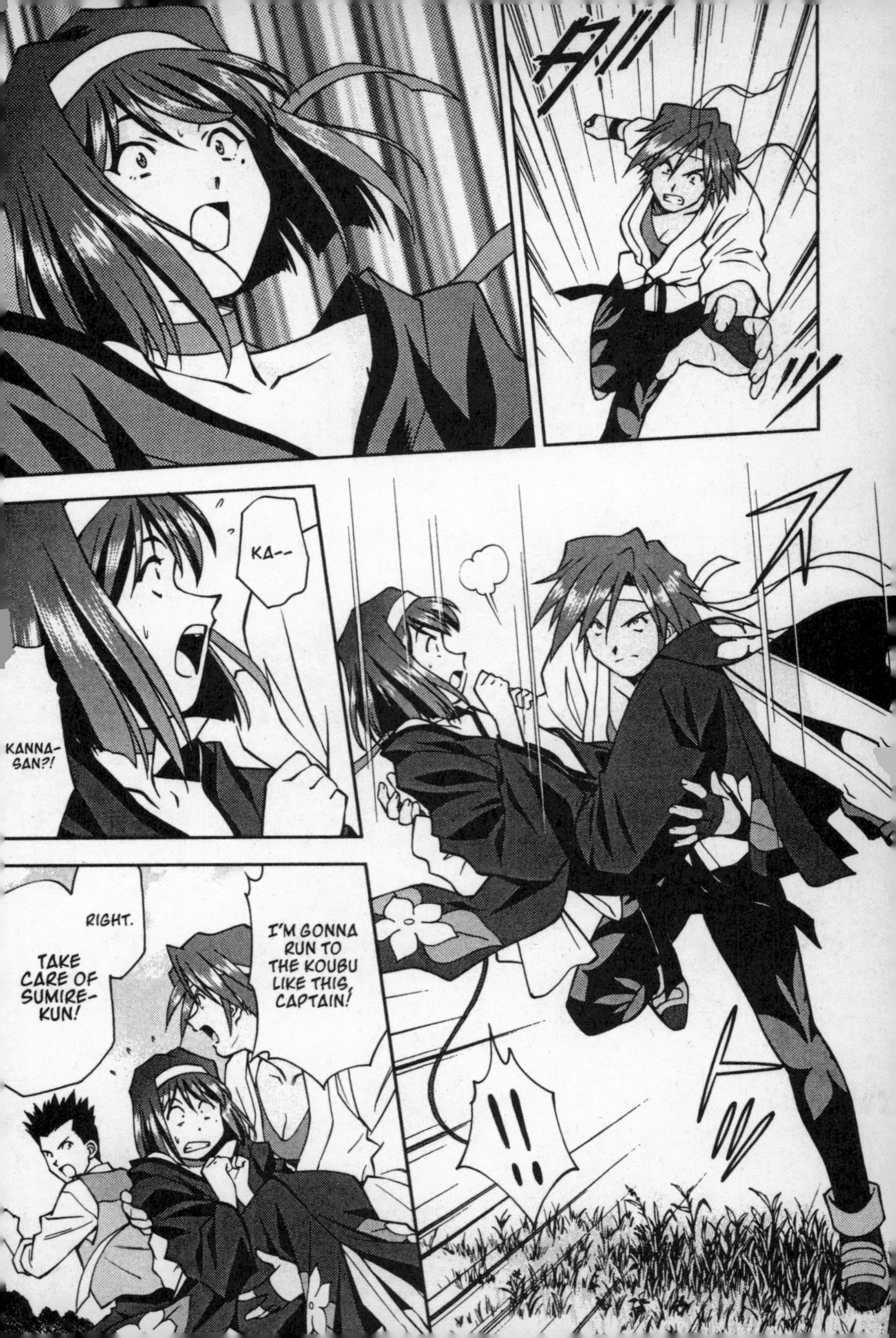
KA--
KANNA-SAN?!
!!
I'M GONNA RUN TO THE KOUBU LIKE THIS, CAPTAIN!
RIGHT.
TAKE CARE OF SUMIRE-KUN!

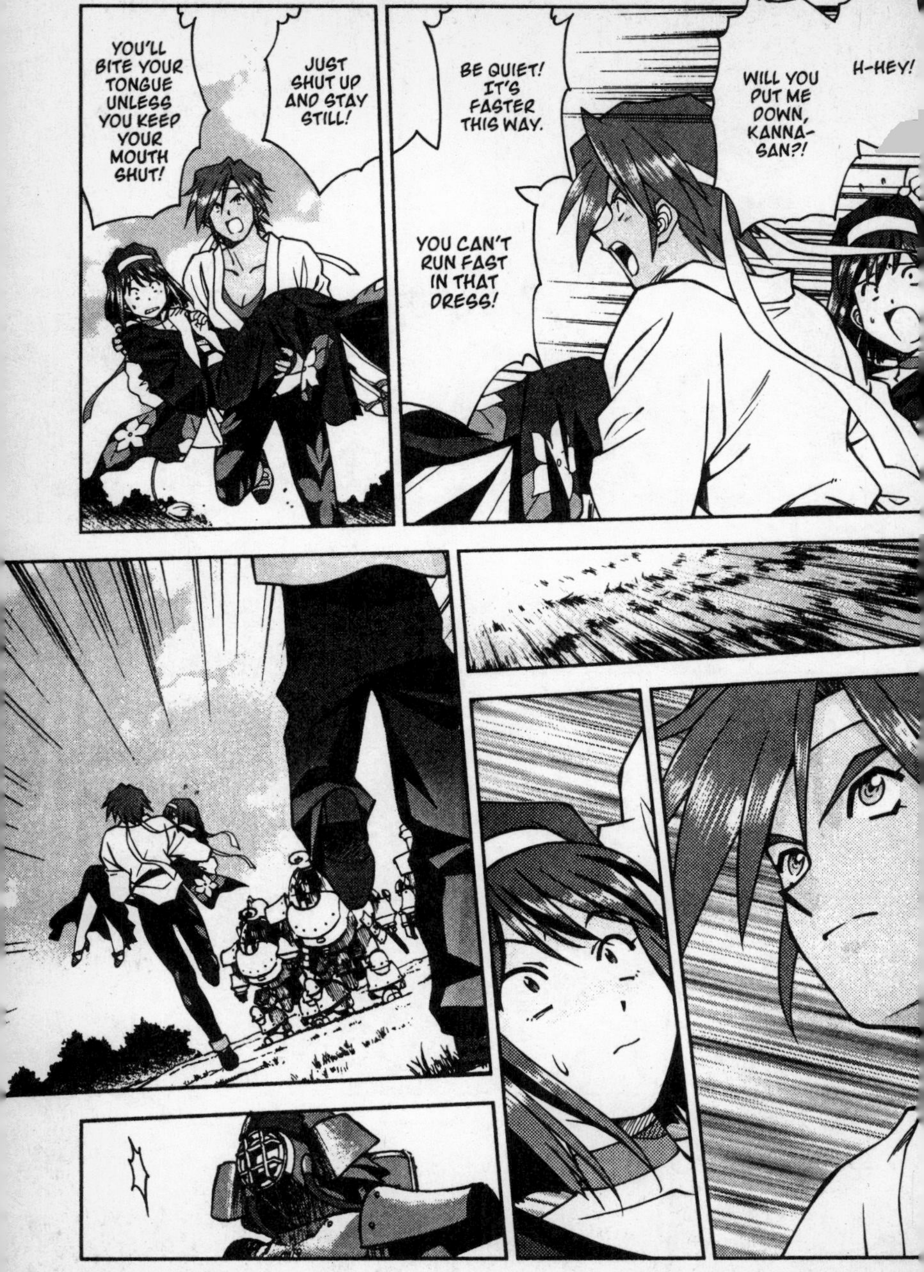
H-HEY!
WILL YOU PUT ME DOWN, KANNA-SAN?!
BE QUIET! IT'S FASTER THIS WAY.
YOU CAN'T RUN FAST IN THAT DRESS!
JUST SHUT UP AND STAY STILL!
YOU'LL BITE YOUR TONGUE UNLESS YOU KEEP YOUR MOUTH SHUT!

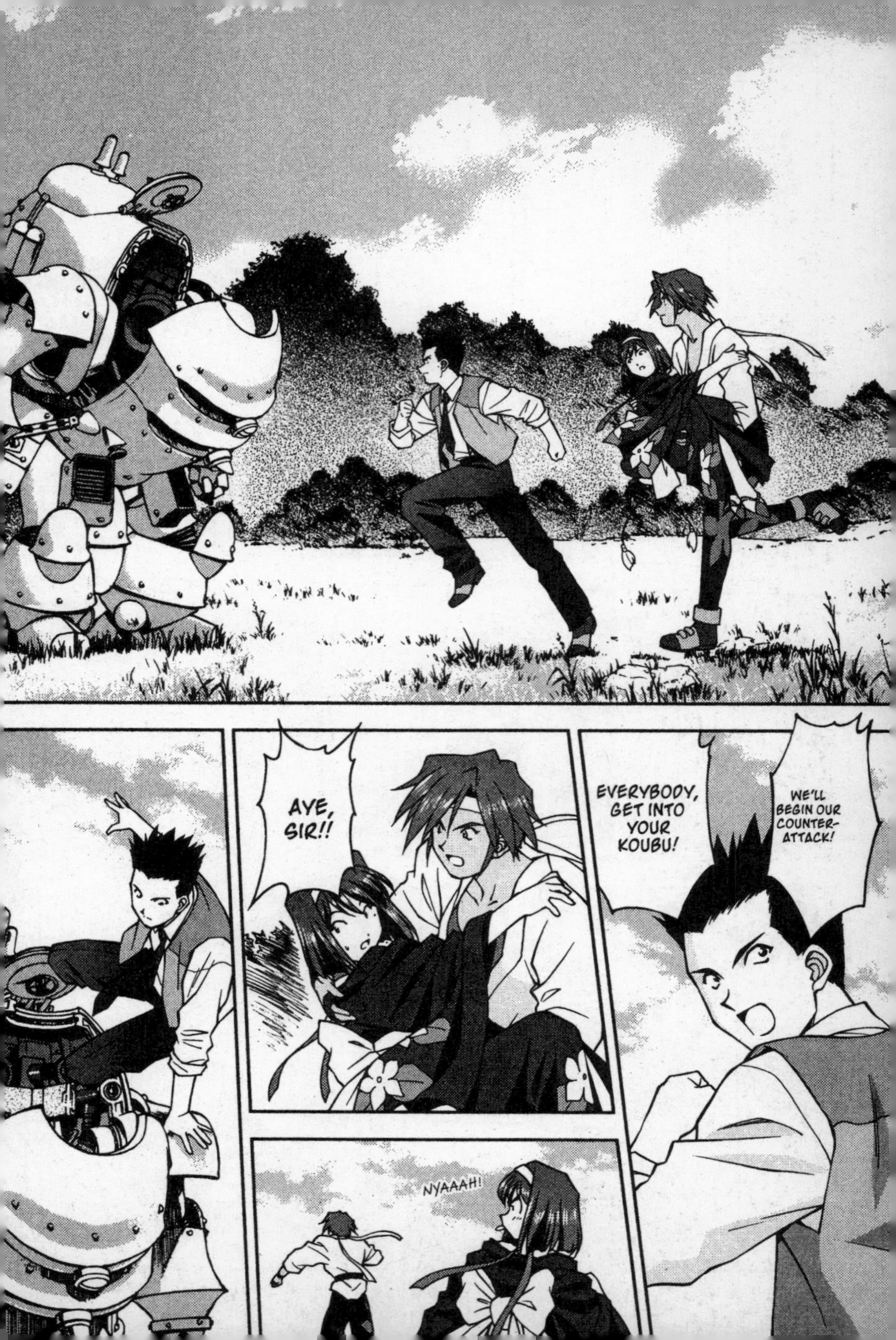
WE'LL BEGIN OUR COUNTER-ATTACK!
EVERYBODY, GET INTO YOUR KOUBU!
AYE, SIR!!
NYAAAH!

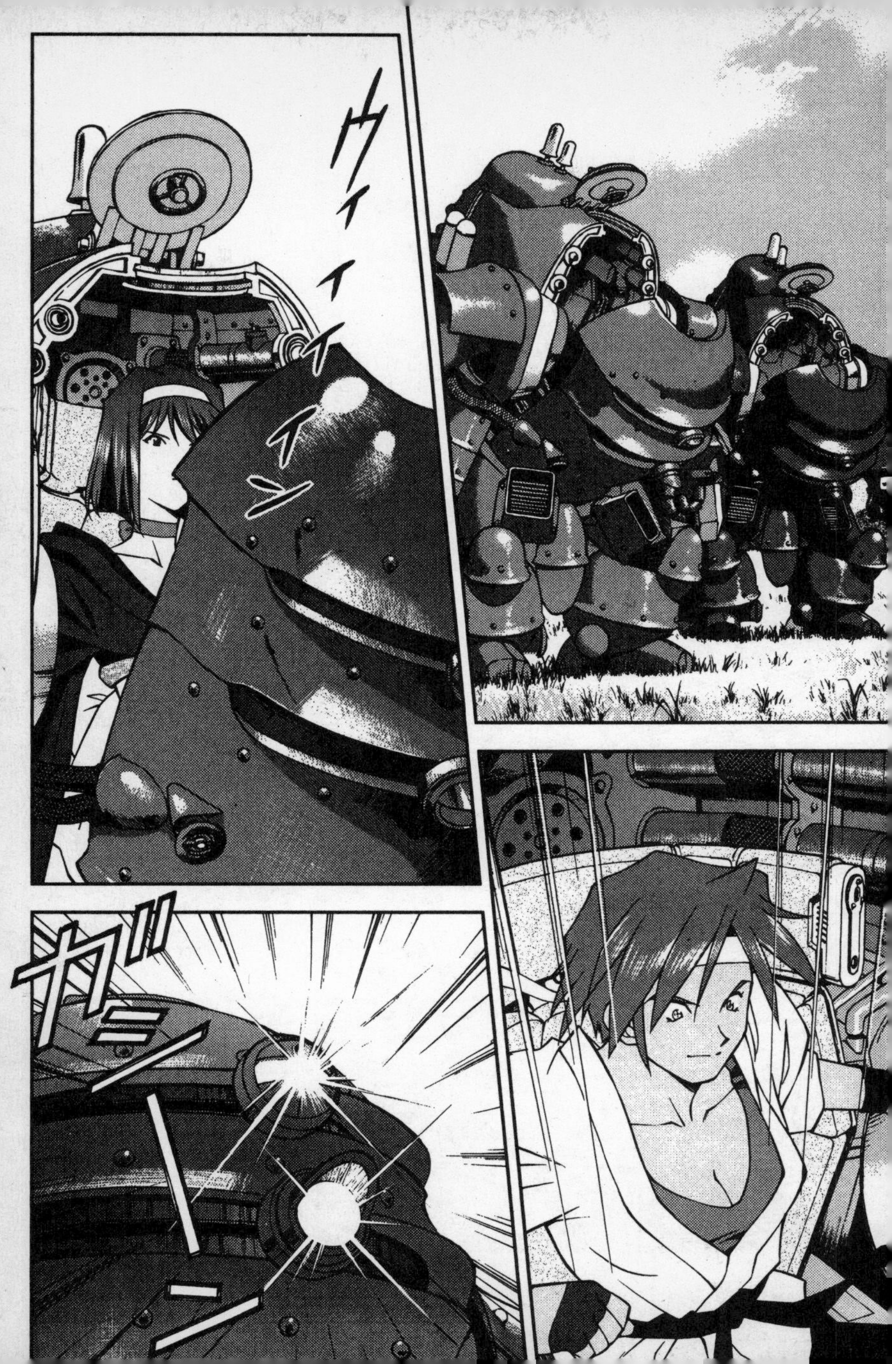
ヴィイイイイン
ガ

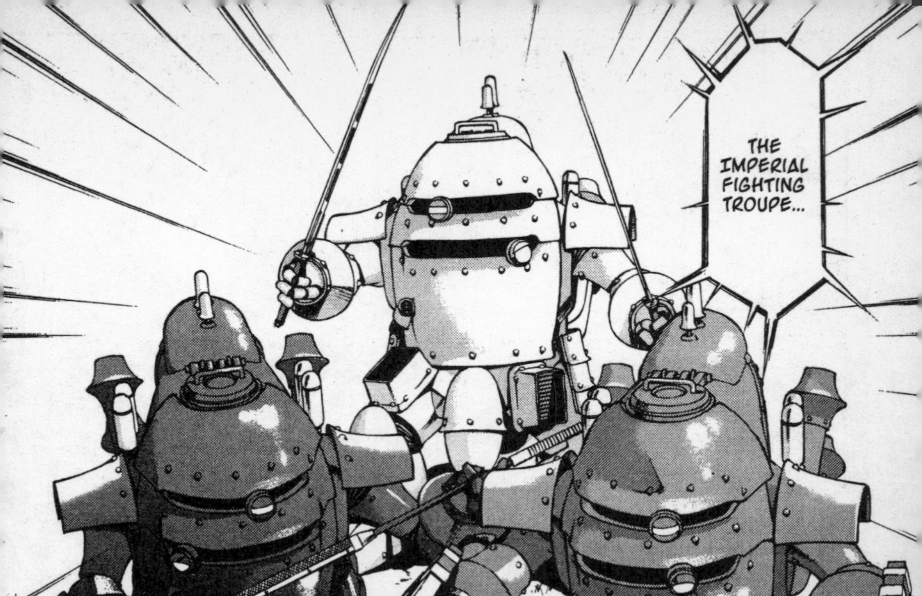
THE IMPERIAL FIGHTING TROUPE...
...IS HERE!
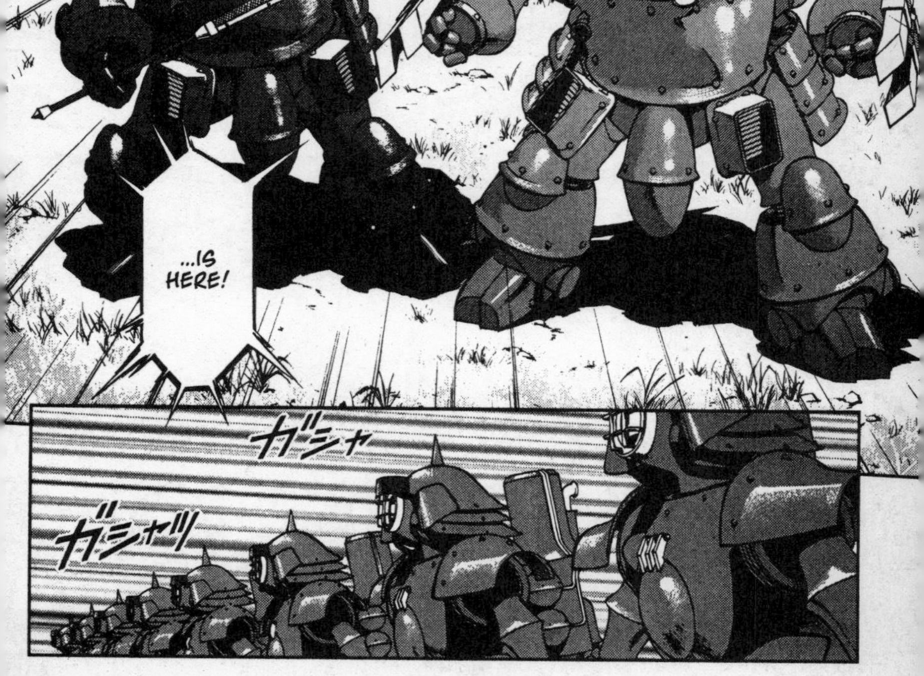
ガシャ
ガシャッ

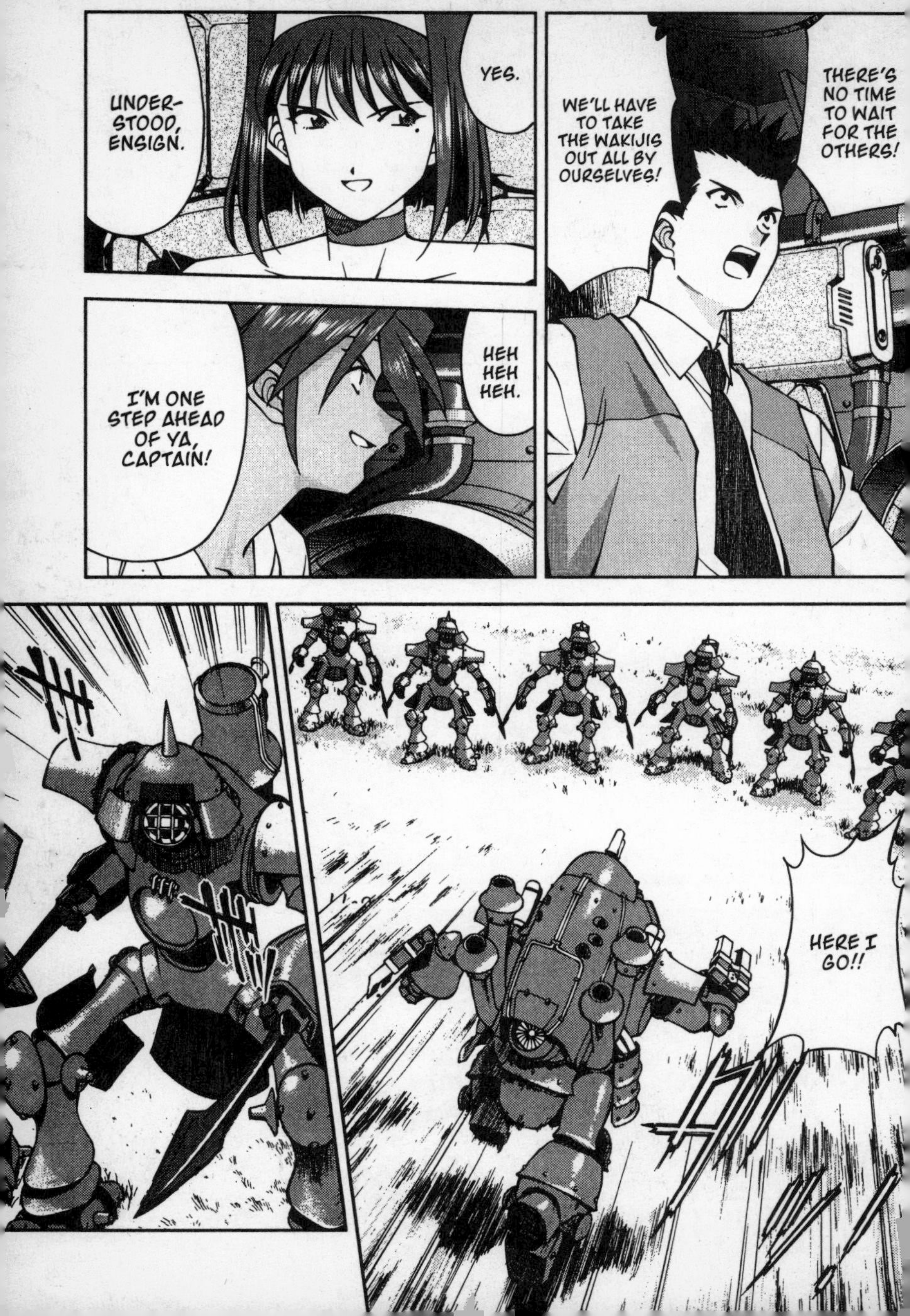
THERE'S NO TIME TO WAIT FOR THE OTHERS!
WE'LL HAVE TO TAKE THE WAKIJIS OUT ALL BY OURSELVES!
YES.
UNDER-STOOD, ENSIGN.
HEH HEH HEH.
I'M ONE STEP AHEAD OF YA, CAPTAIN!
HERE I GO!!

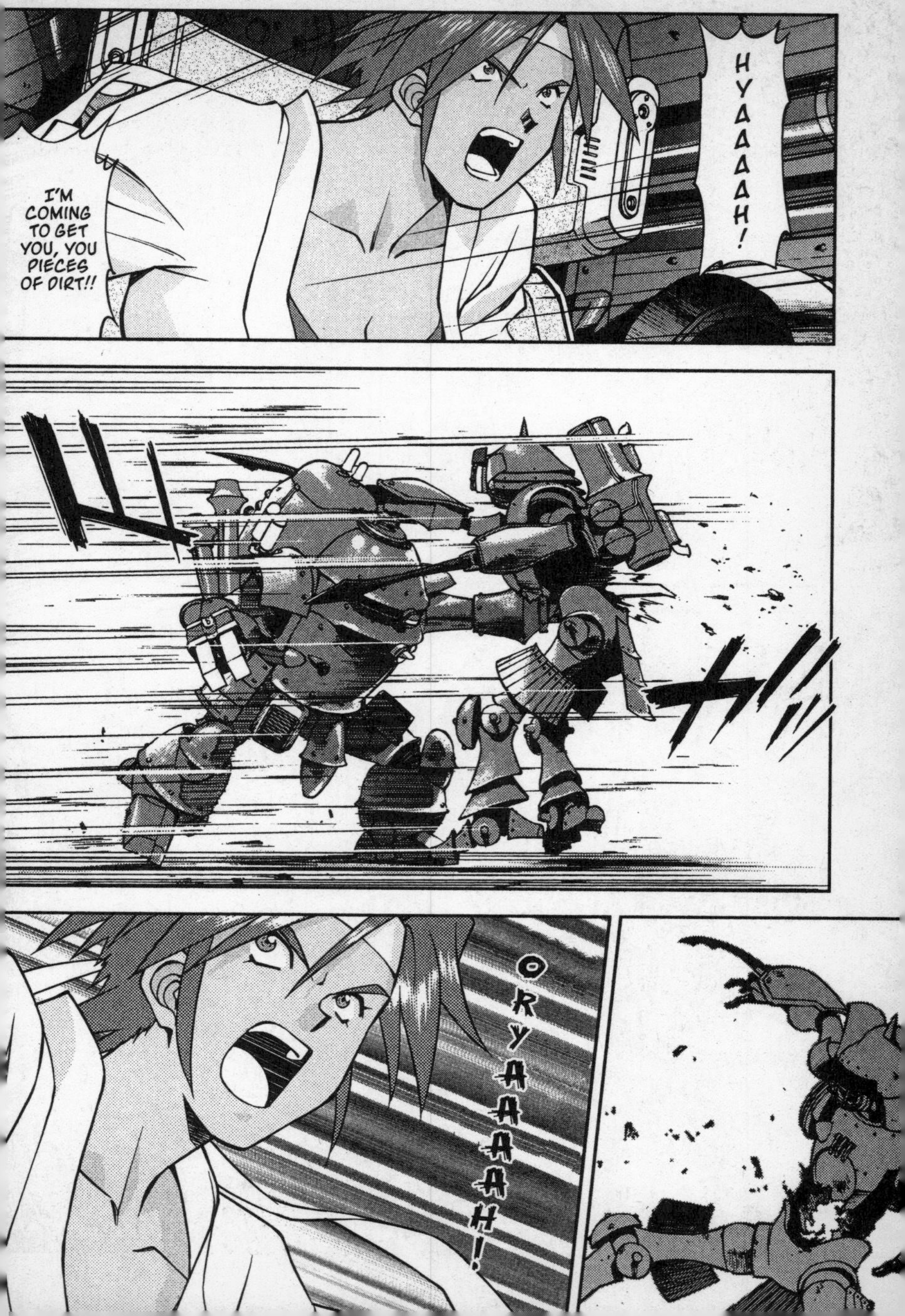
HYAAAAAH!
I'M COMING TO GET YOU, YOU PIECES OF DIRT!!
ORYAAAAAH!

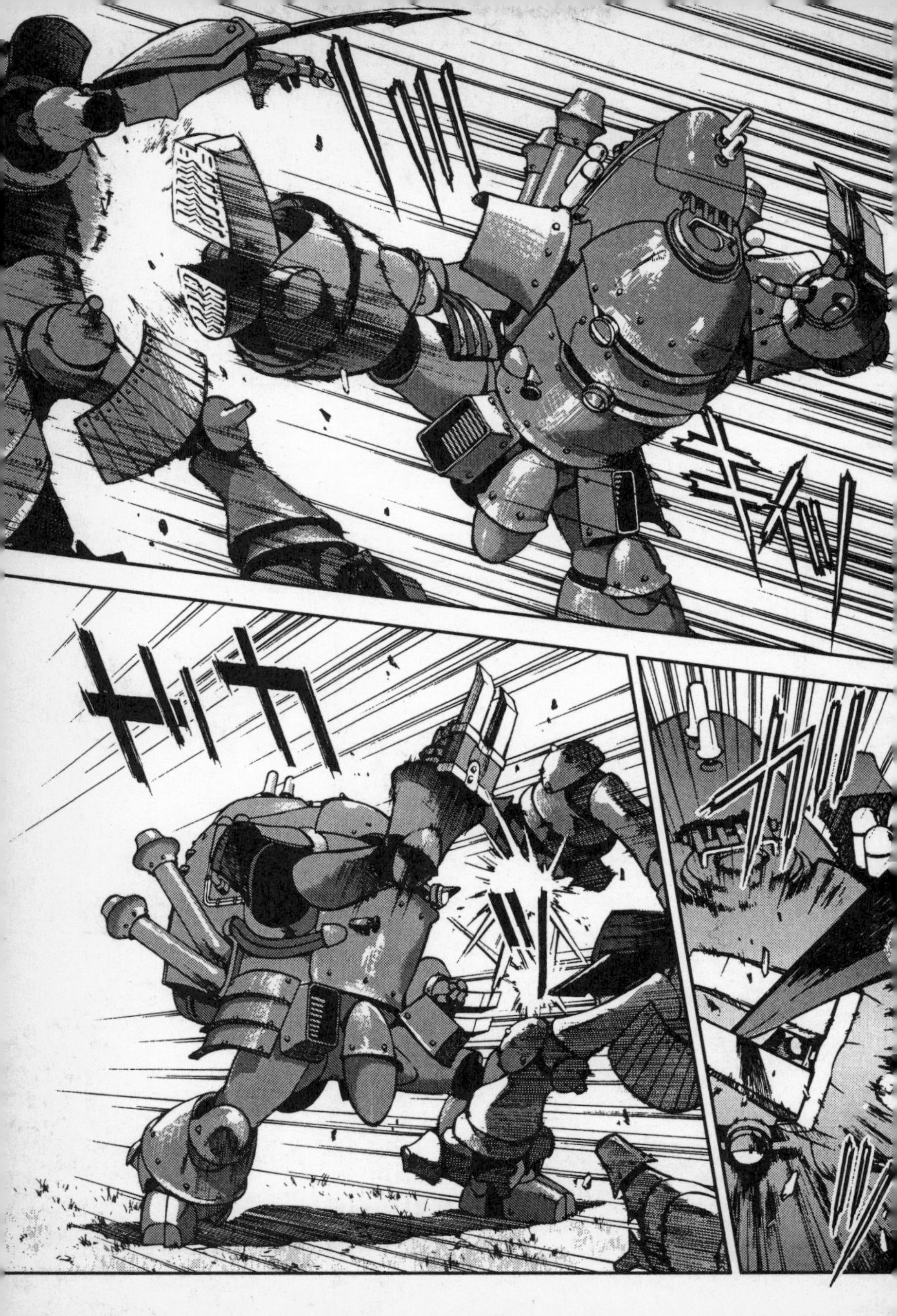

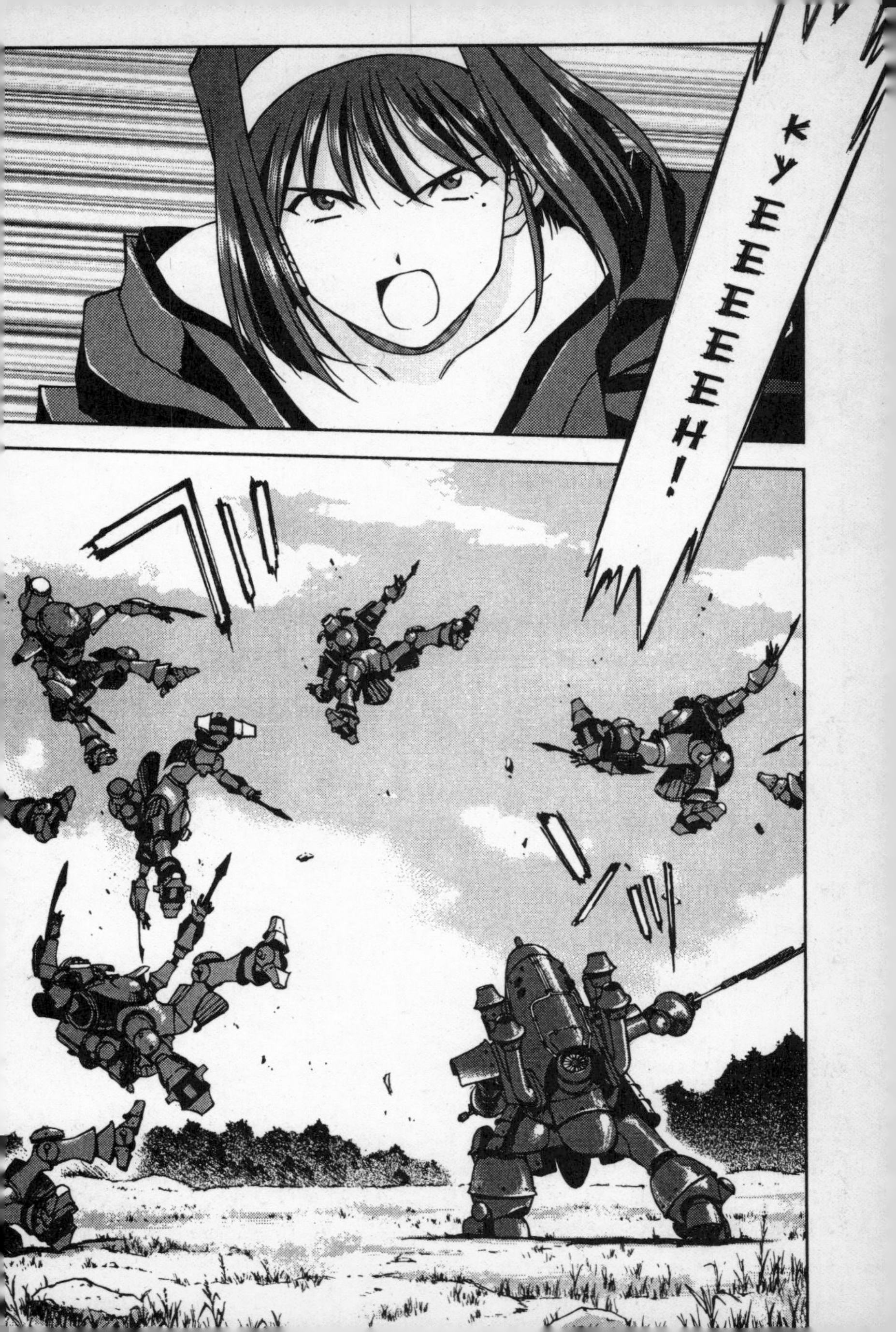
KYEEEEEEEH!

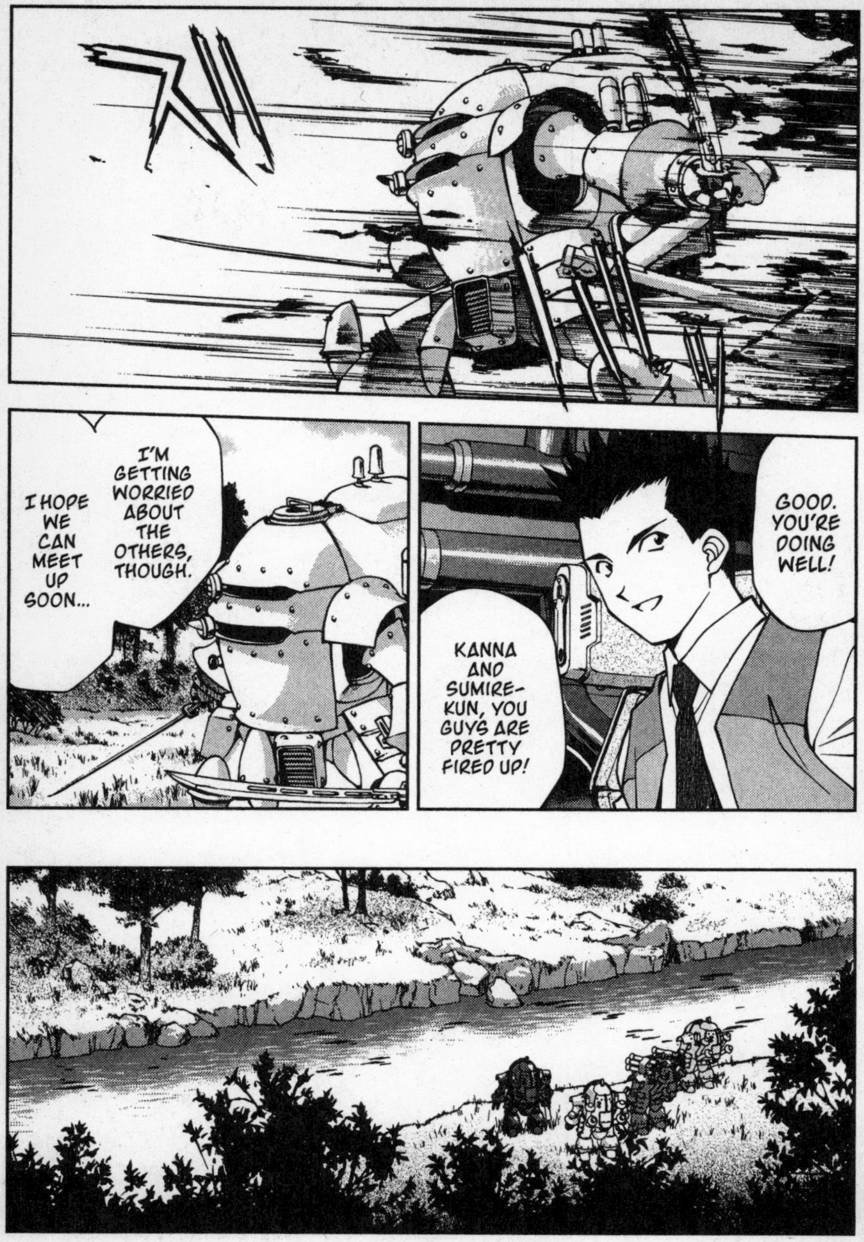
GOOD. YOU'RE DOING WELL!
KANNA AND SUMIRE-KUN, YOU GUYS ARE PRETTY FIRED UP!
I'M GETTING WORRIED ABOUT THE OTHERS, THOUGH.
I HOPE WE CAN MEET UP SOON...

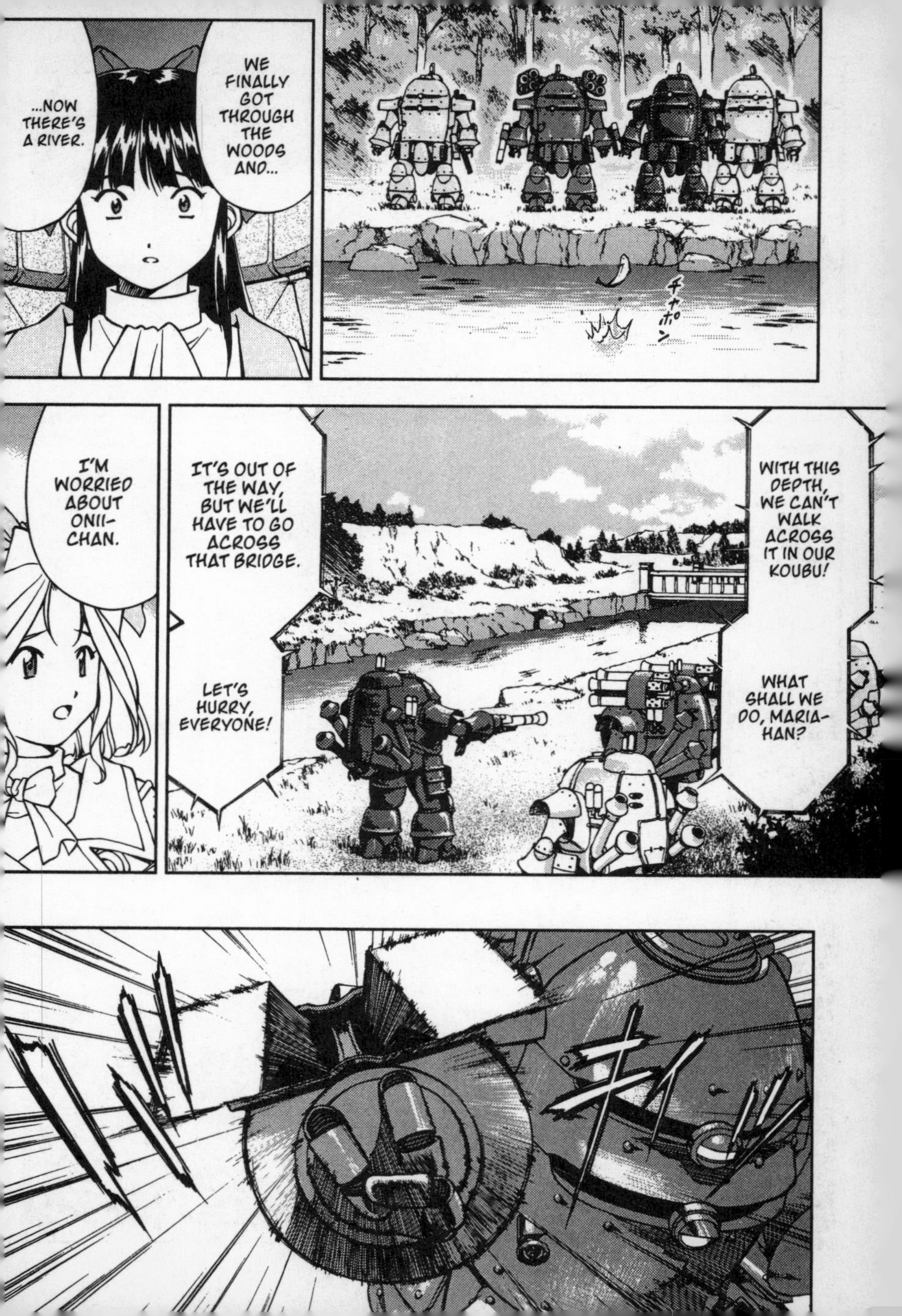
チャポン
WE FINALLY GOT THROUGH THE WOODS AND...
...NOW THERE'S A RIVER.
WITH THIS DEPTH, WE CAN'T WALK ACROSS IT IN OUR KOUBU!
WHAT SHALL WE DO, MARIA-HAN?
IT'S OUT OF THE WAY, BUT WE'LL HAVE TO GO ACROSS THAT BRIDGE.
LET'S HURRY, EVERYONE!
I'M WORRIED ABOUT ONII-CHAN.

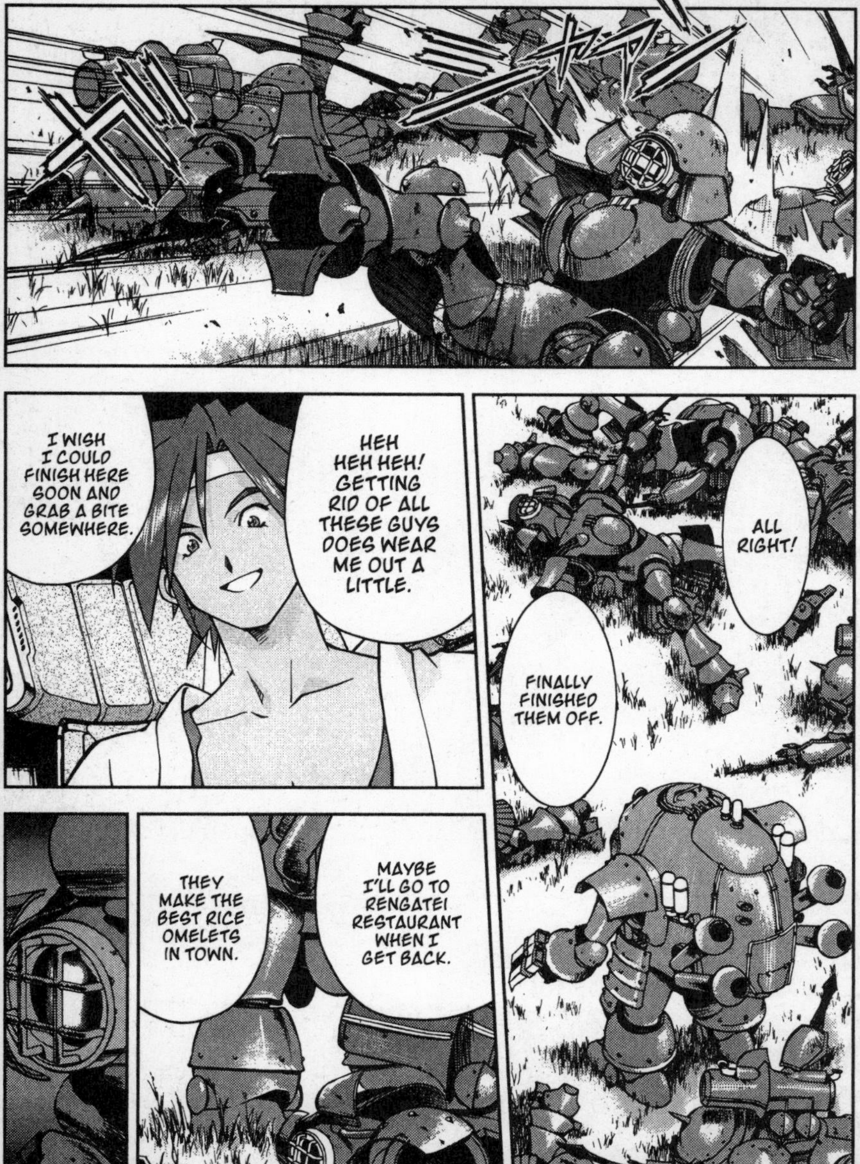
ALL RIGHT!
FINALLY FINISHED THEM OFF.
HEH HEH HEH! GETTING RID OF ALL THESE GUYS DOES WEAR ME OUT A LITTLE.
I WISH I COULD FINISH HERE SOON AND GRAB A BITE SOMEWHERE.
MAYBE I'LL GO TO RENGATEI RESTAURANT WHEN I GET BACK.
THEY MAKE THE BEST RICE OMELETS IN TOWN.

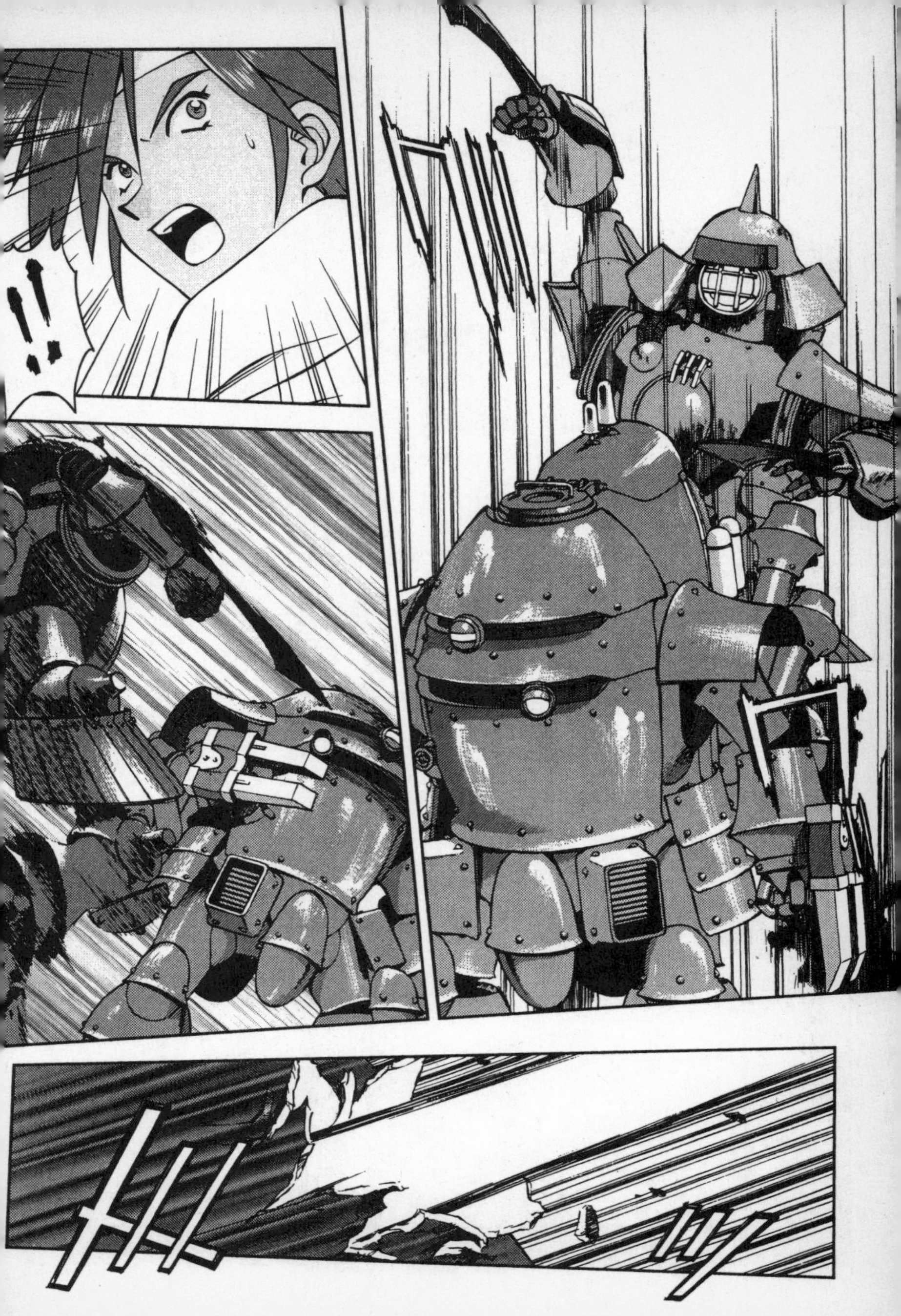
!!

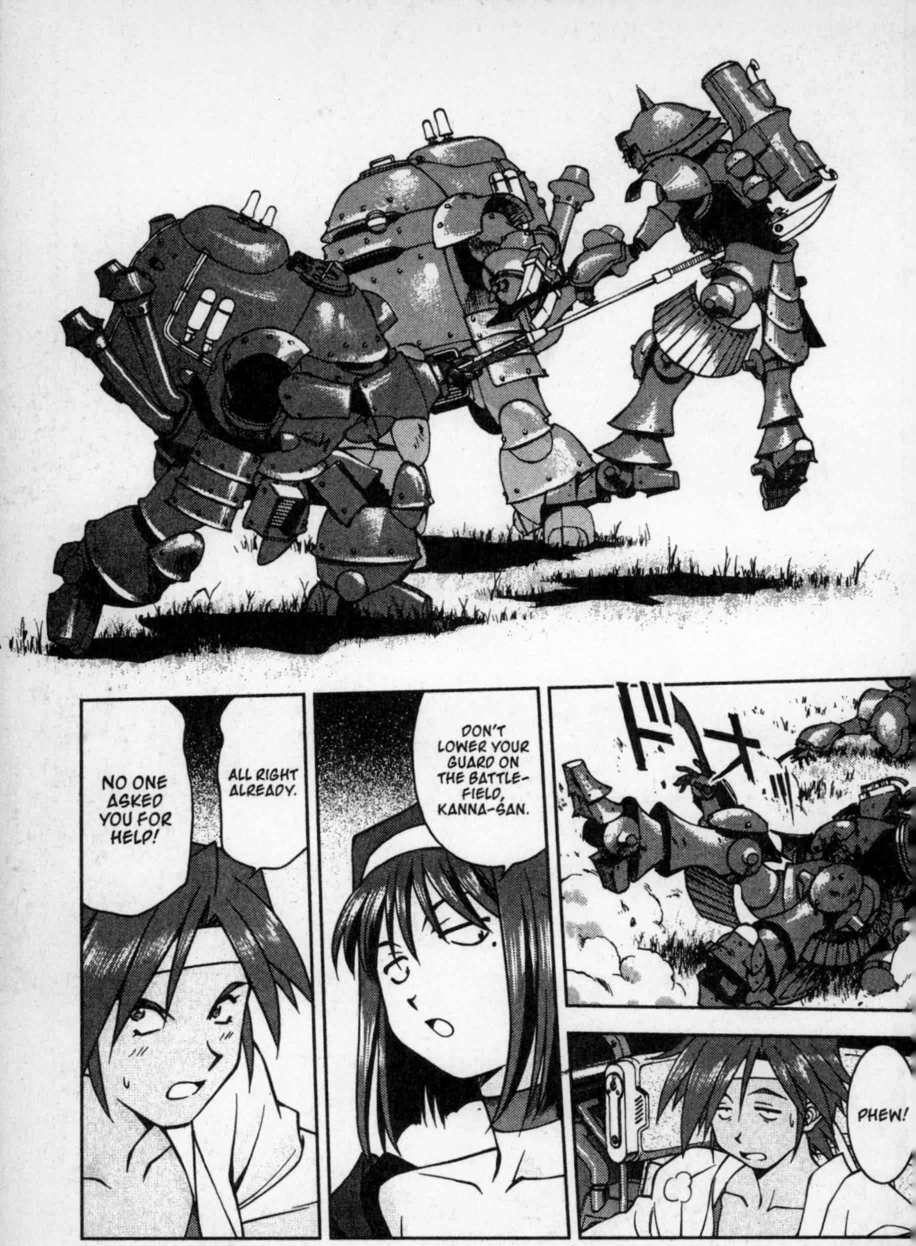
PHEW!
DON'T LOWER YOUR GUARD ON THE BATTLE-FIELD, KANNA-SAN.
ALL RIGHT ALREADY.
NO ONE ASKED YOU FOR HELP!

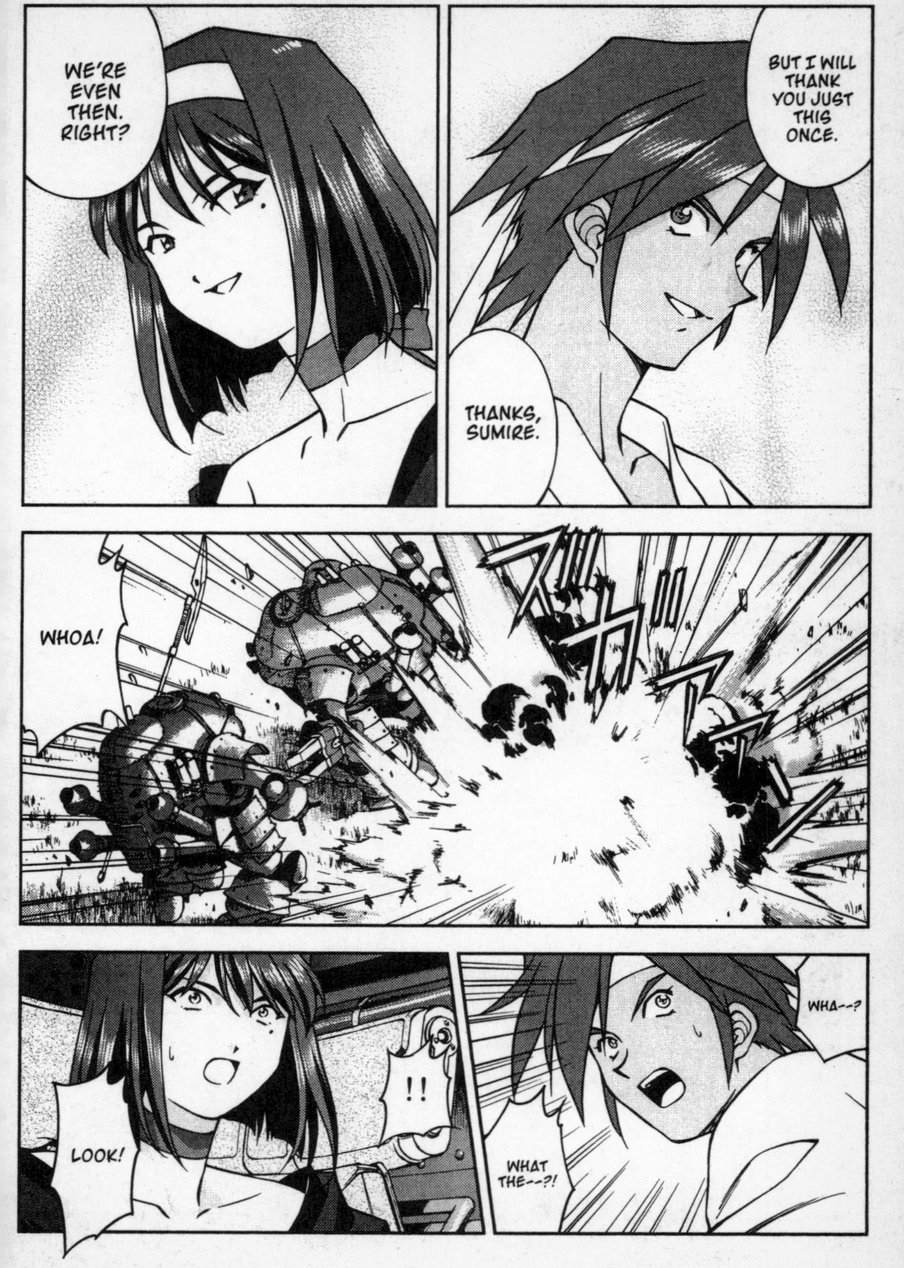
WE'RE EVEN THEN. RIGHT?
BUT I WILL THANK YOU JUST THIS ONCE.
THANKS, SUMIRE.
WHOA!
!!
LOOK!
WHA--?
WHAT THE--?!

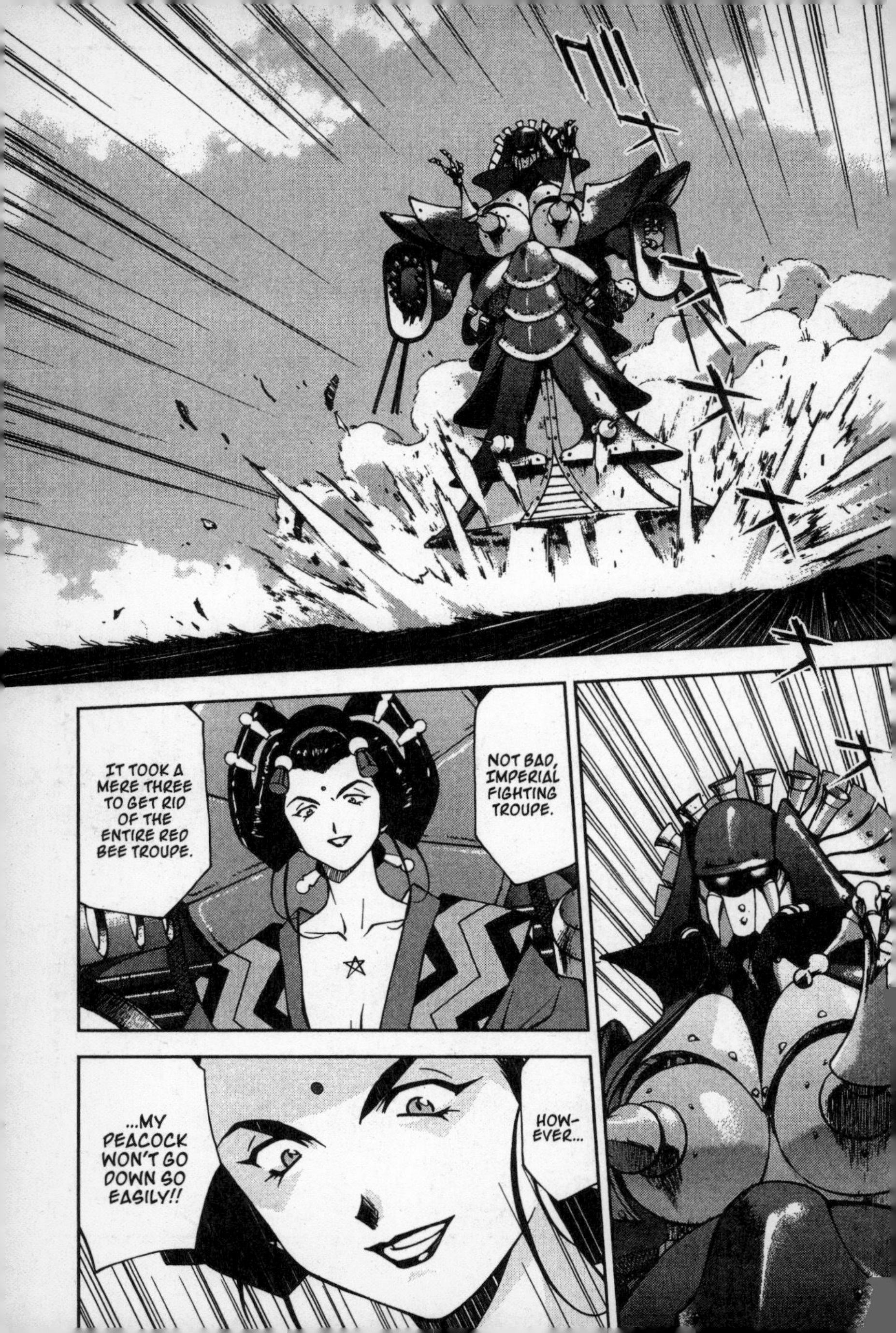
NOT BAD, IMPERIAL FIGHTING TROUPE.
IT TOOK A MERE THREE TO GET RID OF THE ENTIRE RED BEE TROUPE.
HOW-EVER...
...MY PEACOCK WON'T GO DOWN SO EASILY!!

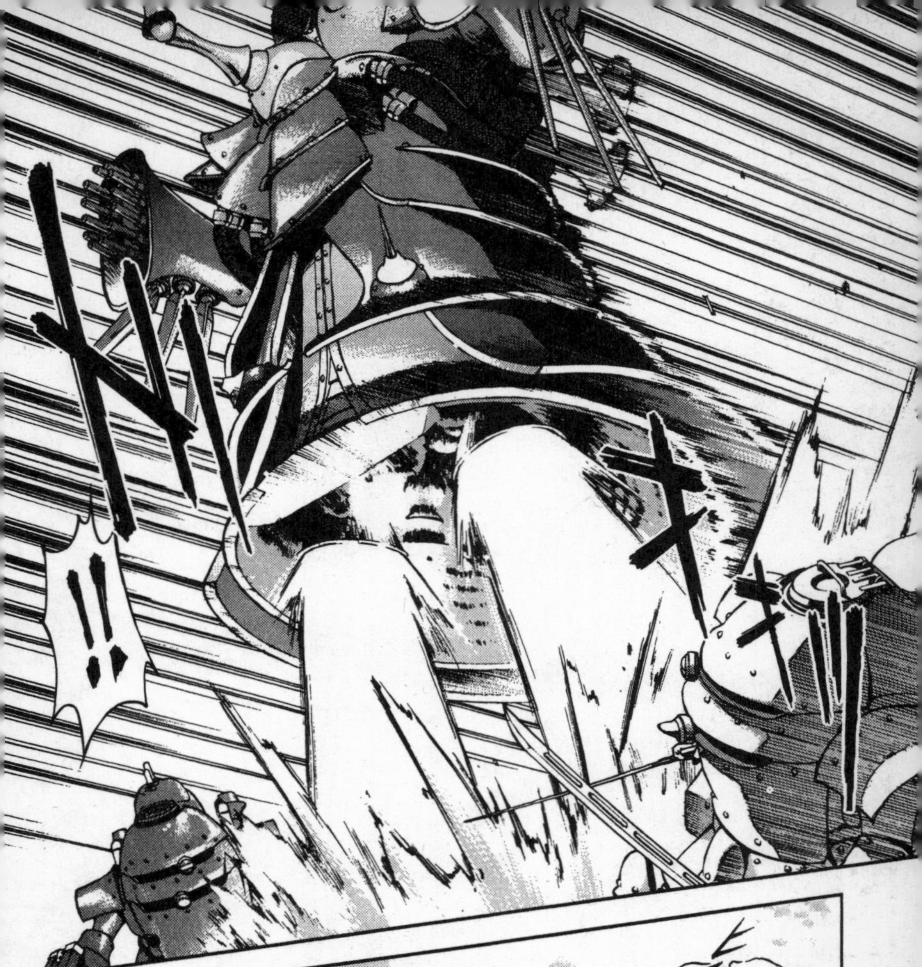
!!
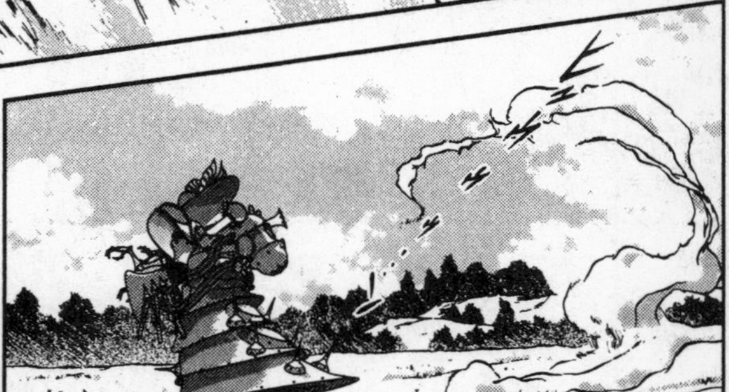
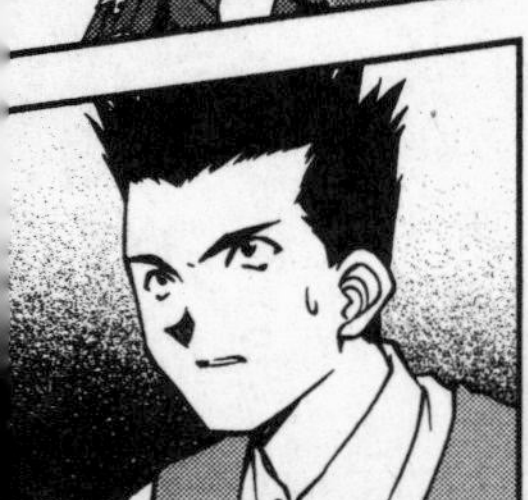
?!

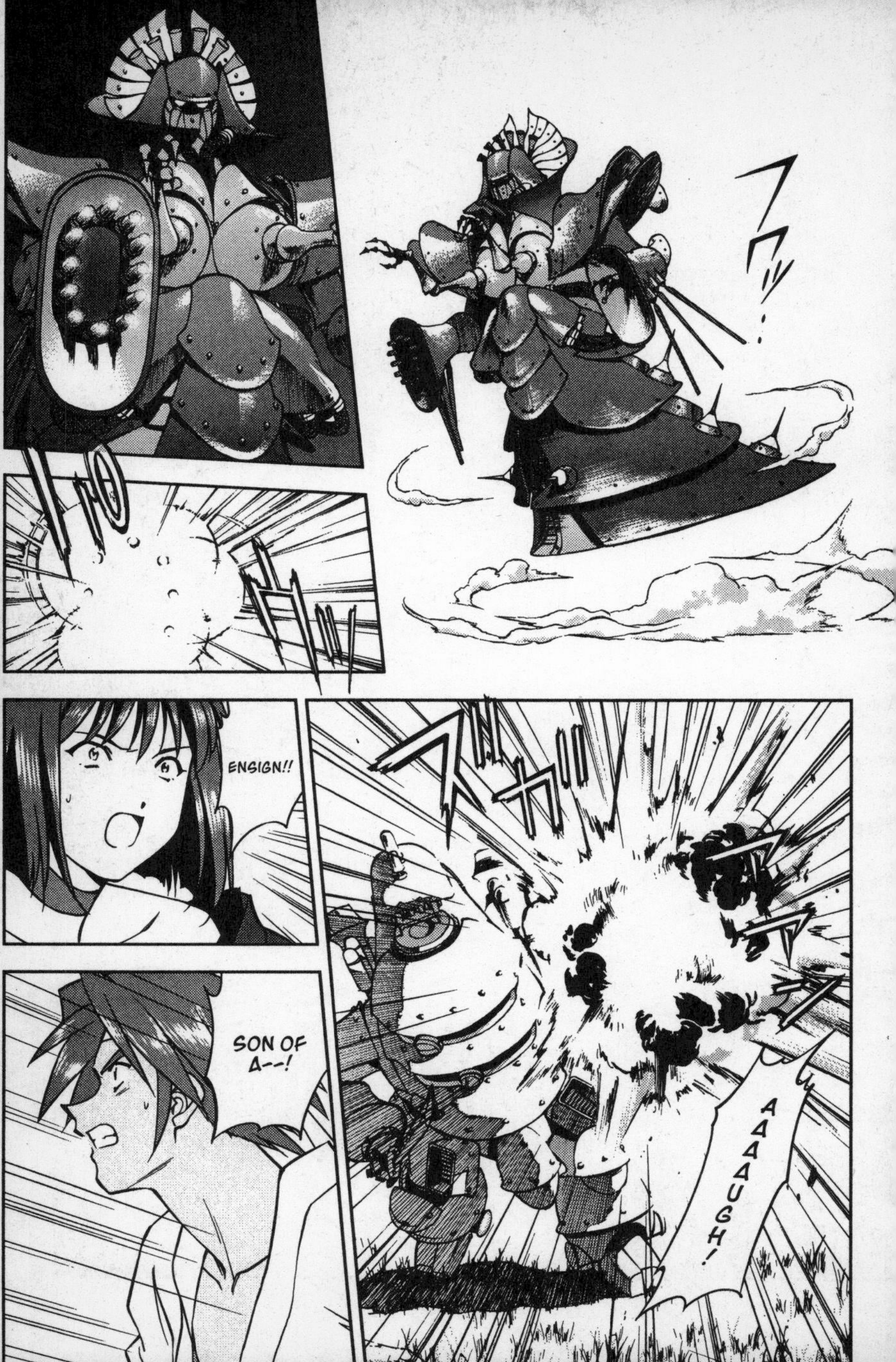
AAAAUGH!
ENSIGN!!
SON OF A--!

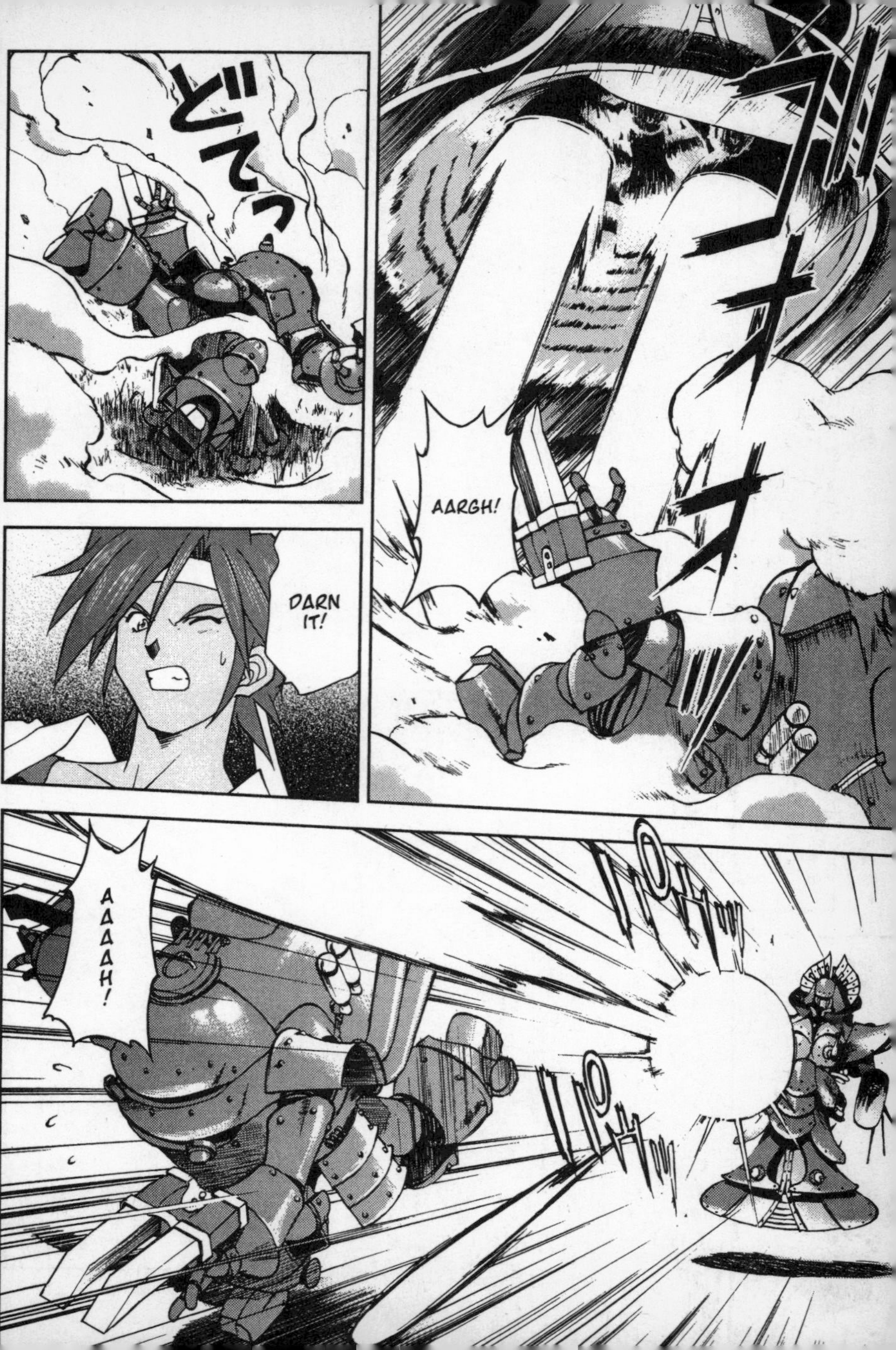
AARGH!
どてっ
DARN IT!
AAAAH!

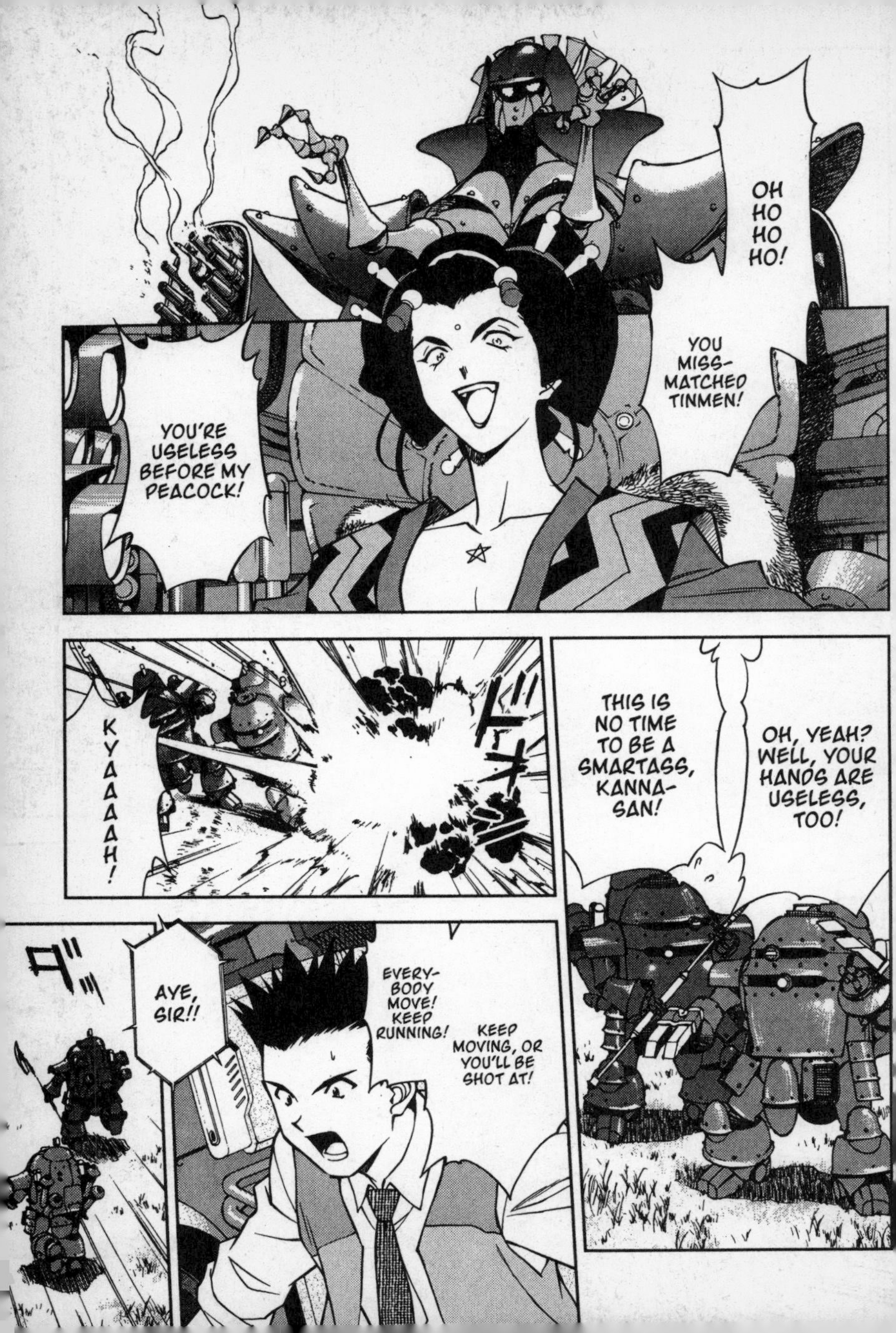
OH HO HO HO!
YOU MISS-MATCHED TINMEN!
YOU'RE USELESS BEFORE MY PEACOCK!
THIS IS NO TIME TO BE A SMARTASS, KANNA-SAN!
OH, YEAH? WELL, YOUR HANDS ARE USELESS, TOO!
KYAAAAAH!
EVERY-BODY MOVE! KEEP RUNNING!
KEEP MOVING, OR YOU'LL BE SHOT AT!
AYE, SIR!!

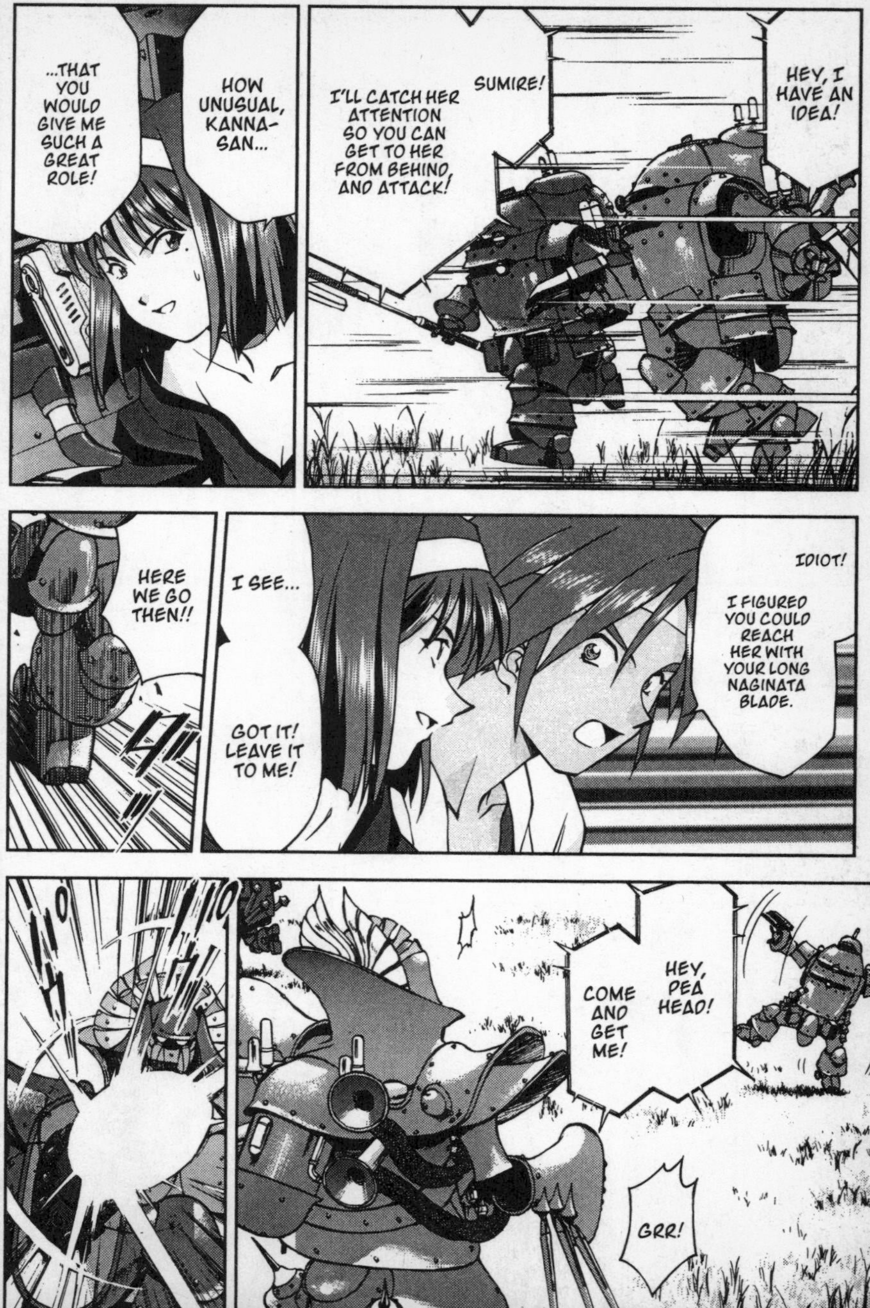
HEY, I HAVE AN IDEA!
SUMIRE!
I'LL CATCH HER ATTENTION SO YOU CAN GET TO HER FROM BEHIND AND ATTACK!
HOW UNUSUAL, KANNA-SAN...
...THAT YOU WOULD GIVE ME SUCH A GREAT ROLE!
IDIOT!
I FIGURED YOU COULD REACH HER WITH YOUR LONG NAGINATA BLADE.
I SEE...
GOT IT! LEAVE IT TO ME!
HERE WE GO THEN!!
HEY, PEA HEAD!
COME AND GET ME!
GRR!

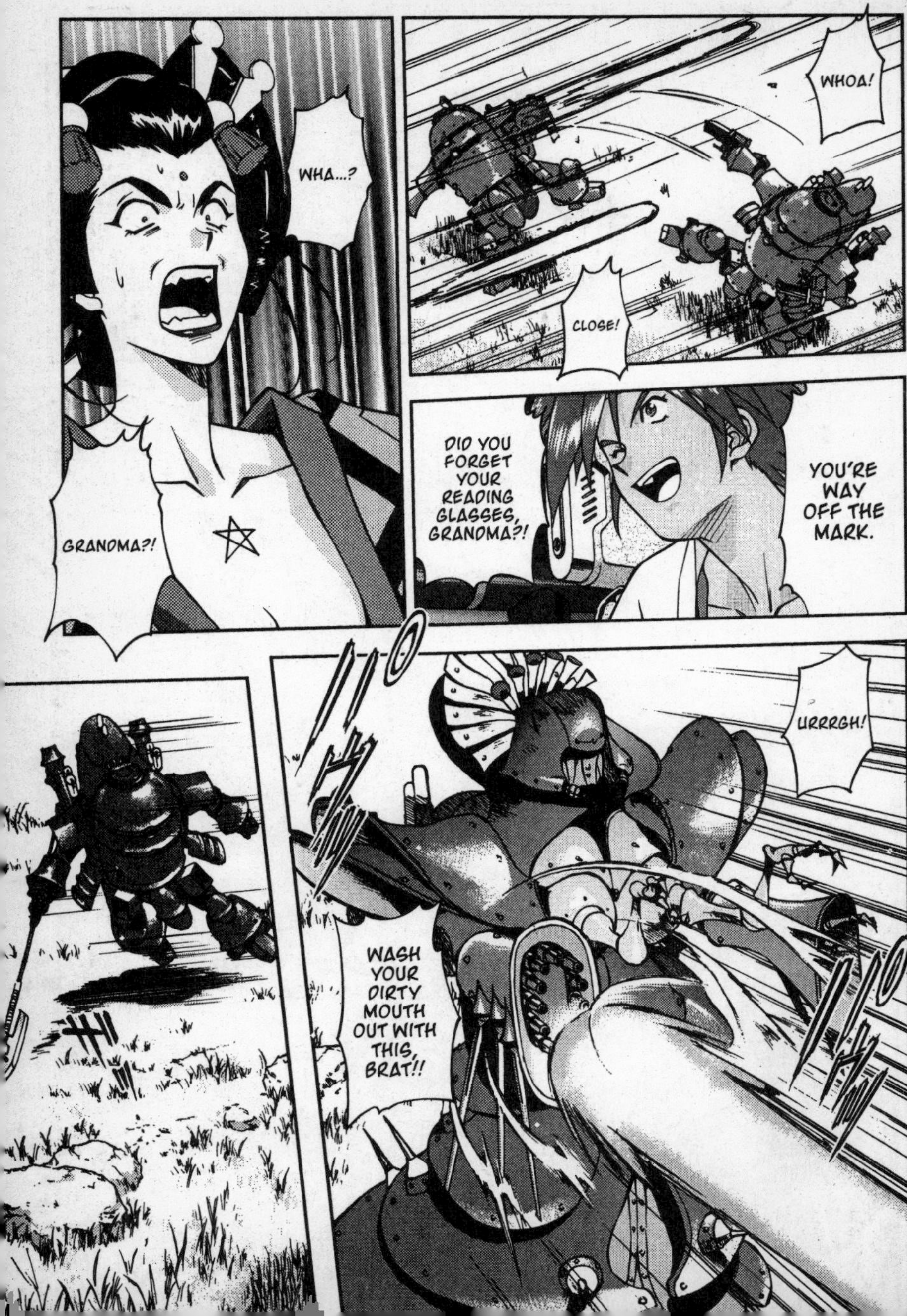
WHOA!
CLOSE!
YOU'RE WAY OFF THE MARK.
DID YOU FORGET YOUR READING GLASSES, GRANDMA?!
WHA...?
GRANDMA?!
URRRGH!
WASH YOUR DIRTY MOUTH OUT WITH THIS, BRAT!!

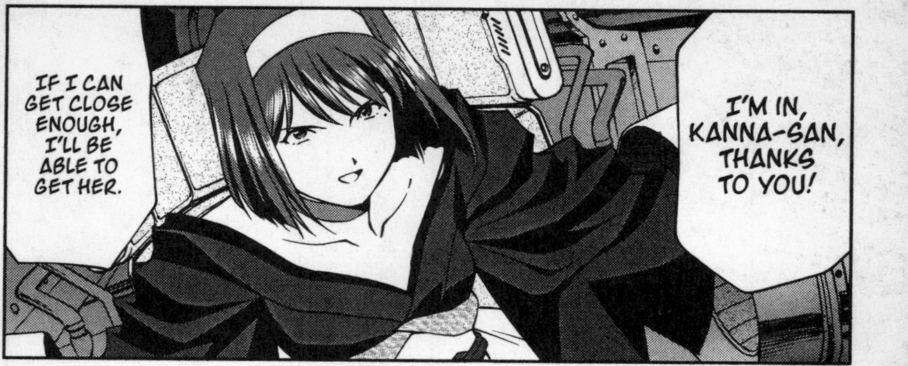
I'M IN, KANNA-SAN, THANKS TO YOU!
IF I CAN GET CLOSE ENOUGH, I'LL BE ABLE TO GET HER.

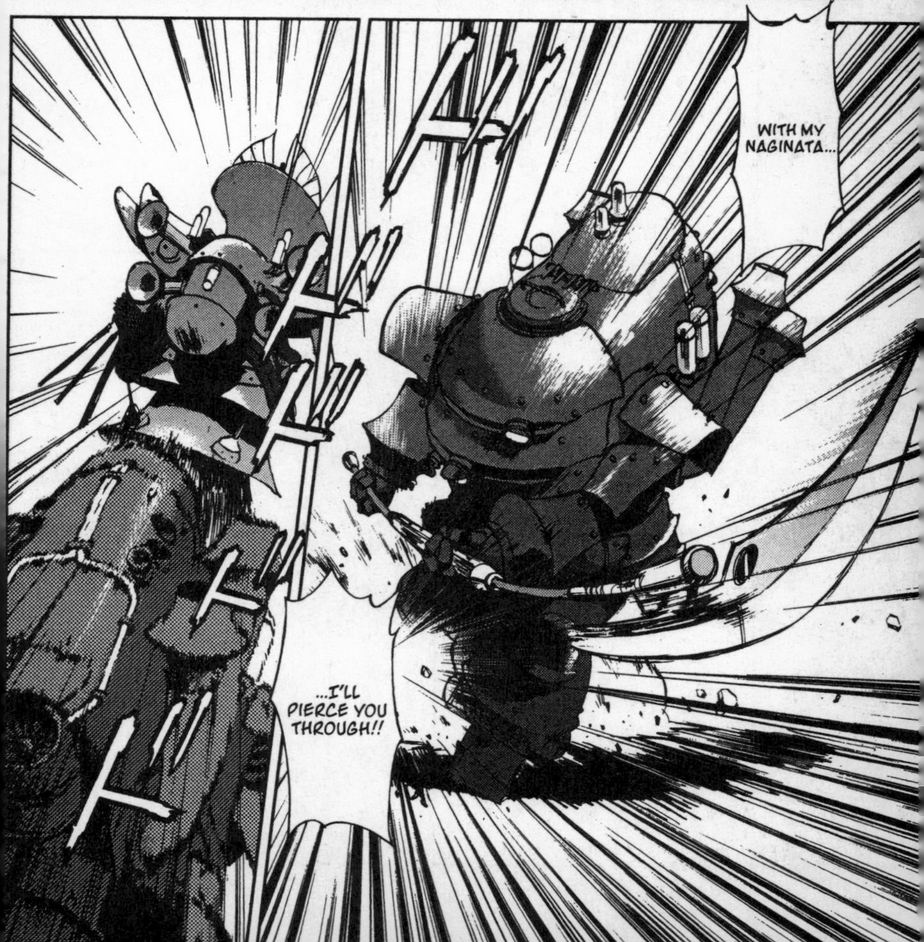
WITH MY NAGINATA...
...I'LL PIERCE YOU THROUGH!!

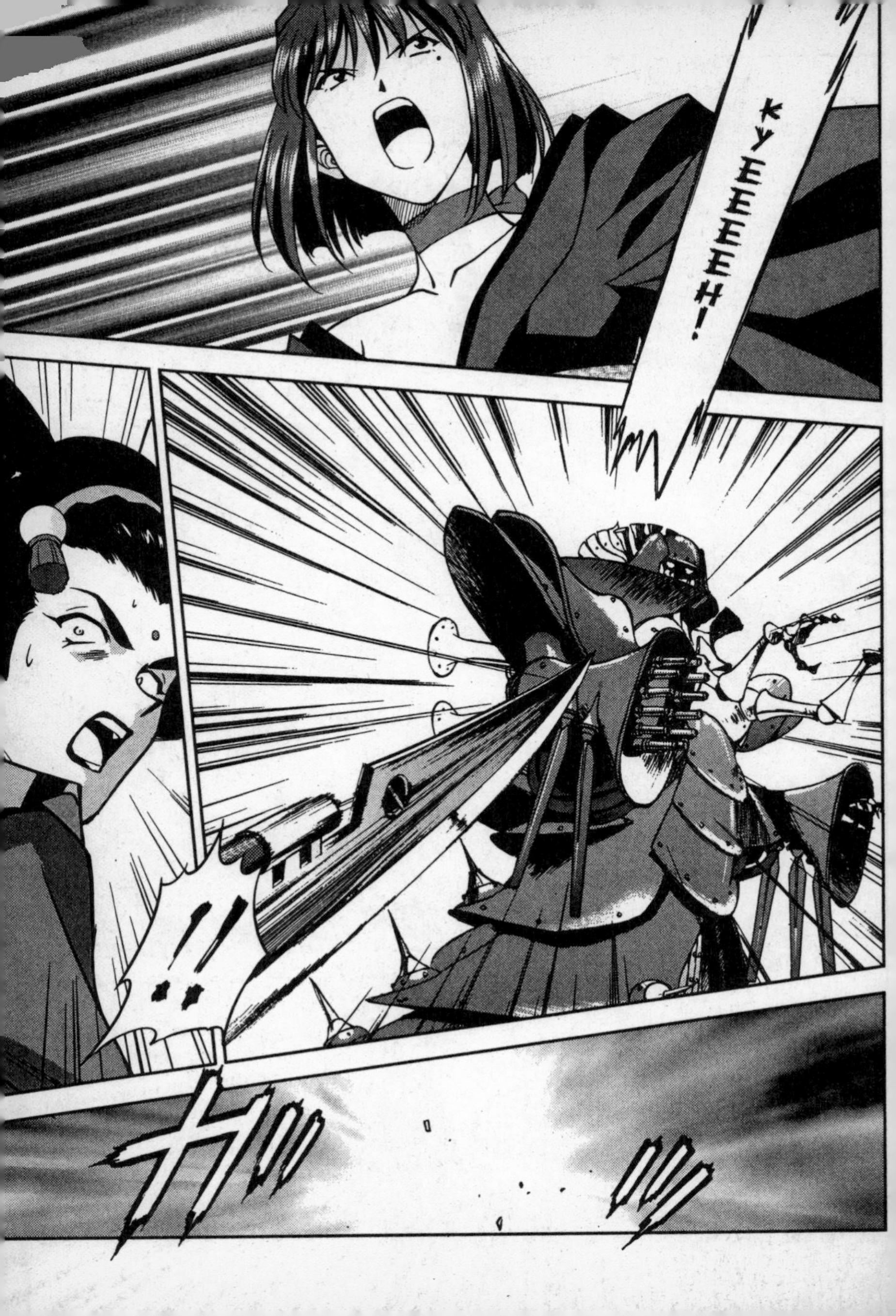
KYEEEEEH!
!!

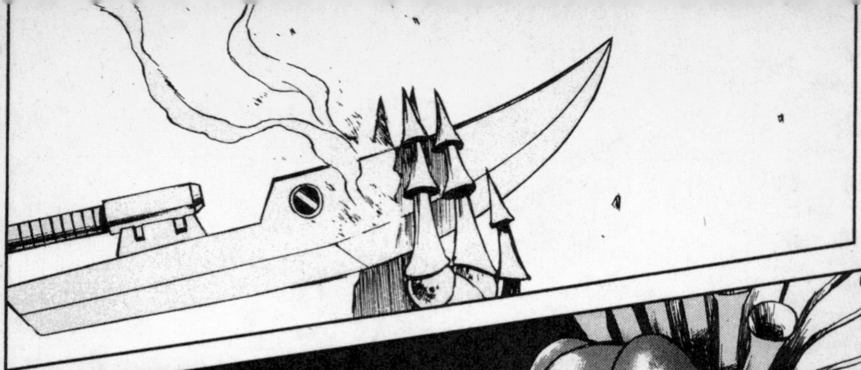
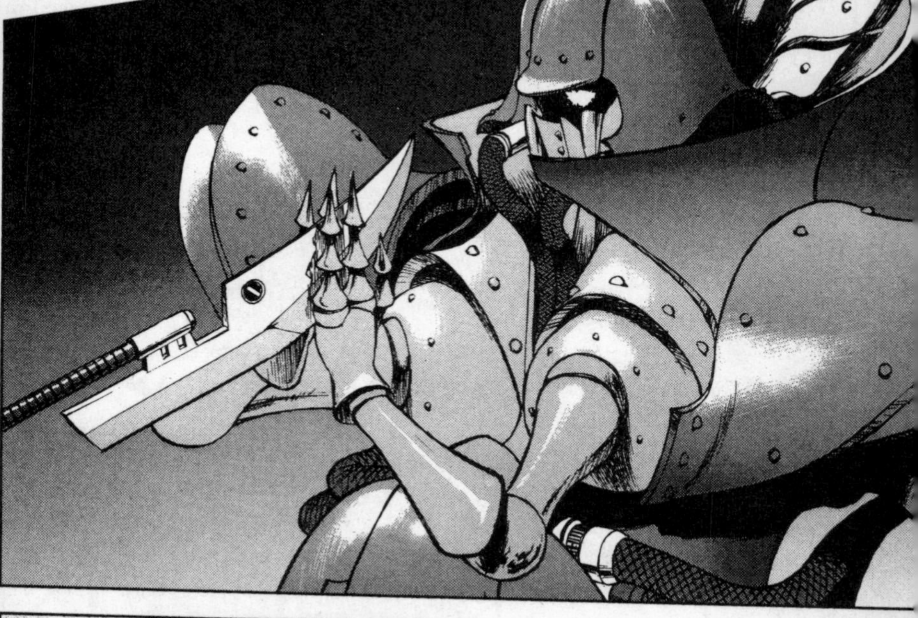
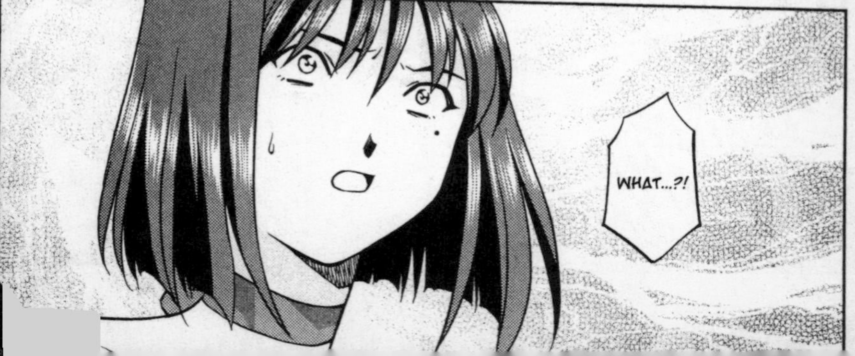
WHAT...?!

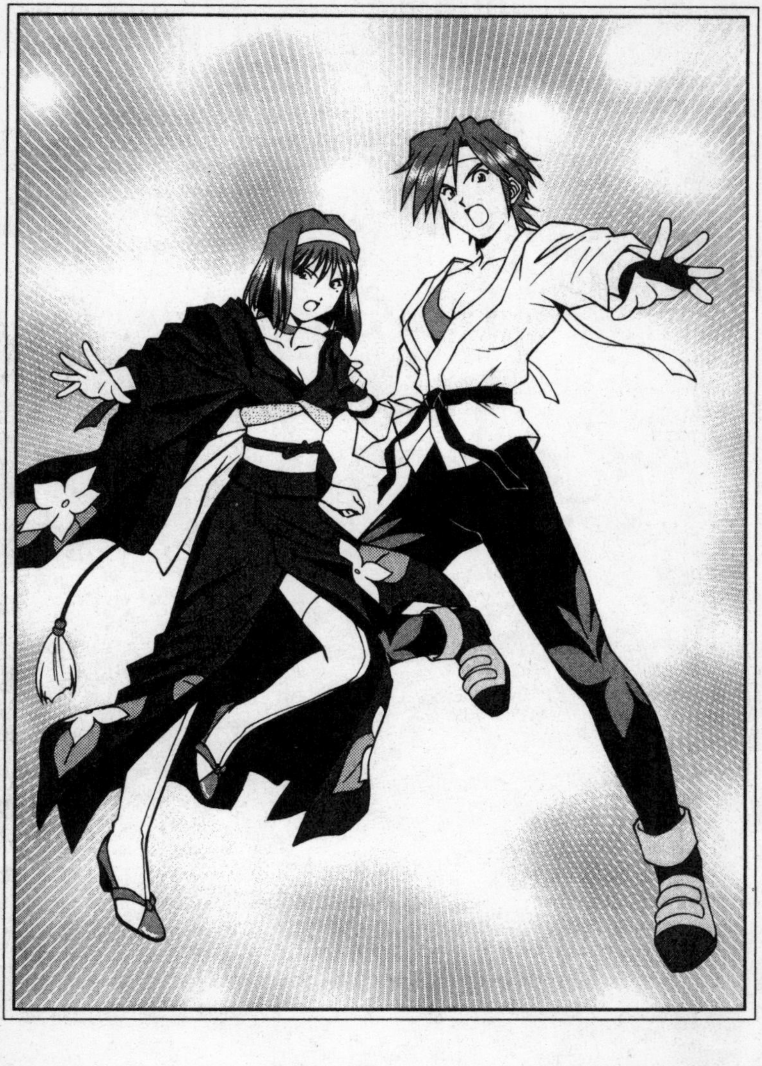

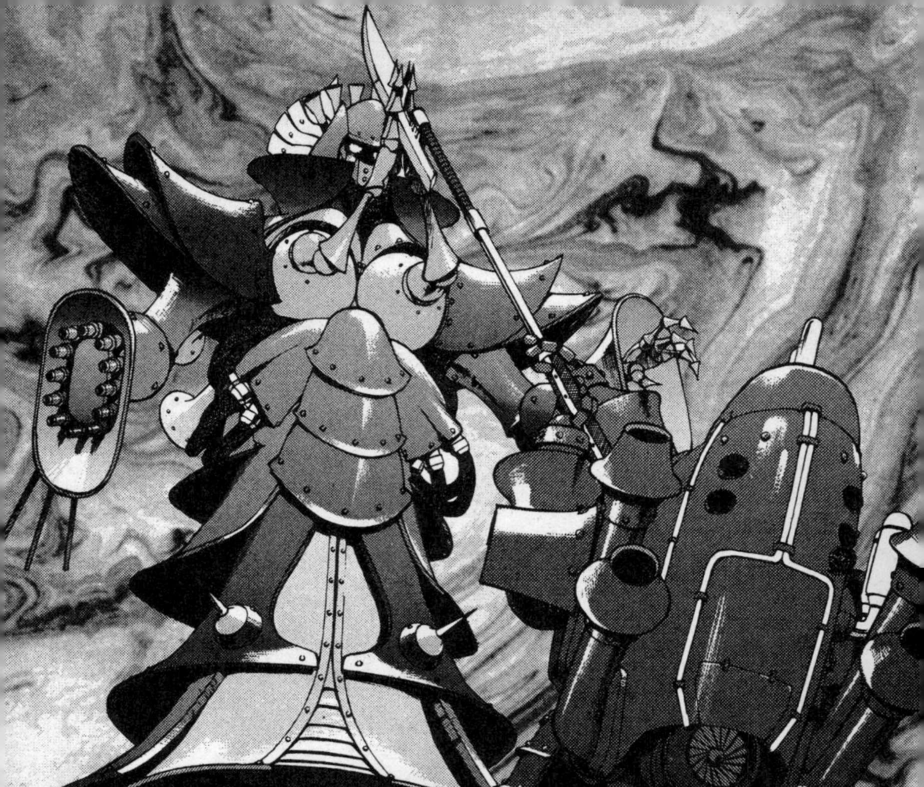

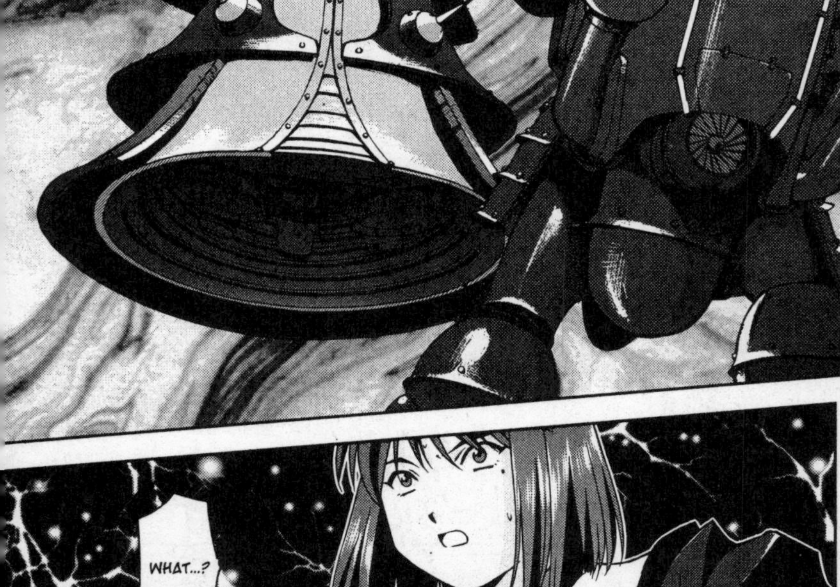
WHAT...?

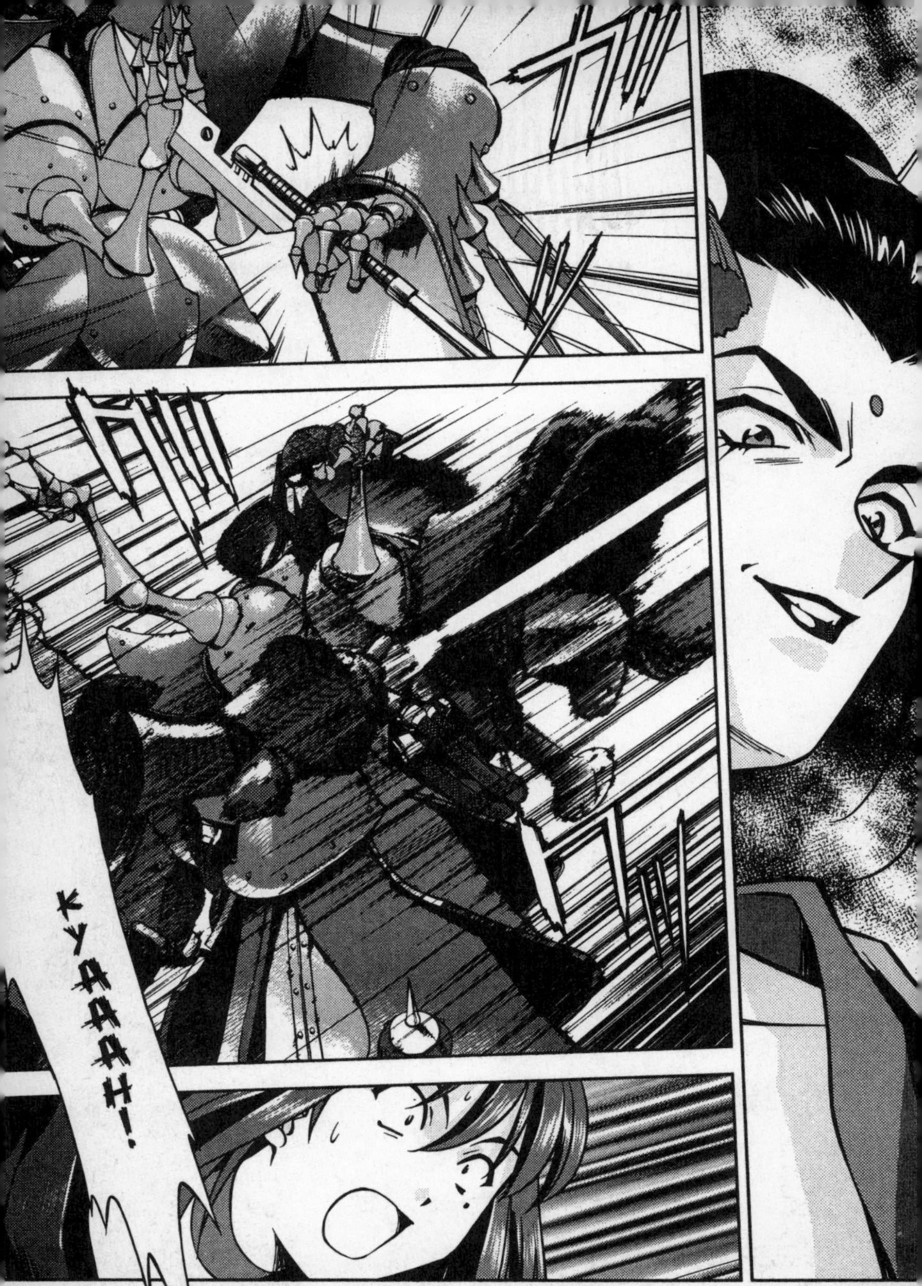
KYAAAH!

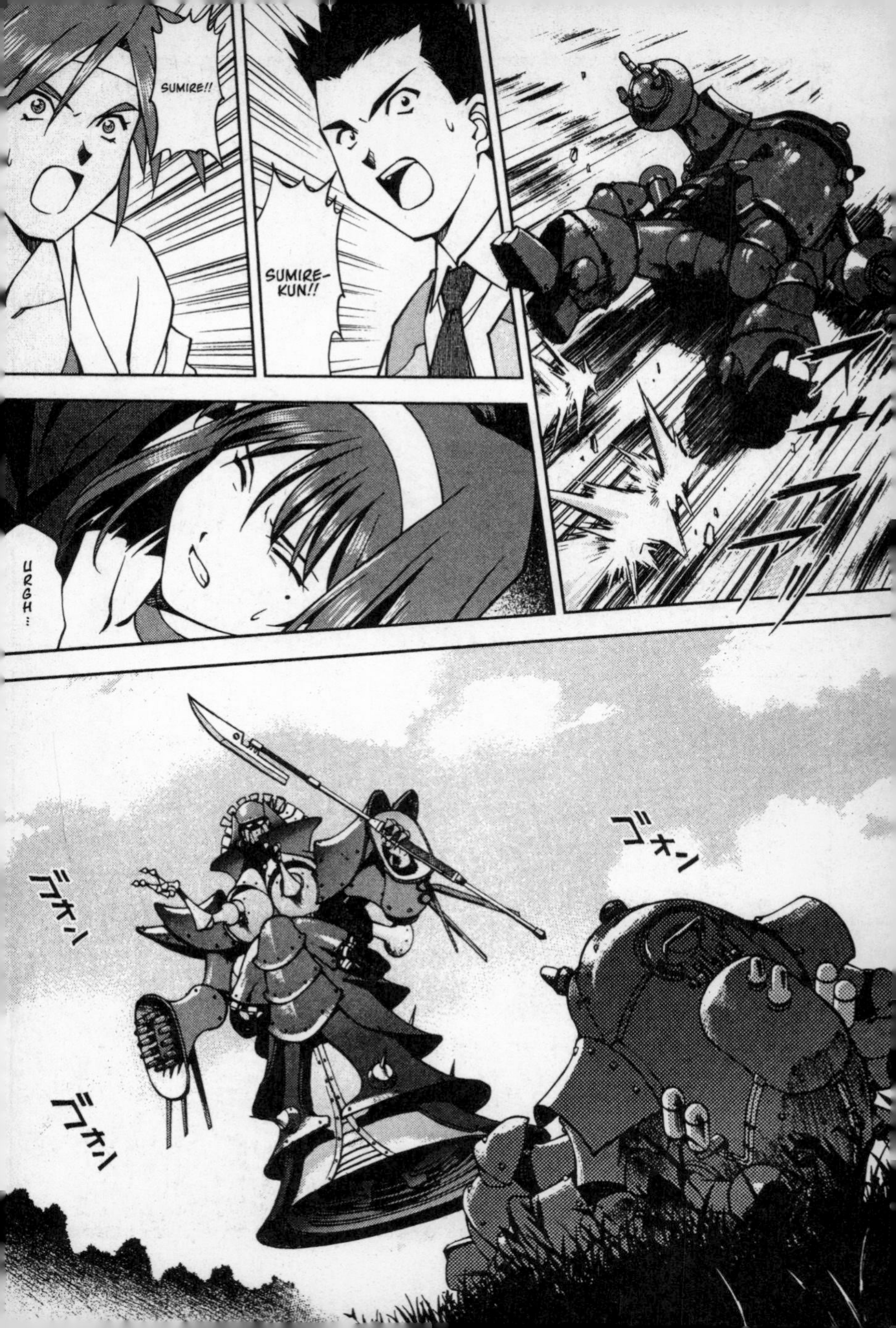
SUMIRE-KUN!!
SUMIRE!!
URGH...
ゴオン
ゴオン
ゴオン

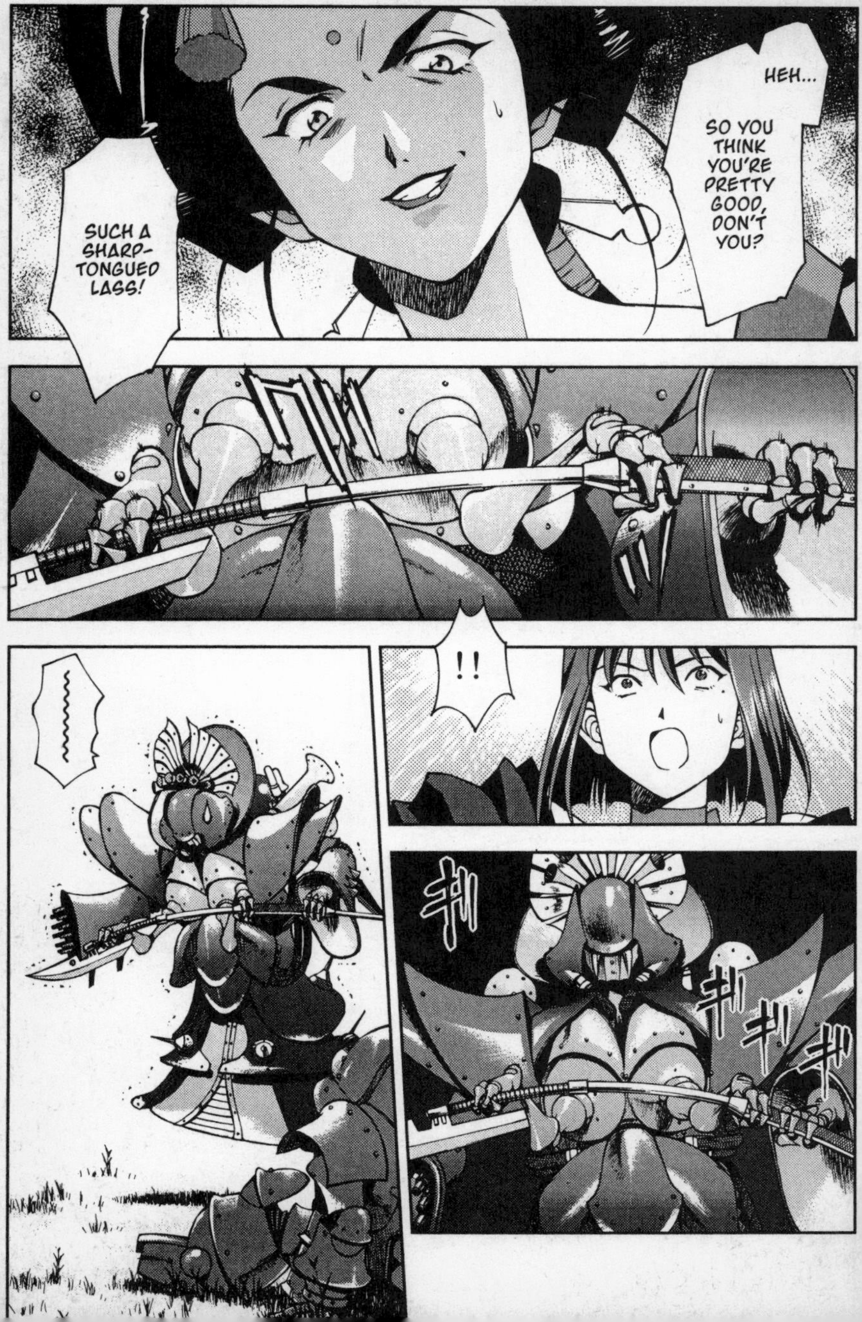
HEH...
SO YOU THINK YOU'RE PRETTY GOOD, DON'T YOU?
SUCH A SHARP-TONGUED LASS!
!!
ギリ
ギリ
ギリ
ギ

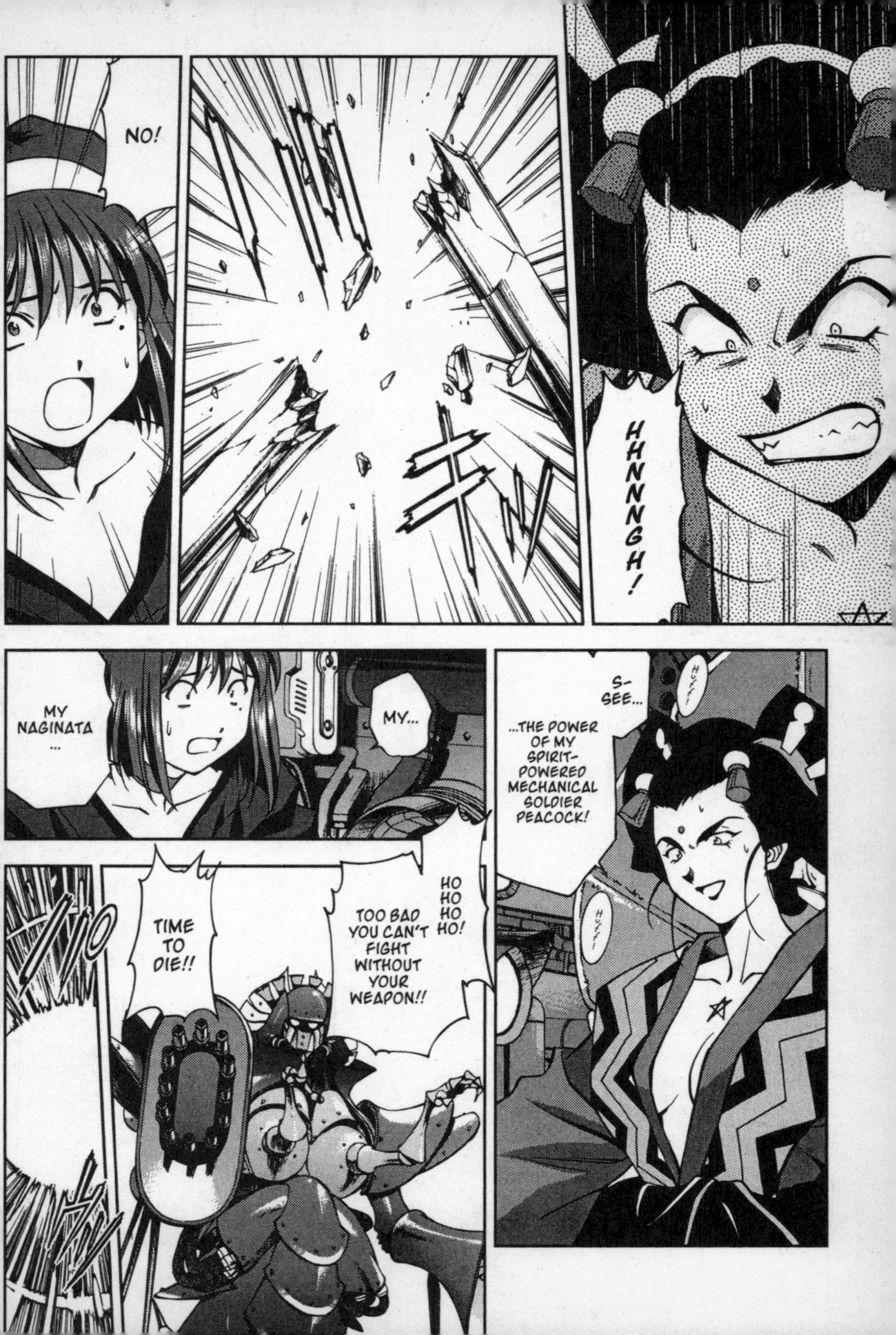
HHNNNGH!
キン
NO!
Huff!
S-SEE...
...THE POWER OF MY SPIRIT-POWERED MECHANICAL SOLDIER PEACOCK!
Huff!
MY...
MY NAGINATA ...
HO HO HO HO HO!
TOO BAD YOU CAN'T FIGHT WITHOUT YOUR WEAPON!!
TIME TO DIE!!

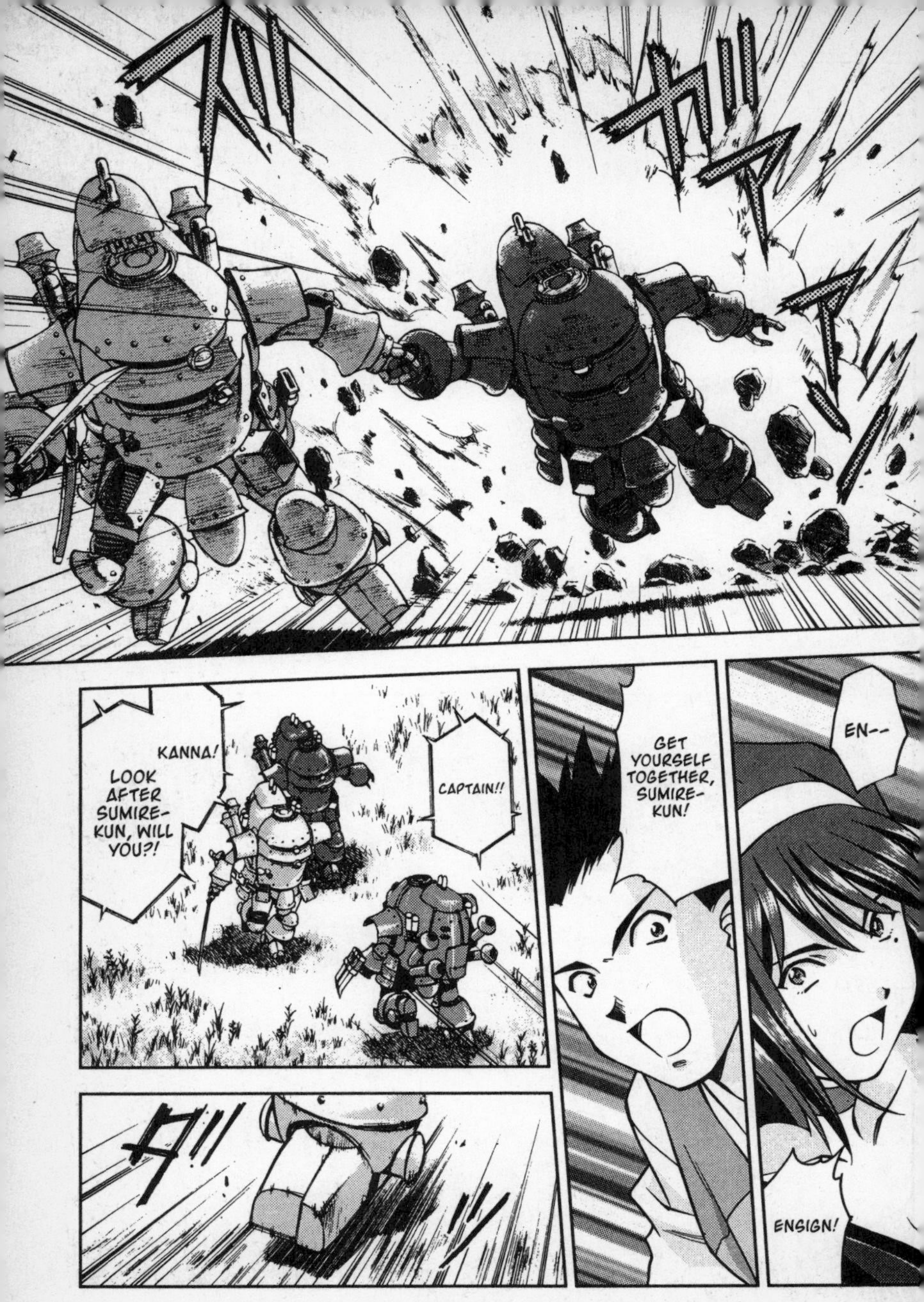
EN--
ENSIGN!
GET YOURSELF TOGETHER, SUMIRE-KUN!
KANNA! LOOK AFTER SUMIRE-KUN, WILL YOU?!
CAPTAIN!!

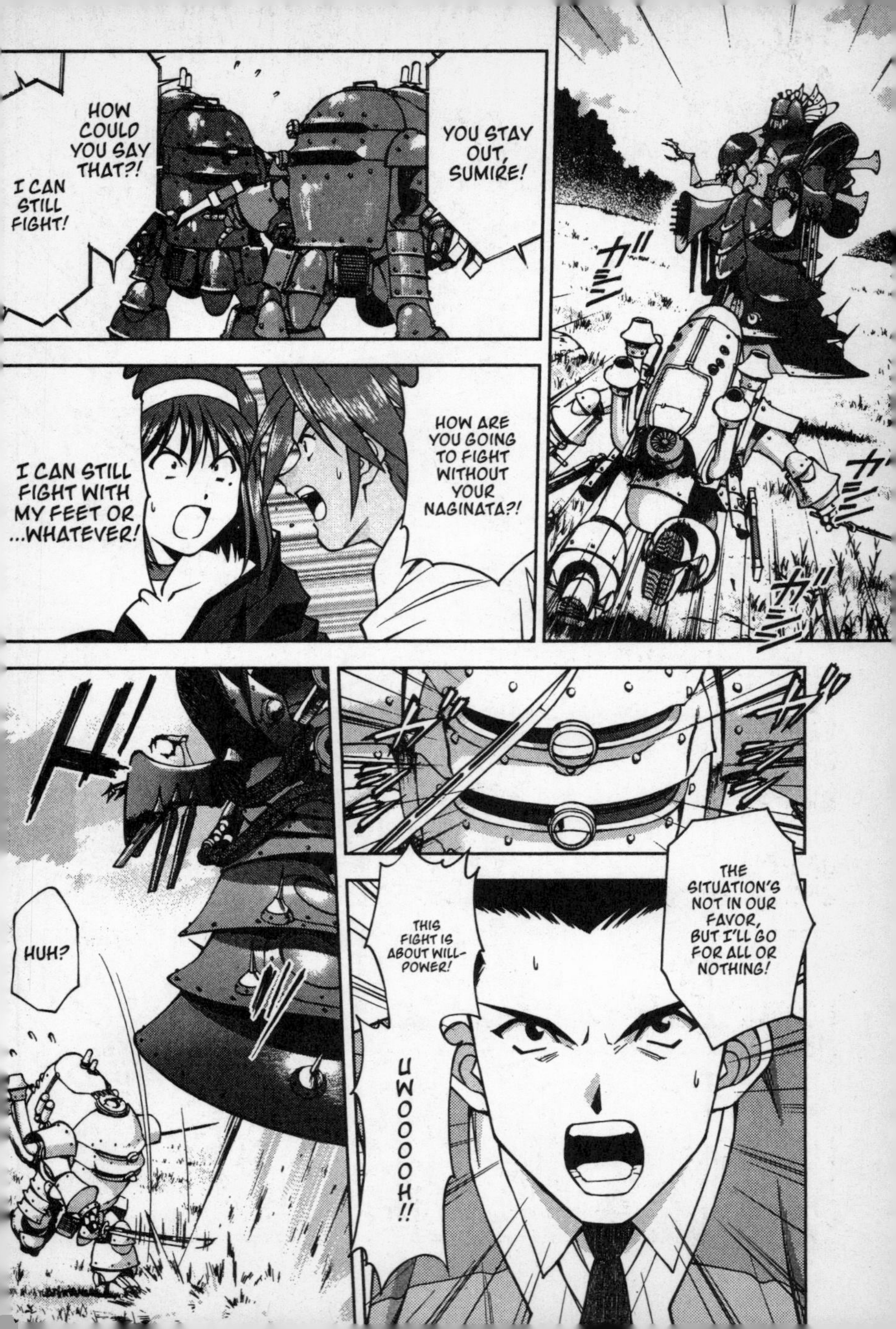
YOU STAY OUT, SUMIRE!
HOW COULD YOU SAY THAT?!
I CAN STILL FIGHT!
HOW ARE YOU GOING TO FIGHT WITHOUT YOUR NAGINATA?!
I CAN STILL FIGHT WITH MY FEET OR ...WHATEVER!
THE SITUATION'S NOT IN OUR FAVOR, BUT I'LL GO FOR ALL OR NOTHING!
THIS FIGHT IS ABOUT WILL-POWER!
UWOOOOOH!!
HUH?

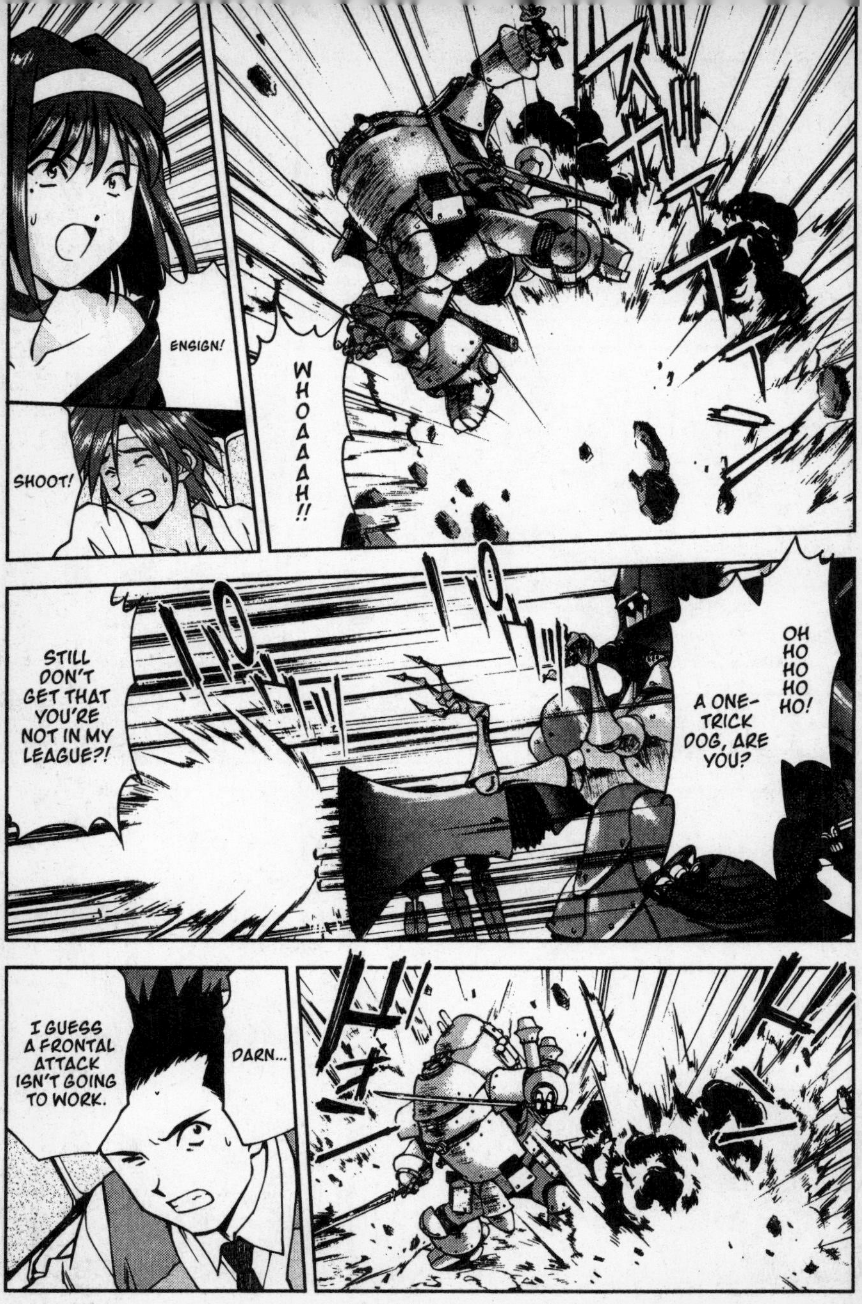
WHOAAAAH!!
ENSIGN!
SHOOT!
OH HO HO HO HO!
A ONE-TRICK DOG, ARE YOU?
STILL DON'T GET THAT YOU'RE NOT IN MY LEAGUE?!
DARN...
I GUESS A FRONTAL ATTACK ISN'T GOING TO WORK.

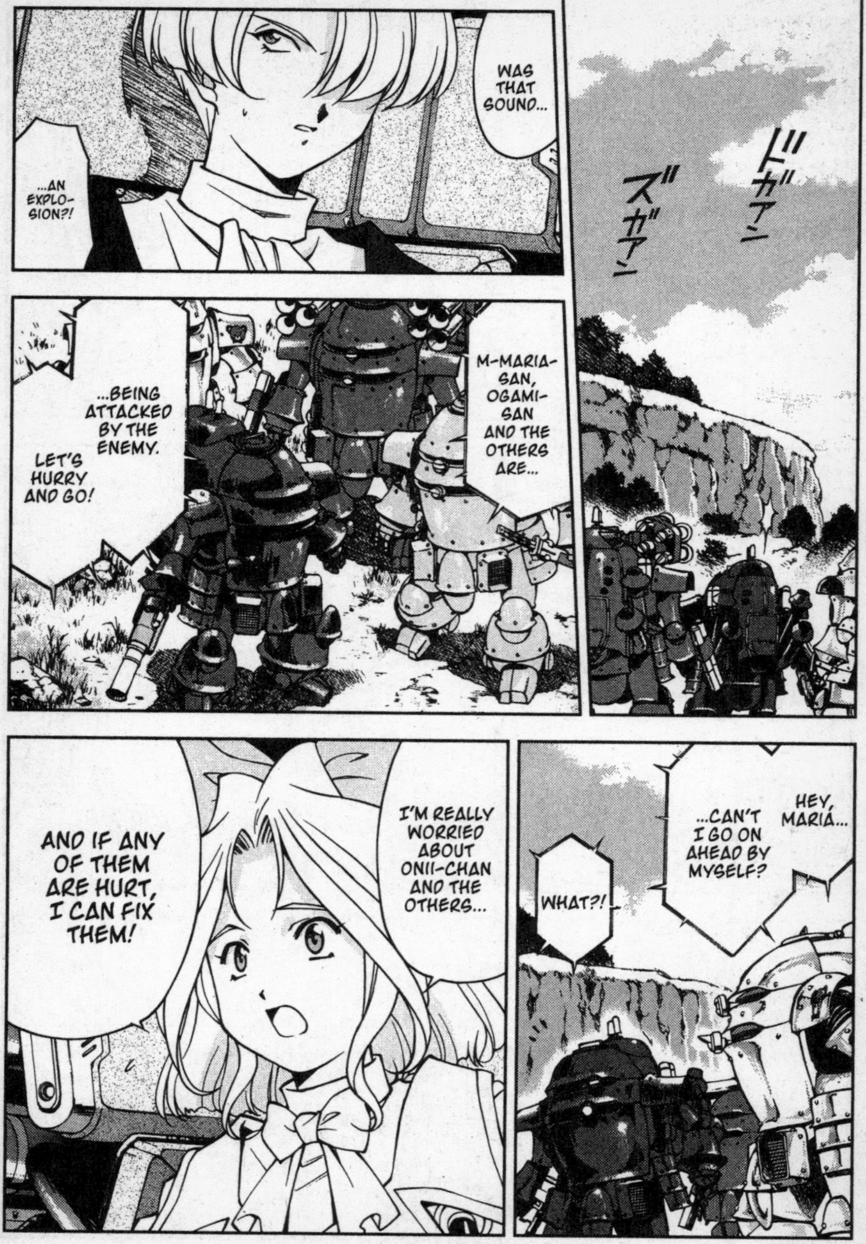
ドガァン
ズガァン
WAS THAT SOUND...
...AN EXPLOSION?!
M-MARIA-SAN, OGAMI-SAN AND THE OTHERS ARE...
...BEING ATTACKED BY THE ENEMY.
LET'S HURRY AND GO!
HEY, MARIA...
...CAN'T I GO ON AHEAD BY MYSELF?
WHAT?!
I'M REALLY WORRIED ABOUT ONII-CHAN AND THE OTHERS...
AND IF ANY OF THEM ARE HURT, I CAN FIX THEM!

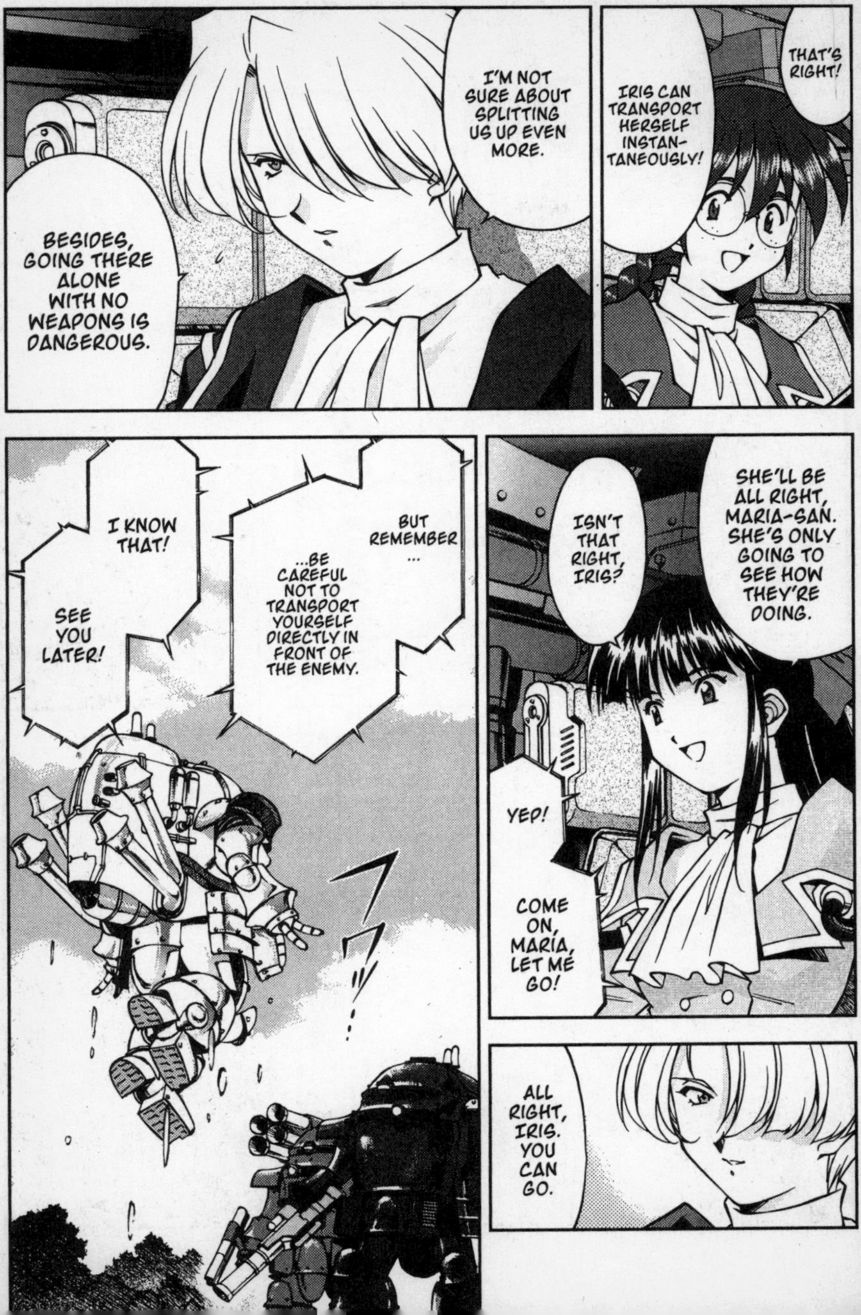
THAT'S RIGHT!
IRIS CAN TRANSPORT HERSELF INSTANTANEOUSLY!
I'M NOT SURE ABOUT SPLITTING US UP EVEN MORE.
BESIDES, GOING THERE ALONE WITH NO WEAPONS IS DANGEROUS.
SHE'LL BE ALL RIGHT, MARIA-SAN. SHE'S ONLY GOING TO SEE HOW THEY'RE DOING.
ISN'T THAT RIGHT, IRIS?
YEP!
COME ON, MARIA, LET ME GO!
ALL RIGHT, IRIS. YOU CAN GO.
BUT REMEMBER ...
...BE CAREFUL NOT TO TRANSPORT YOURSELF DIRECTLY IN FRONT OF THE ENEMY.
I KNOW THAT!
SEE YOU LATER!

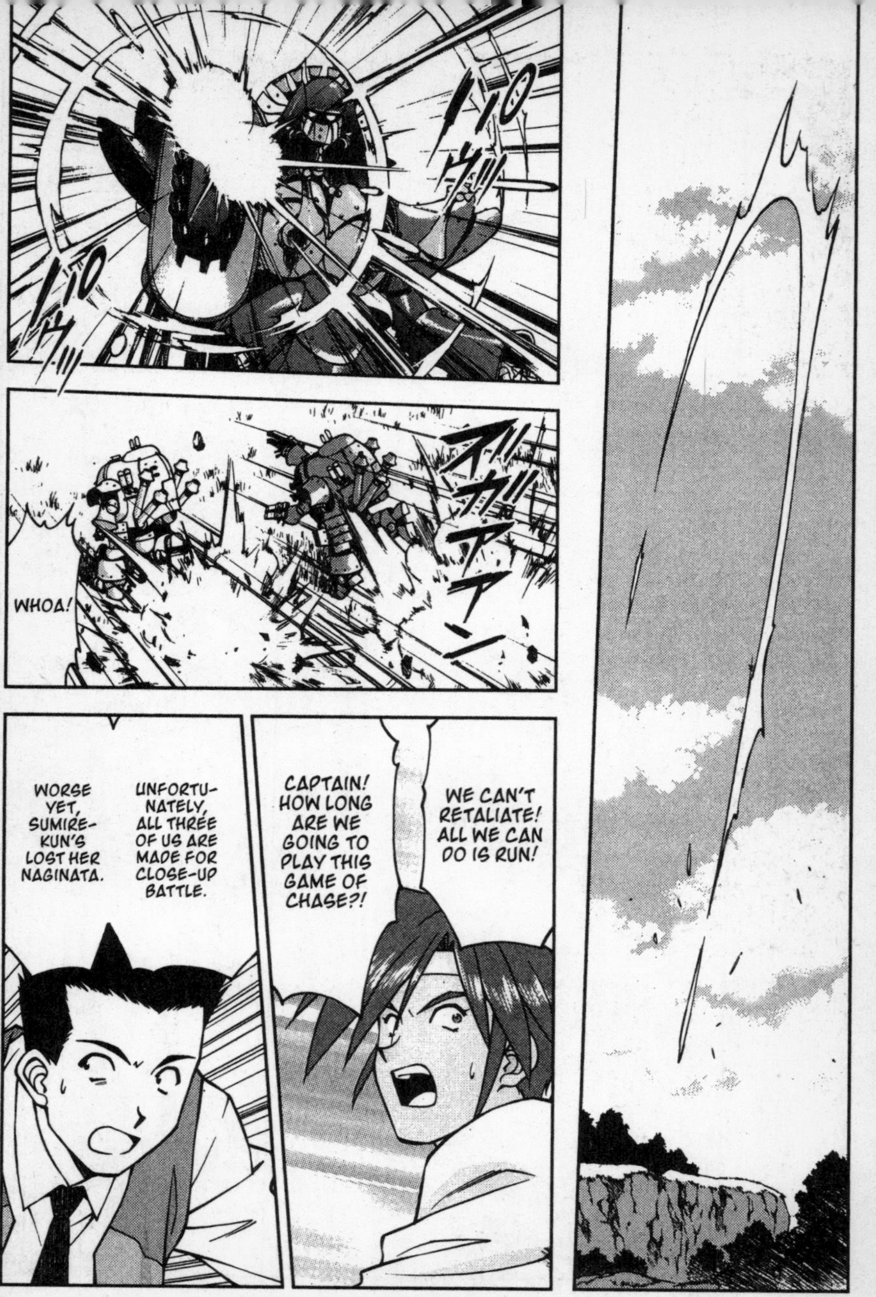
WHOA!
WE CAN'T RETALIATE! ALL WE CAN DO IS RUN!
CAPTAIN! HOW LONG ARE WE GOING TO PLAY THIS GAME OF CHASE?!
UNFORTU- NATELY, ALL THREE OF US ARE MADE FOR CLOSE-UP BATTLE.
WORSE YET, SUMIRE- KUN'S LOST HER NAGINATA.

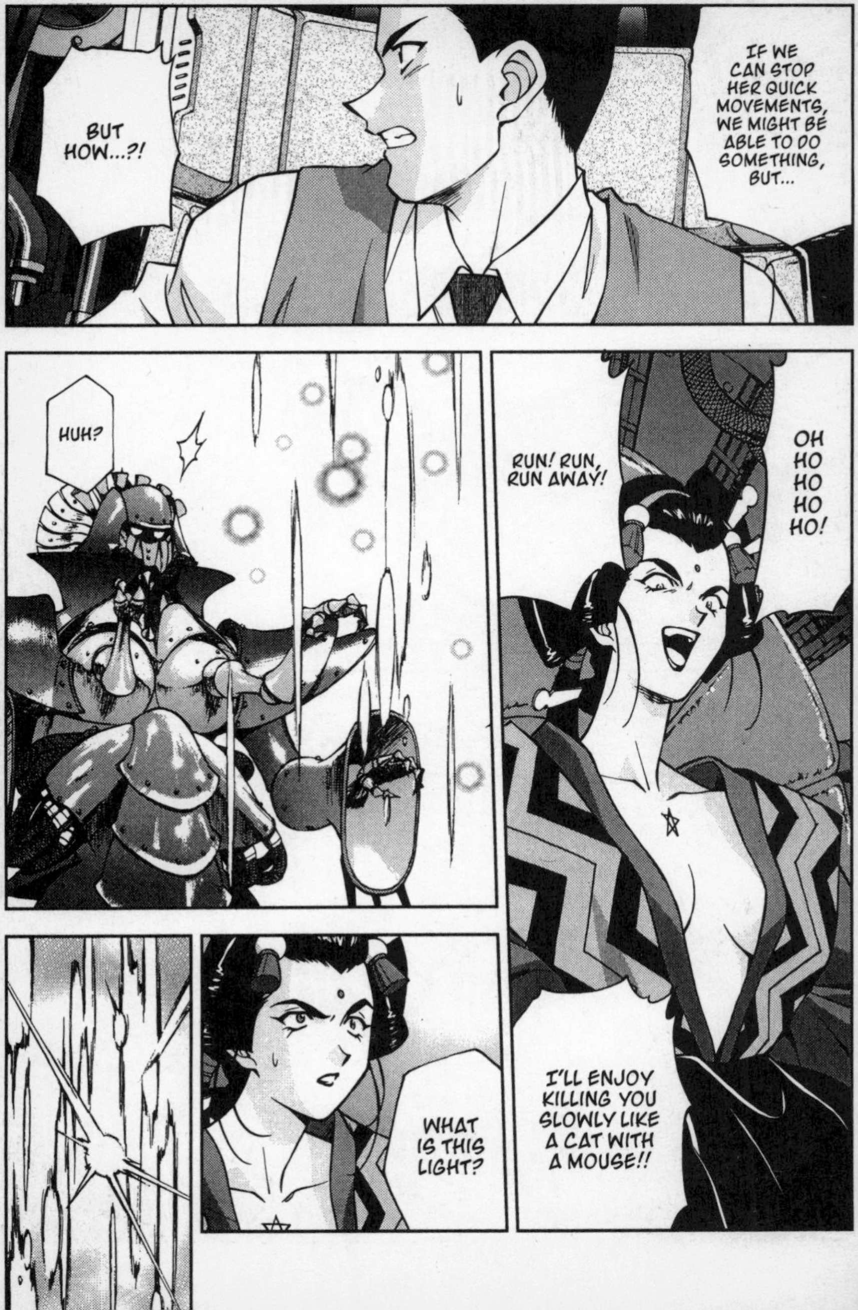
IF WE CAN STOP HER QUICK MOVEMENTS, WE MIGHT BE ABLE TO DO SOMETHING, BUT...
BUT HOW...?!
OH HO HO HO HO!
RUN! RUN, RUN AWAY!
I'LL ENJOY KILLING YOU SLOWLY LIKE A CAT WITH A MOUSE!!
HUH?
WHAT IS THIS LIGHT?

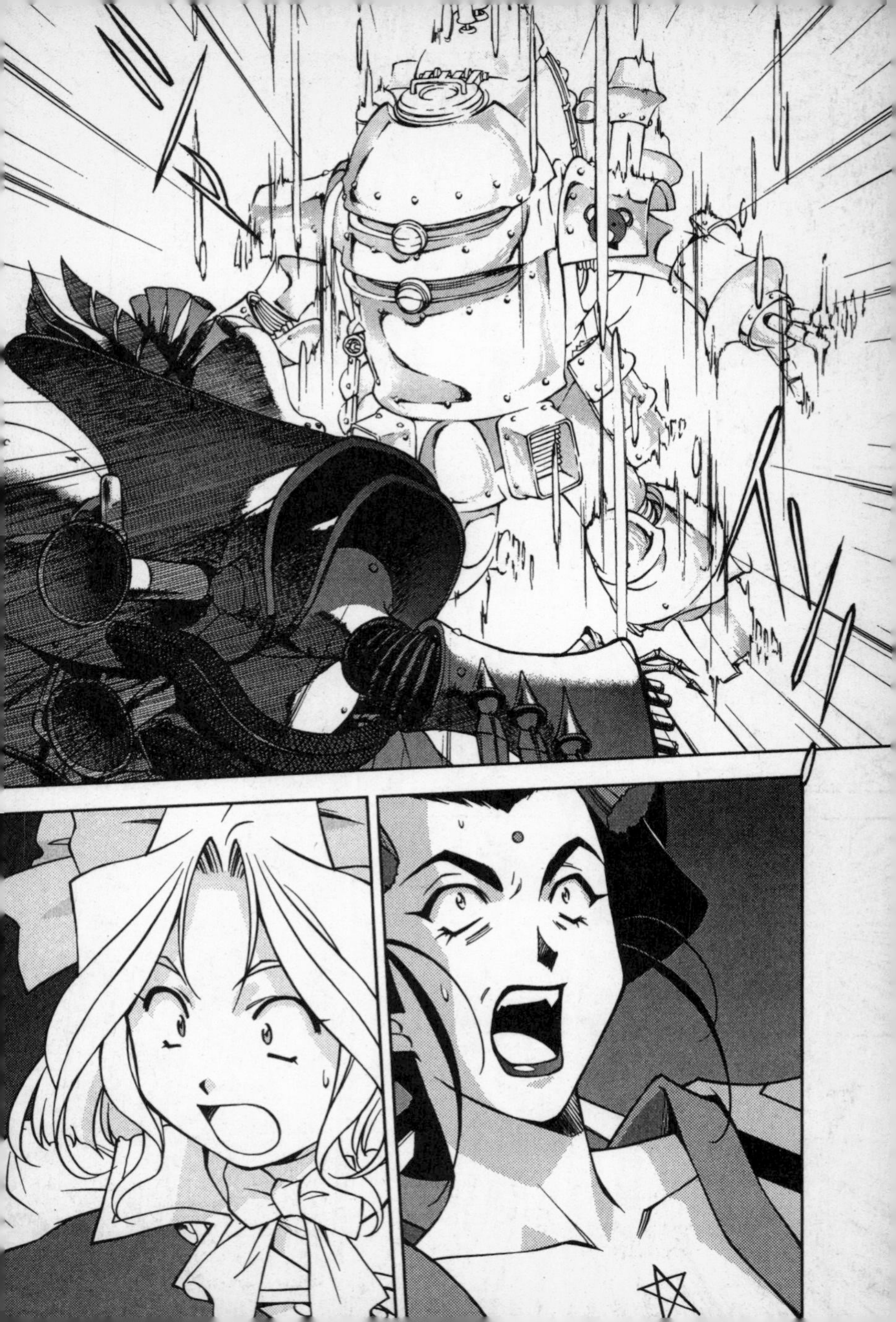

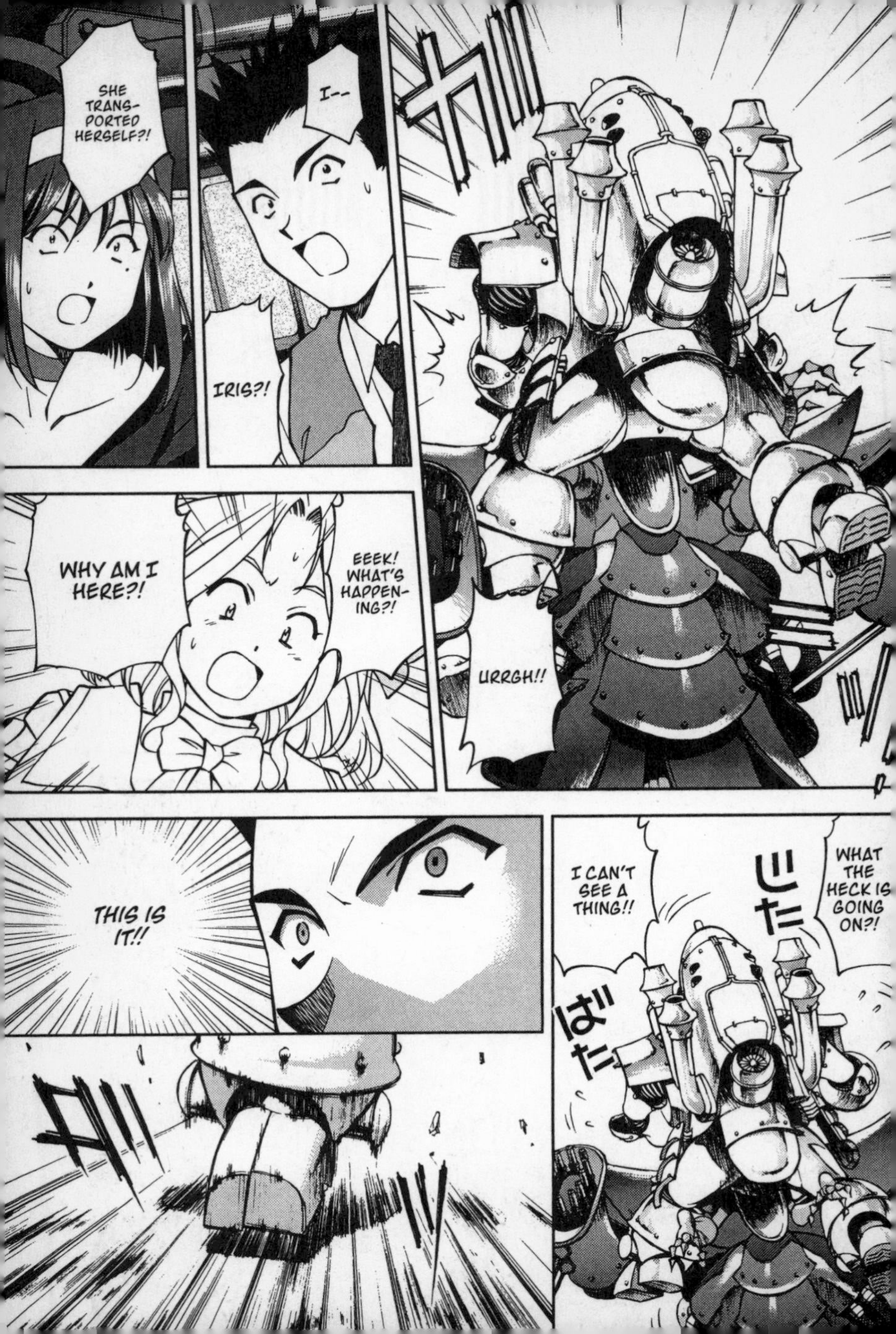
カッ
URRGH!!
I--
IRIS?!
SHE TRANSPORTED HERSELF?!
EEEK! WHAT'S HAPPENING?!
WHY AM I HERE?!
WHAT THE HECK IS GOING ON?!
じた
I CAN'T SEE A THING!!
ばた
THIS IS IT!!

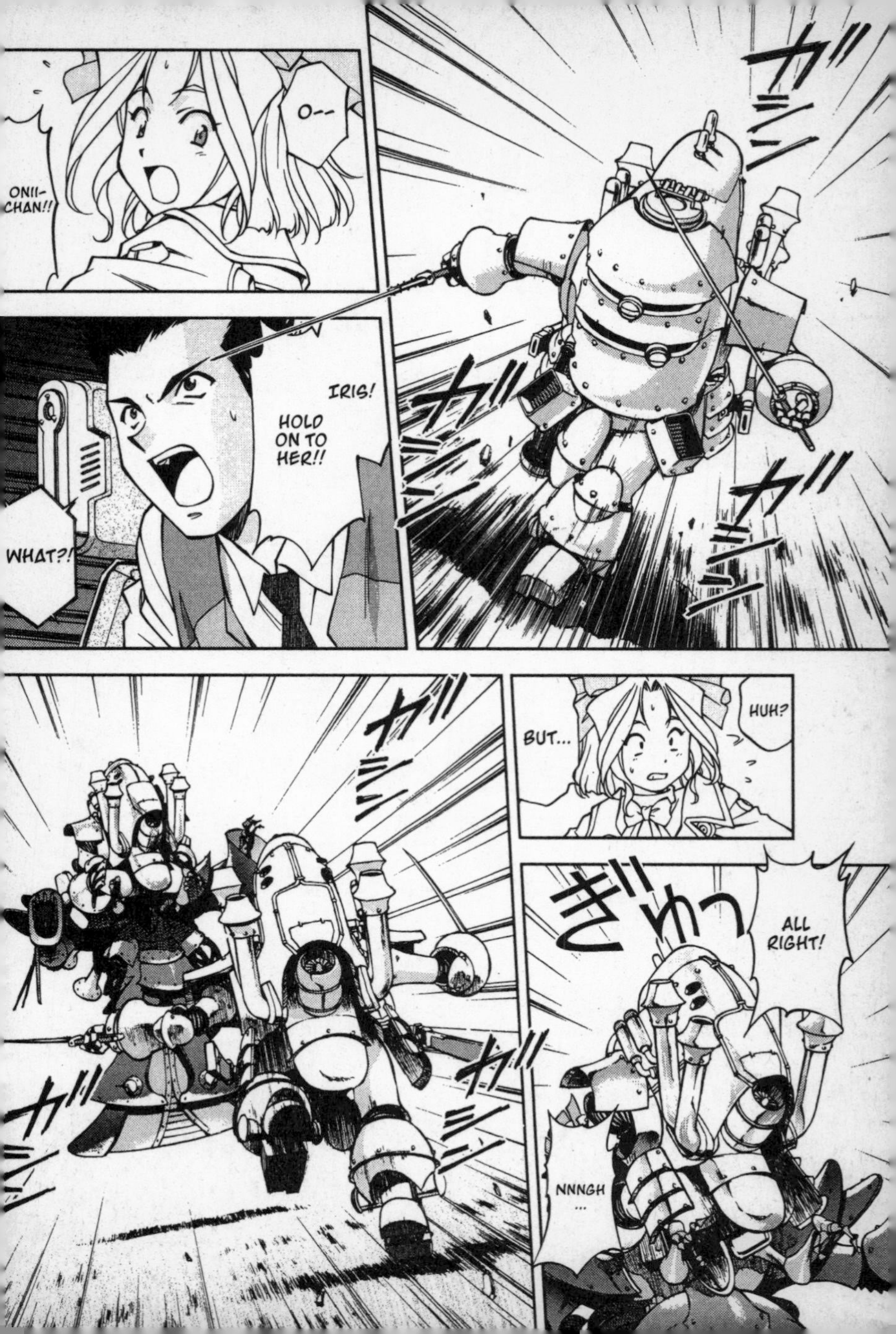

O--
ONII-CHAN!!
IRIS!
HOLD ON TO HER!!
WHAT?!
HUH?
BUT...
ぎゅっ
ALL RIGHT!
NNNGH ...

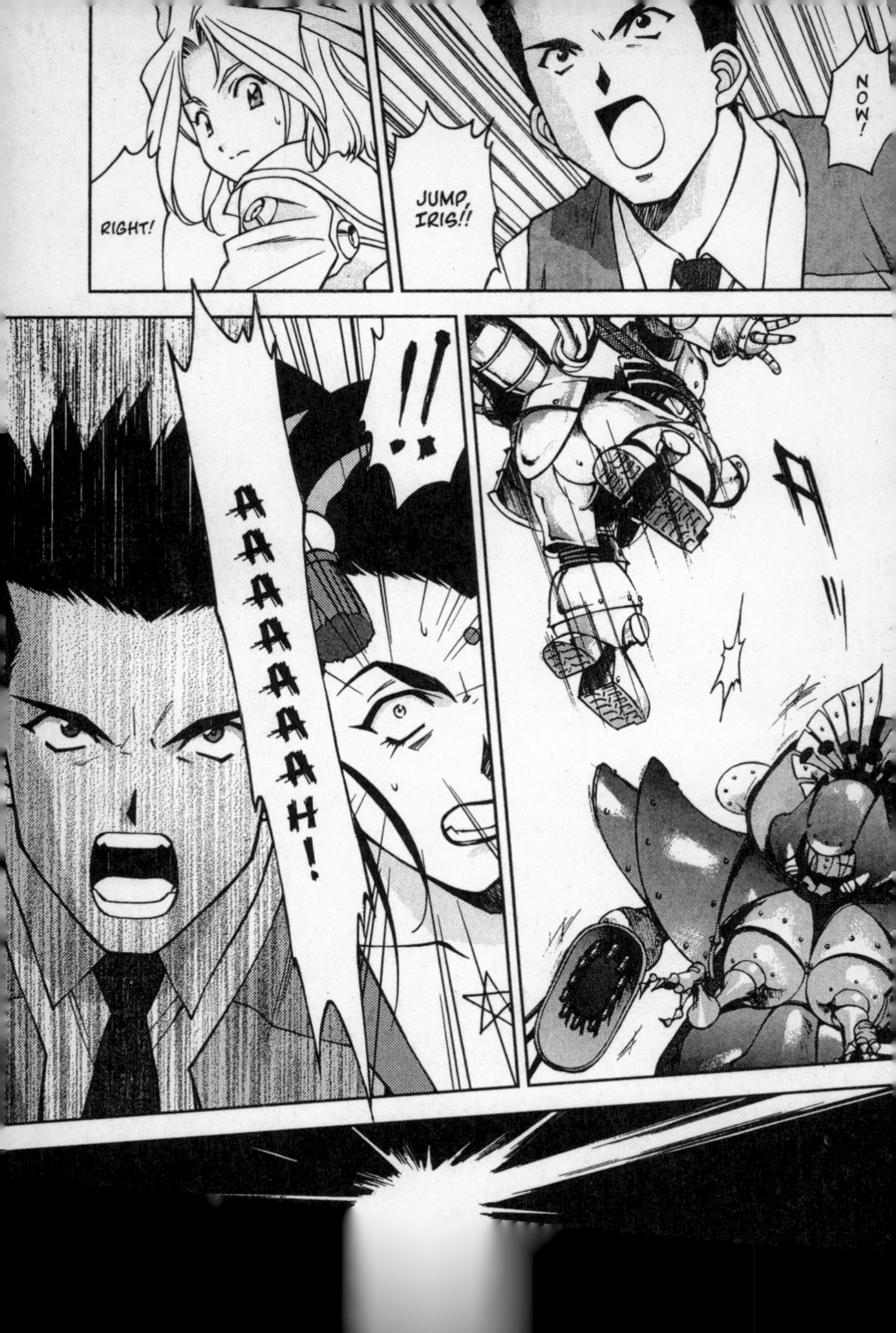
NOW!
JUMP, IRIS!!
RIGHT!
!!
AAAAAAAH!

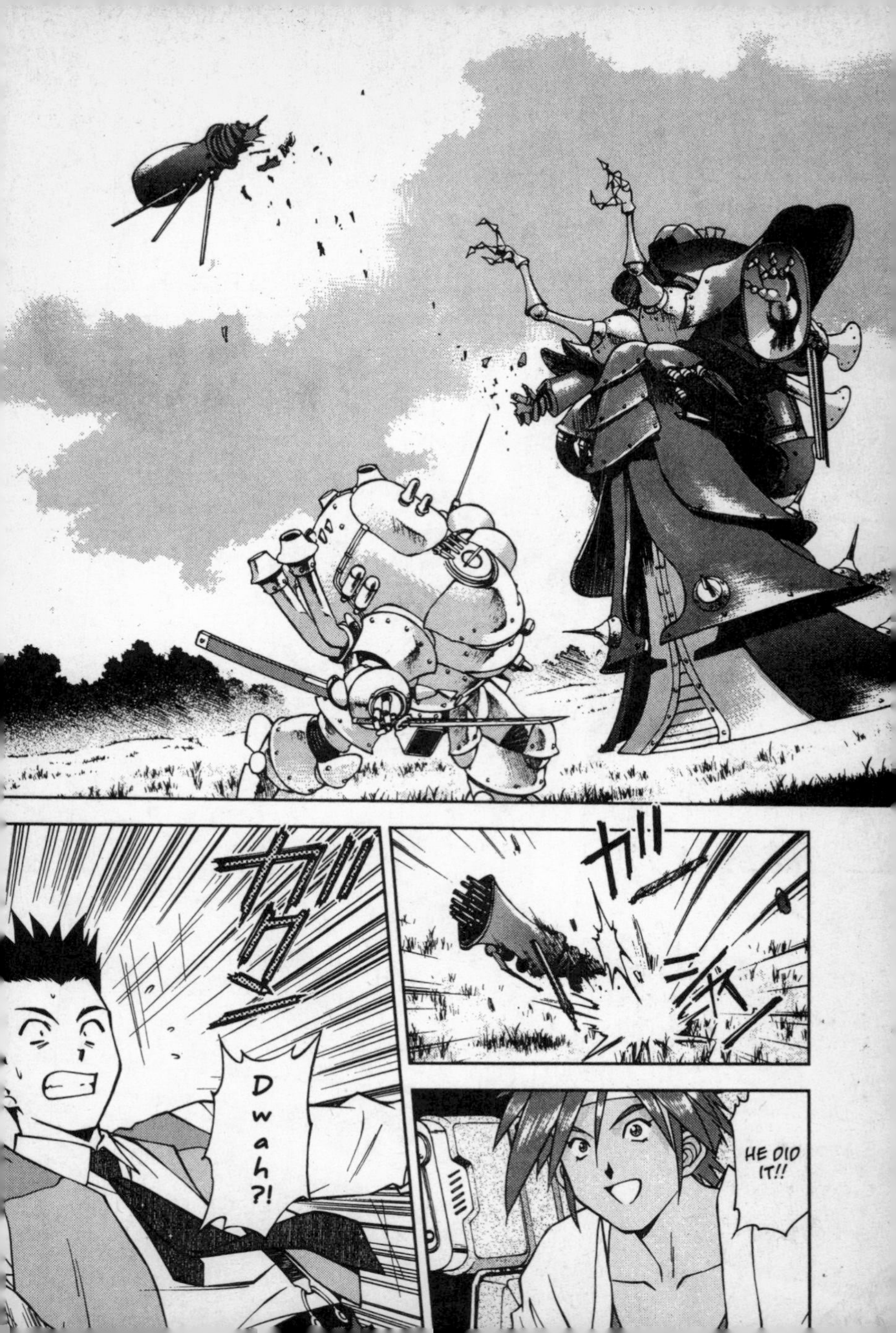
HE DID IT!!
Dwah?!

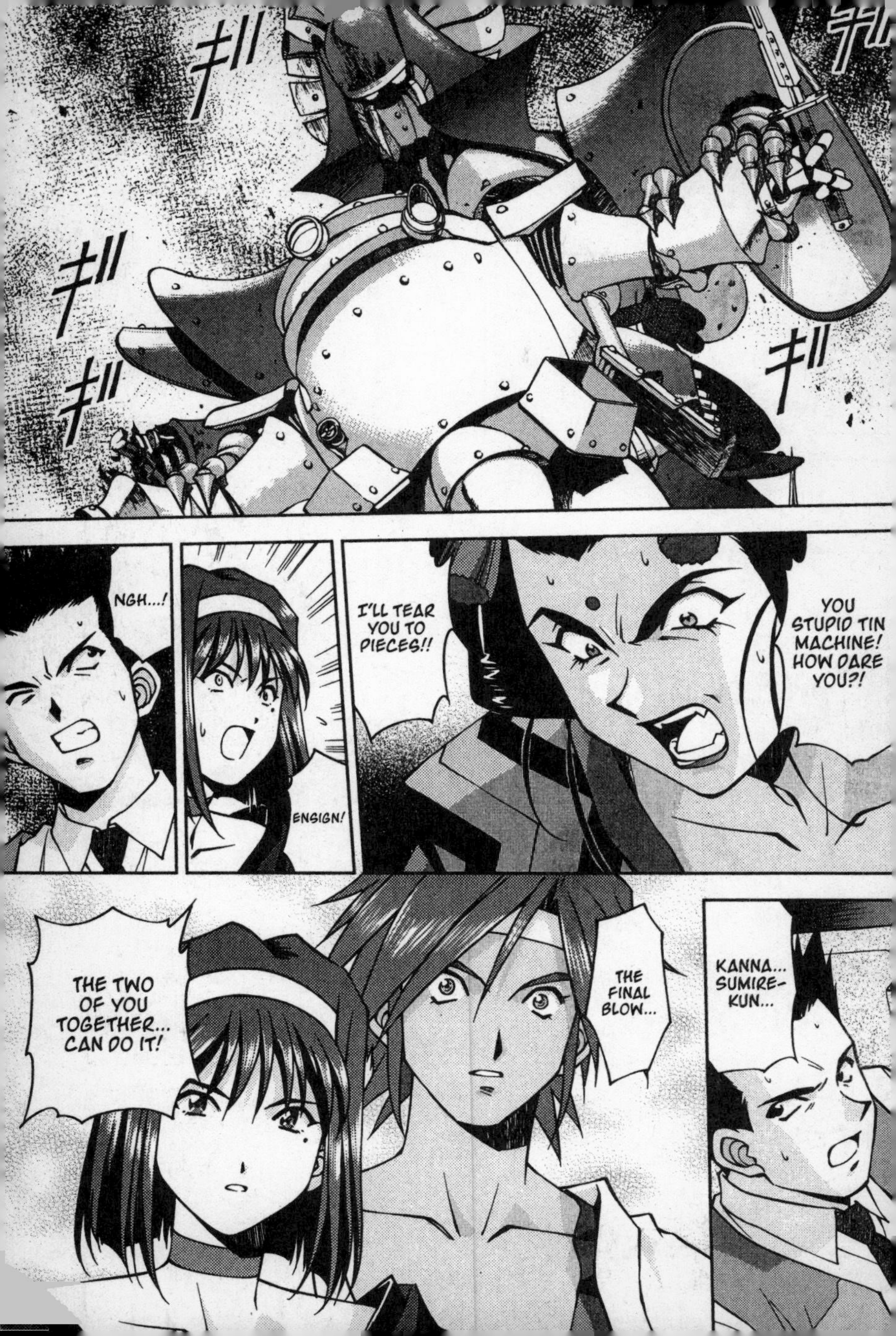
YOU STUPID TIN MACHINE! HOW DARE YOU?!
I'LL TEAR YOU TO PIECES!!
ENSIGN!
NGH...!
KANNA... SUMIRE-KUN...
THE FINAL BLOW...
THE TWO OF YOU TOGETHER... CAN DO IT!

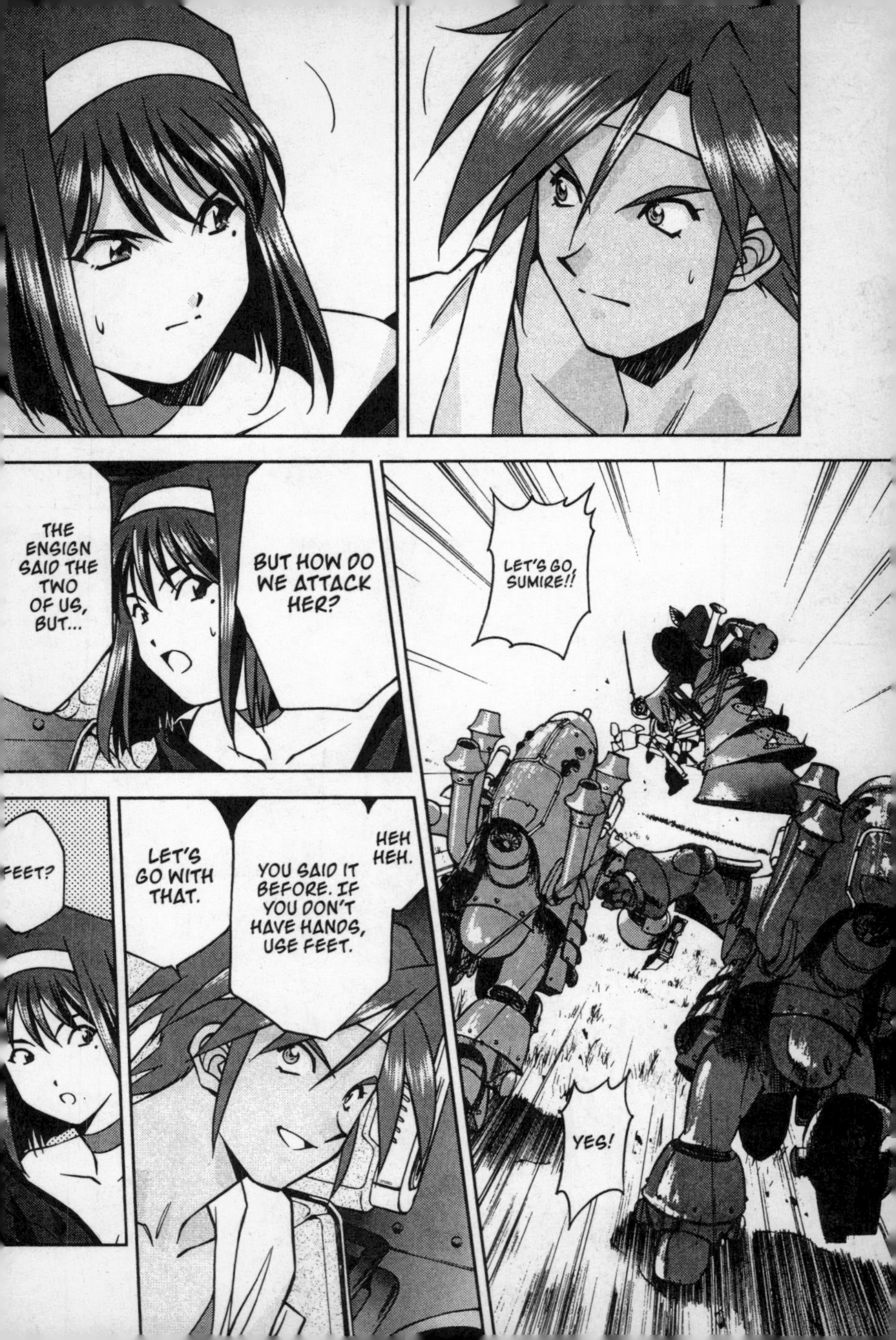
THE ENSIGN SAID THE TWO OF US, BUT...
BUT HOW DO WE ATTACK HER?
HEH HEH.
YOU SAID IT BEFORE. IF YOU DON'T HAVE HANDS, USE FEET.
FEET?
LET'S GO WITH THAT.
LET'S GO, SUMIRE!!
YES!

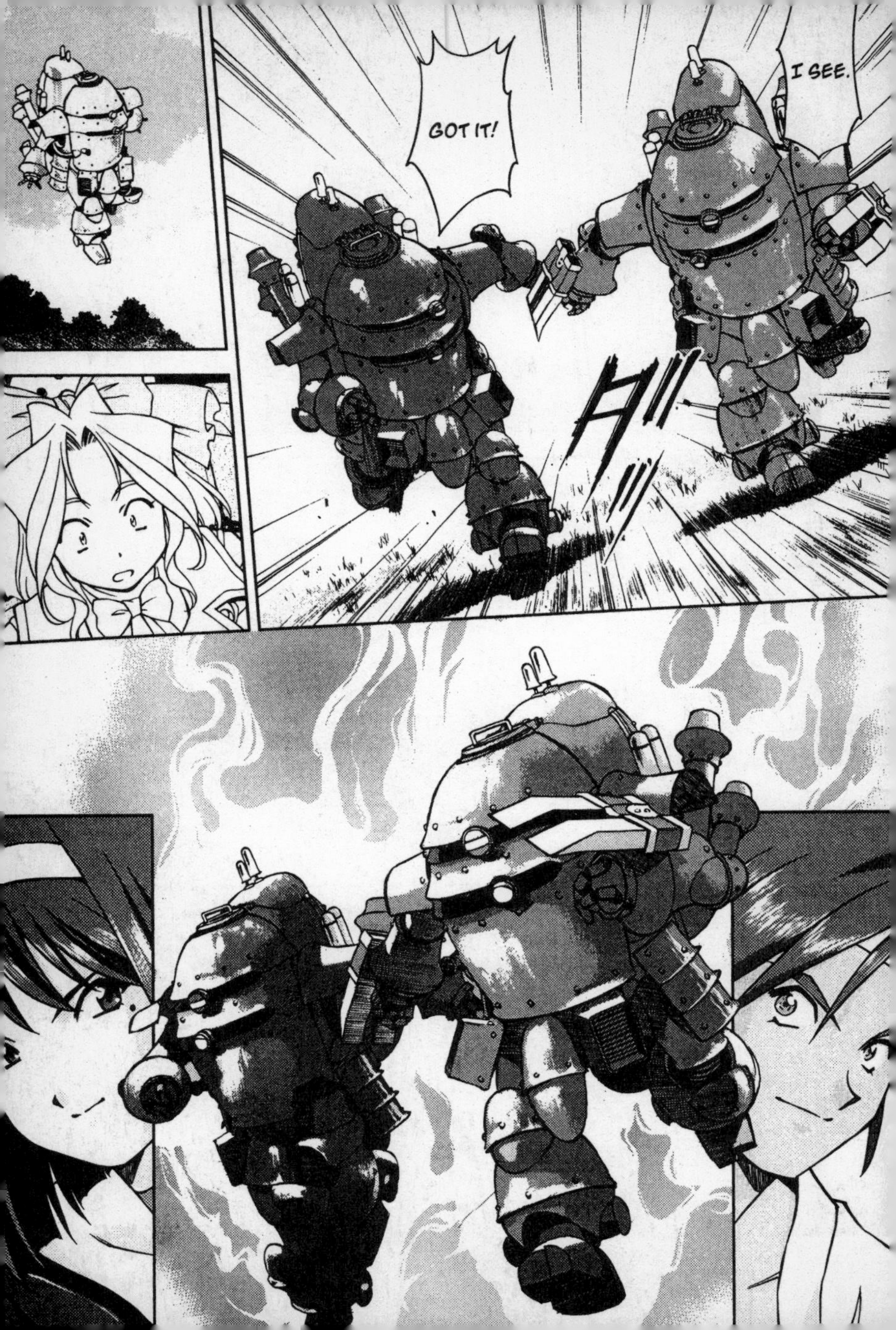
I SEE.
GOT IT!

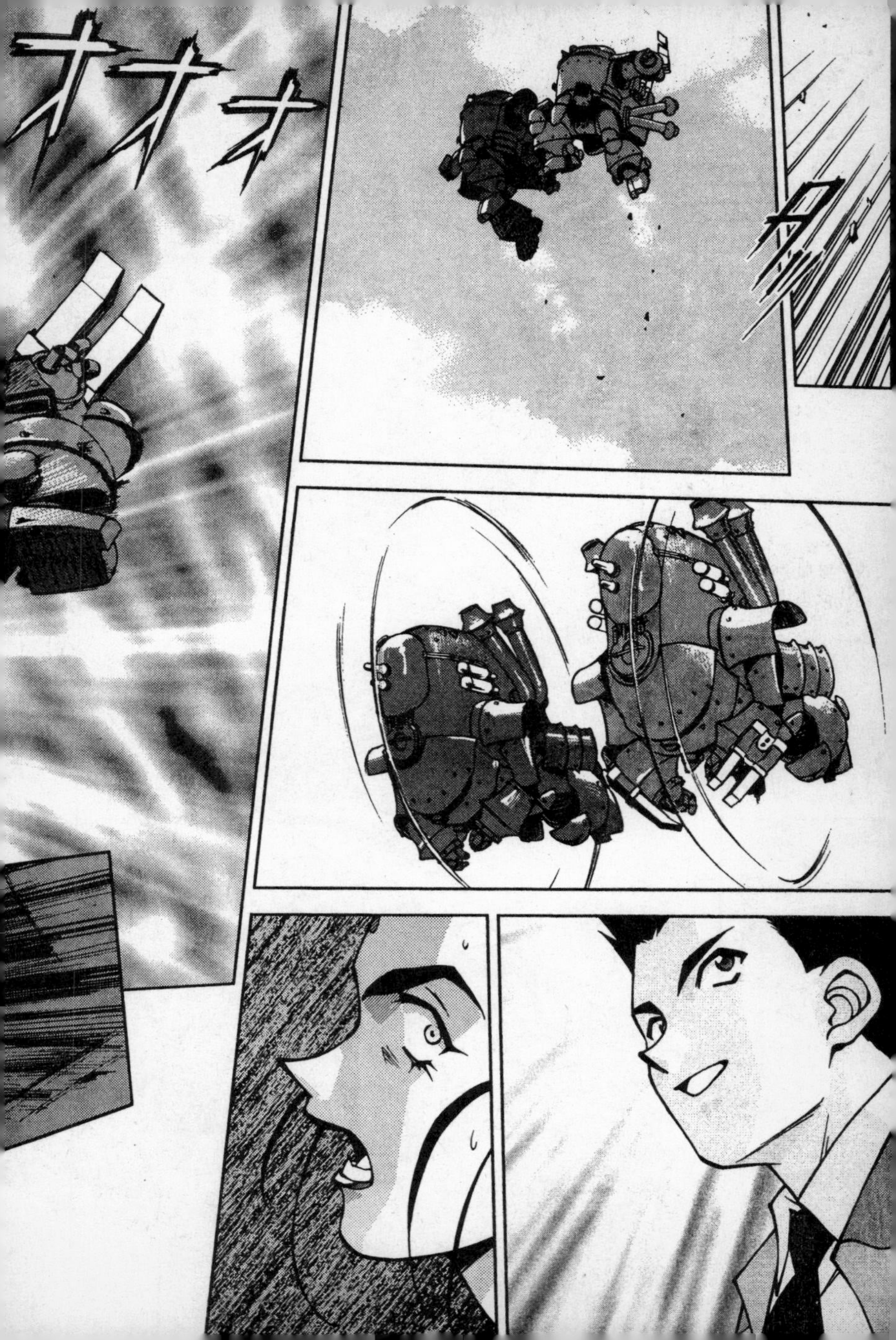
オオオ

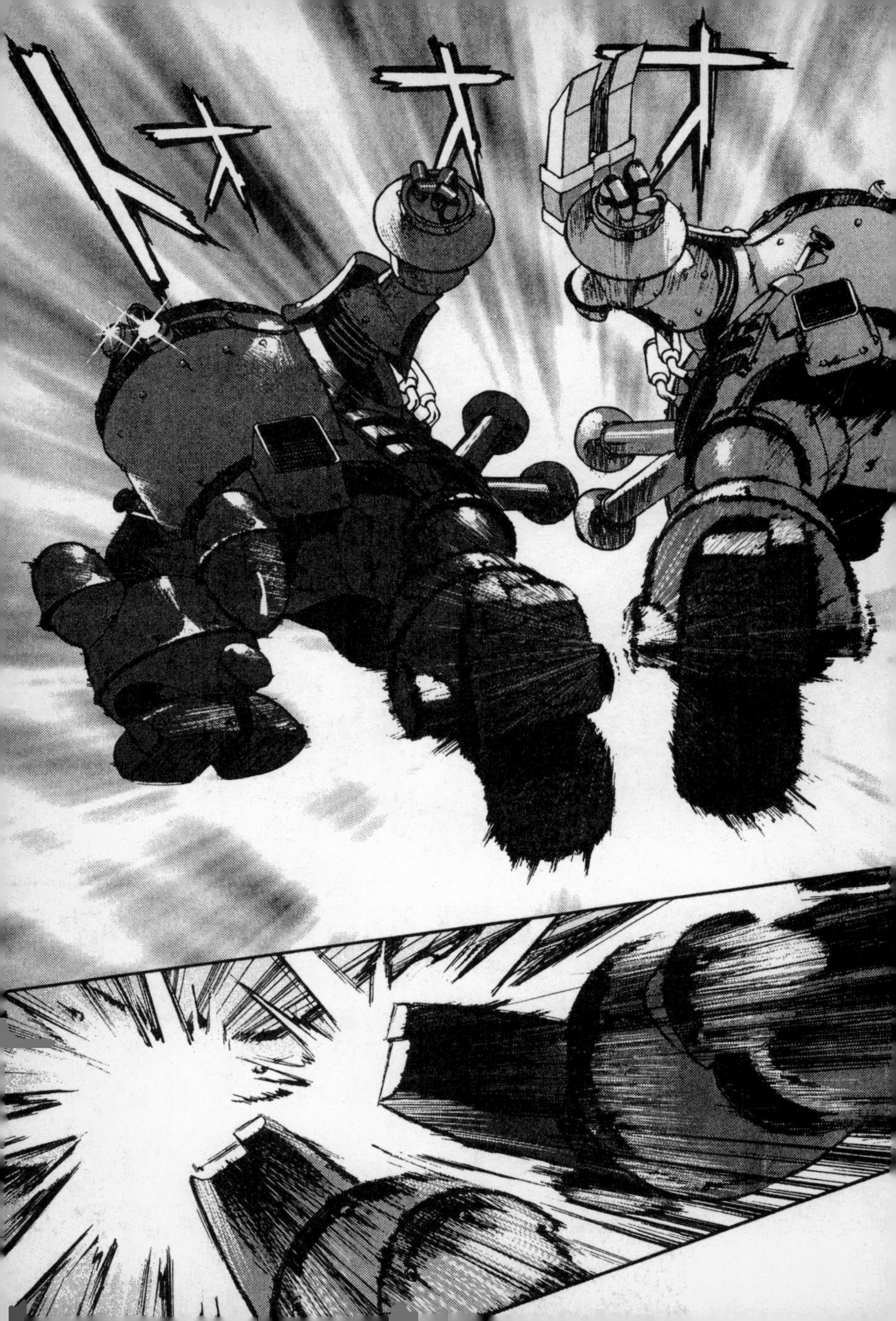

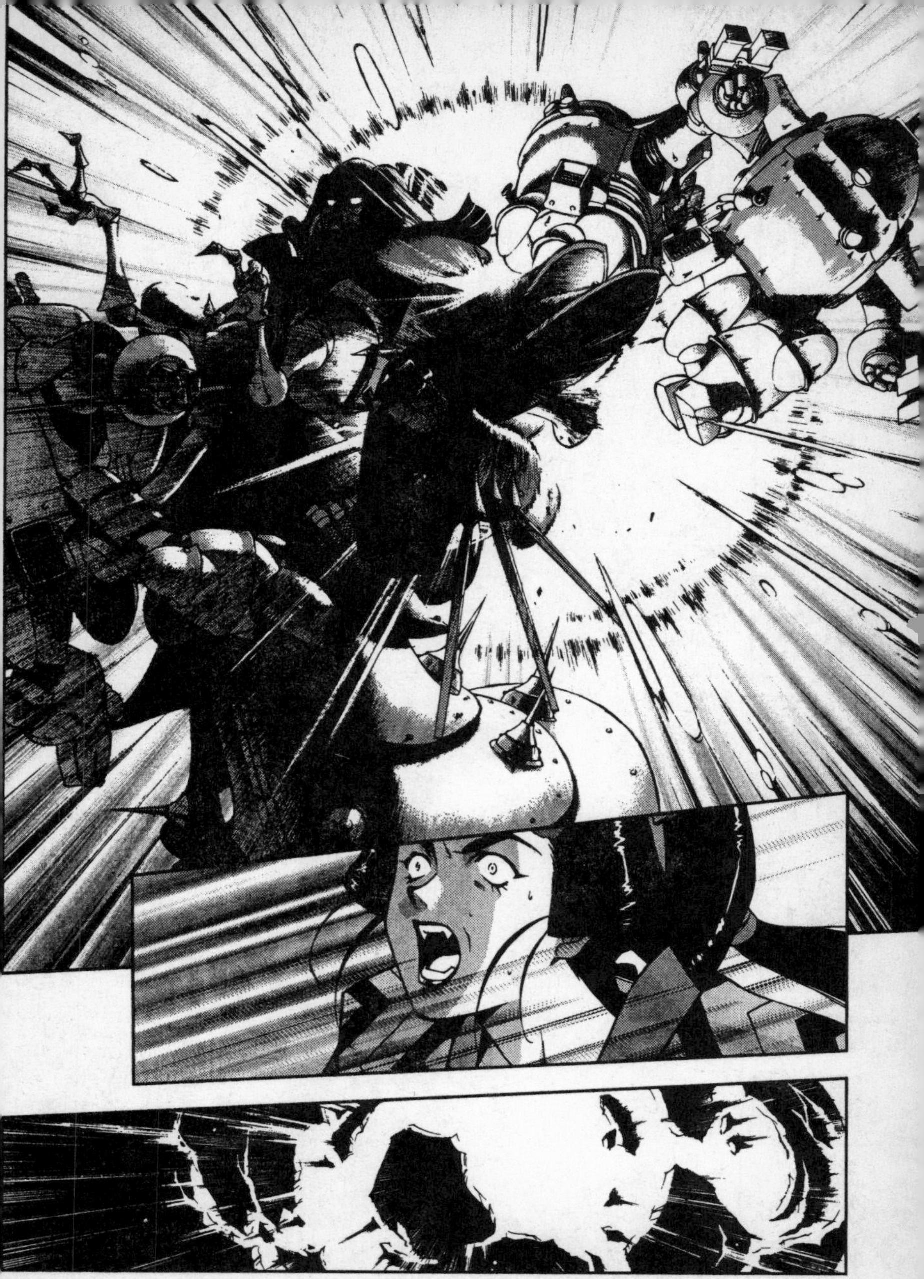

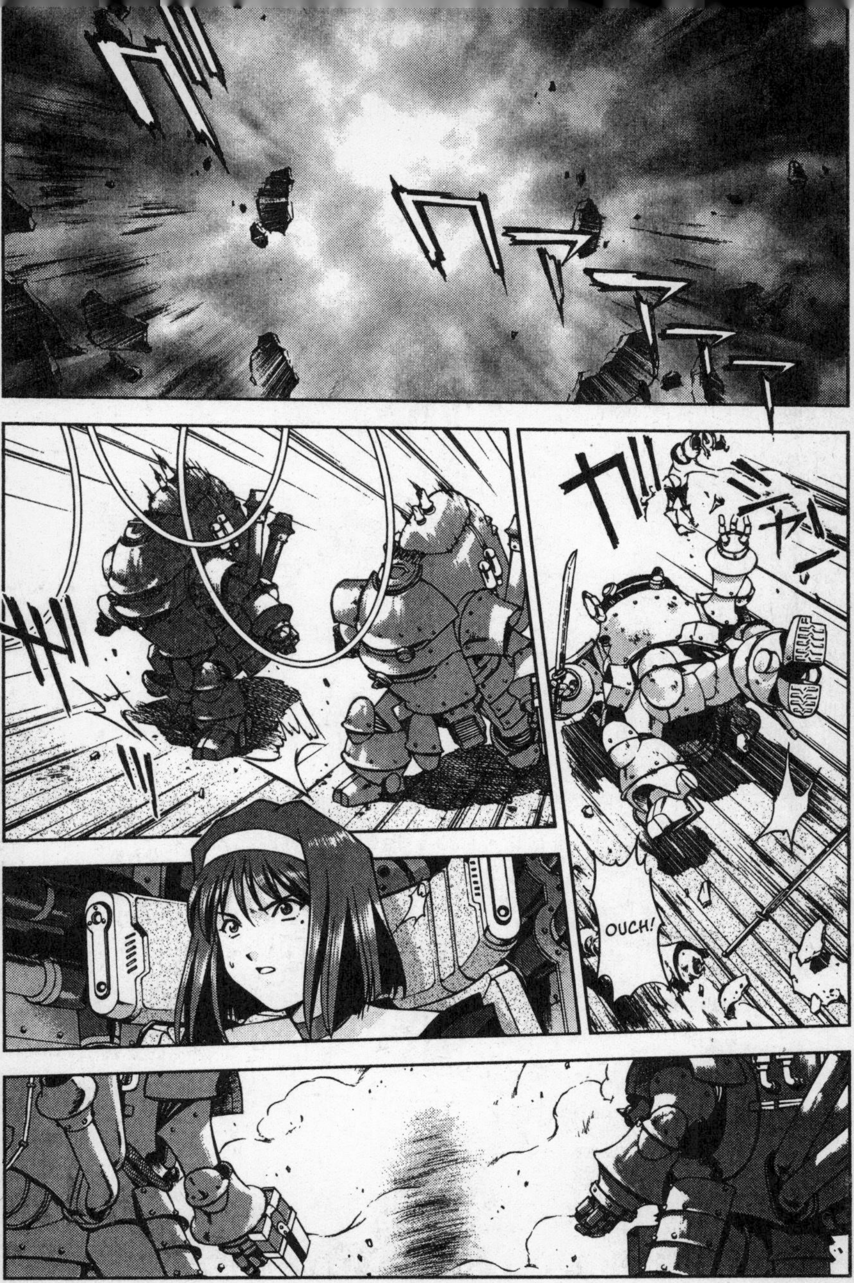
OUCH!

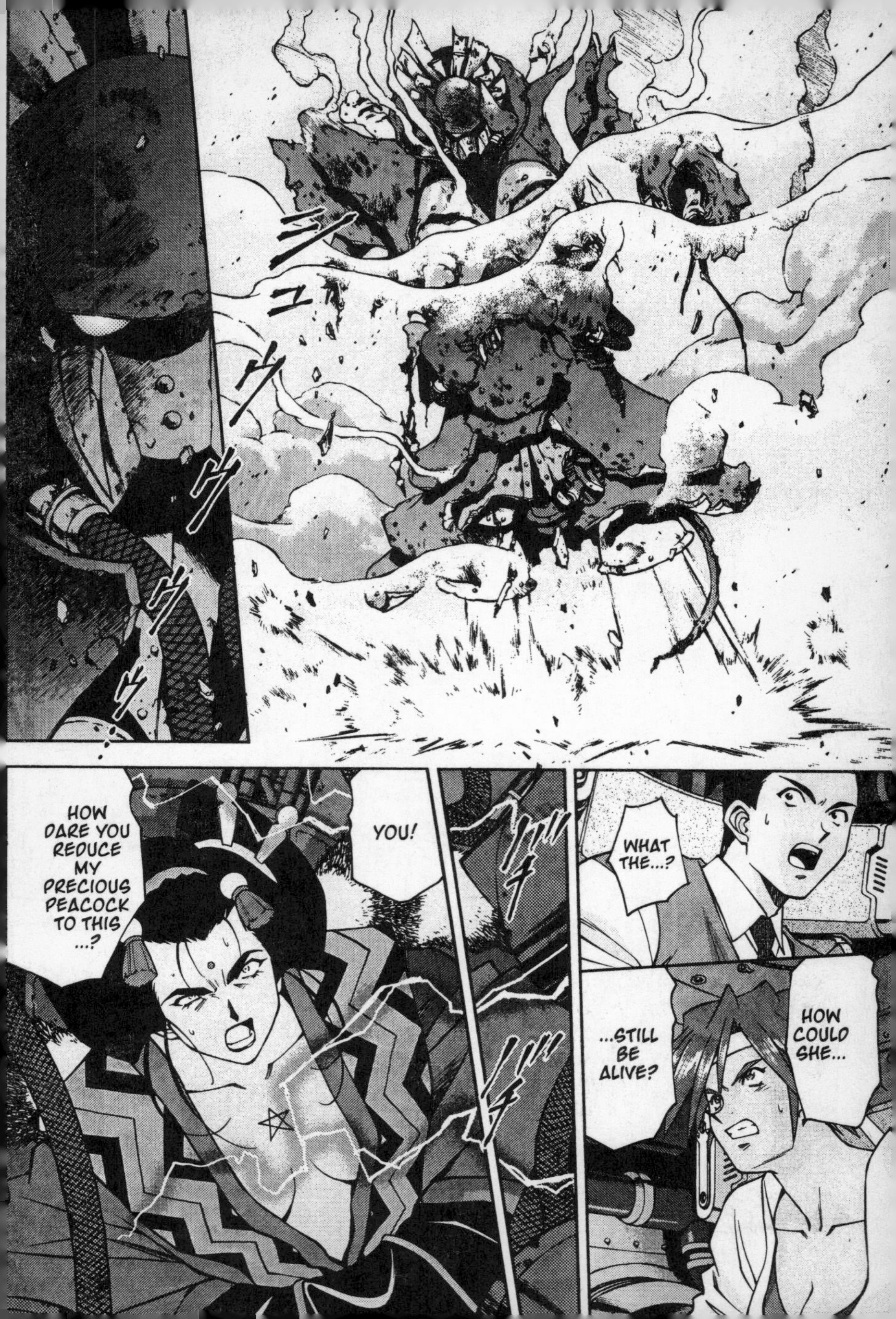
WHAT THE...?
HOW COULD SHE...
...STILL BE ALIVE?
YOU!
HOW DARE YOU REDUCE MY PRECIOUS PEACOCK TO THIS ...?

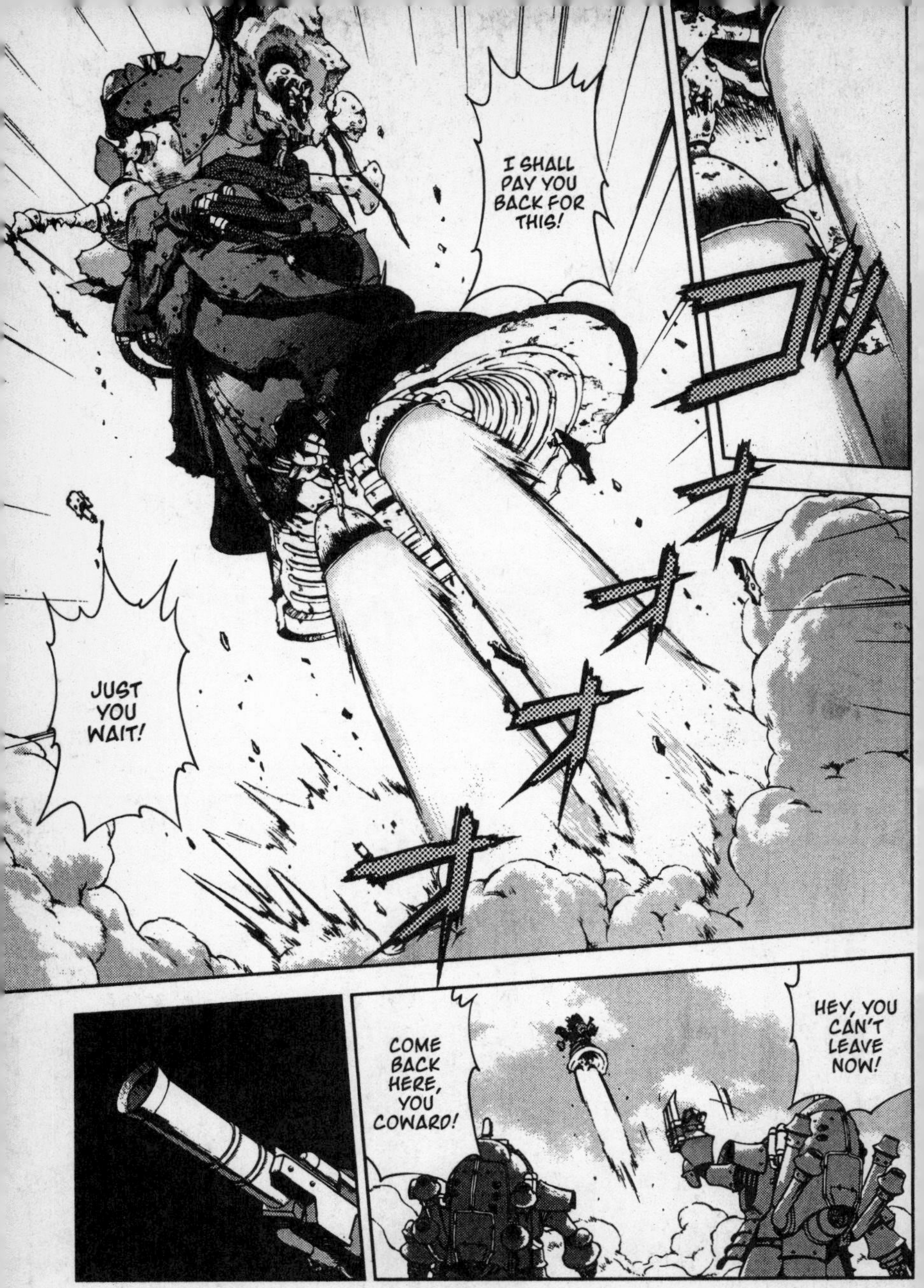
I SHALL PAY YOU BACK FOR THIS!
ゴオオオオ
JUST YOU WAIT!
HEY, YOU CAN'T LEAVE NOW!
COME BACK HERE, YOU COWARD!

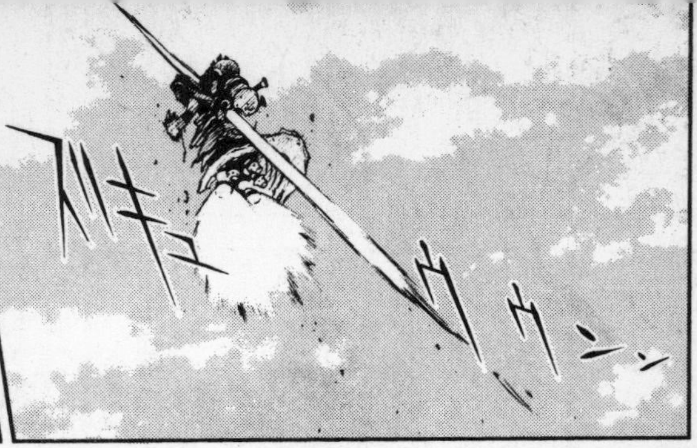
ズキュウウン
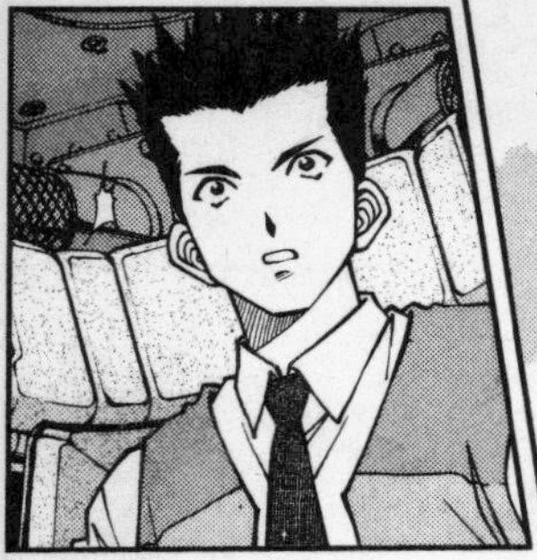
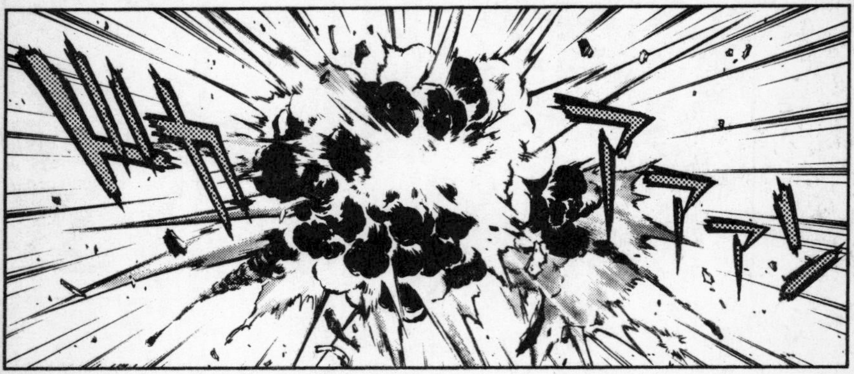
ドッカアアアン
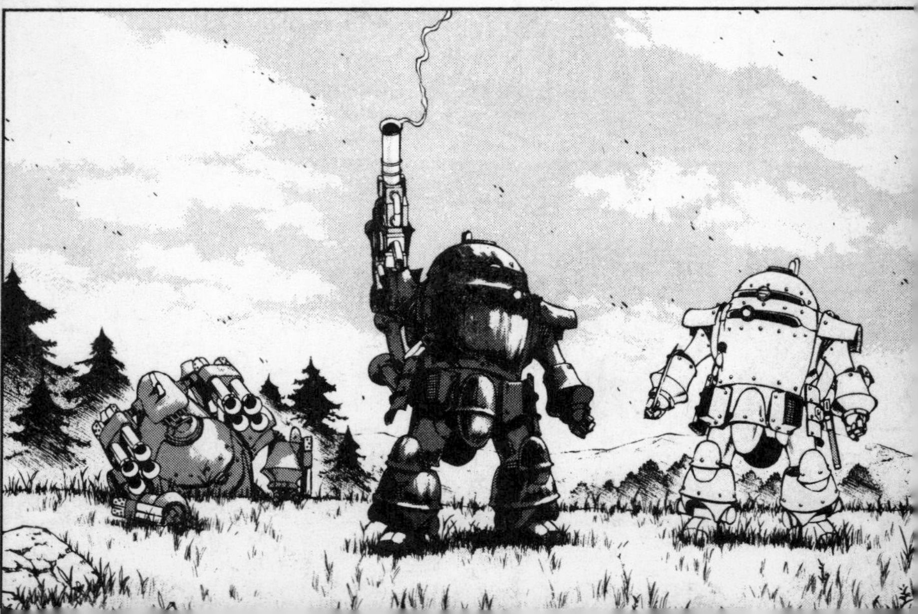

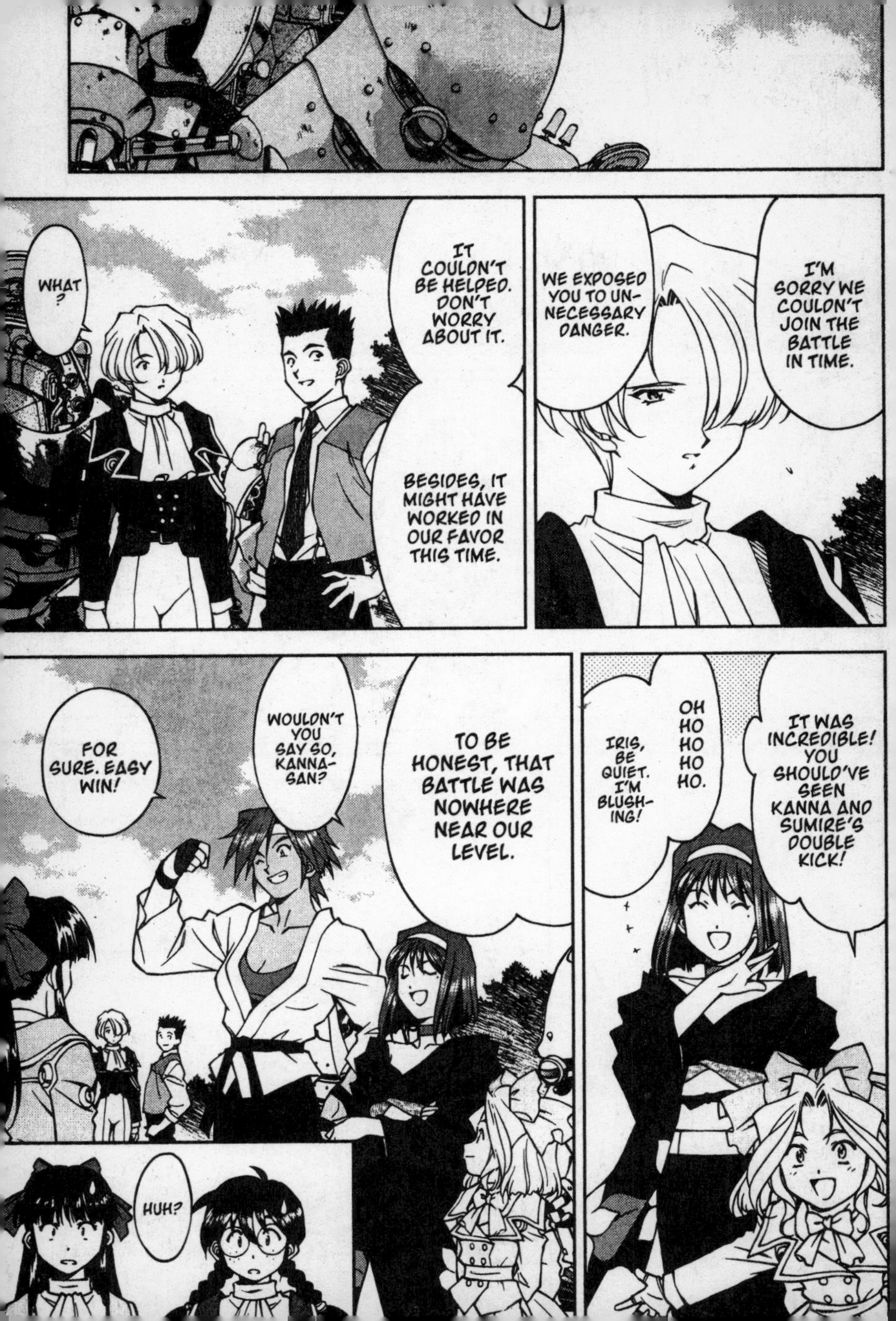
I'M SORRY WE COULDN'T JOIN THE BATTLE IN TIME.
WE EXPOSED YOU TO UN-NECESSARY DANGER.
IT COULDN'T BE HELPED. DON'T WORRY ABOUT IT.
BESIDES, IT MIGHT HAVE WORKED IN OUR FAVOR THIS TIME.
WHAT?
IT WAS INCREDIBLE! YOU SHOULD'VE SEEN KANNA AND SUMIRE'S DOUBLE KICK!
OH HO HO HO HO.
IRIS, BE QUIET. I'M BLUSHING!
TO BE HONEST, THAT BATTLE WAS NOWHERE NEAR OUR LEVEL.
WOULDN'T YOU SAY SO, KANNA-SAN?
FOR SURE. EASY WIN!
HUH?

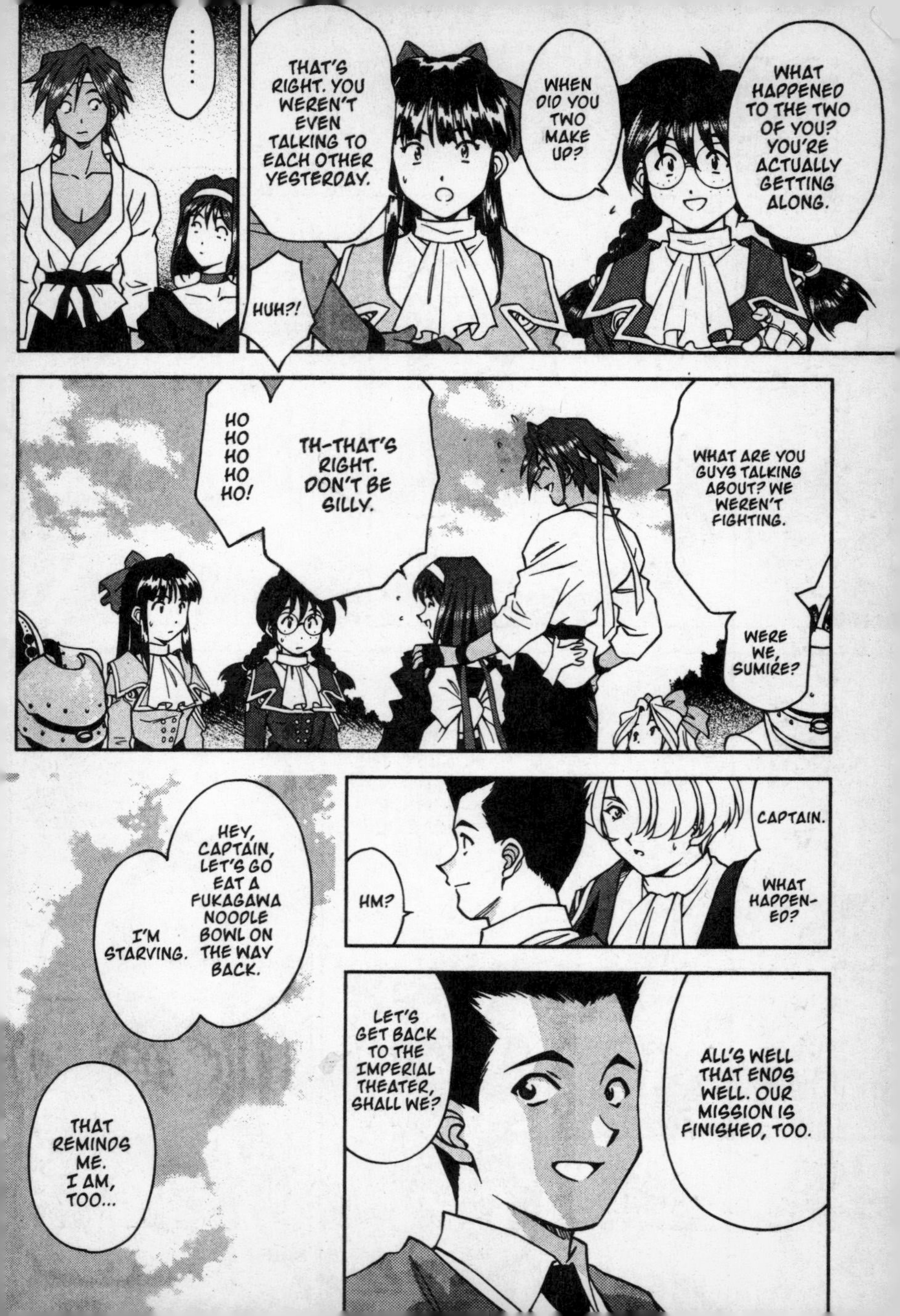
WHAT HAPPENED TO THE TWO OF YOU? YOU'RE ACTUALLY GETTING ALONG.
WHEN DID YOU TWO MAKE UP?
THAT'S RIGHT. YOU WEREN'T EVEN TALKING TO EACH OTHER YESTERDAY.
HUH?!
......
WHAT ARE YOU GUYS TALKING ABOUT? WE WEREN'T FIGHTING.
WERE WE, SUMIRE?
TH-THAT'S RIGHT. DON'T BE SILLY.
HO HO HO HO HO!
CAPTAIN.
WHAT HAPPEN-ED?
HM?
ALL'S WELL THAT ENDS WELL. OUR MISSION IS FINISHED, TOO.
LET'S GET BACK TO THE IMPERIAL THEATER, SHALL WE?
HEY, CAPTAIN, LET'S GO EAT A FUKAGAWA NOODLE BOWL ON THE WAY BACK.
I'M STARVING.
THAT REMINDS ME. I AM, TOO...

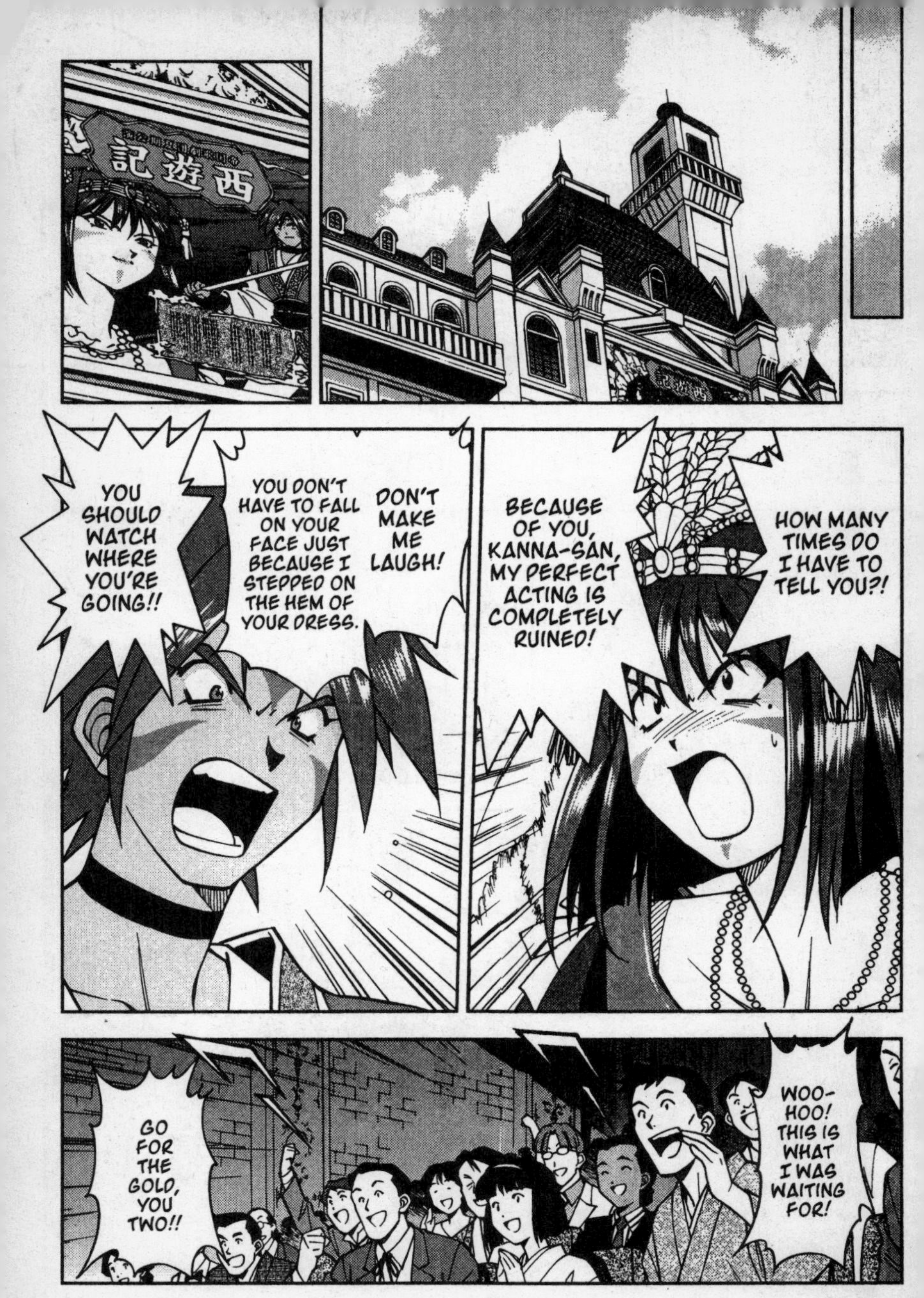
西遊記
HOW MANY TIMES DO I HAVE TO TELL YOU?!
BECAUSE OF YOU, KANNA-SAN, MY PERFECT ACTING IS COMPLETELY RUINED!
DON'T MAKE ME LAUGH!
YOU DON'T HAVE TO FALL ON YOUR FACE JUST BECAUSE I STEPPED ON THE HEM OF YOUR DRESS.
YOU SHOULD WATCH WHERE YOU'RE GOING!!
WOO-HOO! THIS IS WHAT I WAS WAITING FOR!
GO FOR THE GOLD, YOU TWO!!

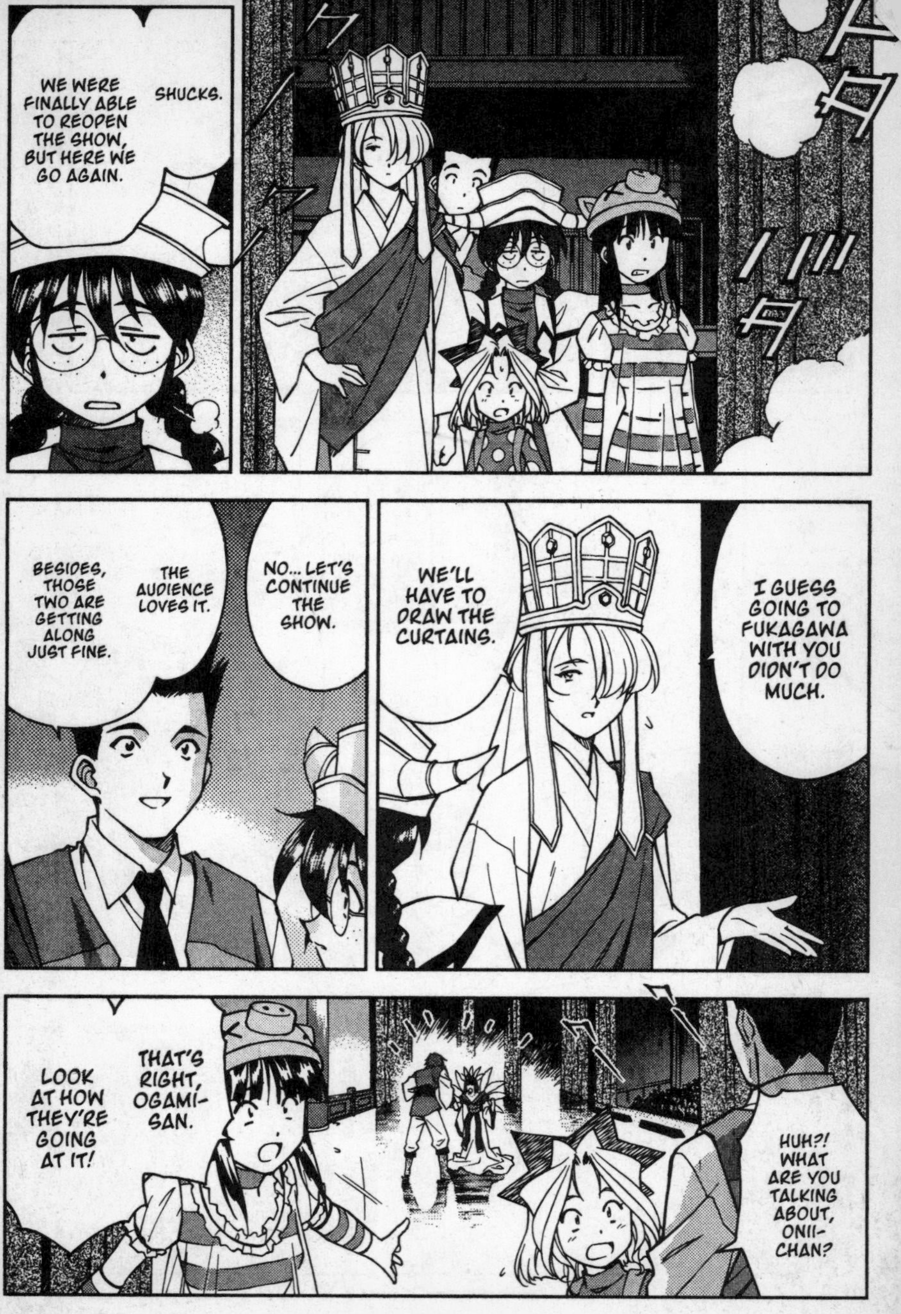
SHUCKS.
WE WERE FINALLY ABLE TO REOPEN THE SHOW, BUT HERE WE GO AGAIN.
I GUESS GOING TO FUKAGAWA WITH YOU DIDN'T DO MUCH.
WE'LL HAVE TO DRAW THE CURTAINS.
NO... LET'S CONTINUE THE SHOW.
THE AUDIENCE LOVES IT.
BESIDES, THOSE TWO ARE GETTING ALONG JUST FINE.
HUH?! WHAT ARE YOU TALKING ABOUT, ONII-CHAN?
THAT'S RIGHT, OGAMI-SAN.
LOOK AT HOW THEY'RE GOING AT IT!

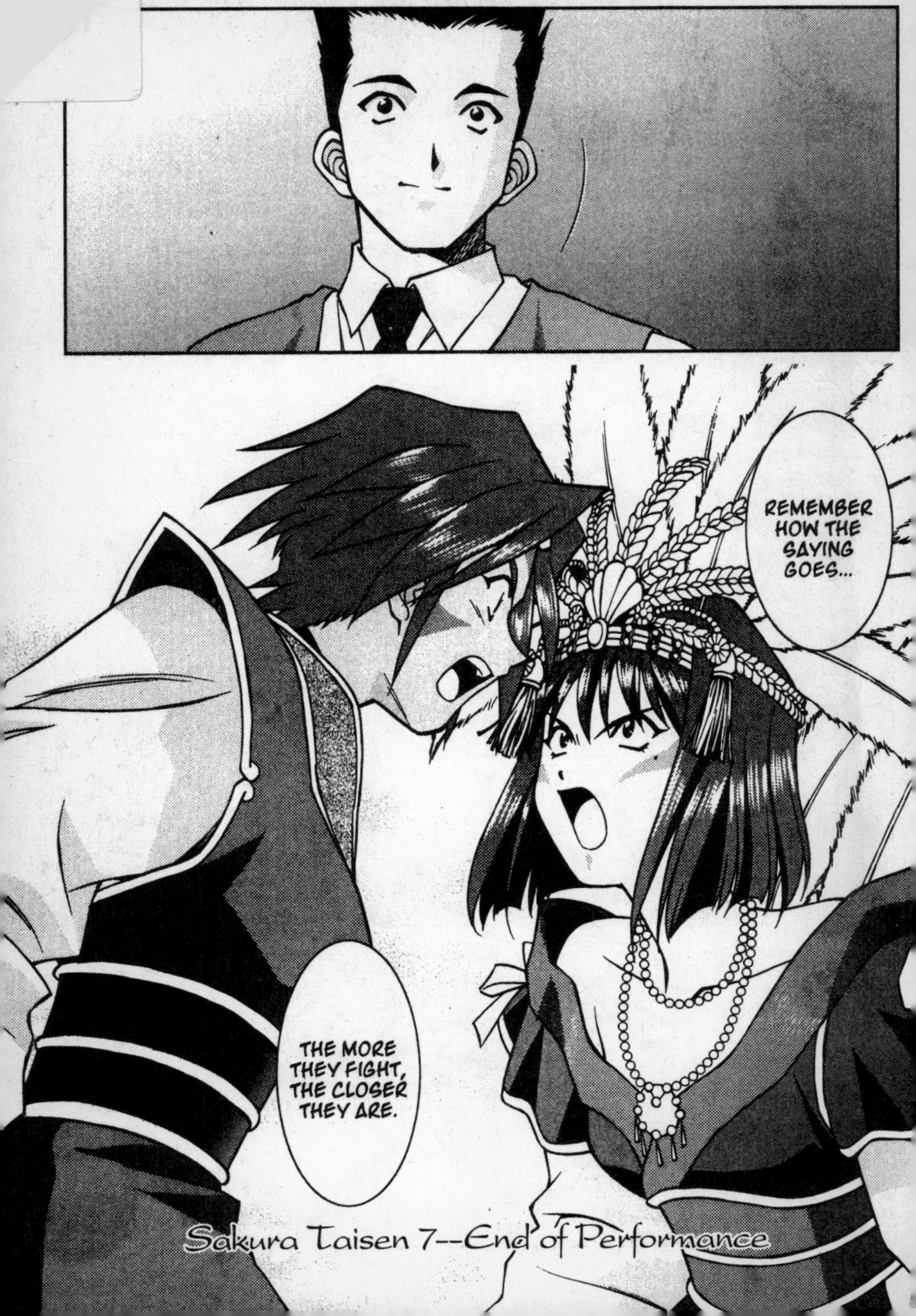
REMEMBER HOW THE SAYING GOES...
THE MORE THEY FIGHT, THE CLOSER THEY ARE.
Sakura Taisen 7--End of Performance

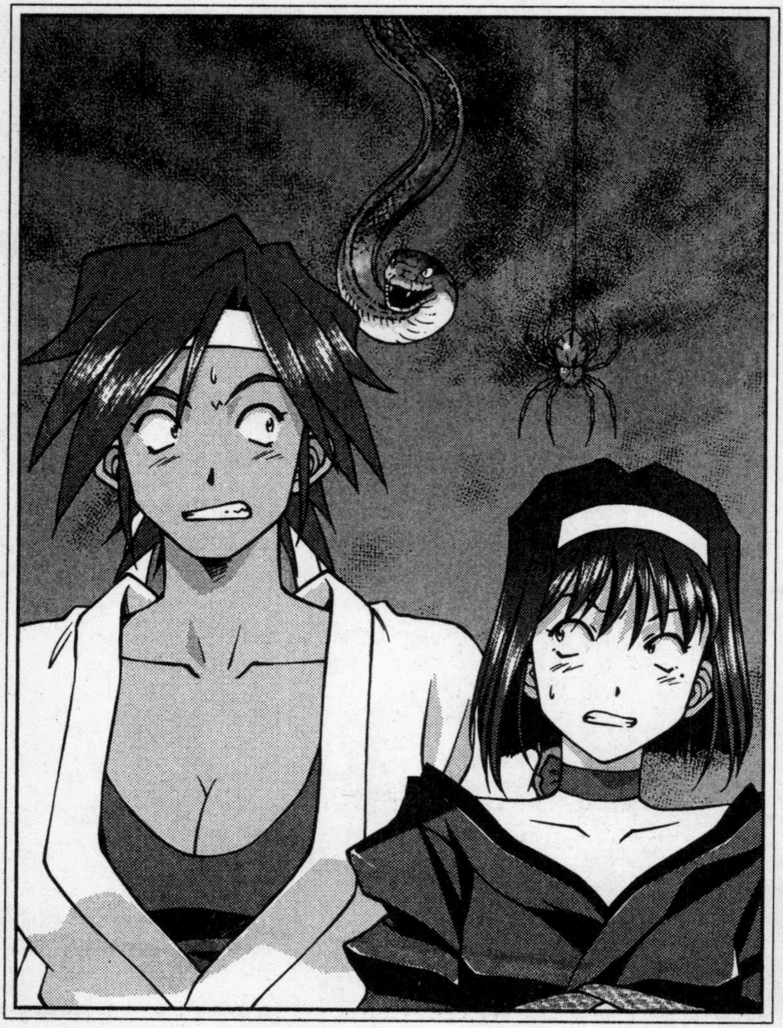

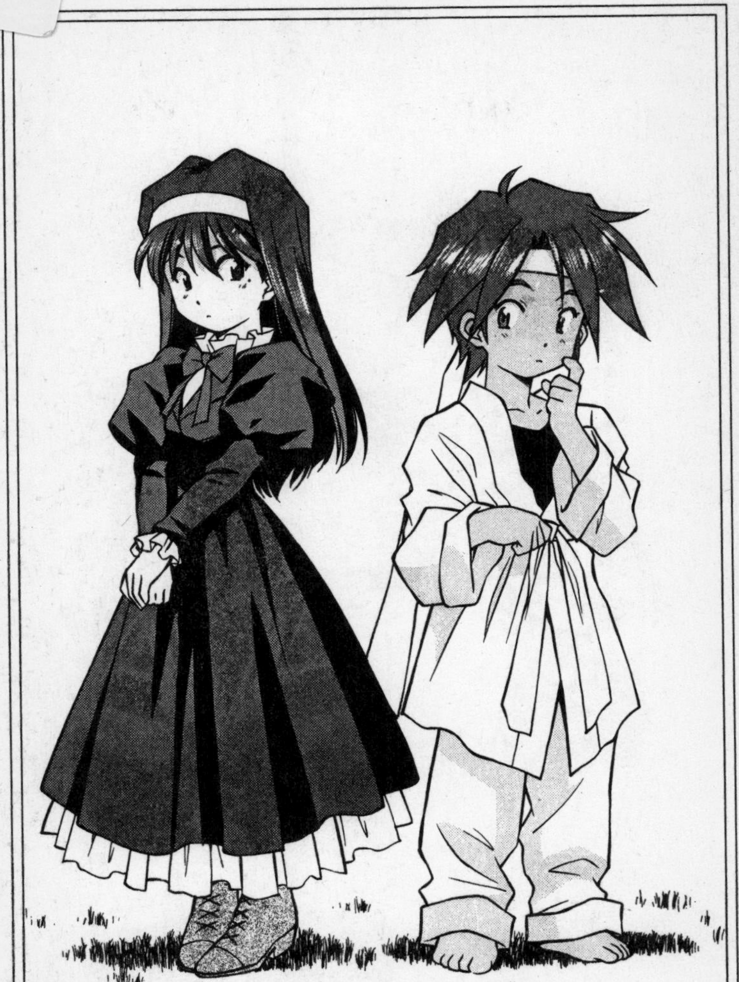

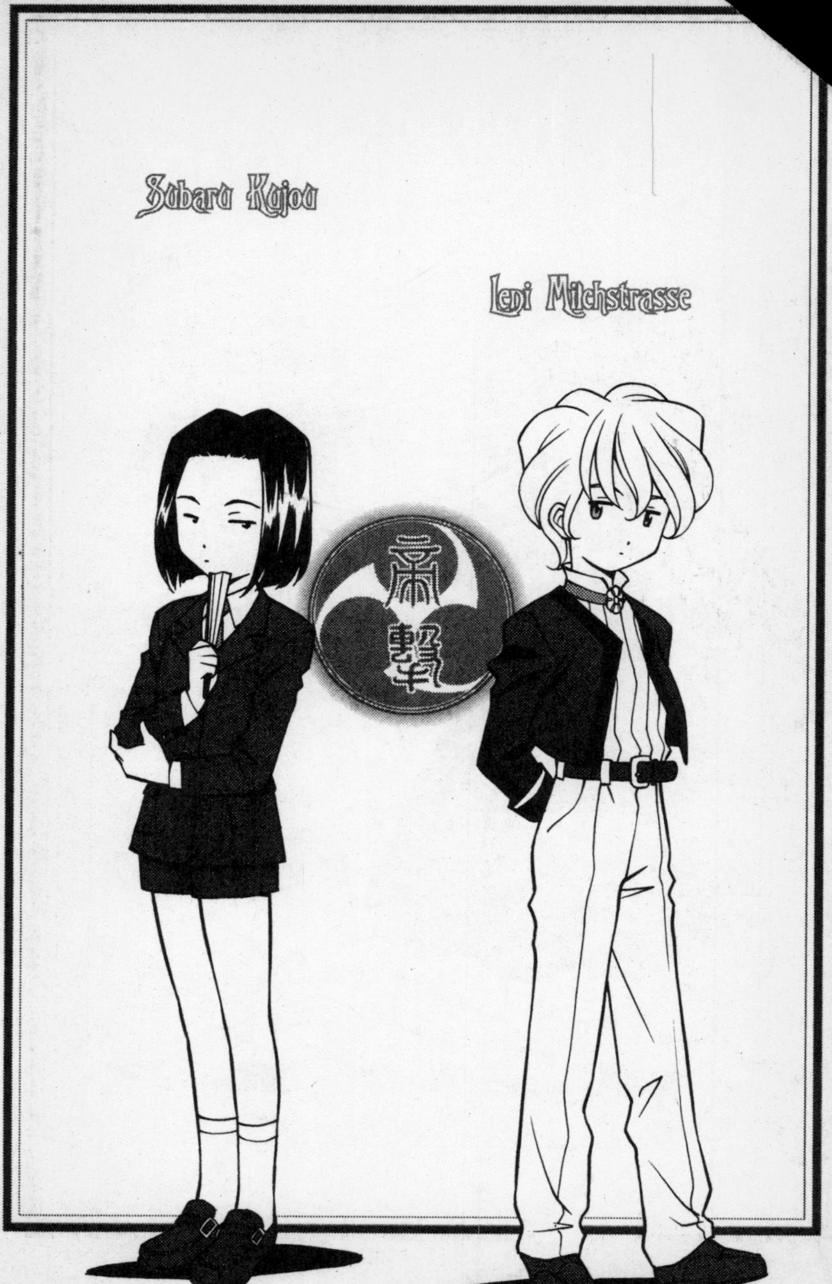
Subaru Kujou
Leni Milchstrasse
帝
撃

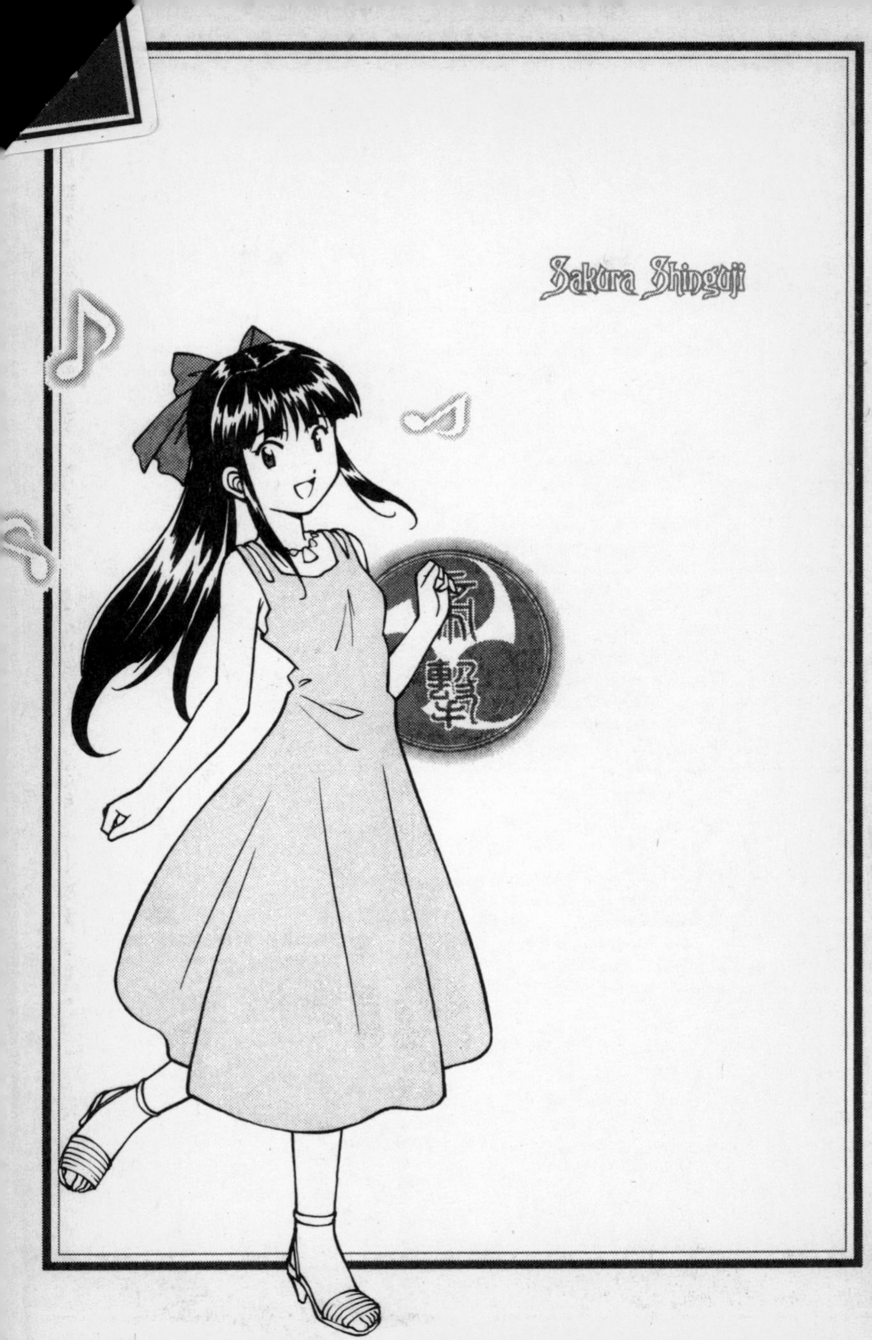
Sakura Shinguji

Bonus Section

**Seventh Installment**

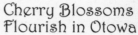

# Cherry Blossoms Flourish in Otowa

By Ohji Hiroi

The blue sea, the forever blue sea. Azure sea.
I can't believe that such a beautiful body of water existed.
As I was overcome with emotion, tears began to flow.
Why do I tear up when I see beauty in nature?
It's strange.

I'm on a small island in the Marshall Islands.
"Marshall Islands is composed of 29 atolls. You can think of an atoll as a gigantic necklace made of coral. On the atolls, there are 1,225 islands and 870 reefs," said Martha Naito. This super buxom woman is a special agent of Kodansha Investigation Department, otherwise known as the **Other** History of Showa.

"So what are you going to do, now that you've brought me here?"
This was no time to shed tears. Suddenly, all my assignments flew though my head. It's true that I tend to wonder about a lot. But I'm usually in areas that are within three hours from Tokyo. When I say I'm going on a trip, it usually means three to four days at the most. Somewhere in the corner of my head, I'm always thinking that someone might call and want me on some job. I'm chicken. It's a testament of being a freelancer.

A freelancer has to be audacious, but also be a wimp.
If you miss a small opportunity, you'll never get a big one.
"Oh, Hiroi-chan, could you come over right away? I have a project for you."
If I miss this kind of call, there won't be another call. Even if it's the most bland pedestrian ad for a supermarket, you have to run over!
If someone asks you if you're busy, never tell the truth and say, "I'm busy." A truthful person always gets the short end of the stick.

Unless you're super top-notch, you'll get more work if you humbly say, "I'm poor!" To be busy and be popular is a wonderful thing. And it's only natural that people want to hire the busiest, most popular freelancers. However, this country runs on envy and jealousy. "How dare that idiot get so popular without saying a thing to me?!"

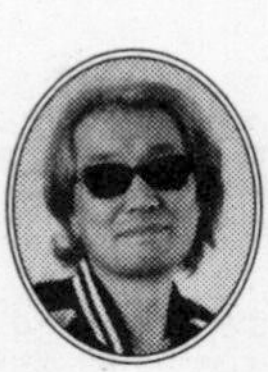

"Fool. I didn't get popular because of you," I want to say, but I can't. It's because I'm a wimp. I worry about not getting work anymore. That's the nature of freelancers.

"I heard you like the ocean. Here, you have only the beautiful ocean. You can write the original story without any distractions." Martha smiled a most beautiful smile.

"How can I write in a place like this?" I pouted.

"You will write. You can't go home unless you write. No matter how much they resist, everyone writes in the end before they go back."

I hate women who are so confident.
Splish splash, went the roaring waves…

It's been three days since I've been here. I write as I listen to the sound of the waves. The pencils are High Uni brand. There is a moment in which the brain cells and the fingertips and the pencil become one. Concentration and unconsciousness. Keeping the world of fiction in balance, I copy down the characters' manners, the backgrounds and their voices. The ultimate technique. A technique that is beyond technique. The moment that God descends upon me. Like automatic writing. The state where one can write for days on end and never feel tired. I think about how that would be, but I can't do it.

My concentration lasts 30 minutes at the most.
I've only written one page of the script.

I was given a shabby hut by the beach. A desk and a chair, a fan and refrigerator were the only furnishings in the hut. The fridge was filled with mineral water and coke. Time to take a breather.

"I love the ocean." I murmured, but the calm was soon interrupted by several rounds being shot into the sand by my feet.
"Eeeeep!" I cried out and jumped up.

"I warn you. Twenty pages. **Then**, a break. Break time lasts only 10 minutes!" A deep male voice from a loudspeaker announced.
"You jerk! You almost hit me!" I yelled back.

"Don't worry. We're aiming at your feet. We won't shoot your head or your hand. If you want to go back unscathed, you'd best heed my warning!"

I hurried back into my hut and stared at the blank writing pad.
I must write, and I must do it quickly. I want to go home.

How many days had it been since I was brought to the island? Ten days? Fifteen? Twenty? My sense of time had gone numb. Write and take a break. Write and eat. Write and sleep. In this monotonous repetition, a vivid story was coming alive.

The day that Sakura parted with her father, Sakura probably knew that it would be the last time she would see her father. The mind of a toddler that stared into the future.

The trembling fingers of Maria who had hit bottom in New York as she held a glass of vodka. The fingers that pull the trigger. The fingers that touch a kitten drenched in the rain.

The smile on Kanna's face as she dances in front of her father's grave. A smile that can blow away any sadness. A sadness brought on by the smile.

The true feelings of Sumire who is ever proud. Her troubles caused by her pride. Because of pride, she endeavors to be the best, and then puts herself up against the greatest odds with her haughty words.

Forced to leave her country because she was orphaned, Kohran learned the importance of compassion in her life of vicissitude. It was not a lesson learned merely for cover, but a philosophy of life and for survival.

Cute and pitiful little Iris. Is it such a crime to be different from others? The paradox of being rejected for being different as people seek uniqueness. Iris's heart trembles, not knowing what is happening.

Ogami, who graduated from the Naval Academy at the top of his class, faces failure and frustration.

Lieutenant General Yoneda's feelings of void as he sends innocent girls out into the frontline.

Chapter Three, Chapter Four, Chapter Five, Chapter Six... The scripts are written. It doesn't matter whether I'm on a southern island or in the middle of a metropolis. I have no need for breaks or meals. I didn't even want to sleep for fear of losing time. The images were right there in front of me. I had things to write about.

How long had I slept? When I came to, I was in a comfortably air-conditioned room. The bed was soft. As I lifted my body, I could see Tokyo Tower shining outside the big window. It seems that I was brought back to Tokyo from the Marshall Islands while I was unconscious.

I heard the sound of the shower running. Who could it be?

I took a cigarette from the side table and lit it. A thin smoke streaked the air of the room.

"Are you up?" The woman who got out of the shower was silhouetted by the backlight. I could tell it was Martha from her voice. The legs that were exposed from the towel that surrounded her body were long and thin as a gazelle's.

"Did I do anything?"
"You slept like an angel."
"What of the script?"
"I gave it to the editorial staff."
"Will I be released?"
"Think of it as a warrior's repose."
"What about you?"
"I'm going back. I have my next assignment to fulfill."
"Will I see you again?"
"Let's hope that we never meet again." Martha smiled. It was a charming smile.
"Will you give me a toast?"
"Sure, with a coke."
"Yes, coke is fine."
After downing the soft drink, Martha put on her clothes and left the room. I was alone in silence. I turned the radio on the bedside table. John Coltrane's "A Love Supreme" filled the room.

**To be continued in the next volume.**

## Me and Ogami

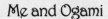

I love the manga version of Sakura Taisen.
As a fan of the Sakura Taisen video game, I love that the
story originates from Ogami's point of view. I've been involved
with Sakura Taisen for 10 years now, but even now, I get
bogged down with preparing for the role. Ogami's character
is quite elusive and difficult to act out. When that happens, the
manga version of the story is a lifesaver! As I say the lines
out loud, Ogami's image starts to form in my head. And Ichiro
Ogami is my ideal. He possesses many things I don't.

### Akio Suyama
### playing
### Ichiro Ogami

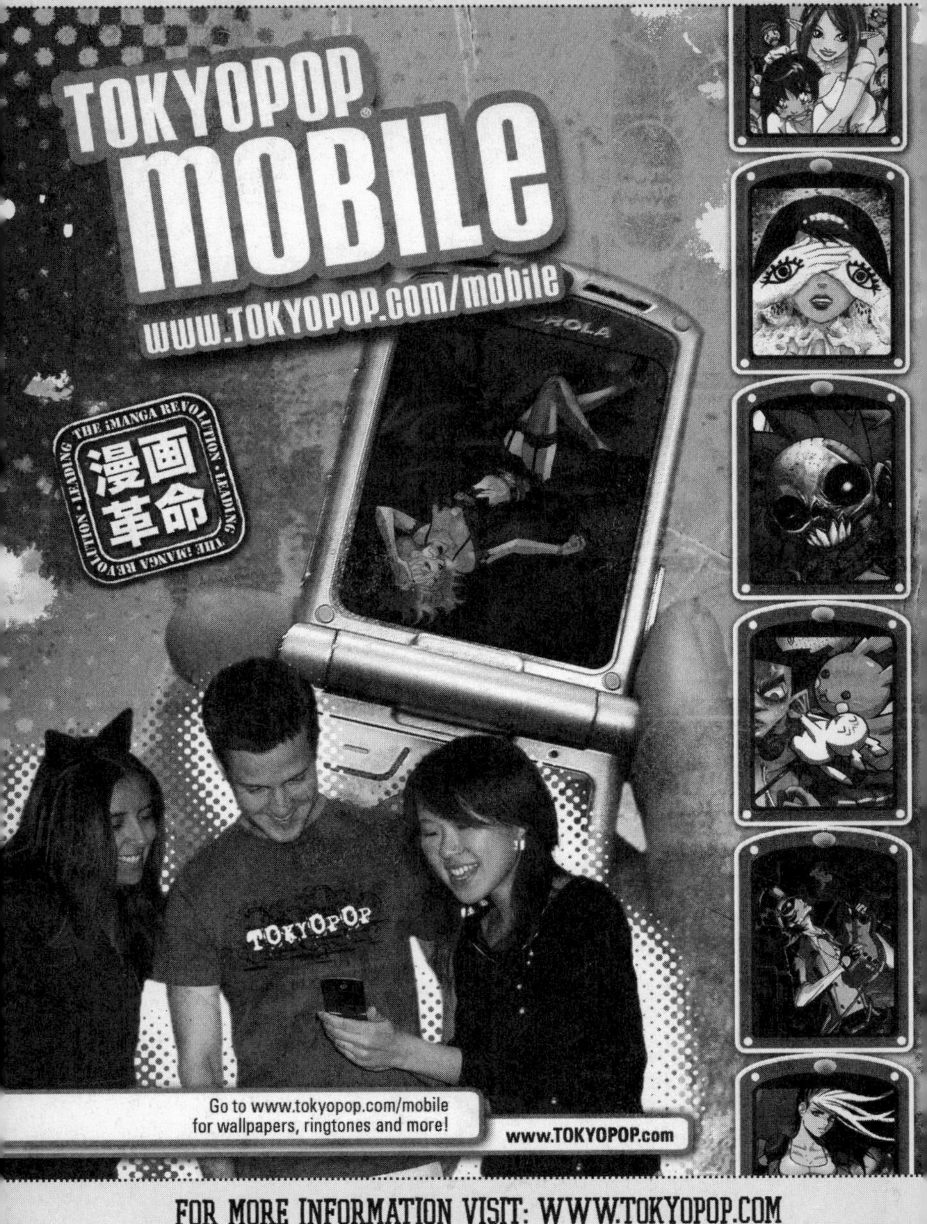
TOKYOPOP® MOBILE
www.TOKYOPOP.com/mobile
THE iMANGA REVOLUTION · LEADING THE iMANGA REVOLUTION · LEADING
漫画革命
TOKYOPOP
Go to www.tokyopop.com/mobile
for wallpapers, ringtones and more!
www.TOKYOPOP.com

# Fruits Basket™
## sticker collection
### stickers, pinups, and temporary tattoos!!

Fruits Basket
sticker collection
The #1 selling shojo manga in America!
Natsuki Takaya
Includes pinups, stickers, and temporary tattoos!

**BEAUTIFY YOUR SURROUNDINGS —AND YOURSELF!— WITH GORGEOUS ART FROM *FRUITS BASKET*!**

Pinup Sample Page | Pinup Sample Page | Temp. Tattoo Sample Page

Winner of the American Anime Award for Best Manga

This limited edition art book includes:
- Pinup art of all your favorite *Fruits Basket* characters
- Stickers
- Temporary Tattoos



FOR MORE INFORMATION VISIT: WWW.TOKYOPOP.COM